Kathy Fry
253 9464
2914

Essentials of MMPI-2 and MMPI-A Interpretation

Essentials of MMPI-2 and MMPI-A Interpretation

James N. Butcher and Carolyn L. Williams

Foreword by Raymond Fowler

University of Minnesota Press
Minneapolis · London

Published by the University of Minnesota Press
111 Third Avenue South, Suite 290, Minneapolis, MN 55401-2520

Fourth printing, 1996

Printed in the United States of America on acid-free paper

Library of Congress Cataloging-in-Publication Data

Butcher, James Neal, 1933–
    Essentials of MMPI-2 and MMPI-A interpretation / James N. Butcher
and Carolyn L. Williams.
      p.   cm.
    Includes bibliographical references and index.
    ISBN 0-8166-2100-4
    1. Minnesota Multiphasic Personality Inventory.   I. Williams,
Carolyn L., 1951– . II. Title.
BF698.8.M5B87   1992
155.2'83 — dc20   94-4277

Dedicated to Warm and Happy Memories of
Neal Glynn Butcher
1965-1985

Contents

Tables

Figures

Foreword
Raymond D. Fowler

Fifteen years ago, I left home on a February afternoon to participate in one of the annual MMPI symposia that Jim Butcher has been organizing and directing since 1965. The weather changed from fog to drizzle to rain and finally to an ice storm that caused long delays on flights connecting through Atlanta. What I had expected to be a two-hour trip had turned into a fourteen-hour ordeal by the time I reached the airport in Tampa at 3:00 a.m. I woke up the driver of the last taxi still left at the airport, negotiated terms, and settled down for a 35-mile ride to St. Petersburg. The taxi driver, now wide awake, was as eager for conversation as I was to get a little sleep.

"What brings you to the Tampa Bay area?" he asked, brightly.

"A meeting," I muttered.

"What kind of meeting?"

"A psychology meeting."

"What kind of psychology meeting?"

(Irritably) "THE MINNESOTA MULTIPHASIC PERSONALITY INVENTORY!"

(Cheerfully) "Are they ever going to restandardize that thing?"

This story, almost too good to be true (the taxi driver, of course, was a Minnesotan), has become a part of the MMPI lore. It seems appropriate to tell it here, since Jim Butcher has told it at dozens of workshops, as have I. Jim and I have been friends and colleagues for almost 30 years, and we have coauthored articles and co-led workshops in various parts of the world. Carolyn Williams, who joined Jim's personal and professional life later, also became a friend and colleague.

For Jim Butcher and Carolyn Williams, and even for their daughter Holly, the MMPI has been a family affair. A 1964 graduate of the University of North Carolina, where he worked with Grant Dahlstrom, Jim went to the University of Minnesota and initiated a flood of MMPI activities, including an active research program, numerous books, the now-famous MMPI symposia and workshops that have instructed thousands of psychologists in the interpretation of the MMPI. Carolyn, who joined the Minnesota faculty in 1981, began her own MMPI research program with an emphasis on adolescents.

Many (including my taxi driver) complained for years about the failure to revise the MMPI, but no one did much about it until Jim Butcher began, almost twenty years ago, to encourage serious discussions among MMPI colleagues about the pros and cons of doing so. The need for a revision of the MMPI was apparent. Almost everyone agreed that it had serious flaws. Poor norms, clumsy wording, and outdated nosology were only a few of the charges leveled at the MMPI by friends and enemies alike. How could one justify the continued use of a test standardized fifty years ago on a population that was nonrepresentative even in the 1940s?

The disadvantages of a revision were just as apparent. How could one change the MMPI to any significant degree without jeopardizing the accumulated research and clinical work of a half-century? The MMPI was the most widely used and most effective multipurpose instrument in the world, and major revisions could change all that. There was another, and entirely understandable, source of concern. Because good graduate courses and interpretation manuals were not available, many psychologists had to develop, through self-study and workshops, their own methods of MMPI interpretation. A new MMPI might threaten this painstakingly developed skill. Besides, why change it if it is working well?

Revising the MMPI took more than intelligence and perseverance; it also took raw courage. The task itself was daunting, requiring major time commitments and organizational skills. But even with the completion of the MMPI-2, the job was not over. As might have been expected, there are many who cling to the original MMPI, and others who suggest using a combination of the two instruments. These are debates that will continue until the rapidly developing MMPI-2 literature confirms the superiority of the revised test beyond question. In a discipline with few trustworthy instruments, we do not easily give up a sure thing.

When I first began to work with psychological tests four decades ago, it was not easy to learn to interpret the MMPI. Neophyte Rorschachers could learn interpretation from excellent books by Walter Klopfer and Samual Beck or choose from numerous interpretive workshops available around the country. Not so for the aspiring MMPI interpreter. There were almost no MMPI courses in graduate programs, and most of the material covered in general testing texts covered the skimpy manual available at that time. There were few, if any, MMPI workshops, and most internships ignored the MMPI completely.

By the late 1950s, a lively underground information network had developed. Brief manuals prepared by relatively experienced interpreters for their own use and notes taken in the few available MMPI courses began to be circulated, usually as smudged mimeographs or, worse, rapidly fading purple ditto copies. Crude as they were, these humble documents taught most early MMPI interpreters their craft.

Most underground manuals of the time were built around the concept of code types determined by the most elevated two or three clinical scales. The effectiveness of code types, demonstrated in a 1949 dissertation by George Guthrie, led to their adoption in much of MMPI research as well as in most MMPI interpretation. This method of classifying MMPI profiles has been the basis of the majority of clinical, actuarial, and computer-based interpretation systems that have been developed to date. The two-point code correlates were presented in Dahlstrom and Welsh's *Handbook* in 1960 and in the first two general MMPI texts by John Graham in 1977 and Roger Greene in 1980.

Users of the MMPI-2 and MMPI-A are fortunate that the first book on interpreting both these second-generation MMPI instruments was written by authors so intimately involved in their development. Jim Butcher played a major role in initiating the MMPI-2 and developing its norms, and he has supported it with extensive research. Carolyn Williams participated in the development of the MMPI-2 and, because of her expertise with adolescents, played a key role in the development of the MMPI-A.

Essentials of MMPI-2 and MMPI-A Interpretation should be in the library of every practitioner who uses these instruments. If such a book had been available for the MMPI, the test would probably have become the overwhelming choice of clinicians even sooner and more decisively than it did. Having such an excellent guide to interpretation should greatly accelerate the adoption of the MMPI-2 and MMPI-A.

Preface

Publication of this book and the release of the MMPI-A marks the end of a decade of research for the MMPI Restandardization Project. How much this project has been a part of our lives was illustrated by a dinner conversation we had with our daughter about a time before she was born. Holly, with all the resoluteness of a three-year-old, informed us that there never was a time before her birth, because she had always existed. Sensing what must have captivated Piaget when he observed his children's cognitive development, we interviewed Holly about the steadfastness of her belief:

> *"But, Holly, we can remember before you were born and you were not here."*
> *"I was too!"*
> *"But we didn't see you."*
> *"Well, I was at my office."*
> *"Who was with you?"*
> *"Nick" (her nephew, Jim's grandson).*
> *"What were you doing?"*
> *"Talking about the MMPI!"*

Our conversation took place almost five years ago. Holly is now eight and Nick, 10.

This decade of MMPI research has been gratifying in numerous ways. Like the development of the original MMPI, work on the MMPI-2 and MMPI-A was carried out through partnerships among university researchers and practitioners in the field. Many psychologists, other mental-health professionals, teachers, and school officials throughout the United States contributed to our studies. They recognized the MMPI's value in understanding and helping individuals in trouble and were quite willing to participate in research to modernize the long-established standard. We hope that this book will benefit our partners in the field as an appreciation for their efforts in our research programs. We are also indebted to the thousands of people who volunteered their time as subjects in the many studies that served to develop the MMPI-2 and MMPI-A.

We are pleased to have been able to follow the steps of Starke Hathaway, J. C. McKinley, and Elio Monachesi. With each passing year of the MMPI Restandardization Project we became more appreciative of the magnitude of their contributions to psychological assessment. That they did it without personal computers, word processing, and fax machines amazes us.

The University of Minnesota Press recognized that the MMPI was no longer just a "Minnesota test" when the MMPI Restandardization Committee was appointed in 1982. W. Grant Dahlstrom of the University of North Carolina and John R. Graham of Kent State University joined a Minnesotan on the committee, James N. Butcher. Auke Tellegen, also from the University of Minnesota, was appointed to the committee in 1986. This committee guided the research that resulted in the publication of the MMPI-2 and eventually the MMPI-A. In 1990 Beverly Kaemmer appointed the Adolescent Project Committee to advise the University of Minnesota Press on the final development of the MMPI-A. Robert Archer of the Eastern Virginia Medical School joined James Butcher and Auke Tellegen on this committee.

We greatly appreciate the assistance of our colleague Auke Tellegen, not only for his substantial contribution to the development of the MMPI-2 and MMPI-A with his uniform T scores and the VRIN and TRIN inconsistency scales, but also for his assistance in the preparation of sections of this book dealing with those topics.

Our work on the MMPI-2 and MMPI-A Content Scales follows a recent tradition in personality assessment that Jerry S. Wiggins so ably pioneered with the Wiggins Content Scales for the original MMPI. His gracious welcome to our new scales and farewell to his own in the foreword of our MMPI-2 Content Scales monograph was moving. Likewise, Craig MacAndrew provided the legacy for our work developing new alcohol and drug problem scales for the MMPI-2 and MMPI-A.

Our computerized interpretive systems for the MMPI-2 and MMPI-A were substantially influenced by Raymond Fowler's innovations in this area. He has contributed in many other ways as well. Over the years he has always been supportive, encouraging, and someone we could rely upon.

Many students volunteered their time in our research projects, worked long hours as research assistants (would you do just one more analysis? How about proofing this table again?), and chose to do their doctoral theses on topics related to the MMPI Restandardization Project. We are very grateful for their contributions. Their intellect, curiosity, and eagerness brought pleasure to our work. We say this even with memories like the time a research assistant neglected to make back-up copies of a data file and left the diskette on the roof of a car driven through the streets of Minneapolis! The student was there afterward, helping us search through streets, alleys, and dumpsters looking for the missing floppy disk. We can laugh now.

We had excellent technical support from Mary Alice Schumacher, Elizabeth Anderson, and Rebecca Turner. We've come to rely on Mary Alice's astute editorial comments. Both Liz and Becky have endured draft after draft after draft . . . with exceptional patience.

We have two very special colleagues, collaborators, and friends who were very much part of this decade of research. John R. Graham, in addition to being on the Restandardization Committee, served many other roles and we benefited greatly from his efforts and thoughtfulness. It would be hard to imagine how these projects could have been completed without him. Yossef S. Ben-Porath joined the MMPI Project a bit later as an exceptionally talented student, quickly becoming an indispensable colleague. Not only are they respected colleagues, but also two of our closest friends—and only a fax or MMPI meeting away!

We close this decade of MMPI research with satisfaction (and relief), although it is likely that the future will see us again "talking about the MMPI."

December 1991
J.N.B. and C.L.W.

Chapter 1

Objective Personality Assessment Using the MMPI-2 and MMPI-A

According to Starke Hathaway (1965), sheer frustration led him and J. C. McKinley to begin research in 1939 that eventually resulted in the publication of the MMPI. They developed the MMPI to assist themselves and others at the University of Minnesota Hospitals in the routine tasks of assessing and diagnosing patients with mental disorders. Other objective inventories of his day were too tied to psychological theories about the structure of personality to be useful, were developed with college students, or measured variables unrelated to psychopathology and thus were of little benefit to Hathaway in his work on an adult psychiatric service.

Despite the MMPI's origins in a single psychiatric service in Minnesota, it became the most widely used and researched objective personality inventory in the world (Lubin, Larsen & Matarazzo, 1984; Lubin et al., 1985; Piotrowski & Lubin, 1990). Its use extended far beyond the University of Minnesota Hospitals into psychiatric clinics and hospitals across the United States. Very soon after its development, the MMPI was employed with patients in general medical settings, adolescents in schools, inmates in correctional facilities, individuals in alcohol- and drug-problem treatment units, military personnel, and eventually with applicants in industrial settings who applied for highly responsible or stressful positions such as airline pilot, police officer, or nuclear power plant operator. It also became the most widely used measure of psychopathology in psychological, psychiatric, and medical research studies.

The late 1940s and early 1950s saw the MMPI crossing national boundaries as well. Some of the first translations of the MMPI were developed for Italy, Germany, and Puerto Rico (Butcher, 1985). By 1976 over 50 foreign-language translations were available (Butcher & Pancheri, 1976). Cheung (1985; Cheung & Song, 1989), reporting her work on a Chinese version of the MMPI, described the advantages of using the MMPI in places like Hong Kong or Beijing where few standardized Chinese instruments existed to assist clinical psychologists in their work. Adopting and adapting a well-established instrument like the MMPI was made possible by others' prior conceptual work and investigations into the test's psychometric properties. Given that other translations of the MMPI had passed cross-cultural methodological scrutiny (Butcher & Pancheri, 1976), Cheung (1985) indicated that adapting and validating the MMPI was more efficient than constructing entirely new indigenous instruments. This is particularly true in places like China, where professional resources are more limited. Others

1

obviously felt the same; we now know of over 140 MMPI translations in 46 countries.

What has contributed to the remarkable success and durability of the MMPI? One obvious answer is that the MMPI provides a useful and practical technique for assessing individuals who report mental-health symptoms and problems. This likely accounts for the large number of research studies documenting the MMPI's reliability and validity. Because it provides information useful in predicting individual clients' problems and behaviors cost-effectively, clinicians are willing to cooperate in research projects using the MMPI. In fact, they frequently contribute to the MMPI research literature.

Starke Hathaway (1965, p. 463) listed several structural features of the MMPI, in addition to its validity, that he thought accounted for its popularity:

> the provisions for some control over undesirable response patterns, detection of invalid records such as those from nonreaders, the use of simple language, the simplicity of administration and scoring, and, finally, the general clinical familiarity of the profile variables.

Other qualities contributed to the MMPI's reputation as a sound psychological assessment procedure. It provided reliable evaluations, that is, its scores were consistent across administrations. As Hathaway (1965) indicated, the MMPI also made it possible to evaluate the credibility of the person's self-report through the use of validity scales. Another important characteristic was that a person's score on an MMPI scale could be interpreted within a normative framework (e.g., the individual under consideration could be compared with others to determine whether his or her scores were low or high, whether the scores were extreme compared with normals, or whether his or her scores matched the pattern of known groups such as those with depression or schizophrenic disorders).

Development of the MMPI

Hathaway and McKinley believed the best way to learn what was troubling an individual was to ask him or her. Consequently, they chose for their inventory statements with which the client could agree or disagree, using a "True" or "False" response. This approach involved a straightforward self-administered task that could be completed by individuals with a relatively low reading level (sixth grade) and in a relatively brief time, usually an hour and a half. Hathaway and McKinley thought that patients who endorsed similar symptoms or items in the MMPI pool were diagnostically more alike than they were different. For example, an individual endorsing many symptoms related to having a depressed mood were likely to be more similar to other depressed patients than to other clinical groups. Hathaway and McKinley also thought that individuals endorsing more symptoms of a particular kind could be viewed as experiencing a more serious problem than those reporting fewer symptoms. To quantify this relationship between numbers of psychological symptoms and diagnostic similarity they developed scales by which individuals could be compared on particular variables. A group of items endorsed in a defined direction constitutes a *scale*.

The MMPI scales were conceived as measurable dimensions that reflect particular problems such as depression or hypochondriasis.

Hathaway and McKinley rejected the view that items should be selected for specific personality scales according to content obviously related to the various personality attributes or symptom clusters. They considered the selection of scale items based on face validity, the general practice of test developers at the time, to be too subjective. Instead, Hathaway and McKinley developed the MMPI on the basis of item and scale validity. That is, they required that any item on a scale be assigned to a scale only if it objectively discriminated a given criterion group (e.g., individuals with depression) from their normative sample (i.e., healthy visitors to the University of Minnesota Hospitals). This approach was referred to as an empirical scale-construction strategy.

Hathaway and McKinley compiled a large pool of potential items (about 1,000) that were, for the most part, indicative of symptoms of mental disorders or other problems treated on their psychiatric service. They had no preconceived notion of whether a particular item was related to the constructs of interest. Instead, they empirically compared the responses of the normal subjects with those of groups of well-classified patients to determine which items would be included on a particular scale. Their objective approach came to be referred to as "blind or dustbowl empiricism." It is important to realize, because it is often overlooked, that Hathaway and McKinley took great care in initially writing and ultimately choosing items for their pool, as well as in selecting their criterion groups. These two important aspects of their procedure should not be considered "blind."

Hathaway and McKinley's empirical scale construction method produced MMPI clinical scales that have high generality across diverse settings (Graham, 1990) and across national boundaries (Butcher & Pancheri, 1976). As mentioned before, the MMPI also became an important criterion measure in the objective study of psychopathology.

The Need to Revise the MMPI

The MMPI was not without its problems. Hathaway (1965, p. 462) indicated that the MMPI could be criticized for "its perpetuation of the Kraepelin-derived diagnostic nosology." These problems became more evident with the changes in psychiatric diagnosis, particularly with the transformations in the *Diagnostic and Statistical Manual of Mental Disorders* (American Psychiatric Association, 1952; 1968; 1980; 1987). Hathaway (1965) also noted problems with their method of selecting items for scales, but he but did not elaborate.

Over time others noted problems with the original MMPI. Butcher (1972), Butcher and Tellegen (1966), and Butcher and Owen (1978) concluded that many of the items in the inventory were out-of-date or objectionable, and recommended that the instrument be revised by deleting obsolete items and broadening the item pool to include more contemporary themes. Use of the original MMPI norms was also questioned. Butcher (1972) pointed out that the normative sample on which the original MMPI scales were based was not appropriate for many contemporary comparisons. The original normative sample was composed essentially of white, rural subjects from Minnesota, while the instrument was used across the United States with broadly diverse clients. Colligan et al. (1983) and Parkison and Fishburne (1984) conducted studies showing that the original MMPI norms were inappropriate for use with today's subjects.

Perhaps because the instrument worked so well and was used so widely, these problems were overlooked for over 40 years, despite calls for a revision. During these years, other objective personality inventories were developed, although none gained the acceptance attained by the MMPI. With the passage of time and a growing awareness of the limitations of the original instrument, the University of Minnesota Press, the copyright holder, decided to revise the MMPI. This revision was framed as a modernization and restandardization of an instrument of demonstrated reliability and validity. Given the extensive research base supporting the use of the MMPI in psychological assessment, an adaptation or restandardization seemed much more appropriate than a radical revision. One of the goals of the restandardization was to maintain the acceptability of the original instrument in its restandardized versions, the MMPI-2 and the newly released MMPI-A for adolescents. Table 1-1 details the reasons the MMPI and the MMPI-2 are so widely accepted in psychological assessment, reasons that suggest the MMPI-A has the same potential.

The MMPI Restandardization Project

In 1982 Beverly Kaemmer, MMPI manager at the University of Minnesota Press appointed a committee to undertake the restandardization of the MMPI. James N. Butcher (University of Minnesota) and W. Grant Dahlstrom (University of North Carolina) began the work, joined later that year by John R. Graham (Kent State University) and in 1986 by Auke Tellegen (University of Minnesota). Beverly Kaemmer represented the University of Minnesota Press. The Restandardization Project's tasks were to modify the original test booklet and to conduct studies to develop new norms for the instrument. Funding for the project was provided by the University of Minnesota Press out of income from the sale of MMPI materials and from the scoring and interpretive services.

In the first year of the project, the committee decided to develop two separate experimental booklets, one for adults (Form AX) and one for adolescents (Form TX), for use in data collection. Each experimental booklet included all the original MMPI items, some with minor wording improvements (Butcher et al., 1989; Butcher et al., 1992). Items measuring new content (e.g., suicidal behavior, treatment readiness, Type A behaviors, problematic alcohol and other drug use) were added to both experimental booklets. In addition, developmentally relevant items were added to the appropriate booklets (e.g., work adjustment items were added to Form AX and school adjustment items to Form TX). James Butcher, Grant Dahlstrom, and John Graham, with consultation from other MMPI experts, wrote the new items for Form AX. James Butcher and John Graham invited Carolyn Williams, experienced in work with adolescents, to participate with them in writing items for the Form TX booklet.

Table 1-1. Reasons for acceptance of the MMPI, MMPI-2, and MMPI-A in psychological assessment

The MMPI, MMPI-2, and MMPI-A are easy to administer, available in printed booklets, on cassette tapes, and by computer administration. It usually takes between one and one and one-half hours for adults to complete and one hour for adolescents.
Individuals self-administer the test by simply responding T (True) or F (False) to items on the basis of whether the statement applies to them. The items are written so that individuals with a sixth-grade reading level can understand them.
Many foreign language versions of the MMPI are in use and several translations of the MMPI-2 are under way in Spanish, Thai, Vietnamese, Chinese, Norwegian, Japanese, Dutch, Hebrew, Italian, and Russian.
The MMPI, MMPI-2, and MMPI-A are relatively easy to score. Item responses for each scale are tallied and recorded on profile sheets. Scoring can be delegated to clerical staff to conserve more costly professional time. Computerized scoring programs are available, which enhance the scoring process (i.e., they reduce errors and score the numerous available scales quickly).
The MMPI-2 and MMPI-A provide several response attitude measures that appraise the test-taking attitudes of the client, including several not available on the MMPI. Any self-report instrument is susceptible to manipulation, either conscious or unconscious; thus, it is imperative to assess what the client's test-taking attitudes were at the time the answer sheet was completed.
Like the MMPI, the MMPI-2 and MMPI-A are objectively interpreted instruments. Empirically validated scales possess clearly established meanings. A high score on an MMPI scale is associated with behavioral characteristics. These scale "meanings" are easily taught and objectively applied to clients. The established correlates for the scales allow them to be interpreted objectively, even by computer.
MMPI, MMPI-2, and MMPI-A scales have good reliability (i.e., are quite stable over time). With well-established scale reliability, the versions of the MMPI are considered effective in settings such as forensic assessments where good test reliability is a necessary characteristic.
The MMPI, MMPI-2, and MMPI-A provide clear, valid descriptions of people's problems, symptoms, and personality characteristics. Scale elevations and code-type descriptions provide a terminology that enables clinicians to describe patients clearly. To say that a client possesses "high 4 characteristics" or exhibits features of a "2-7" communicates very specific information to other psychologists.
MMPI-2 and MMPI-A scores enable the practitioner to predict future behaviors and responses to different treatment approaches, as was the case for the MMPI. For example, if the client's MMPI-2 profile is defined most prominently by scale 2 (Depression), it is likely that treatment, such as cognitive-behavioral therapy or antidepressant medication, will bring about positive change and a commensurate lowering of the scale 2 score.
Similar to the MMPI, the MMPI-2 and MMPI-A profiles provide a valuable method for providing test feedback about personality characteristics, symptoms, and so forth to clients.

The MMPI Restandardization Committee decided that maintaining the integrity of the instrument during its restandardization could best be accomplished by keeping the MMPI validity and standard scales relatively intact. Otherwise, the half-century of research supporting the use of these scales would not be relevant to the restandardized versions. Items comprising the validity and standard scales, except for a few objectionable items on four scales (4 items on F, 1 on Hs, 3 on D, 4 on Mf, and 1 on Si), were retained in the MMPI-2. New items measuring additional clinical problems and applications were added to the inventory, replacing the items from the original booklet that did not score on the validity or standard scales. Thus, broader content coverage, allowing for new scale development, was accomplished without altering the original scales.

To modernize the MMPI, committee members and their collaborators collected extensive normative and clinical data using Form AX with adults and Form TX with adolescents. Data collected during the restandardization allowed committee members to assess what changes needed to be made in the instrument. These data also served as validity information for both the original and the newly developed scales. The decision to develop a separate version for adolescents was also based on data collected during the project. The MMPI Restandardization Committee established several major goals for the project:

1. Revise and modernize the MMPI items by deleting those that are objectionable, nonworking, or outdated, and replacing them with items addressing contemporary clinical problems and applications. Include items on the original validity and standard scales in the first part of the booklet.

2. Ensure continuity with the original instrument by keeping the MMPI validity, standard, and several supplementary scales virtually intact. (Studies show that the MMPI-2 versions of these scales are comparable to the original MMPI versions and thus can be considered equivalent scales [Ben-Porath & Butcher, 1989a; 1989b].)

3. Develop new scales to address problems that were not covered in the original MMPI.

4. Collect new, randomly solicited samples of adults and adolescents, representative of the population of the United States, to develop age-appropriate norms.

5. Develop new normative distributions for the adult and adolescent scales that would better reflect clinical problems and would resolve the problem of nonuniformity in percentile classification that occurred with the original MMPI scales (i.e., T scores at a given value were not equivalent percentiles across scales).

6. Collect a broad range of clinical data for evaluating changes to be made in the original scales and for validating the new scales.

After the publication in 1989 of the MMPI-2 for adults (Butcher et al., 1989), Beverly Kaemmer of the University Press appointed a new committee to determine whether an adolescent form of the MMPI was needed. James N. Butcher, Auke Tellegen, and Robert Archer (Eastern Virginia Medical University) formed this committee. John R. Graham, Carolyn L. Williams, and Yossef S. Ben-Porath continued to work as Butcher's collaborators on several research projects related to the development of the MMPI-A. The MMPI-A manual was published in 1992 (Butcher et al., 1992).

Development of the MMPI-2

The MMPI-2 normative sample consists of 2,600 subjects (1,462 women and 1,138 men, ages 18 through the adult years), sampled from seven regions of the United States (California, Minnesota, North Carolina, Ohio, Pennsylvania, Virginia, and Washington). The normative sample was balanced for gender and demographic characteristics such as ethnic group membership. Normative subjects were randomly solicited, initially contacted by letter, and asked to come to a pre-arranged testing site for completion of the test battery. All subjects were administered the 704-item experimental Form AX of the MMPI, a biographical questionnaire, and a questionnaire assessing significant life events in the past six months.

Heterosexual couples (N = 822) were also included in the normative sample. Each member of the couple was administered Form AX, the Dyadic Adjustment Questionnaire (Spanier & Filsinger, 1983), and a revised version of the Katz Adjustment Scale (Katz, 1968). This information provided validity descriptors for the MMPI-2 scales with nonclinical samples.

In addition to the normative study described in the manual for the MMPI-2, a number of other normative and clinical studies provided validation for the MMPI-2 standard scales and the new Content Scales. These included studies in inpatient psychiatric facilities (Ben-Porath, Butcher, & Graham, 1991); alcohol treatment settings (Greene et al., 1992; Levenson et al., 1990; Weed et al., 1992); mothers at risk for child abuse (Egeland et al., 1991); outpatients in marital distress (Hjemboe & Butcher, 1991); antisocial personalities (Lilienfeld, 1991); post-traumatic stress disordered veterans (Litz et al., 1991); older men (Butcher et al., 1991); military personnel (Butcher, Jeffrey, et al., 1990); and college students (Butcher, Graham, Dahlstrom, & Bowman, 1990).

Present-day subjects, including individuals from the new normative sample, tend to endorse more items in the pathological direction, therefore producing higher mean scores (approximately 5 T-score points on each scale) than the original MMPI normative sample. This probably occurs because a somewhat different set of instructions are used today. Originally, item omissions were allowed, even encouraged. In current practice, test administrators tend to encourage completing all the items. Consequently, the original MMPI norms are inaccurate for today's test usage. The new norms, based on responses obtained using contemporary instructions, should allow for more accurate assessment.

The original MMPI norms were developed using a linear T-score transformation (Hathaway & McKinley, 1940, 1942). In an effort to make the scales comparable, the T-score distributions were assigned a mean of 50 and a standard deviation of 10. This approach was followed during the restandardization, with an important modification that solved the problem of nonequivalency of percentile values across scales that occurred with the original linear T scores.

The MMPI-2 T scores, referred to as uniform T scores, were developed by Auke Tellegen (Tellegen & Ben-Porath, 1992) using the eight clinical scales (1, 2, 3, 4, 6, 7, 8, 9) to constitute a composite distribution. For these scales, raw scores were converted into the corresponding uniform T scores by regressing raw scores on percentile-equivalent uniform T scores. Then uniform T scores were derived, separate for men and women, for the eight clinical scales and the 15 MMPI-2 Content Scales (Butcher et al., 1989).

In interpreting original MMPI profiles, clinicians followed the strategy of considering a T score of 70 the point at which an elevation was clinically significant. This cut-off was selected because it was thought to fall at a percentile rank of 95 for each MMPI scale. However, in practice percentile equivalents for a given T score varied across scales. In clinical studies with the MMPI-2, a T score of 65 proved to be the optimal score level for separating known clinical groups from the MMPI-2 normative sample (Butcher, 1989c; Keller & Butcher, 1991). Consequently, a T score of 65 or greater was chosen to demarcate the "clinical range" on the MMPI-2 (Butcher et al., 1989). On the MMPI-2, a T score of 65 falls uniformly at the 92nd percentile for the eight clinical scales and the MMPI-2 content scales.

Even though the MMPI Restandardization Committee sought to maintain continuity with the original MMPI by keeping the validity and clinical scales relatively intact, the MMPI-2 is a different instrument in several other respects. The revised instrument contains new items and fewer items that are objectionable to test-takers. The MMPI-2 norms are based on a more diverse and ethnically balanced sample and are more appropriate for present-day test users. A number of new scales were added to aid in psychological assessment. New validity scales assessing test-taking attitudes have been incorporated, and several new measures focus on clinical problems (e.g., Addiction Acknowledgment Scale and Marital Distress Scale) not assessed in the original MMPI.

A person's endorsement of content about herself or himself is an important source of clinical information in MMPI-2 and MMPI-A interpretation. Reliance on MMPI item content has increased over the last 20 years, in spite of the "dust bowl empiricism" characterizing its original development. Content scales (i.e., homogeneous groupings of items measuring single dimensions like anger or bizarre thinking) are relatively easy to understand, interpret, and to explain to others (Burisch, 1984). Wiggins (1966) developed a set of homogeneous scales for assessing the content dimensions contained in the original MMPI. However, a number of items on several of these scales were deleted in the MMPI revision process. Moreover, the MMPI-2 contains many new items not represented in the original Wiggins scales.

Content scales for the MMPI-2, described more fully in Chapter 7, were developed by Butcher, Graham, Williams, and Ben-Porath (1990) to assess the main content dimensions in the revised inventory. The new MMPI-2 Content Scales were derived by a multimethod, multistage scale-construction strategy employing both rational and statistical procedures to ensure content homogeneity and strong statistical properties. The new MMPI-2 Content Scales assess symptomatic behavior (Anxiety, Fears, Obsessiveness, Depression, Health Concerns, Bizarre Mentation), personality factors (Type A Behavior, Cynicism), externalizing behavior (Anger, Antisocial Practices), negative self-view (Low Self-Esteem), and clinical problem areas (Family Problems, Work Interference, Negative Treatment Indicators).

The MMPI-2 Content Scales have been shown to have strong internal psychometric properties, along with external validity. For example, comparisons between the MMPI-2 Content Scales and the clinical scales using the same behavioral descriptors show the Content Scales to be of equal or greater external validity than the original MMPI clinical scales (Ben-Porath, Butcher, & Graham, 1991; Butcher et al., 1990).

Development of the MMPI-A

When the MMPI Restandardization Committee initiated the revision of the original MMPI in 1982, they did not immediately decide to develop a separate version of the instrument for adolescents. There was a consensus at the time that several problems limited the use of the original instrument with adolescents. For example, the MMPI items were written from an adult perspective and were administered to adolescents with no modifications; the MMPI scales were not developed using samples of adolescents or considering developmental issues, but were simply assumed to be appropriate for adolescents even though they were derived from samples of adults; originally there were no adolescent norms for the MMPI; and interpretations for adolescents were often based on research with adults. The history of the MMPI's use with adolescents and the problems that arose will be discussed in more detail in Chapter 9. In spite of these problems, committee members recognized that the instrument was used extensively with adolescents. In fact, Starke Hathaway administered the MMPI to over 10,000 adolescents in Minnesota schools, demonstrating its ability to predict delinquency and other problems in youth (e.g., Hathaway & Monachesi, 1953a, 1957, 1963; Hathaway, Reynolds, & Monachesi, 1969).

Committee members decided to study whether a separate version of the MMPI for adolescents would prove useful and valid through the use of the experimental Form TX for adolescents. Since the adolescent normative sample for the original MMPI (Marks, Seeman, & Haller, 1974) was not representative of the ethnic diversity in the United States, an important goal of data collection was to obtain a large, diverse normative sample of youth from several regions of the United States. The subjects for the adolescent MMPI norms were obtained through schools in several regions of the United States including California, Minnesota, Ohio, North Carolina, New York, Pennsylvania, Virginia, and Washington State. These testing locations were chosen to maximize the possibility of obtaining a balanced sample of subjects according to geographic region, rural-urban residence, and ethnic background.

The 704-item Form TX was administered to 815 girls and 805 boys in the normative sample, and was also employed in an extensive clinical evaluation study (see Williams & Butcher, 1989a, 1989b; Williams et al., 1992). The final MMPI-A normative and clinical samples were more diverse in background than were the previous ones that included only white subjects (Marks, Seeman, & Haller, 1974). The MMPI-A normative sample consisted of 805 boys and 815 girls, ages 14-18.

The decision to develop MMPI-A norms beginning at age 14 was pragmatic. Although efforts were made to include youth as young as 12 and 13 in the sample, some school administrators were reluctant to grant permission to test these younger individuals with Form TX for several reasons, including its length, general adult orientation, and objectionable content (particularly items about sexual behavior). Data obtained from the limited sample of 12- and 13-year-olds who were tested revealed more invalid test protocols in this age range. Rather than delaying the publication of the MMPI-A until a larger and more representative sample of 12- and 13-year-olds could be obtained, the committee decided to use the data available to develop the test for 14- to 18-year-olds. The question of the instrument's appropriateness with 12- and 13-year-olds awaits future studies. The shorter and more "adolescent-friendly" MMPI-A test booklet may allow greater cooperation of school officials in normative studies.

The MMPI-A booklet consists of 478 items, many of which were on the original MMPI and were also included in the MMPI-2. However, a number of new items were added to the booklet to address adolescent problems and behaviors such as attitudes about school and parents, peer group influence, and eating problems. These items were distributed throughout the booklet in order to make the instrument more relevant to adolescents. Furthermore, items about youthful behaviors that were worded in the past tense on the MMPI and MMPI-2 were changed to the present tense for the MMPI-A.

Several item level changes were made in the MMPI-2 and the MMPI-A. Of the original items, 82 with problematic wording were rewritten for the MMPI-2; 70 items in the MMPI-A booklet are rewritten versions of original items. MMPI-2 items used to develop the Negative Treatment Indicators Content Scale were included in the MMPI-A, as were additional items about alcohol and drug problems. The objectionable items eliminated from the MMPI-2 were also eliminated on the MMPI-A. In addition, items referring to sexual behavior, objectionable in school settings and not necessarily having the same psychological meaning for adolescents as for adults, were eliminated. Finally, to shorten the MMPI-A booklet, items unique to the Fears Content Scale were eliminated (resulting in this scale's deletion from the MMPI-A), as were some scale 5 and scale 0 items.

Continuity was maintained between the MMPI and MMPI-A for validity scales L and K, the standard scales (the eight clinical scales and scales 5 and 0), the MacAndrew Alcoholism Scale (MAC-R), and supplementary scales A and R (Butcher et al., 1992). The F scale required extensive revision to ensure that it performed as an infrequency measure for adolescents. It was assumed that other MMPI-2 scales simply did not work with adolescents. Statistical analyses using adolescent samples and rational procedures that included a developmental perspective were used in developing the MMPI-A Content Scales and the VRIN and TRIN validity scales. Three of the MMPI-A Content Scales were developed primarily using the new adolescent-specific items (School Problems, Low Aspirations, and Alienation). The Family Problems Scale (A-fam) was improved with the addition of adolescent-specific content. A new scale, Conduct Problems (A-con), was substituted for the MMPI-2 Antisocial Practices (ASP) Scale on the MMPI-A when inadequate empirical validity was found for ASP with adolescents (Williams et al., 1992).

MMPI-A norms, like the MMPI-2 norms, were based on the uniform T-score transformation developed by Auke Tellegen, which insured percentile equivalence across the different MMPI scale scores (Butcher et al., 1992). Both the MMPI-2 and MMPI-A norms were developed using the same target distribution, ensuring percentile equivalence across the two forms. Thus, as a person ages, his or her MMPI-A and MMPI-2 T scores can be compared directly. The same cut-off for clinical interpretations (i.e., a T score of 65) is recommended for the MMPI-A as for the MMPI-2. However, for adolescents, clinicians are advised to consider scales elevated in the 60-64 T-score range as yielding potentially useful descriptors.

The remainder of this book provides information about using and interpreting the MMPI-2 and the MMPI-A. Chapter 2 addresses MMPI-2 and MMPI-A concerns. However, the MMPI-A is sufficiently different from the MMPI-2 that it is dealt with separately in Chapters 9, 10, and 11.

Summary

The MMPI was originally developed by Hathaway and McKinley to aid in diagnostic screening. Hathaway and Monachesi (1953a) provided the following description:

> *The MMPI is a psychometric instrument designed ultimately to provide, in a single test, scores on all the more clinically important phases of personality. In devising the instrument, the point of view determining the importance of a trait was that of a clinical or personnel worker who wishes to assay those traits commonly characteristic of psychological abnormality (p. 13).*

The instrument became the most widely used personality instrument in psychological assessment. Its adoption in numerous countries outside the United States indicates a strong generalization of validity across cultural settings.

Problems with the original MMPI became obvious as the years advanced and as the applications expanded beyond the original purpose of the instrument. In 1982, the test publisher, the University of Minnesota Press, began a program of research and revision that culminated in two separate but overlapping and parallel forms of the MMPI, the MMPI-2 for adults and the MMPI-A for adolescents.

The MMPI-2 is a revised version of the instrument in which the validity and standard scales have been kept virtually intact. In addition, a number of new scales for expanded clinical applications have been developed. New norms, based on a large, representative sample of normals (N = 2,600) provide a more relevant comparison sample for today's test applications. A number of validity studies have documented MMPI-2's effectiveness as a replacement for the original MMPI in the assessment of adults.

The adolescent version of the MMPI, the MMPI-A, was developed to eliminate many of the problems psychologists found in using the original MMPI with adolescents, such as too few items with adolescent-specific content, absence of specific scales for adolescents, and norms that were out-of-date and not representative. The item pool for the MMPI-A does not contain objectionable items, and it includes content relating specifically to adolescent problems. Several new scales, such as School Problems and Conduct Problems, were developed to address difficulties that adolescents experience. Finally, new norms were developed on a contemporary sample of adolescents from several regions of the United States to provide a more relevant comparison group for adolescents.

Chapter 2

Administering, Scoring, Profiling, and Coding the MMPI-2 and MMPI-A

The selection of test administration and processing options for the MMPI-2 and MMPI-A depend upon the practitioner's preference, facilities, equipment, and the time available for processing test results. This chapter provides an overview of the various test administration and processing procedures, detailing the relative merits of each format and indicating possible limitations. Since MMPI-A procedures generally parallel those for the MMPI-2, separate descriptions are provided only when they differ, as they do in administering the test to adolescents.

Selecting the Proper Form

The MMPI-A is recommended for adolescents ages 14 through 18; the MMPI-2 is recommended for use with adults from age 18 onward. An important question arises when the individual to be tested is 18, when either the MMPI-A or the MMPI-2 is appropriate. The practitioner needs to determine which form to administer depending upon the individual's life circumstances (e.g., whether he or she is still in high school, in college, in the military, or living independently from parents). The psychologist may administer either form with confidence, but the individual's T scores and interpretation will vary for a given set of raw scores depending upon which comparison group is chosen. For example, a young man's raw score of 24 on the Pd scale will give a T score of 66 on the MMPI-2 and a T score of 57 on the MMPI-A.

In general, the MMPI-A item content is more appropriate for 18-year-olds still living at home with parents and attending high school. The MMPI-2 is more appropriate for those 18-year-olds living away from their parental home, either in college or employed full time. However, since 18-year-olds are included in the norms for both instruments, either version can be used; the decision lies with the clinician.

Questions may also arise about the appropriateness of administering the MMPI-2 or MMPI-A to individuals outside the age range used to develop the instrument. Is it appropriate to use the MMPI-2 for adolescents 17 years and under or the MMPI-A for adults 19 years and older? In some cases, convenience may argue for substituting the MMPI-2 for the MMPI-A (or vice versa); for example, when clinics serving adults get an occasional younger adolescent for assessment and do not have an MMPI-A booklet or answer sheet available.

Others may have more substantive arguments for substituting for the age-appropriate version of the instrument for a particular client. Consider the case of a 16-year-old boy being tried as an adult for a capital crime. Since the courts determined that the youth is to be treated as an adult in their procedures, should he be evaluated with the adult-based MMPI-2? What about a 23-year-old brain-injured woman whose cognitive abilities and emotional development are estimated to be at a 12- to 13-year-old level? Is the adolescent-based MMPI-A more appropriate?

The test manuals for each instrument are very clear about recommending the use of the MMPI-2 with adolescents or the MMPI-A with adults:

> *It is inappropriate to use either instrument to make individual predictions for those outside the age range of the instrument.*

Although the MMPI-2 and MMPI-A are comparable measures of psychopathology, they are not substitutes for each other. Earlier MMPI research (e.g., Archer, 1987; Hathaway & Monachesi, 1953a; 1963; Marks et al., 1974) and new information from the MMPI Restandardization Project point to the need for separate versions of the MMPI for adults and adolescents (e.g., Butcher et al., 1989; 1992; Williams & Butcher, 1989b; Williams et al., 1992).

Chapter 9 presents more information about the differences in adult and adolescent responding to the MMPI leading to the decision to develop a separate version of the MMPI for adolescents. The descriptors and other interpretive information presented in this book are based on the assumption that the age-appropriate version of the instrument is used. There is no evidence supporting the accuracy of these decriptors and interpretations when the age-inappropriate version of the instrument is used. Convenience, judicial decisions to try an adolescent in an adult court, brain-injured adults, and similar rationales do not provide the necessary empirical support for making predictive statements about the individuals being assessed with the age-inappropriate MMPI version.

In some circumstances the practitioner being asked to provide an MMPI-2 or MMPI-A interpretation might not have been available to ensure that the age-appropriate version was administered and the individual being assessed might not be available to be retested with the appropriate version. The first step in these circumstances is to inform the referral source about this problem in MMPI administration so that it is not repeated with other clients. Next, the client's raw scores can be converted to the age-appropriate version by plotting them on the profile sheet of the appropriate form using the following procedures.

In cases where the MMPI-2 was administered inappropriately to younger adolescents, MMPI-2 raw scores can be converted to usable MMPI-A raw scores by dropping the items from the MMPI-2 that do not appear in the MMPI-A and plotting the standard scale scores on the MMPI-A profile sheet. If MMPI-2 scores are used to plot MMPI-A profiles, the F score presents the greatest complication for the basic scales (see Chapters 9 and 10). In this case the F items from the MMPI-A, appearing mostly on F_1, should be used as the infrequency measure. Remember that the K correction is not used on the MMPI-A profile. A similar process can be followed for some of the supplementary scales and Content

Scales appearing on both versions of the instrument (see Chapter 9). However, the supplementary scales and Content Scales specific to the MMPI-A will not be available (e.g., Alcohol and Drug Problem Proneness, Adolescent-Conduct Problems, Adolescent-School Problems, Adolescent-Low Aspirations, Adolescent-Alienation). The MMPI-2 and MMPI-A manuals provide the information needed about item-scale memberships to accomplish these MMPI-2 to MMPI-A conversions.

In plotting scores from MMPI-A to MMPI-2 profiles, the conversion process is more complicated. Raw scores from some MMPI-A scales will be the same as raw scores for the MMPI-2 (see Tables 9-4, 9-5, and 9-6 in Chapter 9). Scales L, F, Pd, Mf, Sc, and Si need to be prorated since there are fewer items on these scales in MMPI-A than in MMPI-2. The MMPI-2 and MMPI-A manuals provide the information needed to determine item-scale memberships. The raw score for F_1 on MMPI-A should be prorated to become the F scale on MMPI-2; F_2 cannot be converted since many of its items are not in the MMPI-2. However, if F_2 is elevated, the supplementary scales and Content Scales should not be used for interpretation (see Chapter 10). If MMPI-A scores are used to estimate MMPI-2 scores, it is important to K-correct the scores before plotting them on the MMPI-2 profile. Only the supplementary scales and Content Scales with substantial item overlap (see Chapter 9) should be converted with this process. Many of these important scales cannot be converted because of insufficient item overlap. These conversion procedures are cumbersome and have the potential for introducing error into the assessment process, arguing for appropriate instrument choice at the time of administration, not afterward.

Administering the MMPI-2 and MMPI-A

Some general test administration issues warrant discussion before we turn to specific aspects of MMPI-2 and MMPI-A test administration and processing procedures. Since the MMPI-2 and MMPI-A are self-administered inventories, they are relatively easy to use in most settings. However, some general guidelines can be offered to prevent problems from occurring. It is important to make the test situation a professional one in order to communicate a serious, task-oriented test-taking attitude to the subject. Whether the inventory is being administered individually or in a group setting, care needs to be taken to ensure that the individual knows what is expected of him or her and that he or she appropriately defines the test situation.

A comfortable, private, and supervised setting should be provided for the client taking the MMPI-2 or MMPI-A. Although space limitations may restrict or require modifications of test administration procedures, clients should have enough work space so that they feel their responses can be made in private, without concern about their answers being observed. This is especially important if the tests are group administered. The inventory should not be given to individuals to complete in an unsupervised setting since it is not possible to ensure that the person being tested actually took the test (Pope, 1990). It is never appropriate to send an MMPI-2 or MMPI-A booket home with an individual.

The psychologist is unable to ensure the accuracy, privacy, and confidentiality of the responses in these circumstances.

It is desirable to explain the reasons for administering the MMPI-2 or MMPI-A before this is done. In some clinics the testing may be performed by trained personnel before the patient is actually seen by a psychologist or psychiatrist. In such settings, care must be taken to ensure that the person responsible for the assessment communicates clearly to the client the reason for testing. Clients who are simply handed the booklets and told to respond to the test items may misconstrue the purposes of the testing, which could compromise the validity of their self-report.

The test should be administered by someone trained in giving standardized test instructions. Problems in profile interpretation arise if the test-taker has received vague or non-standard instructions. Deviating from the instructions on the booklet should be avoided or else carefully evaluated before decisions based on the test results are made. Consult the MMPI-2 and MMPI-A booklets for test instructions.

Special Administration Considerations for Adults

In some settings, such as personnel screening, use of the MMPI-2 is complicated by defensive response styles or the natural desire for applicants to present themselves in a positive light. For example, applicants for jobs as airline pilots typically do not endorse many psychological problems, tending to be quite defensive. Some assessors, when encountering defensive profiles, attempt to obtain more valid records by having the applicant retake the test after alerting them to the fact that they were initially "too defensive" and produced unusable results. Characteristically, when retested with these instructions, applicants produce less defensive profiles.

In an effort to obtain more cooperative response attitudes in a personnel screening situation, Fink and Butcher (1972) conducted a study with college students taking the MMPI in a simulated personnel situation, in which they altered the test instructions as follows:

> *The following personality inventory is made up of many statements; you are to decide whether the statements are mostly true as applied to you or mostly false, and then fill in the appropriate spot on your answer sheet. In taking the test, some people have been concerned about certain things. For example, some people wonder how honest they have to be in responding to the items. In the development of the inventory, several scales were constructed to allow the interpreter to evaluate test-taking attitudes. In other words, people who give an overly virtuous picture of themselves or people who try to appear more psychologically disturbed than they are, are easily detected. Thus, their test protocols are invalid and have to be discarded.*
>
> *It is also important to realize that this inventory was developed as a way of measuring individual personality traits not just to detect if a person is insane or not. We all know that every person is different, that is, has a different personality, and that they are better suited for certain things because of this.*

This test helps a psychologist understand what an individual's personality is like, and, by this, enable him (or her) to advise and help in a more efficient manner.

Some of the statements may seem unrelated to anything about your personality, and other items may seem too personal. A word then, about how these items were chosen. A large list of statements was given to a group of normal people and to people suffering from many kinds of personality problems. Then, the statements that were answered with different frequency by the two groups were selected as a scale, and it was shown that people who have certain kinds of personality structures will answer these items in similar ways. . . . So the important thing to remember is that test interpretation does not involve reading your specific responses. Scoring involves simply placing a scoring stencil over the answer sheet and counting the responses for each personality scale. This allows us to compare your total responses on each scale with other people.

We hope that you will answer all the items, unless they really do not apply to you.

The experimental group of subjects was given these altered instructions, and a second group of control subjects was given traditional instructions before testing. In addition, subjects were given a follow-up questionnaire:

Imagine that you had been asked to take this test as part of the selection procedure in a job application.

1. *Would you have felt that some of the items were (highly offensive, mildly offensive, not offensive) Circle one.*
2. *In your opinion, would this test constitute an invasion of privacy? (Yes, No, Unsure)*
3. *Would you feel (highly anxious, mildly anxious, not anxious) about the results of the test?*

The results of the study indicated no significant mean MMPI standard scale differences between the two conditions, suggesting that the indicators of psychopathology did not differ significantly. However, the subjects in the special instructions experimental group were less defensive and acknowledged greater willingness to report problems than did the subjects who received traditional instructions. In addition, the special instructions experimental group, in post-test questionnaires, reported that they viewed the test as less offensive and fewer of them thought the test was an invasion of privacy.

Overall, the results of this study showed that special instructions explaining the psychological test and giving reassurance regarding its use decreased resentment toward the test-taking situation. If altered instructions are used, the practitioner needs to address the possible influences of this change in the report so that test report users are aware that non-standard instructions were used.

Special Administration Considerations for Adolescents

As noted earlier, testing with adolescents presents some special problems. Additional care needs to be taken to ensure that an adolescent approaches the test situation with an appropriate, task-oriented mind set and with a clear under-standing of what is expected. Moreover, it is important to ensure that the testing atmosphere, especially in group testing, is conducive to concentration. The fol-lowing special considerations are recommended:

1. Ensure that the adolescent is a willing participant in the testing and approaches the task in a cooperative manner. The test administrator should take time in the beginning to explain the reasons for the testing and answer any questions the adolescent might have.

2. Ensure that the testing situation is private and free from intrusions—for example, from distractions created by other adolescents in the testing room. The adolescent should be given ample time and freedom from interference to concentrate on the questions.

3. Ensure that the adolescent understands the test instructions. The proctor should go over the test instructions carefully, making certain that the adolescent has the directions clearly in mind. It is very important to monitor the adolescent's responses to the questions, making sure that they are being recorded in the proper place.

4. Ensure that the adolescent understands the MMPI-A terminology. The MMPI-A requires about a sixth-grade reading level. However, some items in the booklet may require more than a sixth-grade reading level. Table 2-1 lists the words we received the most questions about in large testing sessions with young adolescents. We developed these standardized definitions and examples for use in test administration. The table can be used and expanded as necessary for use in your settings.

5. Provide sufficient breaks and reinforcement (both social and tangible reinforcers) to maintain cooperation. In some settings having a point system, points are assigned for completion of sections of the MMPI-A. Candy and praise were frequently used with subjects in the MMPI Restandardization samples. It may be useful to administer the MMPI-A in shorter 20- to 30-minute sessions, rather than one longer one.

MMPI-2 and MMPI-A Formats

One of the values of the MMPI-2 and the MMPI-A is that they are relatively easy to administer. A number of different administrative formats have been devel-oped to make the test situation conform to particular patient limitations or to take advantage of particular setting requirements. The item order of the inven-tory is the same for all forms of the test except for the special research form to be discussed later (i.e., the adaptively administered test).

Table 2-1. Standardized definitions and examples for the MMPI-A

Word/Phrase	Definition	Example
Anxiety	Nervous, jumpy, upset	I feel nervous or upset about something or someone almost all the time.
Apt	Likely	I am likely to go home after school.
Benefit	To do good for, to help	If given the opportunity I could do something that would do great good for the world. If I was allowed, I could do something that would greatly help the world.
Brood	Worry	I worry a great deal.
Condemned	Doomed, ruined	I believe I am a doomed person. I believe I am a ruined person.
Crowd	A large number of people	I avoid being with a large number of people.
Disturbed	Interrupted, upset	My sleep is interrupted and upset.
Editorial	Opinion by an editor	I like to read opinions by editors in newspapers.
Excessively	Too much or too great	I have used too much alcohol.
Fault	Problems, criticisms	My parents find more problems with me than they should. My parents criticize me more than they should.
Fitful	Restless	My sleep is restless and disturbed.
Have it in for me	Are unfair, out to get me, treat me worse than others	My teachers are unfair to me.
Judgment	Ability to decide what is right	My ability to decide what's right is better than it ever was.
Lacking in	Do without, do not have	I am certainly without self-confidence. I do not have self-confidence.
Law enforcement	Police, police force	I believe in the police.
Laxative	A mild drug used to relieve constipation or to help a person have a bowel movement (Ex-lax, Feen-a-mint)	Sometimes I use Ex-lax or another medicine so I won't gain weight.
Lecture	An informative talk	I like to attend informative talks on serious subjects.
Loud fun	Noise, activity	I like to go to parties and other affairs where there is lots of noise and activity.
Object	Disapprove of	My parents often disapprove of the kind of people I go around with.
Plotted against	Involves people making secret plans against someone else	I believe others are making secret plans about me.
Quarrels	Disagreements, arguments, fights	I have very few disagreements with members of my family.

Table 2-1. Standardized definitions and examples for the MMPI-A, continued

Word/Phrase	Definition	Example
Self-confident	Belief in one's own abilities, certainty about one's capability	I am entirely certain about my abilities.
Shrink	Avoid	I avoid facing a crisis or difficulty.
Sociable	Outgoing, friendly	I am a very outgoing and friendly person.
Soul	Spritual part of a person. The mind or thinking part	My spirit sometimes leaves my body. My mind sometimes leaves my body.
Spirits	Supernatural beings or creatures like ghosts	Evil ghosts possess me at times. Bad creatures sometimes control me.
Stranger	Outsider, newcomer, someone you do not know	I do not mind meeting newcomers or people I do not know.
Stress	Mental or physical tension	I am not feeling much mental or physical tension these days.
Success	To turn out as hoped for	If people had not had it in for me I would have turned out better.
Tender	Sensitive to pain, frail, weak	The top of my head is sometimes sensitive to pain. The top of my head sometimes feels weak.
Unpardonable	Cannot be forgiven	I believe my sins cannot be forgiven

Paper and Pencil Versions

Perhaps the most frequently used forms of the MMPI-2 and MMPI-A are the printed booklets. Two separate booklets, a softcover and a hardcover, are available. Each has advantages and limitations. The softcover booklet (see Figure 2-1) is more frequently used and can be administered in individual or group sessions. It is durable and reusable. Different answer sheets are available for use with the various test-processing options. It usually takes about one and a half hours to complete the booklet version of the MMPI-2 and about an hour for the MMPI-A.

One limitation of the softcover booklet is that it requires a hard writing surface such as a desk or table. The hardcover booklet was developed to provide a "laptop" administration form. The hardcover booklet is held together by a spiral binding, allowing the client to use the cover as a writing surface. This form requires a specially designed answer sheet (see Figure 2-2) that is attached to the back cover by pegs to prevent it from slipping. The booklet and answer sheet are staged by having the statements printed on pages of gradually decreasing width. The answer sheet is fixed to the back of the booklet so that the appropriate columns of the answer sheet are exposed to view as the booklet pages are turned.

In using the hardcover version, test administrators need to make certain that the answer sheet remains fixed in the appropriate position since the answer sheets can slip out of alignment. This, of course, results in incorrect answer columns being used, thereby invalidating the test. Another setting-specific disadvantage has been noted. A psychologist in a correctional facility pointed out that

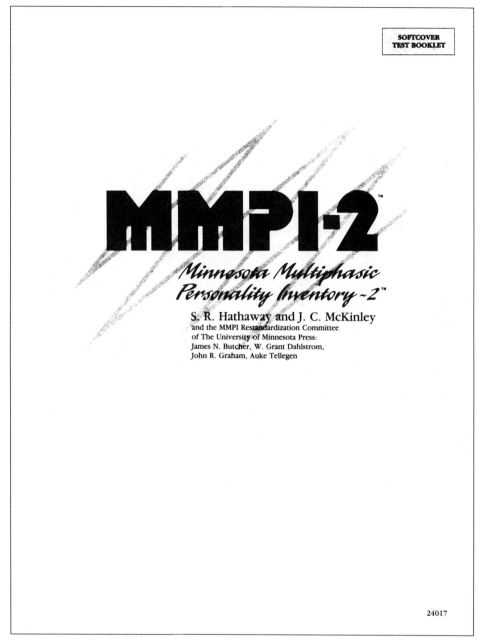

Figure 2-1. MMPI-2 softcover test booklet

his prison system was not able to use the hardcover MMPI-2 booklet because the wire spiral binding was removable and provided a weapon for inmates to attack others or kill themselves!

Whether the softcover or hardcover version is used, the examiner should check each booklet before use to ensure that previous clients have not left mes-

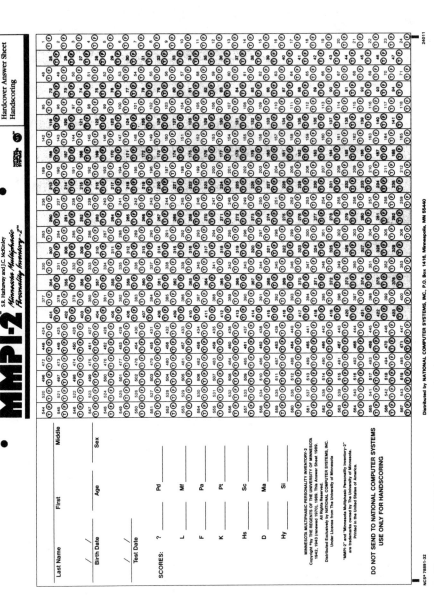

Figure 2-2. MMPI-A hardcover answer sheet

sages, complaints, obscenities, and so forth in the margins. One of the authors once found a booklet in which a number of MMPI statements had been "edited" to suit the previous user and express his generally cynical philosophy of life. Entertaining though it was, it altered the sentence meanings too much to obtain a valid test with other clients. Adolescents seem particularly prone to writing messages in the booklets.

Audiocassette Versions

Audiocassette versions of the MMPI-2 and MMPI-A are available to provide alternative administration formats for individuals with vision problems or reading difficulties. These versions are also useful for individuals who are unable to manipulate the booklet and answer sheets because of a physical disability. The audio form presents each item twice, allowing sufficient time for an individual to record his or her response. Research has shown that the audio version of the MMPI is comparable to the booklet version (Dahlstrom & Butcher, 1964; Reese, Webb, & Foulks, 1968; Urmer, Black, & Wendland, 1960; Wolf, Freinek, & Shaffer, 1964). The use of professionally developed audiocassettes is preferable to reading items to clients. Reading the items increases the likelihood of deviation from standardized item presentations. The audiotapes can seem slow and boring, particularly for adolescents. Careful monitoring with frequent breaks may be necessary to maintain motivation to complete the assessment.

Computer-Administered Versions

The MMPI-2 and MMPI-A can be administered on-line by computer. The test items are presented on a video screen, and the responses are recorded by the individual pressing the appropriate keys, designated as true and false, on a standard keyboard. The computer initially presents all items in their standard order to each subject. If a response is not given in the allotted time, the item is skipped and re-presented later in the sequence.

There are several advantages to this administration format:

1. Many individuals, particularly younger adolescents, enjoy working at a computer terminal and feel comfortable with this format. Those who have never used a computer can be taught quickly and appreciate having the opportunity to get experience with a computer.

2. It actually requires less time to take the standard MMPI-2 by computer than by booklet. Many people can finish the full MMPI-2 in an hour to an hour and 15 minutes since the response required is simply pressing a key rather than manipulating answer sheets, checking one's place, and marking with a pencil. Even less time is required for the MMPI-A in this format.

3. The scales can be readily scored and computer-interpreted immediately after the individual has completed the test. For

example, it is possible to have a complete computer-generated personality report immediately after the individual finishes responding.

One disadvantage of computer administration is that it may not be cost-effective since only one person can be tested at a time. Testing may tie up a computer for too long or require that an expensive computer be dedicated solely to test administration. Psychologists in some settings find it more cost-effective to have the client use the booklet version and have a clerk key punch the answers (requiring about eight minutes) into the computer.

Abbreviated and Short Forms for the MMPI-2 and MMPI-A

Even though experts (Dahlstrom, 1980; Lachar, 1979) point out that testing time is a less important consideration than obtaining sufficient clinical information, some researchers recommend using shortened versions of the MMPI to reduce the testing time for clients. The MMPI has been considered too long and tedious for many patients to complete and, in some clinical settings, time for test administration can be scarce. The stated reason for using short forms (that is, the need to reduce patient testing time) is not well founded. The idea that patients are too busy to respond to the full MMPI, or are otherwise unable to complete the inventory, is questionable (Graham, 1987). For most individuals in inpatient units, taking the full MMPI-2 or MMPI-A does not usually detract from their ongoing activities. Even in outpatient settings, complete assessments can usually be arranged if the staff and patients are informed of the importance of the information. Patients are willing to share information about themselves if they view the questions as relevant to understanding their problems and know that they will be given extensive feedback about the test results. Rarely will clients object to testing if a clinician or staff person explains the purpose of the test. This is especially true if clients are informed that the results will be valuable in treatment planning and that they will be given feedback about test results.

The two strategies for shortening MMPI administration currently available are the abbreviated forms and several so-called short forms. The abbreviated form is created by reducing the number of items by presenting only the items contained on desired scales. For example, scores for the complete validity and standard scales can be obtained by administering only the first 370 items in the MMPI-2 or the first 350 items in the MMPI-A. This is possible because all the items comprising the original standard and validity scales are in the first part of the booklet. The actual number of items administered for each scale, for example the Depression scale, remains the same as when the full test is administered. The scales containing items in the back of the booklet, (e.g., the Content Scales) are not scored. Accurate assessments, although limited to the standard scales, can be obtained with the abbreviated forms. However, it is important to note that many of the adolescent-specific scales of the MMPI-A are not available when the abbreviated version is used.

The term short form is used to describe sets of scales that have been decreased in length from the standard MMPI form. An MMPI short form is a subgroup of items that is hypothesized to be a valid substitute for full scale scores, even though the shortened scales may contain only 4 or 5 items. Research on the ability of MMPI short forms to predict full scale scores is equivocal at best. Most researchers have concluded that the limitations of MMPI short forms are too great to use them for clinical predictions (e.g., Graham, 1987; Greene, 1982; Hart et al., 1986; Helmes & McLaughlin, 1983; Hoffmann & Butcher, 1975; Streiner & Miller, 1986; Wilcockson, Bolton, & Dana, 1983).

Shortened scales are less reliable than the full versions of the MMPI-2 scales. The lower reliability of shortened scales is likely to lessen the validity of the scales (Butcher & Hostetler, 1990). Shortened MMPI scales have been considered to be too inaccurate to employ in clinical evaluations (Dahlstrom, 1980; Graham, 1987; Greene, 1982; Hoffman & Butcher, 1975; and Lachar, 1979). Users of short forms of the MMPI should consider it a new test (Greene, 1982) and employ "honesty in labeling" since shortened scales are not equivalent measures. A considerable amount of clinically valuable information is lost when a short form is used in lieu of the full MMPI-2. Short forms have been developed only for the validity and standard scales, and do not allow for the assessment of supplementary measures.

Computer Adaptive Administration

When a clinician conducts a clinical interview, he or she does not ask the same questions in the same order of all clients. An inflexible interview format would be highly inefficient and would quickly alienate even the most tolerant clients. Practitioners usually vary their interview for each client depending upon the person's response to previous questions. For example, if the client responds "no" to the question "Are you married?" the clinician does not follow with questions about the individual's spouse, but instead branches to a different topic.

Yet personality inventories traditionally pose the same questions, in the same order, to all people regardless of whether they are relevant to the individual tested. Until recently it has not been technically possible to vary item presentation in fixed inventories such as the MMPI-2 or MMPI-A. Item administration contingent upon previous responding is technically possible with personal computers, and research has demonstrated the comparability of the adaptive approach with the booklet version (Roper, Ben-Porath, & Butcher, 1991). This format has not yet been developed for use beyond research projects.

Scoring the MMPI-2 and MMPI-A

Many types of answer sheets are available for the MMPI-2 and MMPI-A because different scoring methods (e.g., handscoring, optical scanning) require different answer forms. The test administrator should determine in advance which scoring option is to be used in order to employ the proper answer sheet. The most frequently used answer sheets are the handscored, optically read, and computer-processed or key-punched versions.

Handscoring

Many practitioners and small clinics have the answer sheet scored by a trained individual and profiles drawn by hand. This is a time-consuming procedure taking from 15 to 40 minutes, depending upon the number of scales scored and the care with which the task is completed. If the practitioner wishes to take advantage of the full range of MMPI-2 or MMPI-A measures (i.e., the validity scales, standard scales, supplementary scales, the Content Scales, and Harris-Lingoes subscales) scoring requires substantial time. Consequently, those using the handscoring option typically score only the validity and standard scales, limiting the interpretation that can be made from the MMPI-2 or MMPI-A.

All MMPI-A and MMPI-2 scales, with the exception of the VRIN and TRIN inconsistency scales, are scored by simply counting the number of items endorsed on the particular scale. Scoring templates are placed over the answer sheet allowing the scorer to visually check the responses for each scale. The responses are then recorded on the appropriate place on the profile sheet.

There are several common errors or problems with the handscoring procedure. Templates frequently are used improperly, for example, by failing to align them properly. Counting errors are so common that it is a good idea for the scorer to count the items twice to ensure accuracy.

Computer Scoring

Several options are available for computer processing of MMPI-2 and MMPI-A protocols. Computer processing will be covered briefly here, and computer intepretation will be discussed in more detail in Chapter 12. The official MMPI-2 distributor, National Computer Systems (NCS) in Minneapolis, provides a number of scoring options for the MMPI-2 and MMPI-A. One computer scoring method involves the on-line administration of the MMPI-2 or MMPI-A described earlier. In this method inventory items are presented on a video display, and the client makes responses by pressing designated keys on the computer keyboard. A second approach is to have the client respond to the items on an answer sheet and to have the responses key entered directly on the computer or onto a disk. The computer can then score item responses and draw profiles.

Computer processing of personality test protocols has become a widely used, cost-effective, and very accessible means of facilitating the use of psychological tests. A note of caution is in order for those who might like to develop their own MMPI-2 or MMPI-A scoring program for their personal computers. The user should be aware that the MMPI-2 and MMPI-A are copyrighted instruments. That is, the items and the norms are protected against duplication or unauthorized use. Any such use requires permission of the publisher.

Mail-In Scoring

Another approach to computer scoring is to have the test-taker use an optically scannable answer sheet, which is then mailed to NCS for processing. The scored and interpreted test is then returned by mail to the practitioner. This service is useful for those who can wait for mailed responses. Scanners are also available for in-office scoring.

Fax Processing Scoring

Many practitioners have not fully computerized their clinical practices and cannot process MMPI-2 or MMPI-A responses by computer in their offices. However, they can obtain immediate test results by using a fax machine. The practitioner simply administers the MMPI-2 or MMPI-A to the client and faxes the answer sheet to National Computer Systems through a toll-free telephone number. The answer sheet is processed and a computer-based score or interpretive report is immediately returned.

Computing Useful Indexes for MMPI-2

A number of indexes, some composed of a combination of several clinical scales, have been developed for special interpretive purposes and are commonly scored for the MMPI-2. Several of these indexes are clinically derived measures, others are actuarially or objectively devised measures, such as the Goldberg Index. Unfortunately, many of these indexes have not been sufficiently studied for adolescents and so are not recommended for use with the MMPI-A.

Percentage True

This index, composed simply of the percentage of items the individual endorsed as True, is used to identify uncooperative subjects who give the same response to all or most questions. An uncooperative response set is indicated if the individual endorses true responses in excess of 80% of the items. It can be used with either the MMPI-2 or MMPI-A.

Percentage False

Similarly, the percentage of items endorsed False can be used to identify subjects who endorse a large number of items in the false direction. An excessive number of false responses (greater than 80%) indicates an uncooperative attitude in taking the test.

F − K Index

The Dissimulation Index (F − K Index), developed by Gough (1947) for the original MMPI, is sometimes used as a measure of response dissimulation or exaggeration of symptoms on the MMPI-2. This index is simply the raw score of F minus the raw score of K. F − K scores beyond + 15 are generally interpreted as faking pathology or claiming excessive psychological problems.

Average Profile Elevation

Another useful MMPI-2 index to compute is the average profile score. The average profile score is simply the mean of the T scores on the clinical scales (Hs,

D, Hy, Pd, Pa, Pt, Sc, and Ma). This index provides a rough indication of the overall degree of maladjustment in the individual's profile. Mean T-score elevations over 60 reflect a high level of psychological symptoms being reported.

Goldberg Index

For the original MMPI, Goldberg (1965) developed an index of severe psychopathology in an effort to discriminate neurotic from psychotic profiles. Using a linear regression model for classifying MMPI profiles, Goldberg found that a simple linear combination of five MMPI scores yielded a prediction formula that classified neurotics and psychotics with greater success than most clinicians rating the profile. The Goldberg Index is computed by simply adding and subtracting the T scores as follows: L + Pa + Sc − Hy − Pt. If the resulting score is greater than 45, a psychotic diagnosis is suggested. The Goldberg Index can serve as a useful sign for discriminating psychotics from neurotics in inpatient mental-health settings using the MMPI.

Megargee Classification System for Criminal Offenders

Megargee and his colleagues (Megargee & Bohn, 1977) developed a very useful classification system for felons that has gained broad use in many correctional settings and is being redeveloped to accommodate MMPI-2 norms (Megargee, Rivera, & Fly, 1991). The authors identified ten types of criminal offenders by using MMPI clinical scale patterns (see Chapter 4 for discussion).

Plotting MMPI-2 and MMPI-A Profiles

To facilitate interpretation, the MMPI-2 and MMPI-A scale scores are plotted on profile sheets that provide a visual summary of the scale elevations and patterns of scores. Separate profiles are used for males and females. The profile sheets are designed so that raw scores, once computed, can be plotted directly in the appropriate place on the graph, thereby converting the raw scores to T scores. There are a number of profile sheets available to facilitate scoring of a broad range of MMPI-2 and MMPI-A scales. The handscoring profile sheets most commonly used for the MMPI-2 are shown in Figure 2-3 and for the MMPI-A in Figure 2-4.[1]

The MMPI Restandardization Committee decided to make both K-corrected and non-K-corrected profile sheets available for MMPI-2 users since there is some indication that the K score is not the most appropriate correction to use for all settings and applications (Weed, Ben-Porath, & Butcher, 1990). Some MMPI users might choose non-K-corrected scores for their MMPI-2 clinical work and research. The K correction is not used on the MMPI-A, hence is not included on the MMPI-A profile sheet.

---

[1]Another profile sheet providing a means of plotting the so-called MMPI-2 subtle and obvious items is also available for the MMPI-2. Since research has not supported the use of these scales, which are based on essentially chance items, we do not recommend plotting or interpreting them (see Chapter 4 for further discussion).

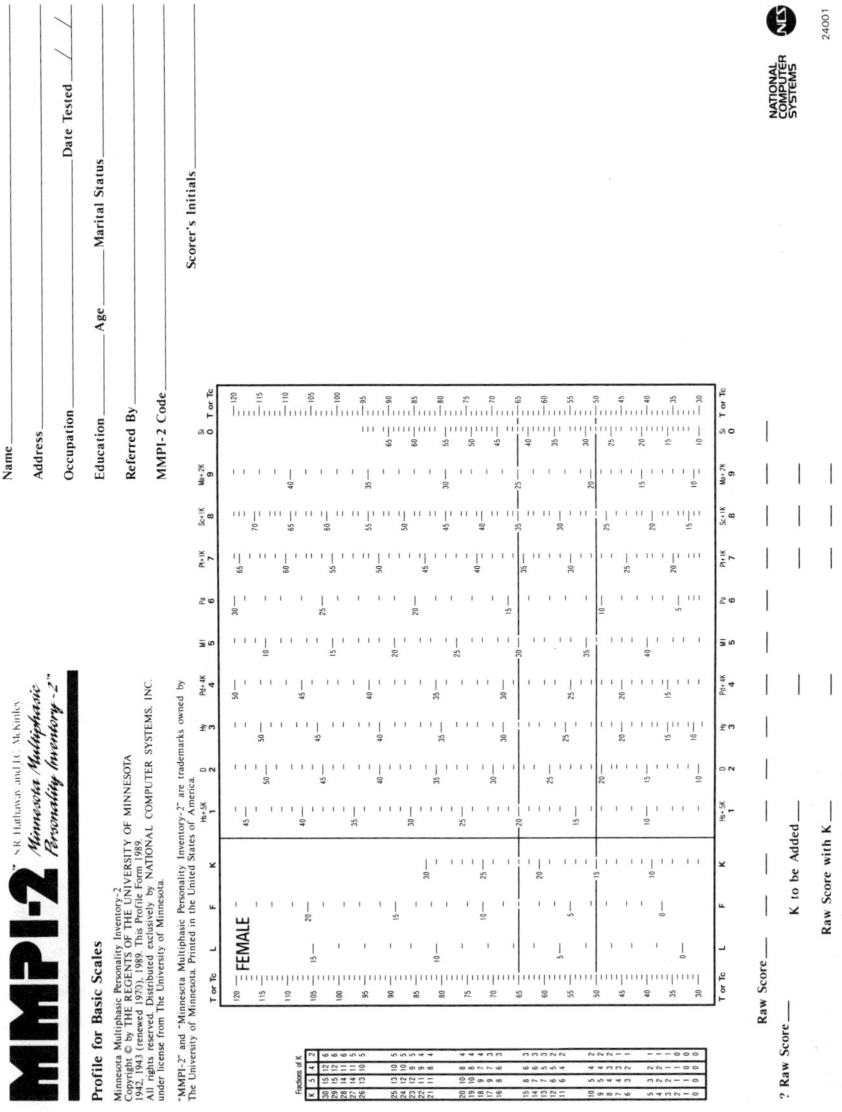

Figure 2-3a. MMPI-2 basic scales profile

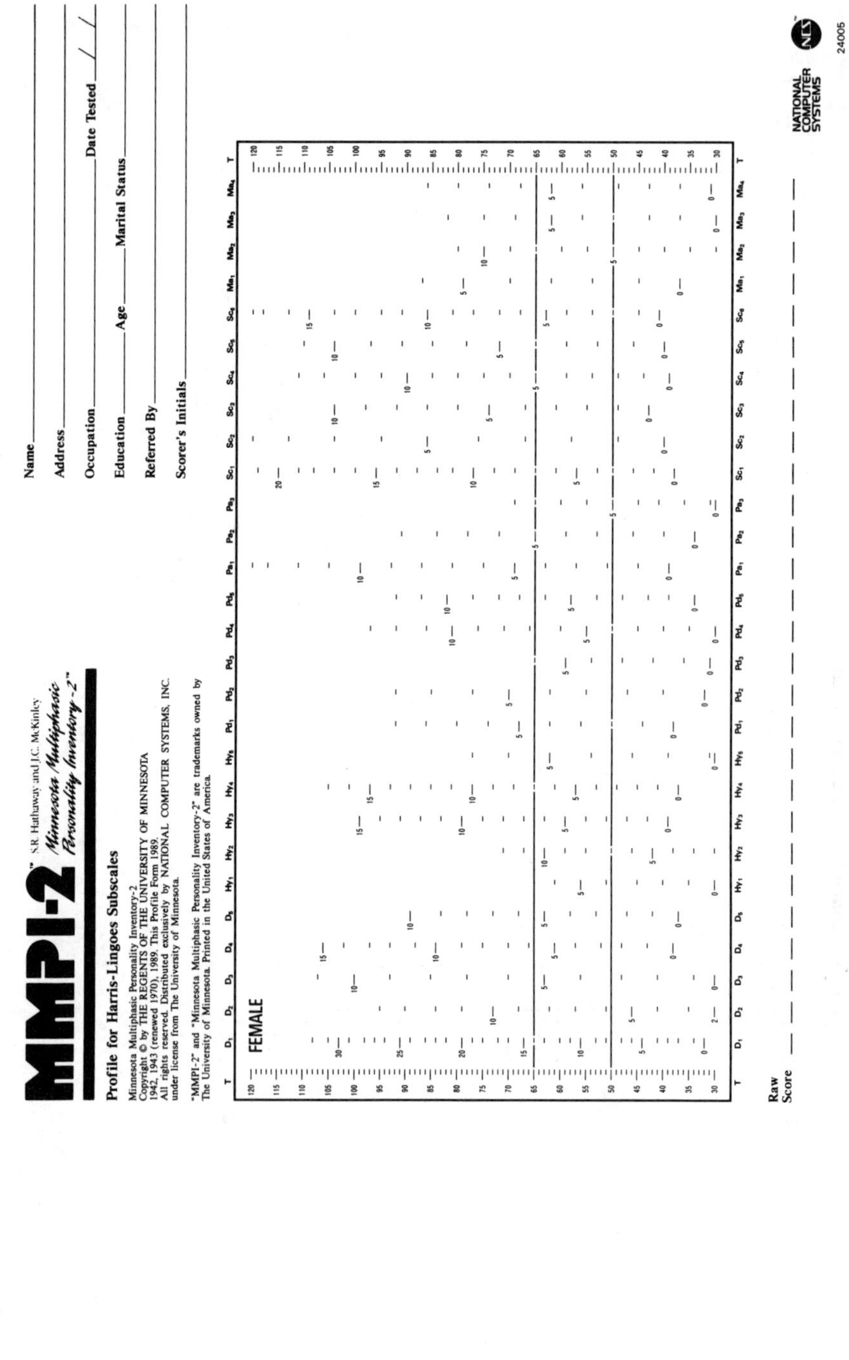
MMPI-2™ S.R. Hathaway and J.C. McKinley
Minnesota Multiphasic Personality Inventory-2™

Profile for Harris-Lingoes Subscales

Minnesota Multiphasic Personality Inventory-2
Copyright © by THE REGENTS OF THE UNIVERSITY OF MINNESOTA
1942, 1943 (renewed 1970), 1989. This Profile Form 1989.
All rights reserved. Distributed exclusively by NATIONAL COMPUTER SYSTEMS, INC.
under license from The University of Minnesota.

"MMPI-2" and "Minnesota Multiphasic Personality Inventory-2" are trademarks owned by
The University of Minnesota. Printed in the United States of America.

Name

Address

Occupation Date Tested / /

Education Age Marital Status

Referred By

Scorer's Initials

FEMALE

T D₁ D₂ D₃ D₄ D₅ Hy₁ Hy₂ Hy₃ Hy₄ Hy₅ Pd₁ Pd₂ Pd₃ Pd₄ Pd₅ Pa₁ Pa₂ Pa₃ Sc₁ Sc₂ Sc₃ Sc₄ Sc₅ Sc₆ Ma₁ Ma₂ Ma₃ Ma₄ T

Raw Score

NATIONAL COMPUTER SYSTEMS

24005

Figure 2-3b. MMPI-2 Harris-Lingoes profile

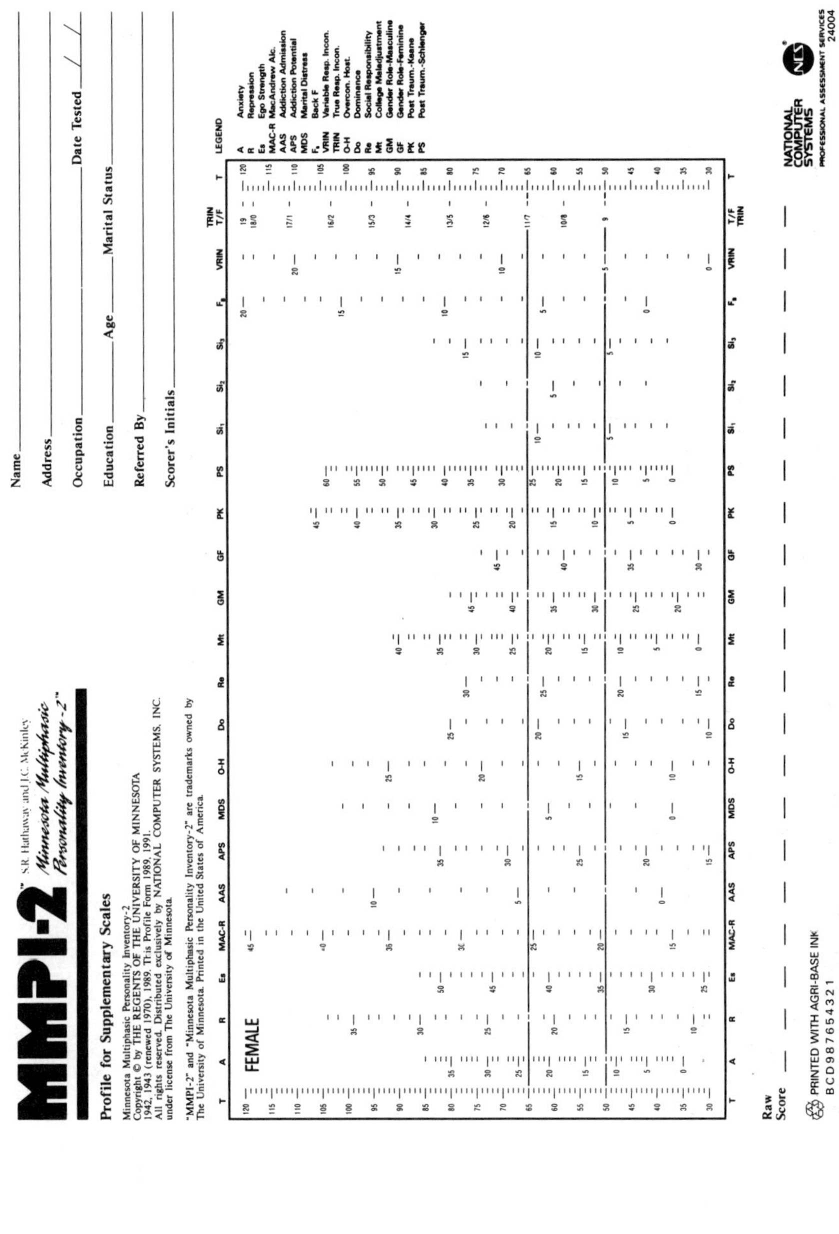

Figure 2-3c. MMPI-2 supplementary scales profile

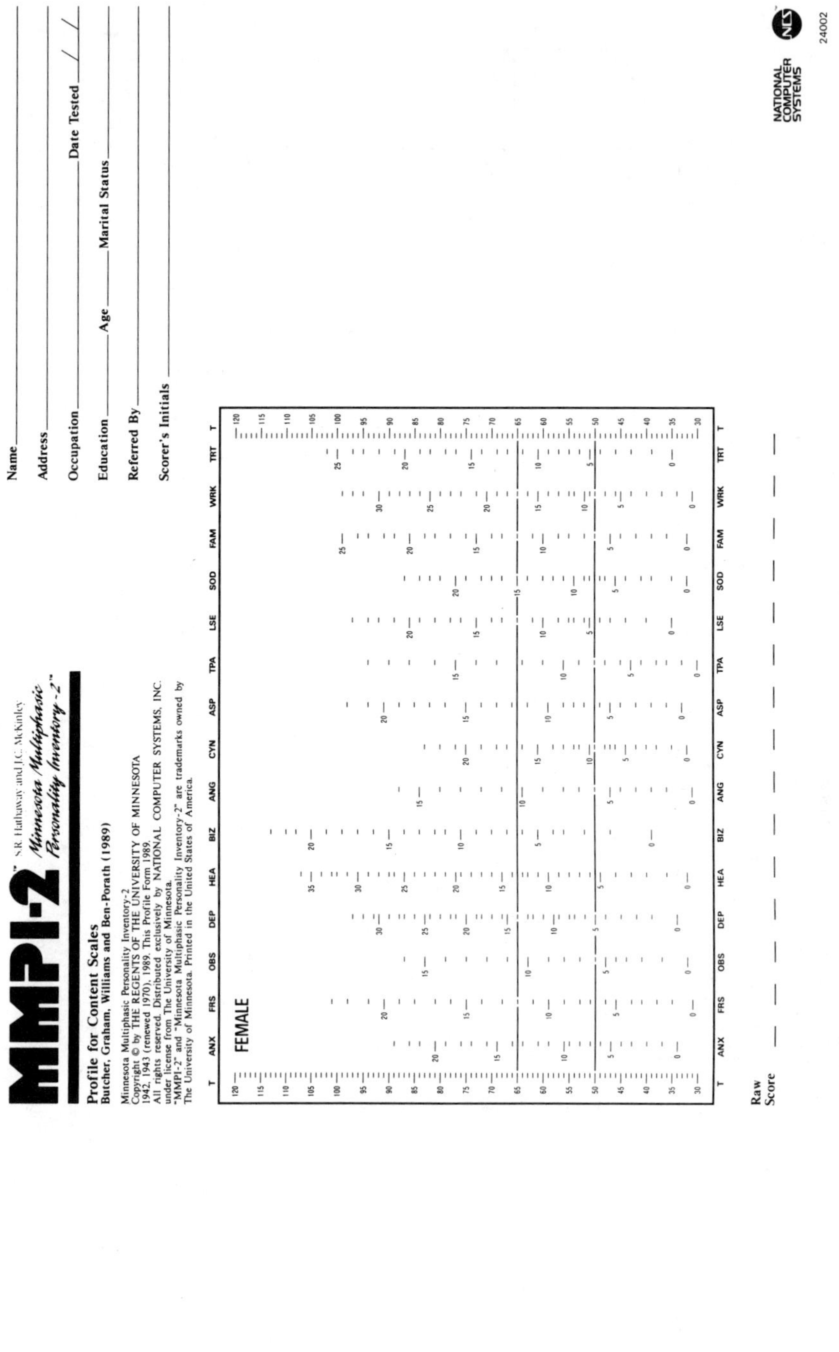

Figure 2-3d. MMPI-2 Content Scales profile

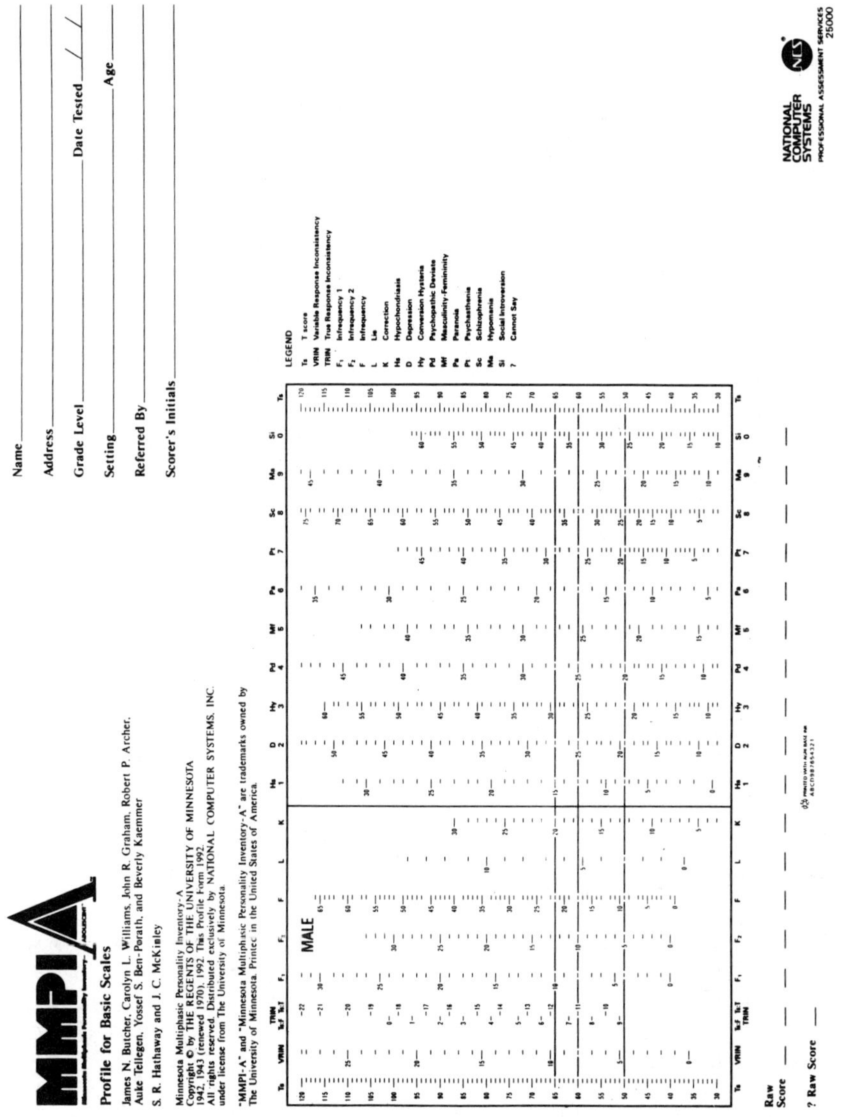

Figure 2-4a. MMPI-A basic scales profile

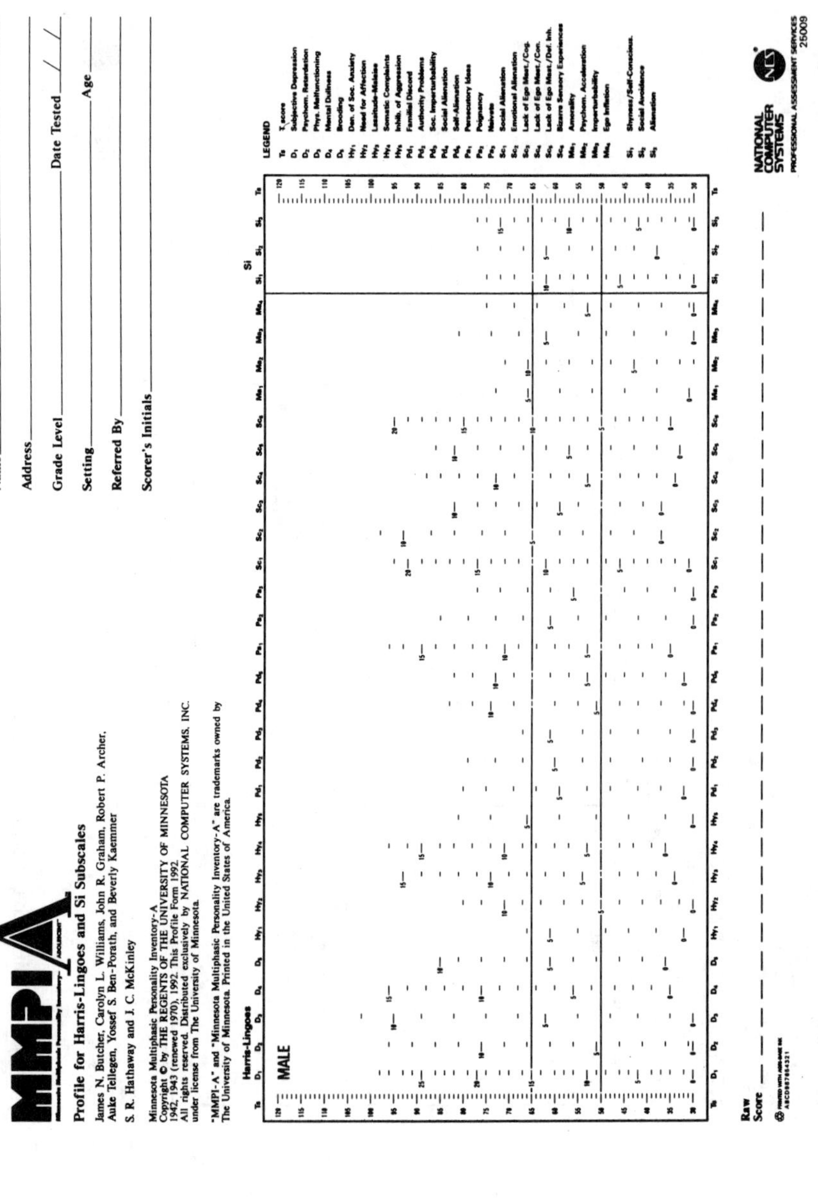

Figure 2-4b. MMPI-A Harris-Lingoes profile

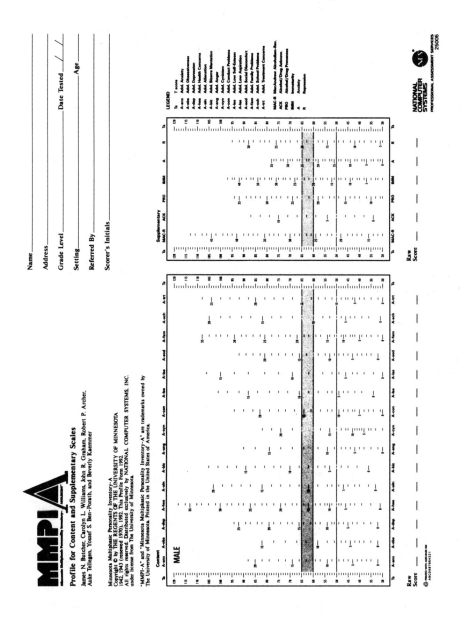

Figure 2-4c. MMPI-A Content and Supplementary Scales profile

Uniform T Scores

The T scores in the original MMPI were somewhat problematic in that they were not uniform across the scales, that is, a T score of 70 would fall at different percentile ranks across the scales. Moreover, T scores were based upon the 1930s normative sample originally assembled by Hathaway and McKinley and a somewhat later, but still dated, adolescent normative sample. The MMPI Restandardization Committee developed norms based on contemporary samples of individuals and followed a procedure, developed by Auke Tellegen and referred to as uniform T scores, that would allow all of the scales to fall at equivalent percentile ranks.

The uniform T scores involved deriving a composite (or average) distribution of the raw scores on the eight clinical scales, and adjusting the distribution of each scale to match the composite distribution. This procedure produced percentile equivalent scales since they are based on distributions that are comparable in terms of skew and kurtosis. This procedure allowed MMPI-2 and MMPI-A scale distributions to retain some of the familiar features of the original MMPI.

The K Correction

Five of the MMPI-2 raw scores on the basic scales profile sheet, Hs, Pd, Pt, Sc, and Ma, are adjusted by adding a correction, based on the K score, in an effort to compensate for test defensiveness. Again, the correction is not used for adolescents on the MMPI-A profile sheet.

Cautions in Plotting MMPI-2 and MMPI-A Profiles

Profiles should be plotted carefully since a number of errors can occur. Before interpreting an MMPI-2 or MMPI-A profile that someone else has plotted, the interpreter should check the profile for possible errors. Several common plotting errors are incorrect application of the K correction, using the wrong profile sheet (e.g., the form for men instead of the form for women), and plotting the scale scores on the wrong scale.

Coding MMPI-2 and MMPI-A Profiles

Profile coding developed early in the MMPI's history as a shorthand technique for communicating the main facets of an MMPI configuration. This facilitated grouping of similar codes by researchers. Coding systems summarize scores from the original MMPI validity and standard scales. Information from other MMPI-2 and MMPI-A scales (e.g., TRIN, VRIN, the Content Scales) are not available from these coding systems. The profile codes are obtained by rank ordering the MMPI-2 and MMPI-A standard scales in order of scale elevation and using symbols to designate level of elevation for each scale. Of the two coding systems that have been published, the Hathaway System (Hathaway, 1947) and the Welsh System (Welsh, 1948; 1951), the Welsh coding system is the most

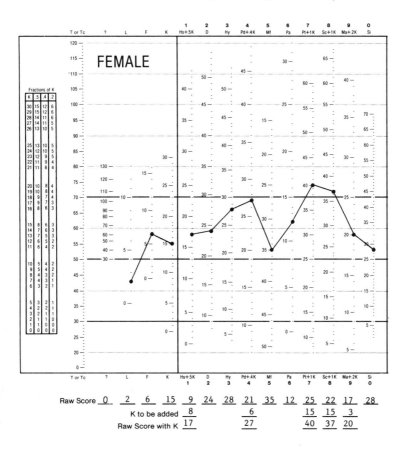

Figure 2-5. Alice. MMPI basic scales profile

widely used. We will begin by describing the Welsh coding system and later discuss modifications for coding the MMPI-2 and MMPI-A.

The Welsh Code

Each of the MMPI-2 and MMPI-A standard scales has a number which serves as the basis for coding. Many MMPI-2 and MMPI-A users routinely refer to the scale numbers, rather than to scale names or abbreviations, to avoid the negative implications that may follow in nonpsychiatric settings. (We use scale numbers, names, and abbreviations interchangeably in this book.) In coding a profile according to the Welsh system, each standard scale is represented by its number so that Hs becomes 1; D becomes 2; Hy, 3; Pd, 4; Mf, 5; Pa, 6; Pt, 7; Sc, 8; Ma, 9; Si, 0 (zero). Much of the early research on MMPI codes did not incorporate the Mf or Si scales since these are technically not considered clinical scales.

Figure 2-5 presents the original MMPI validity and standard scale profile for a young woman named Alice. We will use Alice's MMPI profile to illustrate the Welsh coding system. Alice's standard scale scores are as follows:

Scale:	Hs	D	Hy	Pd	Mf	Pa	Pt	Sc	Ma	Si
Number:	1	2	3	4	5	6	7	8	9	0
T Score:	58	59	67	69	53	64	74	72	58	53

The first step in coding Alice's MMPI profile is to write down the numbers representing the scales in order of T-score elevation, from highest to lowest. The highest scale is Pt with a T score of 74, so 7 will be the first number in the code. The second highest scale is Sc, or scale 8, at 72; the code is now 78. The third highest is Pd, and the code becomes 784. This procedure is followed until all the scales are listed by number in descending order of T scores. The digit sequence for the example is 7 8 4 3 6 2 1 9 5 0. It may be useful to place a small tally mark on the profile form near the T score as the scale number is written down to ensure that all scales are included in the code. Another check for accuracy involves reading through the completed code series in numerical order to determine if a scale has been repeated or omitted.

The second step in coding is to enter the appropriate symbols to denote scale elevation. Scales with T scores of 90 or over will be followed by *, 80 to 89 by '', 70 to 79 by ', 60 to 69 by -, 50 to 59 by /, 40 to 49 by :, and 30 to 39 by #. All scores at 29 or lower are shown to the right of #. When two or more scales fall in the same range of ten T-score points, the elevation symbol follows the digit for the lowest scale. These symbols were selected because they appear on standard typewriters and are familiar to most people.

For Alice's profile, the highest elevation is 74 on the Pt scale, indicating the scale digit 7 should be followed by '. However, because the Sc scale follows closely at a T score of 72, the ' symbol is inserted after scale 8. Next come the Pd scale at 69, the Hy scale at 67, and the Pa scale at 64. The next elevation symbol to be included in the code would be -, which would appear after this group of three scale numbers. The next five scales fall within the same elevation range and are followed by a slash (/). The code is now 78' 436-219 50/:#.

In addition to the standard scales, the validity scales should be coded and placed separately to the right of the standard-scale code. The scores on the validity scales for Alice's profile are:

Scale:	?	L	F	K
T Score:	40	43	58	55

On the original MMPI, the Cannot Say score was profiled along with the other validity scales. As you will see shortly, the Cannot Say score is not coded on MMPI-2. The code is now: 78' 436-219 50/:# FK/L?

Another refinement in the code is sometimes used. Some practitioners choose to begin and end each code with an elevation symbol. Even though the beginning and ending symbols are redundant, their use may allow the practitioner to easily locate cases by the highest (or lowest) score. Since no elevations fall in the 80-89, 90-99, and 100 and above ranges, if we were using this refinement the complete code for Alice's MMPI profile would appear as:

* '' 78' 436-<u>219</u> <u>50</u>/:# FKL/?

Note that we have added underlining. Customarily, when two or more scales are within one T-score point of each other, both code digits are underlined. So Alice's scores on scales 2 (T = 59), 1 (58), and 9 (58) are underlined. When two or more scales have the same T score, they are placed in the usual ordinal sequence and underlined: Note Alice's scores on scales 5 and 0. Another example: If D and Pt are both 65, the code will be 27- rather than 72-. If scales fall into two different ranges but are still within one T-score point, they and the elevation symbol will all be underlined: D=70 and Pt=69 will be 2'7. Some MMPI users have felt that this use of underlining to indicate equivalence of T-score values is arbitrary and overly precise and choose not to employ the procedure.

Other elevation symbols are sometimes used to denote very high scores. Scores from 100 to 109 are followed by **, 110 to 119 by !, and 120 by !!. This practice may be useful if a large number of cases are seen with extreme elevations, for example in an inpatient facility. Profile codes may contain gaps because no scale falls in some elevation ranges. The appropriate elevation symbol for the missing range must be included. If, for example, a 20-point range is skipped, all the symbols marking that range should be included even though the middle symbol is actually redundant.

Modification of the Welsh Coding System for MMPI-2 and MMPI-A

With the publication of the MMPI-2 and MMPI-A, the Welsh system, based upon increments of 10 T-score points, becomes somewhat cumbersome in representing the "critical elevations" in MMPI-2 and MMPI-A profiles. The T-score level at which interpretation is recommended is now at 65, a point at which no Welsh code system is available. Consequently, we have been employing a slight modification of the Welsh code so that the 65 T-score level is immediately recognizable in the profile code. We recommend that a " + " sign be used to demarcate the 65 to 69 T-score level. Profile coding proceeds as follows:

Modified Profile Code

100 or more	**
90-99	*
80-89	''
70-79	'
65-69	+
60-64	-
50-59	/
40-49	:
30-39	#
29 or less	Placed to the right of #

Alice's MMPI-2 profile is presented in Figure 2-6 and will be used to illustrate modifications in the Welsh code for the MMPI-2. Her MMPI-2 standard scale scores are:

Scale:	L	F	K	Hs	D	Hy	Pd	Mf	Pa	Pt	Sc	Ma	Si
Number:				1	2	3	4	5	6	7	8	9	0
T Score:	43	58	50	59	57	63	60	52	59	72	67	51	50

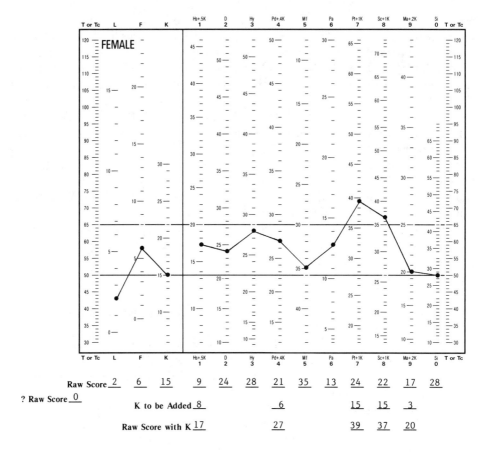

	T or Tc	L	F	K	Hs+.5K 1	D 2	Hy 3	Pd+.4K 4	Mf 5	Pa 6	Pt+1K 7	Sc+1K 8	Ma+2K 9	Si 0	
Raw Score	2	6	15		9	24	28	21	35	13	24	22	17	28	

? Raw Score 0

K to be Added 8   6   15   15   3

Raw Score with K 17   27   39   37   20

Figure 2-6. Alice. MMPI-2 basic scales profile

Alice's code, based on MMPI-2 T scores, would then be modified as

$$*'' \ 7' \ 8 + \underline{34\text{-}16259}0/:\# \ FK/L.$$

The same process is used for coding an MMPI-A profile.

Summary Highlight: The Case of Alice

We will use clinical cases to illustrate elements of MMPI-2 and MMPI-A interpretation throughout this book. Beginning with this chapter and continuing throughout the chapters dealing with the MMPI-2, one case, Alice, will be featured at the end of each relevant chapter to summarize or illustrate the information presented in the chapter. An adolescent boy, Tony, will be highlighted at the end of Chapters 10 and 11. Both cases are included in Chapter 12 about computerized testing.

Alice, the case used to illustrate the elements of MMPI-2 interpretation is an 18-year-old, unemployed, white woman, who was referred to a mental-health center by her family physician following an intense episode of extreme anxiety and panic.

The physician previously evaluated Alice's physical complaints and recommended a psychological evaluation. Alice's anxiety episode occurred after the loss of her most recent job and included feelings of having disappointed her parents. The psychologist's choice of MMPI forms, processing, scoring, and profile coding for Alice illustrates the information provided in this chapter. Alice, at age 18, could have been tested with either the MMPI-2 or MMPI-A. Even though Alice still lived with her parents (making the MMPI-A family content somewhat more relevant), she had graduated from high school several months earlier and was experiencing work-related problems. Because of this, the psychologist chose to administer the MMPI-2, rather than the MMPI-A. The NCS scoring and interpretation service was used (see Chapter 12 for more details).

Alice's basic profile was coded according to both MMPI and MMPI-2 norms to give readers who are converting from the original version of the instrument to the MMPI-2 an idea of the similarities and differences between the two sets of norms. As expected, Alice's profile configuration is quite similar on the two norms, but the scale elevation is somewhat lower on MMPI-2 norms. Relevant extratest information about Alice is described in Chapter 8 on integrating MMPI-2 descriptors. Similar information for Tony is presented in Chapters 10 and 11.

Chapter 3

Assessing the Validity of MMPI-2 Profiles

Because the MMPI-2 and MMPI-A are self-report personality measures, their validity and utility depend upon the cooperativeness of the individual taking them. If an individual wishes to distort responses to the test items to present a particular picture (e.g., one of a seriously disturbed person or of a person in good psychological health), he or she can readily do so. Thus, personality questionnaires would be very difficult and unreliable to use if there were no means of knowing whether a particular test protocol was valid. Fortunately, a number of measures have been developed for the MMPI-2 and MMPI-A to provide the interpreter with information about the individual's cooperativeness, openness, and willingness to share personal information through responses to test items. The answer to the question "Can the MMPI-2 or the MMPI-A be faked?" is, of course, yes. However, in most instances we know when an individual is attempting to distort responses and are able to appraise the person's message and the extent of the response distortion.

Using the measures of response invalidity that have been developed, we can judge whether the individual has distorted the responses to the point of invalidating the test and can, in some cases, correct for test defensiveness to arrive at a more accurate symptomatic picture. Actually, knowing that there is a tendency for some individuals and settings to be associated with invalid MMPI-2 and MMPI-A protocols can be useful information in the interpretive process. For example, individuals who claim damages in a court case because of "psychological maladjustment" may be excessive in their responding and produce very exaggerated symptom patterns that are unbelievable. Some parents in domestic court-custody battles tend to present an overly favorable pattern on the MMPI-2 by excessively denying minor faults that most people would admit to. These extreme patterns of response distortion can provide clues about the test-taker's motivations that might prove valuable in the overall psychological evaluation.

In this chapter, we will discuss the MMPI-2 patterns that provide the interpreter with information about whether the client's profile is valid and interpretable. We will illustrate each of the validity indexes and summarize the conclusions that can be made from them. Similar information is presented about the MMPI-A validity indicators and scales in Chapters 9 and 10.

Table 3-1. Cannot Say interpretive guidelines for the MMPI-2

☐ Cannot Say scores (Cs) ≥ 30 indicate that the individual has produced an invalid protocol that should not be interpreted except under the circumstances noted below. No other MMPI-2 scales should be interpreted.

☐ If most of the Cs items occur toward the end of the booklet (after item 370), the validity and standard scales can be interpreted. However, the supplementary and Content Scales, which contain items in the latter part of the booklet, should not be interpreted.

☐ Possible reasons for item omissions:
  • Defensiveness
  • Indecisiveness
  • Fatigue, low mood
  • Carelessness
  • Low reading skill
  • Perceived irrelevance of items

Measures of Defensiveness

Cannot Say Score (?)

The MMPI-2 contains a Cannot Say score (?), a measure of test validity, that gives the interpreter information about the subject's cooperativeness with the psychological evaluation. The Cannot Say (Cs) score is simply the total number of items the test-taker did not answer. Uncooperative or defensive individuals may fail to respond to some of the test items; this situation attenuates the scale scores, producing an underestimation of psychological problems (Brown, 1950). If the individual has omitted more than 30 items within the first 370 items, the protocol is considered invalid. (Remember that the validity and standard scales can be scored from items 1-370.) If the item omissions occur beyond item 370—if, for example, the individual did not complete the full MMPI-2—the basic scales can be interpreted but scores on some supplementary scales and scores for the MMPI-2 Content Scales will likely be attenuated and should not be interpreted. Cs interpretive guidelines are presented in Table 3-1.

Lie Scale (L)

The L (Lie) scale is a measure of the tendency of some individuals to distort their responses by claiming that they are excessively virtuous. The scale is based on the idea that individuals who are attempting to claim excellent psychological adjustment will endorse items that indicate extremely high moral character—more than most individuals would claim. The 15 items comprising this scale (14 on MMPI-A) are obvious in content and center around the assertion of great virtue, for example, "At times I feel like swearing" (False) and "I do not always tell the truth" (False). Scores elevated above a T score of 65 suggest individuals who are presenting themselves in an overly positive light by attempting to create an unrealistically favorable view of their moral character and psychological adjustment.

Table 3-2. L interpretive guidelines for the MMPI-2

☐ T scores ⩾ 65 indicate possible profile invalidity owing to an overly virtuous self-presentation.

☐ T scores of 60 through 64 suggest a good-impression response set was used.

☐ Elevated L scale scores can be associated with other elevated and interpretable MMPI-2 scale scores.

☐ The TRIN scale (inconsistent true or false responding) can aid the interpreter in determining whether an elevated L score is due to a false or "nay-saying" response set or a true and "yea-saying" response set.

☐ Descriptors associated with elevations on L:
  • Unwilling to admit even minor flaws
  • Unrealistic proclamation of virtue
  • Claims adherence to excessively high moral standards
  • Naïve self-views
  • Outright effort to deceive others about motives or adjustment
  • Personality adjustment problems

In the MMPI-2, as in the original instrument, the L scale is a measure of co-operativeness and willingness to endorse negative self-views. Individuals who score high on this scale, T greater than 60, are presenting themselves as having no faults. If the L score is greater than 65, the individual is claiming virtue not found among people in general.

In addition to serving as an indicator of response distortion or invalidity, the L scale is also associated with personality characteristics that suggest naïveté, lack of psychological mindedness, rigid thinking, an unrealistic self-image, and neurotic defensiveness. Table 3-2 summarizes the guidelines for interpreting L.

Infrequency Scales: F and F_B

The F Scale

Hathaway and McKinley (1942) considered symptom exaggeration or faking an important response tendency to detect in self-report assessment. They developed a simple yet highly effective means of detecting the tendency to claim an inordinate number of psychological symptoms or to exaggerate one's adjustment problems. The idea underlying the F or Infrequency scale was that individuals who are attempting to claim psychological adjustment problems they do not have will actually go to extremes and endorse symptoms from broad and inconsistent problem areas. Moreover, the exaggerated responding is actually in excess of what most actual patients would endorse. To assess this tendency of claiming excessive symptoms, originally referred to as "plus-getting," Hathaway and McKinley developed a scale made up of a broad range of psychological symptoms, symptoms that cover such a wide range of problems that they do not reflect a consistent picture. Hathaway and McKinley conducted an item analysis and selected items that were infrequently endorsed in the normal adult sample, usually by less than 10%. The authors assumed that an individual who subscribed to a large number of these rarely endorsed symptoms would be claiming too many problems. Actual patients do not usually endorse a broad range of F items, but more selectively respond to symptoms.

The F scale in the MMPI-2 contains 60 items representing a wide range of symptoms and aberrant attitudes. Adults from normal samples usually endorse fewer than five items. If test-takers endorse a large number of these extreme items, they are presenting an extreme symptomatic picture not found in the general population. As we will see in Chapter 9, F did not work as intended with adolescents.

The F scale also provides a good indication of random responding to MMPI-2 items. If an individual has endorsed approximately 30 items in the scored direction, the possibility of random item endorsement or an error in response recording (i.e., putting answers in the wrong place on the answer sheet) should be suspected. Thirty items are indicative of random responding because there are 60 items on the F scale; if a two-choice response format, such as True or False is provided, and if the individual is responding randomly, he or she will endorse about 30 items by chance.

The F score can provide a valuable index of the individual's cooperativeness and ability to provide useful information about himself or herself. Suggested meanings of F-scale elevations include:

T < 50:   Little symptom expression. No symptom exaggeration.

T 51-59:   Accessible and open to discussion of problems if F is higher than L and K.

T 60-64:   Valid profile; some symptom expression.

T 65-80:   Likely a valid profile but some symptom exaggeration is possible; presenting a wide range of psychological problems; the subject is open and accessible to discussing problems.

T 81-90:   Borderline validity; suggests possibly confused and disoriented pattern; likely exaggeration of complaints; use of symptoms to gain services, sympathy, etc.

T 91-99:   High-ranging profiles, which should be interpreted very cautiously.

T 100-109: Probably invalid, but some profiles, of inpatient psychiatric patients and incarcerated felons who have recently been admitted, can be interpreted up to 109 if VRIN is in the valid range.

In sum, high-ranging F scores may reflect any of the following conditions. The interpreter should evaluate the situation further to determine which condition is most likely in a given client's case:

1. *Possible recording error*. The individual may have produced an invalid or spoiled test owing to improper recording of answers.

2. *Random responding.* The individual may have responded randomly to the test items. Some uncooperative subjects may take the easy way of completing the MMPI-2 by random or near random responding. The MMPI-2 F scale detects this response attitude well (Berry, Wetter, Baer, Widiger, Sumpter, Reynolds, & Hallam, 1991).

3. *Possible disorientation.* The individual may be confused and disoriented, unable to follow directions or track the meaning of the items, perhaps owing to toxicity, organic brain syndrome, or extreme anxiety. However, in some settings high-ranging profiles, between 90 and 109, are common and should not be treated as invalid. For example, in inpatient psychiatric settings or in prison settings new admissions often present with a highly exaggerated but interpretable pattern of symptoms.

4. *Severe psychopathology.* In some cases, particularly among newly admitted inpatients and inmates in correctional facilities, intense problems and disorientation may be suggested. Gynther (1961); Gynther, Altman, and Warbin (1973d); Gynther and Petzel (1967); and Gynther and Shimunkas (1965) have provided a great deal of information about high F-scoring inpatients. Megargee and Bohn (1977) have shown that incarcerated felons taking the MMPI at admission to prison often produce high F scores that have interpretable utility. Consequently, they recommend the cut-off score for suggesting invalidity for F to be 100+. Graham, Watts, and Timbrook (1991) suggest that it may be useful to interpret profiles at 110 T in inpatient settings.

5. *Possible malingering.* The individual may be consciously exaggerating to reflect some serious disturbance (to present the view that he or she is seriously disturbed) in order to benefit from services. High F responding occurs frequently among individuals who want to convince professionals that they need psychological services. This pattern is also found among individuals who need to claim problems to influence the court (Schretlen, 1988). Grossman et al. (1990) found that police officers who did not want to return to work produced higher F scores than those who wanted to return to duty.

6. *Different cultural background.* Cross-cultural research with the MMPI has shown that individuals whose cultural backgrounds are very different from the MMPI normative group, particularly in Asia, may produce higher F scale scores. This higher F elevation occurs even in samples of individuals who are motivated and cooperative with the testing (Butcher & Pancheri, 1976). Although inadequate test translation could be implicated, these F scale differences might result from cultural factors as well. Cheung, Song, and Butcher (1991), in a study of the MMPI in Hong Kong and mainland China, found that several of the traditional F items did not operate as infrequency items in Chinese samples. That is, their endorsement

Table 3-3. F interpretive guidelines for the MMPI-2

☐ T scores ≥ 110 indicate an uninterpretable profile because of extreme item endorsements.

☐ T scores of 90 through 109 are possible indicators of an invalid protocol. Some high F profiles are obtained in inpatient settings and reflect extreme psychopathology. VRIN T scores ≤ 79 can be used to rule out inconsistent profiles.

☐ T scores of 80 through 89 indicate an exaggerated response set, which probably reflects an attempt to claim excessive problems. VRIN T scores ≤ 79 can be used to rule out inconsistent responding.

☐ T scores of 60 through 79 indicate a problem-oriented approach to the items.

☐ Interpretive hypotheses for elevated F scores:
  • Possible symptom exaggeration
  • Faking psychological problems
  • Malingering
  • Confusion, reading problems
  • Random responding (refer to VRIN)
  • Severe psychopathology

percentages were very different from those in the United States. Some items were found to work in the opposite direction than they do in the United States. Cheung, Song, and Butcher (1991) developed a more effective infrequency scale for use in China following item-response criteria similar to those Hathaway and McKinley used with the original MMPI items. Test translators should be aware that F items need to be carefully evaluated for possible cultural influences in other countries. Interpretive guidelines for F are provided in Table 3-3.

The F_B Scale

An additional index of test invalidity, the F_B scale or F Back scale, was developed for the revised version of the MMPI to detect possibly deviant or random responding in the latter part of the booklet. Some subjects may alter their approach to the items part way through the item pool and begin answering in a random or unselective manner. Since the items on the F scale occur earlier in the test, before item number 370, the F scale may not detect deviant response patterns occurring later in the booklet. The F_B scale was developed using the same method that Hathaway and McKinley employed to develop the original F scale, that is, by including items infrequently endorsed by the normal population.

Suggested interpretations of the F_B scale include the following:

1. If both the F_B and F scales are elevated above T = 110, no additional interpretation of F_B is indicated since the clinical and Content Scales may be invalid by F scale criteria.

2. If the T score of the F scale is valid (that is, below 89) and F_B is below T = 89, then a generally valid approach is indicated throughout the booklet.

Table 3-4. F_B interpretive guidelines for the MMPI-2

☐ Like the F Scale, F_B assesses exaggerated responding by examining infrequent responses to items in the latter part of the MMPI-2 booklet.

☐ If F scale is valid and $F_B \geq 90$, the standard scales are probably interpretable but the scales containing items in the latter part of the booklet (e.g., the Content Scales) should not be interpreted.

☐ Interpretive hypotheses for elevated F_B scores:
  • Possible symptom exaggeration
  • Faking psychological problems
  • Malingering
  • Confusion, reading problems
  • Random responding
  • Severe psychopathology

3. If the T score of the F scale is valid (that is, below 89) and the F_B is above 90 (that is, the individual may have dissimulated on later responses), then an interpretation of F_B is needed. In this case, interpretation of the validity and standard scales is possible, but interpretation of scales that require valid response to later items, such as the MMPI-2 Content Scales, needs to be deferred. The F_B interpretive guidelines are in Table 3-4.

The K Scale and Its Relationship with F

The K Score

The K scale (often referred to as a suppressor scale because it is associated with lowering psychopathology on the clinical scales) was developed as a measure of test defensiveness. This scale, developed empirically by Meehl and Hathaway (1946) to improve the classification of patients who were defensive on the MMPI, is used both as an indicator of test defensiveness and as a correction for the tendency to deny problems. As a corrective factor, K modifies five MMPI scales: Hs, Pd, Pt, Sc, and Ma. The fractions of K to be added to the clinical scales were empirically determined to improve test-based diagnostic assessment.

The K scale contains items that are much less "obvious" in content than the L scale, such as "Criticism or scolding hurts me terribly" (False), "I frequently find myself worrying about something" (False), and "At times I feel like swearing" (False). Most of the items on the scale are endorsed False, reflecting the scale's function as a measure of problem denial.

The K scale has been shown to assess an individual's willingness to disclose personal information and discuss his or her problems. High scores (T above 65) reflect an uncooperative attitude and reluctance to disclose personal information. Low scores (below a T of 45) suggest openness and frankness.

The K scale appeared to operate for MMPI-2 normative subjects much as it did for the original MMPI subjects. Consequently, the K weights originally derived by McKinley, Hathaway, and Meehl (1948) were maintained in the MMPI-2.

Table 3-5. K interpretive guidelines for the MMPI-2

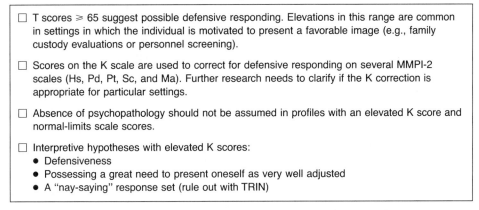

☐ T scores ≥ 65 suggest possible defensive responding. Elevations in this range are common in settings in which the individual is motivated to present a favorable image (e.g., family custody evaluations or personnel screening).

☐ Scores on the K scale are used to correct for defensive responding on several MMPI-2 scales (Hs, Pd, Pt, Sc, and Ma). Further research needs to clarify if the K correction is appropriate for particular settings.

☐ Absence of psychopathology should not be assumed in profiles with an elevated K score and normal-limits scale scores.

☐ Interpretive hypotheses with elevated K scores:
• Defensiveness
• Possessing a great need to present oneself as very well adjusted
• A "nay-saying" response set (rule out with TRIN)

This scale is positively correlated with intelligence and educational level, which should be taken into account when interpreting the scores. A change in the norms for K in the MMPI-2 make the scale somewhat less elevated for individuals of higher socioeconomic status (SES) than it was in the original MMPI. In the past, interpreters had to take SES into account and mentally adjust scores for the SES level of the individual. Since the new normative sample has a generally higher SES level, adjustment of higher SES subjects' scores is not necessary. Some adjustment is probably necessary for individuals who have less than a high-school education—modulating the interpretation of low K scores for individuals in this range is suggested (Butcher, 1990b).

Some debate has been waged over whether the K score actually improves discrimination in the way that Hathaway and Meehl had hoped (Colby, 1989; Silver & Sines, 1962; Weed, Ben-Porath, & Butcher, 1990). It is likely that future research will further examine K as a suppressor variable. In the meantime, the MMPI-2 Committee decided to provide both K-corrected and non-K-corrected profiles for the MMPI-2 since some psychologists might be interested in using non-K-corrected scores. Table 3-5 summarizes the K interpretive guidelines.

The F − K Index

Gough (1950) developed the F − K or Dissimulation Index for the original MMPI to assess the extent to which an individual dissimulated or claimed nonexistent problems and the tendency to exaggerate complaints. Gough thought that extremely high symptom checking (i.e., high F elevation) along with low defensiveness (i.e., low K) suggested an invalid or dissimulated performance. This index is determined by subtracting the raw score of the K scale from the raw score of the F scale. Gough recommended an F − K score of 9 or greater as an indication that the profile was invalid because of symptom exaggeration. Others (e.g., Lachar, 1974) recommended an F − K score of 12 or higher as invalid since the score suggested by Gough (9) was so low that it eliminated too many interpretable profiles.

The F — K index works well in differentiating individuals who have presented an inordinate number of psychological symptoms through the F scale. However, the index K — F (subtracting F when K is the higher scale) to assess "fake good" profiles has not worked out well in practice and is not recommended for clinical use. Too many valid and interpretable protocols are rejected by this index when K is greater than F.

Response Inconsistency Scales (VRIN and TRIN)

True Response Inconsistency

Auke Tellegen (1988) developed the True Response Inconsistency or TRIN scale to assess the tendency for some individuals to respond in an inconsistent manner to items that should, to be consistent, be endorsed in a particular way. TRIN is made up of 23 pairs of items to which the same response is inconsistent. For example, answering both "Most of the time I feel blue" and "I am happy most of the time" True or False is inconsistent. Fourteen of the 23 item pairs are scored inconsistent only if the client responds True to both items. Nine of the item pairs are scored inconsistent only if the client responds False to both items.

The scoring for TRIN is somewhat more complicated than the scoring of other MMPI-2 scales. First, the number of True and False inconsistent responses is determined. One point is added to the subject's score for each of the 14 item pairs in which a True response is inconsistent. One point is subtracted for each of the 9 item pairs if a False response is endorsed. Next a constant of nine points is added to the scale in order to avoid negative numbers. For example, if a subject endorsed four of the True item pairs and six of the False item pairs on TRIN, his/her score would be 4 − 6 + 9 or 7(F). This suggests a tendency to say False to items rather than to pay attention to content. If a subject endorsed twelve of the True pairs and two of the False pairs inconsistently, the score would be 12 − 2 + 9 or 19(T), suggesting that there is a tendency to say True in an inconsistent manner. Extreme scores on either end of this range reflect a tendency to either indiscriminantly answer False—nay saying—at the low end of the range, or indiscriminantly answer True—yea saying—at the upper end of the distribution. Raw scores are converted to linear T scores based on the new normative sample. When scoring TRIN, the score is designated as T or F to indicate the direction of the indiscriminate responding. Table 3-6 provides guidelines for interpreting TRIN.

Variable Response Inconsistency

The VRIN scale, also developed by Tellegen, is made up of 67 pairs of items for which one or two of four possible configurations (True-False, False-True, True-True, False-False) represent inconsistent responses. For example, answering True to "I do not tire quickly" and False to "I feel tired a good deal of the time," or vice versa, are inconsistent responses. The scale is scored by summing the

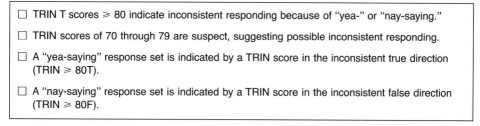

Table 3-6. TRIN interpretive guidelines for the MMPI-2

☐ TRIN T scores ⩾ 80 indicate inconsistent responding because of "yea-" or "nay-saying."

☐ TRIN scores of 70 through 79 are suspect, suggesting possible inconsistent responding.

☐ A "yea-saying" response set is indicated by a TRIN score in the inconsistent true direction (TRIN ⩾ 80T).

☐ A "nay-saying" response set is indicated by a TRIN score in the inconsistent false direction (TRIN ⩾ 80F).

number of inconsistent responses. The VRIN scale may help to interpret a high F score. For example, a high F in conjunction with a low to moderate VRIN score rules out the possibility that the former reflects random responding or confusion. The VRIN scale can also be used in place of the Test-Retest (TR) scale, from the original MMPI, which consisted of the 16 repeated items which no longer appear on MMPI-2.

An interesting example of how the VRIN scale can add to our interpretation of a client's MMPI-2 scores through refining our understanding of how consistently or inconsistently he or she has endorsed the items is shown in Figure 3-1. The MMPI-2 profile is that of a 32-year-old man in psychiatric inpatient treatment. Examination of the F scale would suggest that the profile is uninterpretable since the T score is 110, indicating possible random responding. However, the VRIN scale is at a T score of 69, indicating that the individual has endorsed the items in a consistent manner and ruling out an interpretation of randomness as suggested by T scores greater than 80. The patient's clinical profile would be interpreted as indicating a large number of symptoms either as a result of a psychotic process or else as a consistent pattern of symptom exaggeration to draw attention to himself. Although it has been possible to rule out random responding or carelessness as an explanation of his high F scale elevation, further evaluation, for example, an interview with the client, would be needed to determine which of the alternative explanations is more likely. VRIN interpretive guidelines are provided in Table 3-7.

All-True or All-False Pattern

Another useful index for assessing invalidity of MMPI-2 profiles is the Percentage of True or False Responses in the record. An extremely low true or false percentage, less than 20%, reflects a highly distorted response pattern such as conscious manipulation or careless responding to the items. Records with such a low percentage of true or false responses produce uninterpretable profiles. The effect of an all-true response pattern is shown in Figure 3-2 for the clinical scales and Figure 3-3 for the MMPI-2 Content Scales. The effect of an all-false pattern on clinical scales is provided in Figure 3-4 and for Content Scales in Figure 3-5.

The all-true response pattern provides an invalid and uninterpretable clinical profile with extreme elevation on the scales measuring severe psychopathology (Pa, Pt, Sc, and Ma). The resulting validity scale pattern is of interest. Notice that

Table 3-7. VRIN interpretive guidelines for the MMPI-2

☐ VRIN T scores ⩾ 80 indicate inconsistent random responding that invalidates an MMPI-2 protocol.

☐ VRIN T scores of 70 through 79 suggest a possibly invalid profile owing to inconsistent responding.

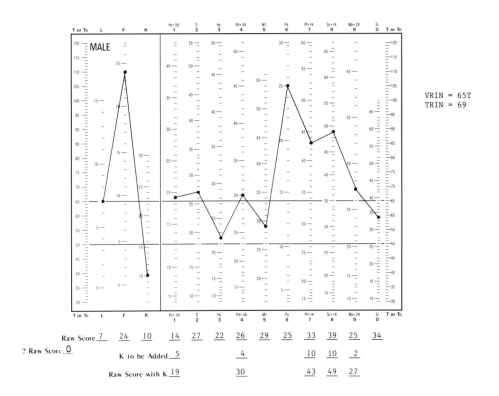

VRIN = 65T
TRIN = 69

	L	F	K	Hs+5K 1	D 2	Hy 3	Pd+4K 4	Mf 5	Pa 6	Pt+1K 7	Sc+1K 8	Ma+2K 9	Si 0
Raw Score	7	24	10	14	27	22	26	29	25	33	39	25	34
? Raw Score 0													
K to be Added				5			4			10	10	2	
Raw Score with K				19			30			43	49	27	

Figure 3-1. 32-year-old male. MMPI-2 basic scales profile

the F scale elevation is very high (a T score of 120), reflecting a clearly uninterpretable profile. The L and K scores are extremely low, reflecting the fact that the items on these two scales are predominantly endorsed in the false direction. The all-true response pattern also significantly affects the scores on the MMPI-2 Content Scales. All but one scale (SOD) are significantly elevated, since many of the Content Scale items are endorsed true.

The all-false response pattern produces a somewhat different, though equally invalid, profile. The L and K scores are extremely elevated, showing a clearly invalid configuration. Interestingly, the F scale is also elevated (a T score of 95), suggesting an unselective response to the items. Notice too that the all-false response pattern produces a more "neurotic" appearing profile with very high elevations on the Hs and Hy scales and high elevations on most of the scales employing a large K correction, such as Sc and Pt. Most of the MMPI-2 Content

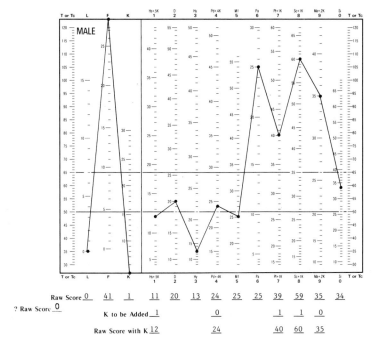

Figure 3-2. All-true pattern. MMPI-2 basic scales profile

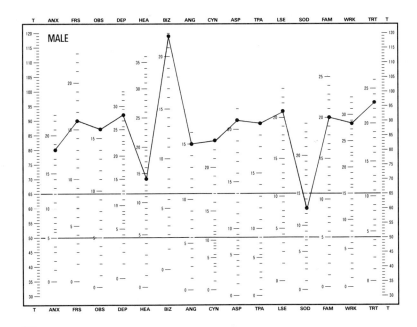

Figure 3-3. All-true pattern. MMPI-2 Content Scales profile

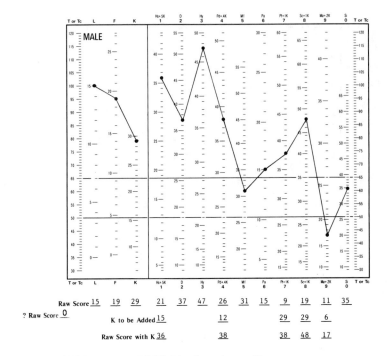

Figure 3-4. All-false pattern. MMPI-2 basic scales profile

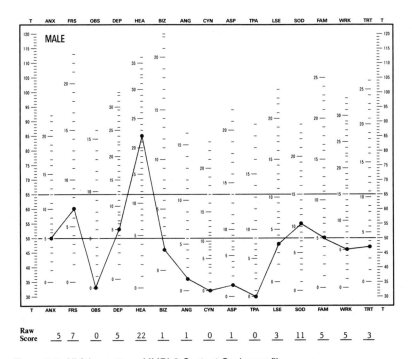

Figure 3-5. All-false pattern. MMPI-2 Content Scales profile

Scales are attenuated with an all-false response pattern; the one scale that is elevated is HEA.

Patterns of Response Invalidity

In assessing an individual's response attitudes to MMPI-2 items, it is valuable to view the configuration of validity scale scores. Very distinctive validity scale patterns emerge with different invalidating response sets. We will examine several of the most common invalidating patterns to discern the conditions under which such response patterns are frequently produced.

Fake-Good Profile

The profile shown in Figure 3-6 provides a good example of a relatively unsophisticated effort to distort MMPI-2 results by presenting an overly favorable self-view or a "good impression" pattern.

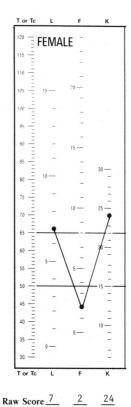

Raw Score 7   2   24

Figure 3-6. Fake-good pattern. MMPI-2 validity indicators

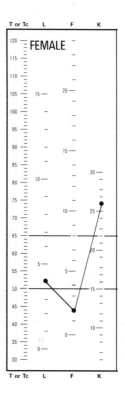

Raw Score 4   2   26

Figure 3-7. Defensive pattern. MMPI-2 validity indicators

In this configuration the elevated L score is prominent, suggesting that the individual has, perhaps consciously, endorsed many items that claim highly virtuous personality characteristics which, in their extreme, are very unlikely and create suspicion about the individual's willingness to cooperate with the evaluation. Assessment situations that frequently produce this pattern include child-custody evaluations, personnel screening, and physical-injury litigation in which the individual is attempting to proclaim a great deal of personal virtue and few or no psychological symptoms. The response set claiming excessive personal virtue is associated with an unwillingness to endorse psychological problems on the clinical scales; however, in some settings (worker's compensation evaluations) physical problems may be claimed readily.

Defensive Profile

The configuration presented in Figure 3-7 shows a high K profile in which the individual does not respond to the rather obvious L items or endorse psychological symptoms through the F scale. This response pattern is more consistently found among individuals who are psychologically inaccessible or unwilling to disclose much personal information about themselves—for example, reluctant therapy cases or individuals being assessed against their will.

This type of defensive profile does not provide a clear picture of the individual's adjustment problems, and both the basic and Content Scale profiles are likely to reflect few problems. A cautious statement about the individual's reluctance to report problems should be made in the report.

However, it is possible for some individuals to produce basic or Content Scale elevations even with this defensive response set. In these cases, when basic or Content Scale elevations occur in the context of a defensive record, the results should not be considered invalid, but should be interpreted with the understanding that the test profiles are likely to underrepresent psychological problems.

Exaggerated Symptom Pattern

The validity configuration shown in Figure 3-8 is a marginally valid profile that should be interpreted only with great caution. As noted earlier, the F scale should be below a T score of 79 to reflect a selective problem orientation. When the F score exceeds 80 the individual probably has endorsed an excessive number of psychological problems and is likely to be confused about the task or exaggerating psychological symptoms. However, this profile is valid and interpretable, though any discussion of the case should be prefaced with the caution that the individual clearly intended to present more problems or to appear more psychologically disturbed than he may be.

The highly exaggerated profile shown in Figure 3-9 was obtained in a worker's compensation case in which the individual was claiming a physical injury (neurological symptoms assumed to be related to toxic exposure) when no work-related injury incident had been reported and no organic basis could be dis-

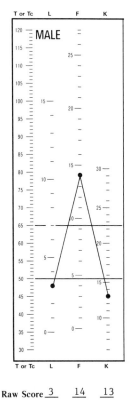

Raw Score _3_   _14_   _13_

Figure 3-8. Exaggerated symptom pattern.
MMPI-2 validity indicators

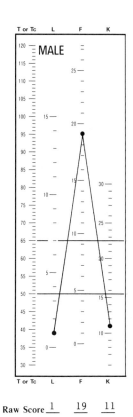

Raw Score _1_   _19_   _11_

Figure 3-9. Exaggerated symptom pattern.
MMPI-2 validity indicators

cerned for the injury in the physical examination. The individual presents a rather mixed and confused clinical picture in which a number of extreme and perhaps unrelated symptoms are endorsed.

Invalid Exaggerated Pattern

The extremely exaggerated profile shown in Figure 3-10 is an invalid pattern that should not be interpreted except to indicate that it is likely to be an exaggerated or faked record. The individual has endorsed a broad range of unrelated symptoms that do not reflect a clear and consistent pattern of psychopathology. His high score on the VRIN scale (T = 92) further supports the interpretation that he has not responded in a consistent, selective, problem-oriented manner on the test.

Highlight Summary: Alice's Validity Pattern

As we have seen in this chapter, the validity and utility of the MMPI-2 is dependent upon the cooperativeness of the individual taking the inventory. To appraise the individual's test-taking attitudes, a number of measures have been developed to pro-

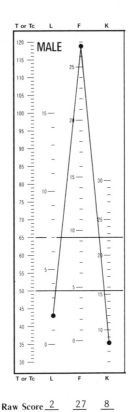

Raw Score 2   27   8

Figure 3-10. Invalid exaggerated symptom
pattern. MMPI-2 validity indicators

vide the interpreter with information about the individual's cooperativeness, openness, and willingness to share personal information through responses to the test
items. We will evaluate Alice's validity scale scores to determine whether her approach to the items provides a clear picture of her current personality functioning
and symptoms. (See validity profile on p. 40.)

The Cannot Say score provides information about how well a person cooperates
with the evaluation and complies with the instructions. Alice answered all the
MMPI-2 items. Moreover, her approach appears to be honest, based upon her responses to the L scale. Her average L score suggests that she did not attempt to
proclaim an unrealistic amount of rectitude. Her K score reflects a lack of defensiveness.

The F scale, a measure of response infrequency, needs to be evaluated to determine if the individual has endorsed an unrealistic number of problems. Alice has
endorsed a few F items, indicating that she reports some extreme symptoms. Her
T score of 80 on the F scale is considered consistent with appropriate problem expression (most patients endorse some items on F) and does not reflect a tendency
to exaggerate or falsely claim mental illness. Alice's response to the TRIN and

VRIN scales shows a pattern of consistent responding to test items. These validity scale scores and their relative elevations indicate that Alice's approach to the MMPI-2 items was valid and cooperative, and that her test protocol is likely to be a good indication of her present personality functioning and symptoms.

Chapter 4

Interpreting the MMPI-2 Standard Scales

After determining whether an MMPI-2 profile is valid, the next step in interpretation is to evaluate the client's scores on the standard scales. This step involves comparing the client's raw scores to those of people in general (i.e., to the MMPI-2 normative sample) by converting them into standard T scores. Scale interpretation involves assessing the elevation of each of the standard scales in the profile (see Figure 4-1) and applying the appropriate, established descriptors or correlates for the scale.

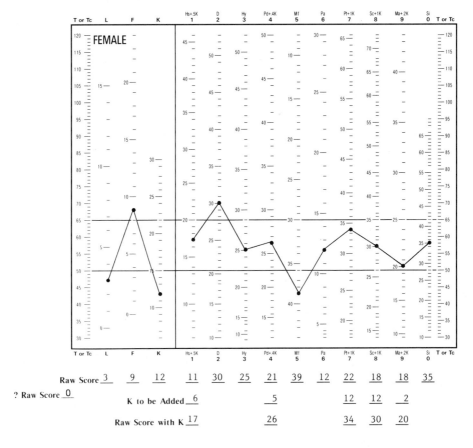

Figure 4-1. MMPI-2 K-corrected basic scales profile

As noted, converting the raw scores to T scores allows the interpreter to compare a client's score with the scores of the normative sample. Each T-score distribution has a mean score of 50 and a standard deviation of 10. The dark line on the profile sheet at the 65 T-score level, which uniformly across scales corresponds to the 92nd percentile, is the point at which elevation takes on clinical meaning. For example, in Figure 4-1 the highest standard scale score (and the only scale elevation in the clinically interpretable range) is on scale 2, the Depression scale (D), at a T score of 70, which falls at the 96th percentile. Since the client's score on the Depression scale is significantly elevated above the norm, the correlates of this scale could be applied to this individual with considerable confidence. An elevation on a particular scale reflects the likelihood that the individual "belongs" to the criterion group. A T score of 70 on scale 2 indicates that less than 4% of the population will score that high (at that degree of scale elevation) and the individual responds in a manner similar to the criterion group of depressed patients.

Low scores on most standard scales are not interpreted as possessing particular qualities. The exceptions to this interpretive rule are scales 0 (Social Introversion, Si) and 5 (Masculinity-Femininity, Mf), which are bipolar in meaning. That is, the Mf and Si scales convey interpretive information in the low end of the scores as well as in the elevated range. Low scores on Si, for example, reflect opposite behaviors from high scores (i.e., extroverted as opposed to introverted behavior). Linear T scores, not the uniform T scores of the clinical scales, are used to interpret scales 5 and 0, another reflection of the bipolar nature of these two scales. Some interpretive meanings of low scores are provided for scales 6 and 9 as well.

To interpret the MMPI-2 standard scales effectively it is necessary to understand and appreciate how the scales derive their meaning from the network of empirical correlates. Our discussion of each standard scale will highlight aspects that explain how the scale operates in describing clients' behavior: a) scale development procedures, b) item content, c) illustrative research underlying the scale, and d) a summary of the descriptors found to be associated with it. The first two aspects are relevant for the MMPI-A as well as for MMPI-2. MMPI-A scale descriptors are described in Chapters 10 and 11.

Scale Development Procedures

An adequate understanding of the MMPI-2 standard scales depends, in part, upon the interpreter's awareness of how they were developed. In most cases, the MMPI standard scales were derived using an empirical-contrast method. The original test authors, Hathaway and McKinley, collected a sample of "normal" subjects and a sample of patients fitting a clear, homogeneous diagnostic pattern. Items that differentiated the clinical from the normal group were included on a scale to define membership in a clinical-diagnostic group. In some cases noted below, further refinement of the scale was necessary to improve prediction.

Content

Most of the MMPI-2 standard scales contain heterogeneous item content. This complexity of the scales makes it difficult to interpret them strictly from the perspective of content. The task of interpreting the standard scales is made easier by evaluating the relative contribution of the specific content subscales, developed by Harris and Lingoes (1955), to the total elevation on the scale. Harris and Lingoes developed their content themes for scales 2, 3, 4, 6, 8, and 9 by rationally grouping the items on the scale into similar content groups. This strategy was developed to enable the interpreter to understand a particular scale elevation by evaluating the individual's response to specific item content. A similar set of subscales was more recently developed for scale 0. Content interpretation will be discussed more fully in Chapter 7. However, we are introducing the content homogeneous subscales in this chapter because they help the MMPI-2 interpreter understand how specific item content can contribute to the standard scale elevation. Although T scores are available for the Harris-Lingoes subscales, many of the item groups are too small to rely on for psychometric prediction. The subscales are also problematic measures because of the item overlap among them. However, they can be indicators of the relative weight of specific item content groups on the standard scale but should be consulted only if the T score on the parent standard scale (2, 3, 4, 6, 8, 9) is at least moderately elevated (i.e., ⩾ 60). The Harris-Lingoes subscales should not be used if the T score on the standard scale is 59 or less. Likewise, the Si subscales should be consulted only when the Si score is greater than or equal to 60. Harris-Lingoes subscales are interpreted at high elevations only (i.e., T scores greater than or equal to 65) because many of them are short.

Illustrative Empirical Research

As previously noted, an MMPI-2 standard scale obtains its meaning from the research studies that relate scale elevations to measured behavior. Several studies illustrating the characteristics that define each scale will be discussed. Numerous other general resources are available (e.g., Dahlstrom, Welsh, & Dahlstrom, 1975; Graham, 1990; Greene, 1991; Hedlund, 1977).

Scale Descriptors

The correlates for each of the scales were adapted from research findings and written in a style that can be used for generating interpretive statements from elevated scale scores. In our discussion of scale elevations, we will refer to a T score of 65 or greater as a high elevation unless otherwise specified. A T-score elevation between 60 and 64 is considered to be moderately elevated.

Much of the information presented in this chapter is also relevant to the MMPI-A standard scales, discussed in more detail in Chapter 10. The above descriptions of the meaning of T-score elevations, scale-development procedures, and item content apply equally well to the MMPI-A standard scales. As we'll see in Chapter 9, the standard scales are relatively intact in both restandardized versions of the instrument. For many years research and empirical descriptors derived from studies of adults were simply assumed to apply to adolescents. In some cases this assumption has been substantiated (e.g., Archer, Gordon, Giannetti, & Singles, 1988; Williams & Butcher, 1989a), in other instances it has not (e.g., Williams & Butcher, 1989b). This results in somewhat different interpretive guidelines for the MMPI-2 standard scales, which are covered in the present chapter, and the MMPI-A standard scales, described in Chapter 10.

Scale 1: Hypochondriasis (Hs)

Development Procedures

McKinley and Hathaway (1940) chose to use the clinical construct of hypochondriasis to develop the first scale of their multiphasic inventory because of the pervasiveness of this problem in medical and mental-health settings and because the disorder is clear-cut and relatively easy to diagnose. They defined hypochondriasis as "abnormal, psychoneurotic concern over bodily health." Most of the patients included in the criterion group were adults who were excessively concerned about bodily processes even though there was no organic basis to their problems. Because the authors were particularly interested in cases in which hypochondriacal concern was central to the clinical picture, they excluded those individuals whose somatization symptoms were part of a psychotic process.

Hathaway and McKinley (1940) were able to identify 50 cases of relatively "pure" hypochondriasis for the initial scale development. The patients included in the criterion group were homogeneous, selected to exclude individuals at age extremes and those who were actively psychotic. The "normal" control samples were composed of two groups. One included 109 men and 153 women ages 26-43 years. All were married and were visitors to the University of Minnesota Hospitals. A second group of 265 normal college students served as a control sample for the item selection to compensate for differences obtained in marital status, age, or socioeconomic level. Items initially selected for the scale were those that empirically differentiated the hypochondriacal patients from the normals. The authors also included a correction factor for individuals suffering from severe psychiatric disorders who presented with somatic symptoms. Originally there were 33 items on the Hs scale. Scale 1 of the MMPI-2 contains 32 of these original items; one item was deleted during the revision because of objectionable content. This same item was deleted from the MMPI-A.

Content

The items on Hs represent a broad range of physical symptoms. Scale 1 items are obvious and overlap primarily with the other neurotic scales (i.e., scales 2, 3, 7), particularly scale 3 which includes 20 Hs items. The items are not restricted to one body system or symptom pattern; rather, they include general aches, pains, weakness, fatigue, and ill health; stomach problems; breathing difficulties; poor vision and other sensory problems; coughing; sleep difficulties; dizziness; and numbness. Because its item content is so homogeneous, centering strictly around somatic complaints, Harris and Lingoes did not develop subscales for scale 1.

Illustrative Empirical Research

Hs has been widely researched and found to be related to excessive medical complaints, chronic pain, and extreme hypochondriacal concern. Although some research suggests that patients with actual physical disorders score with moderate elevations (i.e., T scores of 60-64) on Hs (Greene, 1954), elevated scores (i.e., T scores ≥ 65) generally reflect excessive somatic responding without a physical basis. Several recent studies support the traditional correlates of Hs as a measure of somatization. Lichtenberg, Skehan, and Swensen (1984) found that personality, as measured by Hs, was the most powerful predictor of pain compared with other measures such as arthritic severity or life stress. In a prospective study, Fordyce (1987) found that scale 1 and job dissatisfaction were more significantly related to employees' later development of low back pain than other personality, ergonomic, or life-event variables.

Individuals in a psychiatric inpatient facility who score high on Hs may be experiencing severe cognitive symptoms centering around hypochondriacal problems. Graham and Butcher (1988) found that psychiatric inpatients obtaining high scores on the MMPI-2 Hs were rated by clinicians as showing somatic concern, having unusual thought content, and exhibiting hallucinatory behavior.

Keller and Butcher (1991) found the MMPI-2 scale 1 was a prominent elevation among chronic pain patients. Scale 1 discriminated well between clinical groups characteristically having a great deal of somatic concern. Figure 4-2 shows how chronic pain patients responded to the Hs items in contrast with the MMPI-2 normative sample. The two groups produce very distinct response distributions. The level of scale elevation providing optimal group separation appeared to be at about a T score of 65.

The traditional interpretation of elevations on scale 1 as indicating somatic concern among general population subjects was confirmed in the couples rating study of the MMPI Restandardization Project (Butcher et al., 1989). The correlates of Hs for men and women in the normative sample, as rated by their spouses, centered around worries over health, reporting headaches, stomach trouble, and other ailments, and appearing generally worn out.

Descriptors

High scorers have excessive bodily concerns, numerous vague somatic symptoms, and undefined complaints such as gastric upset, fatigue, pain, and physical weakness. Their longstanding health concerns result in periods of reduced efficiency even though they are not incapacitated with a major illness. In addition to these physical complaints, they are likely to be selfish, self-centered, and

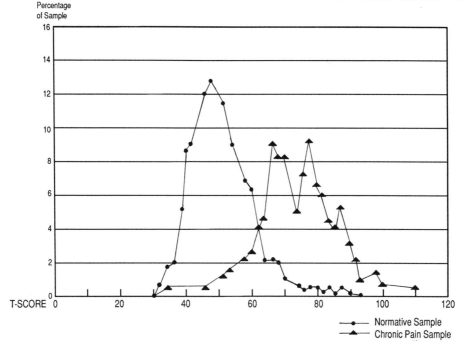

Figure 4-2. Uniform T-score distributions for Hs for normative and chronic pain men

narcissistic. Pessimism, a defeatist attitude, and cynicism also characterize them. They typically are dissatisfied and unhappy, tending to make others feel miserable with their complaining, whining, demanding, and critical behavior. They appear to lack manifest anxiety though they may report feeling tense. These individuals may express hostility indirectly, rarely acting out. Others may view them as dull, unenthusiastic, unambitious, and ineffective in verbal communication. Individuals who score high on scale 1 are viewed as not very responsive to psychological therapy, tend to seek only "medical" treatment, and tend to terminate therapy because the therapist is seen as not giving them enough attention and support.

Table 4-1 summarizes the interpretive guidelines for scale 1.

Scale 2: Depression (D)

Development Procedures

The second standard scale on the basic profile sheet, the Depression or D scale, provides the interpreter with a measure of symptomatic depression. The clinical picture assessed by the D scale is that of a generally negative frame of mind in which the individual has reported poor morale, lack of hope in the future, dissatisfaction with life, and a low mood.

In developing the original MMPI D scale, Hathaway and McKinley (1942) obtained 50 patients who were mostly in the depressed phase of a manic-depressive disorder. They used several contrast groups to develop scale 2, including:

Table 4-1. Scale 1 interpretative guidelines for the MMPI-2

☐ High elevations on scale 1 are T scores ≥ 65. The probability that the descriptors listed below apply to a given individual increases with higher scale elevations.

☐ Moderate elevations on scale 1 are T scores of 60-64, inclusive. Elevations in this range may be associated with some of the descriptors listed below. Many individuals with known medical disorders also obtain scores in this range.

☐ Descriptors for elevated scores:
  ● Excessive bodily concerns
  ● Vague somatic symptoms
  ● Epigastric complaints, fatigue, and pain
  ● Selfish, self-centered, and narcissistic
  ● Pessimistic, defeatist, and cynical outlook on life
  ● Dissatisfied and unhappy
  ● Whining and complaining
  ● Attention demanding
  ● Critical of others
  ● Expresses hostility indirectly
  ● Rarely acts out
  ● Functioning at a reduced level of efficiency but without major incapacity
  ● Tends to be difficult to engage in psychological therapy

139 normal married men and 200 normal married women between the ages of 26 and 43 years; 265 college students; and 50 patients without clinical depression. Initially, scale 2 was developed by determining which of the MMPI items significantly discriminated the depressed patients from the normal group. A number of additional items were included in the scale to minimize elevations on the scale for patients who were not diagnosed as depressed, but suffered from some other disorder. In the MMPI-2, three objectionable items were deleted from scale 2. The same deletions were made on the MMPI-A version of D.

Content

Most of the items on D contain content that is obviously related to low mood, low self-esteem, lack of interest in things, and feelings of apathy. Harris and Lingoes found several distinct subsets of item content on the MMPI D scale. They suggested the following subcategories of item content to help interpreters understand the meaning of scale 2 elevations. Again, these Harris-Lingoes subscales are interpreted only if the elevation on scale 2 is greater than or equal to 60 and the subscale's score is greater than or equal to 65.

D_1—*Subjective Depression* (32 items)
  High scorers on this subscale endorse content indicating that they feel depressed, unhappy, nervous, lack energy, and have few interests. They feel they do not cope well with problems and have difficulties concentrating and giving attention to daily tasks. They feel inferior, lack self-confidence, and are often shy and uneasy in social situations.

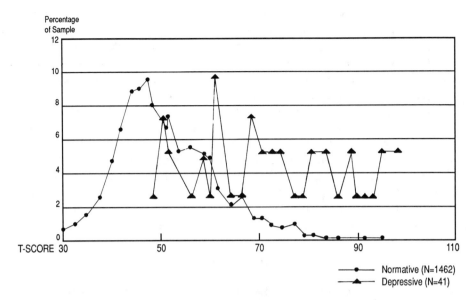

Figure 4-3. Uniform T-score distributions for D for depressed inpatients and normals

D_2 — *Psychomotor Retardation* (14 items)
High scorers on this subscale report being immobilized, listless, withdrawn, lacking energy, and avoiding people.

D_3 — *Physical Malfunctioning* (11 items)
High scorers on this subscale report that they are preoccupied with physical functioning, deny good health, and have a wide variety of somatic complaints.

D_4 — *Mental Dullness* (15 items)
High scorers endorse items suggesting lack of energy, tension, concentration problems, and attention deficits. They seem to lack self-confidence and feel that life is empty. They are apathetic.

D_5 — *Brooding* (10 items)
High scorers tend to brood and ruminate a great deal, and deny feeling happy. They feel inferior and report that life is not worth living. They feel easily hurt by criticism and feel that they are losing control of their thought processes. They report feeling useless.

Illustrative Empirical Research

The MMPI D scale has been found to be related to the presence of mood disorder (Endicott & Jortner, 1966; Nelson & Cicchetti, 1991). Butcher (1989d) showed that the MMPI-2 D score clearly differentiated depressed inpatients from normals, with a T score of 65 providing good separation between the two groups (see Figure 4-3).

In an inpatient psychiatric sample, Graham and Butcher (1988) found that psychiatric patients scoring high on the MMPI-2 D scale were rated by clinicians as having a depressed mood, feeling low, experiencing guilt feelings, and having hallucinations. Ben-Porath, Butcher, and Graham (1991) found that the MMPI-2 D score was the most effective standard scale for differentiating depressives from schizophrenics in an inpatient population.

Interpretation of elevated scale 2 scores for individuals from the general population received substantial empirical support from the couples rating study in the MMPI Restandardization Project (Butcher et al., 1989). Men and women who scored high on D were viewed by their spouses as generally maladjusted, lacking energy and self-confidence. Their spouses reported that they tended to get sad or blue easily, give up on tasks too quickly, and were overly concerned that something bad was going to happen. They were seen as lacking an interest in things and tended to be viewed as bored and restless.

Descriptors

High scorers are seen as depressed, unhappy, dysphoric, pessimistic, self-deprecating, guilt-prone, and sluggish. They report having somatic complaints, weakness, fatigue, low energy, and tension. These individuals are prone to worry, indecisive, and low in self-confidence. They report feeling useless and are unable to function effectively much of the time. They feel inadequate and report feeling like a failure at school or on the job. Individuals with high scores on D are viewed as introverted, shy, retiring, timid, reclusive, and aloof. They tend to maintain psychological distance and avoid interpersonal involvement. They are seen as cautious, not impulsive, and conventional. They are usually viewed as passive and unassertive and tend to make concessions in interpersonal relations to avoid conflict. High scorers tend to be motivated to receive treatment.

Table 4-2 summarizes the interpretive guidelines for scale 2.

Scale 3: Hysteria (Hy)

Development Procedures

In developing the original MMPI, Hathaway and McKinley were interested in providing an objective measure of a complex clinical phenomenon referred to as conversion hysteria, which today we call conversion disorder. Conversion disorder patients often manifest an unusual pattern of personality characteristics composed of denial and flamboyant social assertiveness. Yet, under environmental or relationship stress the individual may become suddenly disabled by physical problems, usually vague and of unknown origin. The patients used in the development of this scale were 50 cases with a clinical diagnosis of psychoneurosis (hysteria). Most were diagnosed as conversion hysteria (for example, aphonia or anesthesia). The normal group employed in the item analysis to de-

Table 4-2. Scale 2 interpretative guidelines for the MMPI-2

☐ High elevations on scale 2 are T scores ≥ 65. The probability that the descriptors listed below apply to a given individual increases with higher scale elevations.

☐ Moderate elevations on scale 2 are T scores of 60-64, inclusive. Elevations in this range may be associated with some of the descriptors listed below.

☐ Elevations on scale 2 can be more fully understood by examining the item content, as assessed by the Harris-Lingoes subscales, contributing to the scale elevation. The scale 2 Harris-Lingoes subscales are:
  - Subjective Depression
  - Psychomotor Retardation
  - Physical Malfunctioning
  - Mental Dullness
  - Brooding

☐ Descriptors for elevated scores:
  - Depressed, unhappy, and dysphoric
  - Pessimistic about the future
  - Self-deprecating, lacking in self-confidence
  - Often feels guilty
  - Sluggish, weak, easily fatigued, and reporting low energy
  - Having many somatic complaints
  - Agitated, tense, high-strung, and irritable
  - Prone to worry
  - Feels useless, unable to function, and like a failure
  - Typically introverted, shy, retiring, and timid
  - Aloof, withdrawn, or distant
  - Avoids interpersonal involvement
  - Cautious and conventional
  - Difficulty making decisions
  - Nonaggressive, overcontrolled, non-impulsive
  - Makes concessions to avoid conflict
  - Typically motivated for therapy

velop the Hy scale included 139 men and 200 women from the original MMPI normative sample and 265 college students. The final Hy scale contained 60 items, all of which were carried over into MMPI-2 and MMPI-A.

Content

The content of scale 3 is complex, composed of several seemingly unrelated item clusters. The items describe somatic complaints, denial of psychological problems, and social extroversion or social facility. Scale 3 items were grouped by Harris and Lingoes into five subscales, which are interpreted only when scale 3 is moderately or highly elevated (T scores ≥ 60) and the subscale score is high (T scores ≥ 65).

Hy_1—*Denial of Social Anxiety* (6 items)
   High scorers endorse items indicating that they are socially extroverted and comfortable in social settings. They deny being shy or having difficulty talking to others.

Hy_2—*Need for Affection* (12 items)
High scorers report having strong needs for attention and affection. They feel they are sensitive, optimistic, and trusting of others. They indicate that they tend to avoid confrontations and deny negative feelings toward others.

Hy_3—*Lassitude-Malaise* (15 items)
High scorers feel physically uncomfortable and in poor health. They deny being happy. They endorse feeling tired, weak, and fatigued, and report having concentration difficulties. They may claim to have a poor appetite, sleep disturbance, and feel vaguely unhappy.

Hy_4—*Somatic Complaints* (17 items)
High scorers report multiple somatic complaints such as headaches, dizziness, or problems with balance. They tend to use repression and conversion of affect in conflict situations.

Hy_5—*Inhibition of Aggression* (7 items)
High scorers deny hostile and aggressive impulses. They feel they are sensitive toward others, and deny irritability.

Several items on Hy may seem contradictory or inconsistent, but they reflect the incongruities in the conversion disorder itself. In nonclinical cases, these seemingly conflicting item groups are usually not endorsed together. However, in some clinical cases where the individual possesses these seemingly disparate characteristics, a particular clinical pattern emerges. This clinical pattern, made up of psychological denial, social facility, and manifestation of vague somatic complaints, is seen as a distinctive clinical syndrome centering around somatization. For example, in diagnostic disorders such as conversion disorder or psychogenic pain disorder, many of these disparate items are endorsed together resulting in marked elevations on scale 3.

Illustrative Empirical Research

Moderate elevations on Hy (60-64) are commonly produced by individuals who are attempting to put their best foot forward in a job application. They are not responding to content related to physical symptoms but, instead, are endorsing the items on Hy related to social facility and denial of problems (Butcher, 1979).

However, when Hy scores are highly elevated (T score $\geq$ 65), the meaning of the scale changes, reflecting the likely endorsement of vague, physical problems and health concerns. High elevations on Hy reflect a proclivity toward developing somatic complaints in response to stressful events. Individuals with elevated Hy scores are usually presenting somatic symptoms of a vague undefined nature. Research has found that a subtype of patients in chronic-pain programs produce high Hy scores often paralleling the elevation on Hs (Keller & Butcher, 1991). Thus, the Hy scale often forms an interesting configuration with other scales (to be discussed in the next chapter) in which *both* denial of psychological problems and manifestation of vague somatic complaints occur together. This pattern is sometimes associated with malingering, either conscious or unconscious, and physical problems (Butcher & Harlow, 1985).

Graham and Butcher (1988) found that psychiatric inpatients obtaining high scores on the MMPI-2 Hy scale showed other psychological problems in addition to their somatic concerns, which included clinician ratings of depression and low self-esteem.

Descriptors

Individuals who score high on Hy tend to react to stress by developing physical symptoms such as headaches, chest pains, weakness, and tachycardia. Symptoms appear suddenly and abate relatively quickly. Individuals with high Hy scores are seen as lacking in insight about the underlying etiology of their symptoms and about their own motives and feelings. They also tend to lack anxiety, tension, and depression, although in some settings and when other scales (such as D and Pt) are elevated, these symptoms can appear.

Individuals with Hy as their highest score are found to be psychologically immature, childish, infantile, self-centered, narcissistic, and egocentric. They seek and expect attention and excessive affection from others, and use indirect and manipulative means to get it. They are interpersonally indirect and do not express hostility and resentment openly. They tend to be socially extroverted, friendly, talkative, and enthusiastic, though somewhat superficial in interpersonal relationships. They may occasionally act out in a sexual or aggressive manner with little apparent insight into their behavior. High Hy scorers rarely report delusions, hallucinations, or suspiciousness. They may show initial enthusiasm about treatment, but efforts to change their behavior are often ineffective. They are seemingly slow to gain insight into the causes of their own behavior and are resistant to psychological interpretations. They have been found to respond well to direct advice or suggestion, if their defenses are not threatened.

Table 4-3 summarizes the interpretive guidelines for scale 3.

Scale 4: Psychopathic Deviate (Pd)

Development Procedures

This scale was developed by McKinley and Hathaway (1944) as a measure of antisocial tendencies or psychopathic behavior. The criterion groups that McKinley and Hathaway used in the original scale development were composed of young men and women (N = 78) from an inpatient university hospital and 100 inmates from a federal prison reformatory (all had received a psychiatric diagnosis of psychopathic personality). Their offenses included such acts as truancy, promiscuity, run-away, and theft. Their responses to the MMPI items were contrasted with 294 normal men and 397 normal women. The items on the MMPI-2 Pd scale are the same items (with minor rewording) as on the original MMPI Pd scale. One item ("My sex life is satisfactory."), deemed inappropriate for adolescents, was dropped from the MMPI-A Pd scale.

Table 4-3. Scale 3 interpretative guidelines for the MMPI-2

☐ High elevations on scale 3 are T scores ≥ 65. The probability that the descriptors listed below apply to a given individual increases with higher scale elevations.

☐ Moderate elevations on scale 3 are T scores of 60-64, inclusive. Elevations in this range may be associated with some of the descriptors listed below for scale 3.

☐ Elevations on scale 3 can be more fully understood by examining the item content, as assessed by the Harris-Lingoes subscales, contributing to the scale elevation. The Harris-Lingoes subscales for scale 3 are:
  ● Denial of Social Anxiety
  ● Need for Affection
  ● Lassitude Malaise
  ● Somatic Complaints
  ● Inhibition of Aggression

☐ Descriptors for elevated scores:
  ● Reacts to stress and avoids responsibility through development of physical symptoms
  ● Has headaches, chest pains, weakness, and tachycardia
  ● Symptoms often appear and disappear suddenly
  ● Lacks insight about causes of symptoms
  ● Lacks insight about own motives and feelings
  ● Shows low anxiety, tension, and depression
  ● Rarely reports delusions, hallucinations, or suspiciousness
  ● Psychologically immature, childish, and infantile
  ● Typically self-centered, narcissistic, and egocentric
  ● Expects attention and demands affection from others
  ● Uses indirect and devious means to get attention
  ● Does not express hostility and resentment openly
  ● Socially involved, friendly, talkative, and enthusiastic
  ● Superficial and immature in interpersonal relationships
  ● Typically slow to gain insight into causes of own behavior
  ● May be resistant to psychological interpretations
  ● May be initially enthusiastic about treatment and might respond to direct advice or suggestion

Content

The item content of Pd is quite heterogeneous, making interpretation of the scale somewhat complex. However, the total score is highly correlated with external behaviors indicating family or behavior problems of an aggressive, interpersonally manipulative, and impulsive nature. The Harris-Lingoes subscales can help facilitate the interpretation of elevations on scale 4:

Pd₁—Familial Discord (11 items)
> High scorers endorse items suggesting they view their home situation as unpleasant and lacking in love, support, and understanding. They view their family as critical and controlling. They indicate a desire to leave home.

Pd₂—Authority Problems (10 items)
> High scorers report that they resent authority and have had trouble with the law. They report definite opinions about right and wrong,

and tend to stand up for their beliefs. They report a history of behavior problems in school. They admit stealing, problematic sexual behavior, and problems with the law.

Pd_3—*Social Imperturbability* (12 items)

High scorers report feeling comfortable and confident in social situations. They acknowledge being exhibitionistic and opinionated.

Pd_4—*Social Alienation* (18 items)

High scorers report feeling misunderstood, alienated, isolated, and estranged from others. They report loneliness and unhappiness, and being uninvolved. They blame others for their problems. They report being self-centered, insensitive, and inconsiderate. They may also indicate some regret and remorse over their past actions.

Pd_5—*Self-Alienation* (15 items)

High scorers report feeling uncomfortable and unhappy with themselves. They seem to have problems in concentration. They report finding life uninteresting or unrewarding. They find it hard to settle down to life. They may report excessive use of alcohol.

Illustrative Empirical Research

High Pd elevations have been found to be related to membership in many deviant groups, including psychopathic personalities (Guthrie, 1952), delinquents (Rempel, 1958), shoplifters (Beck & McIntyre, 1977), prisoners (Panton, 1959), and drug addicts (Hill, Haertzen, & Glaser, 1960). These individuals tend to manifest considerable antisocial features. However, research has also shown the Pd score to be related to personality characteristics in normal groups as well. Moderate scale elevations occur among diverse groups, such as applicants for police department positions (Saccuzzo, Higgins, & Lewandowski, 1974), individuals with poor driving records (Brown & Berdie, 1960), skydivers (Delk, 1973), and actors (Taft, 1961). Assuredly, these moderate elevations appear to be due to the willingness to take risks and to unconventional or extroverted lifestyles among these individuals.

Several recent studies have been devoted to refining the characteristics measured by scale 4 in the MMPI-2. Lilienfeld (1991), using a sample of college students who had been assessed for the presence of DSM III-R characteristics of antisocial personality, reported that Pd was more closely associated with negative emotionality, especially alienation, than it was with other aspects of antisocial behavior. Interestingly, the Content Scale ASP (to be discussed in Chapter 7) is only modestly correlated (.37) with Pd (Butcher, Graham, Williams, & Ben-Porath, 1990), indicating that Pd and ASP are not assessing the same personality dimension. As noted above, scale 4 is a very heterogeneous scale containing many behaviors that are not antisocial, while ASP is a more direct measure of antisocial behaviors and attitudes.

Two other recent studies provided additional information about the meaning of elevations on scale 4. Pd was found to be highly related to the presence of marital problems. Couples in marital therapy had significantly higher MMPI-2 scale 4 elevations than did normal couples (Hjemboe & Butcher, 1991). Pd was also found to be prominent in mothers who were at risk for abusing their children (Egeland, Erickson, Butcher, & Ben-Porath, 1991).

Interpretation of elevated scale 4 scores for individuals from the general population received empirical substantiation from the couples rating study in the MMPI Restandardization Project (Butcher, et al., 1989). Subjects from the MMPI-2 normative sample who scored high on Pd were viewed by their spouses as antisocial, impulsive, moody, and resentful. They were reported to take drugs other than those prescribed by a doctor, have sexual conflicts, and show negative behavior such as swearing.

Descriptors

High scorers on scale 4 are found to engage in antisocial behavior, have rebellious attitudes toward authority figures, have stormy family relationships, tend to blame their parents for their problems, and show a history of underachievement in school or poor work history. If married, they tend to have marital problems. The high Pd scorer is viewed as impulsive, strives for immediate gratification of impulses, does not plan well, acts without considering the consequences, is impatient, shows limited tolerance of frustration, has poor judgment, and takes risks others avoid. Moderate range scores on Pd (60-64) should not be interpreted as reflecting the more extreme antisocial personality features.

High Pd people are viewed as immature, childish, narcissistic, self-centered, and selfish. In social situations they are seen as ostentatious, exhibitionistic, and insensitive. They seem to be interested in others only in terms of how they can use them for their own purposes. They usually are likeable and create a good first impression, although they are shallow and superficial in relationships. They seem unable to form warm attachments to others. They are viewed as extroverted, outgoing, talkative, active, energetic, spontaneous, and self-confident.

High Pd scorers are found to be hostile, aggressive, sarcastic, cynical, resentful, rebellious, and antagonistic. They may display aggressive outbursts, engage in assaultive behavior, and show little guilt over their negative behavior. Many individuals with this profile type may feign guilt and remorse when in trouble. They are usually seen as being free from disabling anxiety, depression, and psychotic symptoms. Those with high elevations are likely be diagnosed as personality disordered (antisocial or passive-aggressive).

As to potential for change, high scorers on scale 4 are viewed as unable to profit from experience and lacking in definite goals. They show an absence of deep emotional response and may not form a treatment relationship. They tend to be unmotivated and report feeling bored and empty. Their treatment prognosis is usually considered poor since they are resistant to change in therapy. They tend to blame others for problems and to intellectualize their problems. Al-

Table 4-4. Scale 4 interpretative guidelines for the MMPI-2

☐ High elevations on scale 4 are T scores ≥ 65. The probability that the descriptors listed below apply to a given individual increases with higher scale elevation.

☐ Moderate elevations on scale 4 are T scores of 60-64, inclusive. Elevations in this range may be associated with some of the descriptors listed below for scale 4.

☐ Elevations on scale 4 can be more fully understood by examining the item content, as assessed by the Harris-Lingoes subscales, contributing to the scale elevation. The Harris-Lingoes subscales for scale 4 are:
  • Familial Discord
  • Authority Problems
  • Social Imperturbability
  • Social Alienation
  • Self-Alienation

☐ Descriptors for elevated scores:
  • Antisocial behaviors
  • Rebellious toward authority figures
  • Stormy family relationships
  • Blames others for problems
  • History of under-achievement or work problems
  • Marital or other relationship problems
  • Impulsive behavior
  • Strives for immediate gratification
  • Does not plan well, acts without considering consequences of actions
  • Impatient, limited frustration tolerance
  • Poor judgment, takes many risks
  • Does not seem to profit from experience
  • Reportedly immature, childish, and self-centered
  • Often ostentatious and exhibitionistic
  • Insensitive to the needs of others
  • Tends to use other people for own gain
  • May be initially likeable, but tends to be superficial in relationships
  • May be unable to form warm attachments
  • Extroverted, outgoing, talkative, active, spontaneous
  • Lacks definite goals
  • May be hostile, aggressive, sarcastic, cynical, resentful, and rebellious
  • May act out in an aggressive manner
  • Shows little guilt over negative behavior, but may feign guilt and remorse when in trouble
  • Usually free from disabling anxiety, depression, and psychotic symptoms
  • Dissatisfied with life and feels bored and empty
  • Absence of deep emotional response
  • Poor prognosis for change in therapy

though they may agree to treatment to avoid punishments such as jail or some other unpleasant outcome, they are likely to terminate psychological therapy before change is effected.

Table 4-4 summarizes the interpretive guidelines for scale 4.

Scale 5: Masculinity-Femininity (Mf)

Development Procedures

The Masculinity-Femininity scale is different from the other standard scales in several ways. The construct underlying its development is not a clinical syndrome. Instead, scale 5 was designed to identify personality features of "male sexual inversion" or homosexual men who had a feminine interest pattern (Dahlstrom & Welsh, 1960; Hathaway, 1956). The criterion group used in the scale's development was quite small compared to the other standard scales and included only 13 homosexual men with gender identification problems (i.e., "male sexual inverts"). Hathaway (1956) was somewhat unclear about the procedures used for item selection, but Constantinople (1973) suggested the following progression:

1)   Retention of all items from the original MMPI pool which discriminated men from women;

2)   Deletion from this subpool of all items which failed to discriminate the responses of the 13 homosexual men forming the criterion group, as well as an unspecified number of men with high inversion scores on the Terman Inversion Scale, from 54 "normal" soldiers (all men);

3)   A check for men-women discrimination using both the original group of normals and smaller groups of soldiers (men) and airline employees (women).

The original MMPI Mf scale consisted of 60 items: 37 from the MMPI item pool and 23 suggested by the work of Terman and Miles (1936).

Hathaway attempted to improve Mf by using a criterion group of women "whose personal problems included homosexuality" (Hathaway, 1956). It was derived using a process similar to the procedures used for scale 5 and was designated Fm. However, Fm was highly correlated with Mf and did not perform well on cross-validation. Fm was abandoned in favor of using Mf for both men and women by reversing the T-score conversions for women. Thus, high T scores for men and women indicated a deviation from the interest patterns assumed to be typical for their gender (i.e., feminine interests in men and masculine interests in women).

Scale 5 was maintained on the MMPI-2 with four item deletions to eliminate objectionable content (i.e., those with religious themes) or irrelevant content (e.g., the item asking about "drop-the-handkerchief"). Additional item deletions on Mf were made on the MMPI-A, as described in Chapter 9.

Perhaps because of the basic assumptions underlying scale 5's development and the procedures followed, it is one of the more difficult standard scales to interpret. Homosexuality is no longer in the psychiatric nomenclature, nor are homosexuals considered more likely to have mental disorders than others. Thus, there is no need for a clinical measure to identify homosexuals. However, some, including the test authors, indicated that scale 5 also was a measure of "the tendency toward masculinity or femininity of interest pattern" (Hathaway & McKinley, 1942).

Constantinople (1973) provided cogent arguments against the use of scale 5 as a measure of masculine and feminine interests that we believe remain valid. First of all, the scale's item selection and validation procedures demonstrate that its major aim was to identify sexual inversion in men:

> *its derivation should produce some caution since homosexuality is explicitly included in the definition of the construct (p. 395).*

Constantinople also questioned the scale's underlying assumptions of unidimensionality and the bipolarity of its construct. Scale 5 assumes that masculinity-femininity is a single bipolar dimension ranging from extreme masculinity at one end to extreme femininity at the other. Furthermore, the Mf scale is based on the hypothesis that masculinity-femininity is a unitary, rather than a multidimensional, trait. Constantinople (1973) reviews several studies demonstrating that both rationally derived categories (Dahlstrom & Welsh, 1960) and factor analyses of scale 5 items (Graham, Schroeder, & Lily, 1971) indicate that the Mf-defined constructs of masculine and feminine interests are not opposite ends of a single bipolar continuum, but separate categories or factors. She also points to Cronbach's (1960) assessment of the overall weakness of scale 5.

Our concerns about the use of scale 5 in contemporary assessment are not limited to those expressed almost 20 years ago. Scale 5 items are not substantially different in the revisions of the MMPI because of the decision to maintain continuity in the standard scales between the MMPI and its successors, the MMPI-2 and MMPI-A. However, masculine and feminine interests have not remained stagnant since the Mf items were written in the 1930s and '40s. Items would have to be added to the MMPI item pool to adequately assess this construct. Furthermore, as indicated in the discussion above, responses from homosexual men were the predominant method of selecting items defining feminine interests in the original item pool. Decades of research on gender differences indicate that this is no longer an acceptable scientific practice.

Content

Scale 5 items are heterogeneous, most of them relating to interests and occupational choices, with very few indicating psychological problems or symptoms. Only five of the original 60 items deal with sexual concerns or practices. The occupational choices are very stereotypically feminine (e.g., librarian, nurse, artist who draws flowers) or masculine (e.g., soldier, sports reporter, forest ranger). Scale 5 item content is quite obvious to the test-taker, who can readily choose whether to admit to items indicating gender-based interests or sexual concerns.

A factor analysis by Graham et al. (1971) revealed six separate factors for this 60-item scale. A set of subscales for Mf using the results of this factor analysis was presented by Serkownek (1975) and gained popularity among users of the original MMPI. However, Graham (1990) described several methodological problems in the development of these subscales that resulted in their deletion from the MMPI-2.

Peterson (1989) developed two gender-role scales for the MMPI-2: GM (Masculine Gender Role) and GF (Feminine Gender Role). GM and GF were developed using the experimental item pool for the MMPI-2. However, this experimental item pool did not include new items designed to assess contemporary gender issues. These scales have not been sufficiently validated to use in clinical assessment.

Illustrative Empirical Research

Scale 5 has not been as extensively researched as many of the other standard scales. Constantinople (1973) indicated that several studies documented consistently large mean score differences between men and women. However, Murray (1963) found that 20 of the 60 items did not discriminate between the genders and deletion of those items brought men's scores largely into the normal range. Although extreme Mf scores have been interpreted as a possible indication of gender-identity problems or homosexuality in men, no support for such an interpretation for women has been documented (Constantinople, 1973).

Some of the earliest research findings demonstrate the influence of education on scale 5 scores. Goodstein (1954), for example, showed that college men scored one-half to one standard deviation above the mean reported for the Minnesota normals. Other characteristics such as intelligence and socioeconomic status have also been found related to Mf scores (Graham, 1990), which further complicates the scale's ability to predict gender-identity concerns.

Education remains important in the interpretation of MMPI-2 scale 5. The correlation between years of education and scale 5 T scores is .35 for men and $-.15$ for women (Butcher, 1990b). Mf scores range, on average, about five points lower for men with less than a high-school education and five points higher for men with postbaccalaureate degrees (Butcher, 1990b). Long and Graham (1991) failed to find any useful correlates for the MMPI-2 Mf scale. Greene (1991) also noted the relative paucity of behavioral correlates for scale 5.

Descriptors

The above descriptions of the development, content, and supporting research base for scale 5 indicate that a different interpretive approach is needed for this scale. Since the publication of the MMPI-2, we have begun to question the appropriateness and utility of continuing this scale on newer versions of the MMPI. As discussed in Chapter 10, we recommended that it be considered for deletion from the MMPI-A (Williams & Butcher, 1989a). However, this was thought to be too radical a departure from the original MMPI by several committee members. In any event, a cautious interpretive strategy is warranted unless additional research suggests otherwise.

The Mf scale is not a "symptom scale," as are most of the other standard scales. Elevations on this scale reflect interests, values, and personality characteristics. It can have meaning with both high and low scores, whereas most of the standard scales are interpreted at high elevations only. Interpretation of scale 5 differs by gender, educational level, socioeconomic status, and elevation levels. The meaning of elevated scores differs somewhat on scale 5 compared with the other standard scales. The more items endorsed by a male in the deviant direction, the greater his interests differ from the stereotypically defined masculine pattern. Because the feminine end of the scale has been defined primarily by responses from men, we refrain from making a similar statement for women.

College-educated men often obtain scores in the 60-65 T-score range. A moderately elevated MMPI-2 score for men with college backgrounds would be between 65-70. More extreme scores would be greater than or equal to 70. Greene (1991) suggests that these highly elevated scores in college men cannot be attributed solely to a humanistic and liberal arts background, but include gender conflicts as well.

Men with a high-school education or less typically achieve lower elevations. Thus, elevations that are considered moderate for men with a college education would be more extreme for those without such experiences. Low scores in men are defined as less than a T score of 40.

Elevated scores are somewhat unusual in women from the general population (e.g., only 6.6% of the women from the MMPI-2 normative sample score ≥ 65 T score on Mf). Elevated scores may be more likely from women in psychiatric settings. We observed that 14.7% of 191 women in a psychiatric setting had T scores ≥ 65 on scale 5. Low scores typically are defined for women as less than a T score of 40. However, it is important to keep in mind that highly educated women often score between 40-50.

Descriptors for Men

High elevations on scale 5 in men traditionally are interpreted as indicating more feminine interest patterns and behaviors, and a denial of stereotypically masculine interests. This interpretation must be tempered by the man's educational background and socioeconomic level. With more extreme elevations, high-scoring men may have conflicts about sexual identity, may be insecure in masculine roles or effeminate in manner. The high scorer likely endorses a variety of aesthetic and artistic interests. He may be seen as intelligent and valuing cognitive pursuits. Sensitivity, tolerance of others, and nurturance are other likely characteristics of high-scoring men. Submissive qualities may be apparent and acting-out behaviors are unlikely.

Low-scoring Mf men can be characterized as "macho." They endorse extremely masculine values, overemphasizing strength and physical prowess. They may be viewed as inflexible, coarse, crude, or vulgar. It has been suggested that extremely low scores indicate those with doubts about their masculinity, limited intellectual ability, narrow range of interests, and inflexible and unoriginal problem-solving abilities. However, low scores should not be over-interpreted in men without a high-school education.

Descriptors for Women

Women who score high on scale 5 are unusual compared with other women. They endorse items that are typically seen as representing extremely masculine interests. In the past, high scores in women were interpreted with positive characteristics such as assertiveness, vigorousness, competitiveness, being logical, and self-confidence. Other descriptors included aggressive, dominating, coarse, and rough. Women from the general population with high Mf scores have been described as blunt, unemotional, and unfriendly. Women in psychiatric settings with elevated scale 5 scores may be psychotic.

Women with lower Mf scores endorse more items indicative of what have been described as stereotypically feminine interests. Negative personality characteristics have been included as descriptors for low scale 5 scores including passivity, submissiveness, insecurity and doubts about their femininity, yielding and deferential behaviors. However, these descriptors of low scores were not validated in women who were highly educated (Graham, 1990).

Given the lack of studies, the scale's questionable developmental strategy as a measure of feminine interests in women, and the conflicting findings with educated women, we recommend considerable caution in making interpretive statements for women until more adequate studies are completed that demonstrate Mf's validity with women. At present we recommend only the interpretive statements appearing in Table 4-5.

Scale 6: Paranoia (Pa)

Development Procedures

Scale 6 assesses the behavior pattern of suspiciousness, mistrust, delusional beliefs, excessive interpersonal sensitivity, rigid thinking, and externalization of blame commonly found in paranoid disorders (Hathaway, 1956). These symptoms often occur with paranoid states, paranoid schizophrenia, or other severe paranoid disorders. The 40 items comprising Pa were obtained by empirical discrimination between a group of individuals diagnosed as having paranoid disorders or paranoid features in their clinical picture and normal individuals.

Scale 6 was initially found to work well in identifying many individuals in clinical settings with paranoid behavioral features. However, one problem that has been observed with Pa is that some individuals with clear paranoid features may second-guess the test and not endorse items that would produce a high Pa score. Instead, they answer the items in a wary, excessively sensitive, and mistrustful manner in keeping with their symptomatic behavior, actually producing low scale 6 scores.

The fact that some highly suspicious and mistrustful individuals do not score high on this scale raises the need for interpretive caution. If the Pa score is elevated above a T score of 65, interpret the profile as suggesting suspicion, mistrust, and possible paranoid ideation. However, the absence of scale elevation

Table 4-5. Scale 5 interpretive guidelines for the MMPI-2

☐ Interpretation of scale 5 differs by gender, educational level, socioeconomic status, and elevation levels. It is not a symptom scale and elevations reflect interests, values, and personality characteristics.

☐ College-educated men often obtain scores in the 60-65 T-score range. A moderately elevated MMPI-2 score for men with college backgrounds is 65-70. More extreme scores would be ≥ 70.

☐ Men with less than a high-school education typically achieve lower elevations. Thus, elevations that are considered moderate for college-educated men are more extreme for those without such experiences. Low scores in men are defined as less than a T score of 40.

☐ High elevations on scale 5 in men are interpreted as indicating more stereotypically feminine interest patterns and behaviors and a denial of stereotypically masculine interests. With more extreme elevations, high-scoring men may have conflicts about sexual identity, insecurity in masculine roles, or be effeminate in manner. The high scorer likely endorses a variety of aesthetic and artistic interests. He may be seen as intelligent and valuing cognitive pursuits. Sensitivity, tolerance of others, and nurturing are other likely characteristics. Submissive qualities may be apparent and acting-out behaviors are unlikely.

☐ Low-scoring men endorse extremely stereotypically masculine values, overemphasizing strength and physical prowess, often called "macho." They may be viewed as inflexible, coarse, crude, or vulgar. Lower scores suggest possible doubts about masculinity, limited intellectual ability, narrow range of interests, and inflexible and unoriginal problem-solving abilities.

☐ Elevated scores in women are somewhat unusual and can be defined as T scores ≥ 65. Low scores in women typically are defined as T scores < 40. Highly educated women often have T scores of 40-50.

☐ Until there is more evidence supporting the use of scale 5 with women, the scores should be interpreted cautiously:
- Women who score high on scale 5 describe interests that are typically seen as stereotypically masculine or "macho." This pattern is unusual compared to other women.
- Low-scoring women endorse more items reflecting interests that have been described as stereotypically feminine.

does not indicate the opposite, especially in inpatient facilities where low Pa scores can be found in individuals with paranoid disorders. The item content of Pa was not changed in the MMPI-2 or MMPI-A.

Content

Harris and Lingoes identified three subgroups of item content in Pa. These subscales can be used to clarify elevated scores on scale 6:

Pa₁—Persecutory Ideas (17 items)
High scorers report that their world is threatening and they have feelings of being misunderstood, unfairly blamed, or punished. They feel suspicious, distrust others, and tend to blame others for their problems. Elevations above 65 suggest delusions of persecution.

Pa₂—Poignancy (9 items)

High scorers see themselves as high-strung and sensitive. They seem to feel more intensely than others. They feel lonely, misunderstood, and distant from others. They may look for risk and excitement.

Pa₃—Naïveté (9 items)

High scorers endorse extremely naïve and optimistic attitudes about others. They seem to feel overly trusting and vulnerable to being hurt. They report having high moral standards and deny hostility.

Illustrative Empirical Research

Research on the MMPI in clinical samples indicates that Pa is related to severe psychopathology. Guthrie (1952) found that paranoid schizophrenics produce high elevations on Pa. Graham and Butcher (1988) found that psychiatric inpatients obtaining high scores on scale 6 were rated by clinicians as suspicious, having unusual thoughts, being anxious, and showing emotional withdrawal.

Interpretation of elevated Pa scale scores for normals received empirical substantiation from the couples rating study in the MMPI Restandardization Project (Butcher, et al., 1989). As viewed by their husbands, women from the MMPI-2 normative sample who scored high on Pa were moody, had tendencies to get sad and blue, lacked emotional control, cried easily, and had bad dreams.

Descriptors

The correlates for Pa change markedly at different levels of elevation, which differs somewhat from many of the other standard scales. Individuals with very high elevations (T > 80) often show frankly psychotic behavior, disturbed thinking, delusions of persecution or grandeur and ideas of reference. They tend to feel mistreated, picked on, and are angry and resentful. They harbor grudges toward others and use projection as a defense mechanism. The most frequently applied diagnoses of extremely high Pa individuals are schizophrenia, paranoia, or paranoid personality.

Individuals with high elevations (T = 65-79) often manifest a paranoid predisposition. They are hypersensitive and overly responsive to reactions of others, feel they get a raw deal from life, rationalize and blame others, are suspicious and guarded, and are hostile, resentful, and argumentative. High scorers are viewed as moralistic and rigid and tend to overvalue rationality. They are viewed as having a poor prognosis for therapy, since they do not like to talk about emotional problems, and usually have difficulty establishing rapport with a therapist.

Individuals with moderate elevations (T scores of 60-64, inclusive) show no specific correlates. It should be noted that some individuals obtain scores in this range on the basis of endorsing the interpersonal sensitivity items on the scale. Interpretation of elevations in this range can be clarified by reference to the Harris-Lingoes subscales.

Very low scores (T < 35) should be interpreted with caution, because some individuals with paranoid problems can obtain scores in this range. Low Pa scores (especially in an inpatient context) are viewed as functionally paranoid if the following conditions are found:

(a) the Pa score is below a T score of 35

(b) the Pa score is the lowest scale on the profile

(c) at least one standard scale score is above a T score of 65

(d) the validity configuration is defensive (i.e., both L and K are above 60 T and above F).

Under these conditions, low Pa scores suggest a frankly psychotic disorder, delusions, suspiciousness, ideas of reference, and symptoms that are less obvious than for high scorers. They tend to be evasive, defensive, guarded, shy, secretive, and withdrawn.

Table 4-6 summarizes the interpretive guidelines for scale 6.

Scale 7: Psychasthenia (Pt)

Development Procedures

Scale 7 was originally developed to assess a psychological disorder (psychasthenia) that today we would describe as anxiety disorder with obsessive-compulsive features. Hathaway and McKinley (1942) obtained a criterion group of patients (20 patients with clear diagnoses) who possessed behavioral features of anxiousness, severe ruminations, and obsessive-compulsive features. The patients' MMPI responses were contrasted with those of the normal Minnesota sample (139 men and 200 women ages 26-43) to obtain the provisional scale. Then internal consistency statistics were used to eliminate items that were not highly correlated with the total score. This procedure resulted in a final scale with high internal consistency and a clear relationship with the first factor (anxiety) of the MMPI. Even though the clinical diagnosis of psychasthenia does not exist in today's psychiatric nomenclature, the features central to the syndrome (anxiety, ruminations, feelings of insecurity, etc.) are very much apparent in most clinical settings. Scale composition for Pt is the same in MMPI-2 and MMPI-A as it is in the original instrument.

Content

There are no specific content subscales for Pt since the items on this scale are homogeneous, measuring a single dimension. As noted above, this scale was developed, in part, by internal consistency procedures (that is, only items with a high correlation with the total score were included on the scale). Consequently, scale 7 contains items that assess anxiety or general maladjustment.

Table 4-6. Scale 6 interpretive guidelines for the MMPI-2

☐ Very high elevations on scale 6 are T scores ≥ 80. High elevations on scale 6 are T scores of 65-79, inclusive.

☐ Elevations on scale 6 can be more fully understood by examining the item content, as assessed by the Harris-Lingoes subscales, contributing to the scale elevation. The Harris-Lingoes subscales for scale 6 are:
- Persecutory Ideas
- Poignancy
- Naïveté

☐ Descriptors for very high elevations:
- May show frankly psychotic behavior and disturbed thinking
- Delusions of persecution and/or grandeur likely
- Ideas of reference
- Tends to feel mistreated and picked on
- Tends to be angry, resentful, and harbors grudges
- Uses projection as a defense
- Most frequently diagnosed as schizophrenia or paranoid state

☐ Descriptors for high elevations:
- Paranoid predisposition
- Overly sensitive and responsive to reactions of others
- Feels that he or she is getting a raw deal from life
- Tends to rationalize and blame others
- Shows suspicious and guarded behavior
- Hostile, resentful, and argumentative
- Tends to be moralistic and rigid
- Overemphasizes rationality
- Does not like to talk about emotional problems
- Has difficulty establishing rapport with therapist
- Tends to have a poor prognosis for therapy

☐ In some cases (see text for more details), individuals with extremely low T scores (≤ 35) may have paranoid disorders and are so suspicious and distrustful that they respond evasively to the scale 6 items. In clinical settings these low scores, coupled with a defensive validity pattern, suggest:
- Frankly psychotic disorder, delusions, or suspiciousness
- Ideas of reference
- Symptoms are usually less obvious than for high scorers
- Evasive, defensive, guarded individual
- May be shy, secretive, withdrawn

Illustrative Empirical Research

Research on scale 7 has shown it to be associated with severe and debilitating anxiety. For example, Schofield (1956) found Pt to be the peak score among neurotic outpatients diagnosed as having anxiety-state or obsessive-compulsive disorders.

In inpatient psychiatric settings with a large percentage of severe affective disorders and schizophrenics, the behavioral correlates for the MMPI-2 Pt scale suggest disabling psychological symptoms. Graham and Butcher (1988) found that the MMPI-2 Pt scale had several significant correlates in inpatient psychiatric settings including severe guilt, low energy, depressed mood, and hallucinations.

Scale 7 has been shown to have clear behavioral correlates in the normal range of subjects as well. In the MMPI-2 normative study, Pt received substantial empirical support from the couples rating comparisons (Butcher et al., 1989). Normal men and women with high Pt scores were rated by their spouses as having many fears, being nervous and jittery, being indecisive, lacking in self-confidence, and having sleeping problems.

Descriptors

People who score high on Pt tend to be anxious, tense, and agitated. They report great discomfort, worry, and feelings of apprehension. They are considered to be high-strung, depressed, jumpy, and have concentration difficulties. They report being introspective, ruminative, indecisive, obsessive, and compulsive. They feel insecure and inferior, lack self-confidence, are plagued by self-doubt, are self-critical, self-conscious, and self-derogatory. They are viewed as rigid and moralistic since they profess high standards for themselves and others, are overly perfectionistic, conscientious, and guilt-prone. They lack ingenuity and originality in problem solving, are dull and formal, and vacillating. They tend to distort the importance of problems and overreact to minor situational problems. They usually are shy and do not interact well socially. They are hard to get to know, yet worry about their popularity and acceptance. They are sensitive, show insight into problems, tend to intellectualize and rationalize. They are often described as neat, orderly, organized, meticulous, persistent, and reliable. They are somewhat resistant to interpretations in therapy, express hostility toward their therapist, remain in therapy longer than most patients, and usually make slow, gradual progress in therapy.

Interpretive guidelines for scale 7 are provided in Table 4-7.

Scale 8: Schizophrenia (Sc)

Development Procedures

The development of the Schizophrenia scale (Sc) differed somewhat from the development of the other MMPI standard scales. Hathaway (1956) indicated that he and McKinley attempted to develop several separate scales for the four recognized subtypes of schizophrenia identified at the time (i.e., catatonic, paranoid, simple, and hebephrenic) using two partly overlapping groups of 50 patients who had been diagnosed as having schizophrenia. However, since they could not differentiate successfully between the different subtypes of schizophrenia, Hathaway and McKinley simply merged all the items into a single scale for schizophrenia. Consequently, the resulting Sc scale is quite long and complex. It contains the same items in the MMPI-2 as in the original MMPI, although one item was dropped from the MMPI-A version.

Table 4-7. Scale 7 interpretative guidelines for the MMPI-2

☐ High elevations on scale 7 are T scores ≥ 65. The probability that the descriptors listed below apply to a given individual increases with higher scale elevations.

☐ Moderate elevations on scale 7 are T scores of 60-64, inclusive. Elevations in this range may be associated with some of the descriptors listed below.

☐ Descriptors for elevated scores:
  ● Anxious, tense, and agitated
  ● Discomfort, worry, and apprehension
  ● High strung and jumpy
  ● Difficulties in concentrating
  ● Introspective, ruminative, obsessive, and compulsive
  ● Feels insecure and inferior
  ● Lacks self-confidence, has great self-doubts
  ● Self-critical, self-conscious, and self-derogatory
  ● Rigid and moralistic
  ● High standards for self and others
  ● Overly perfectionistic and conscientious
  ● Tends to be guilty and depressed
  ● Often orderly and meticulous
  ● Persistent and performs tasks in a stereotyped manner
  ● Often constricted in action and lacks ingenuity and originality in problem-solving
  ● Indecisive
  ● Overreacts to minor problems
  ● Shy and does not interact well socially
  ● Hard to get to know, but worries about popularity and acceptance
  ● Reports physical complaints
  ● May show some insight into problems
  ● Intellectualizes and rationalizes
  ● Resistant to interpretations in therapy
  ● Remains in therapy longer than most patients
  ● Makes slow but steady progress in therapy

Content

As indicated above, the procedures used in the development of scale 8 produced a rather long and heterogeneous scale. A high score on this scale reflects a number of diagnostic possibilities since individuals with many disorders can receive high elevations, including schizophrenics, chronic psychiatric patients with affective disorders, persons with organic brain disorders, or severe personality disorders, normal individuals with severe sensory impairment, unconventional, rebellious, and counterculture people (e.g., the hippies of the 1960s).

Interpretation of Sc can be facilitated by examining the relative contributions of the different content subgroups to the total score. Harris and Lingoes, in their rational categorization of the item content for scale 8, suggest the following subcategories:

Sc₁—Social Alienation (21 items)
> High scorers endorse items that suggest feelings of being misunderstood and mistreated. They report their family situation is lacking in love and support, and they feel hostility and hatred toward

their family members. They feel lonely and empty, having never experienced a love relationship. They feel that they are being plotted against.

Sc_2—*Emotional Alienation* (11 items)
High scorers report feelings of depression and despair. They may wish they were dead and are frightened and apathetic.

Sc_3—*Lack of Ego Mastery, Cognitive* (10 items)
High scorers fear losing their mind. They report having strange thought processes, feelings of unreality, and problems with concentration and attention.

Sc_4—*Lack of Ego Mastery, Conative* (14 items)
High scorers feel that life is a strain. They report having depression, despair, and worry. They have problems coping with everyday life. Life is not interesting or rewarding for them. They seem to have given up hope and may wish they were dead.

Sc_5—*Lack of Ego Mastery, Defective Inhibition* (11 items)
High scorers report feeling out of emotional control. They are impulsive, restless, hyperactive, and irritable. They may have laughing or crying spells and may not remember previously performed activities.

Sc_6—*Bizarre Sensory Experiences* (20 items)
High scorers feel their body is changing in unusual ways. They may have blank spells, hallucinations, or unusual thoughts, or external reference. They report skin sensitivity, weakness, and ringing in ears. They report having peculiar and strange experiences.

Illustrative Empirical Research

The Sc scale has been shown to be empirically related to a number of extreme personality characteristics and symptomatic behaviors, including the diagnosis of schizophrenia (Lewinson, 1968; Moldin et al., 1991; Wauck, 1950; Rosen, 1958). Shaffer, Ota, and Hanlon (1964) found that Sc was associated with the severity of the disorder. More recently, with the MMPI-2, Graham and Butcher (1988) found that psychiatric inpatients obtaining high Sc scores were rated by clinicians as having suspiciousness and unusual thought content.

Descriptors

Given this scale's complexity and the large number of personality and symptomatic behaviors it assesses, interpretation may change somewhat depending upon scale elevation. It is possible, for example, for an individual to obtain a moderate elevation (e.g., 60-65) on the scale if he or she has a sensory impairment or lives a rather unconventional life. Possible interpretation of scale elevations in this range should be verified with reference to demographic or admitting complaint information. However, marked elevation on the scale (greater than 70) suggests significant personality problems and symptoms.

Individuals who score 65-69 on Sc tend to have an unconventional life-style and feel somewhat alienated from others. They feel distant and different from others and may tend toward reclusiveness. They tend to feel inferior and socially different from others and may appear aloof and uninterested. They tend to employ fantasy as a defense against unpleasant situations and may daydream a great deal. High Sc scorers are somewhat immature and self-preoccupied. They may be non-conforming and reluctant to go along with conventions. Some high scale 8 individuals are impulsive, aggressive, or anxious.

Very high scorers (70-79) tend to have a schizoid life-style, do not feel a part of the social environment, are isolated, alienated, and misunderstood. They report feeling unaccepted by peers and are often seen as withdrawn, reclusive, secretive, and inaccessible. They avoid dealing with people and new situations, and are seen as shy, aloof, and uninvolved. These individuals are anxious, resentful, hostile, and aggressive. They are unable to express their feelings and tend to react to stress by withdrawing into fantasy and daydreaming. They have difficulty separating reality and fantasy, have great self-doubts and feel inferior, incompetent, and dissatisfied. They may manifest sexual preoccupation and experience sex-role confusion. They are nonconforming, unusual, unconventional, and eccentric. Others view them as stubborn, moody, opinionated, immature, and impulsive. Some high-scoring Sc persons are also reported to be imaginative, abstract, and have vague goals. They often appear to lack basic information for problem-solving, have a poor prognosis for therapy, and are reluctant to relate in a meaningful way to a therapist. They may stay in therapy longer than most patients, and may eventually come to trust their therapist.

Extremely high scorers (T > 80) may show blatantly psychotic behavior, confusion, disorganization, and disorientation. They typically report unusual thoughts or attitudes, delusions, hallucinations, and poor judgment.

Table 4-8 summarizes the interpretive guidelines for scale 8.

Scale 9: Hypomania (Ma)

Development Procedures

McKinley and Hathaway (1944) were interested in developing a measure of manic or hypomanic behavior, the tendency to act in euphoric, aggressive, and hyperactive ways. The Ma scale was developed initially by contrasting a group of 24 individuals who were experiencing manic (usually less intense hypomanic) episodes of euphoria. All of the patients were in an inpatient facility and had been clearly diagnosed as having manic or hypomanic behaviors. A total of 46 items were found to significantly discriminate the clinical cases from normals. All 46 items were retained in the MMPI-2 and MMPI-A.

Table 4-8. Scale 8 interpretive guidelines for the MMPI-2

☐ Extremely high elevations on scale 8 are T scores ⩾ 80. Very high elevations on scale 8 are T scores of 70-79, inclusive. High elevations are 65-69, inclusive. Different descriptors are associated with these differing levels.

☐ Elevations on scale 8 can be more fully understood by examining the item content, as assessed by the Harris-Lingoes subscales, contributing to the scale elevation. The Harris-Lingoes subscales for scale 8 are:
  • Social Alienation
  • Emotional Alienation
  • Lack of Ego Mastery, Cognitive
  • Lack of Ego Mastery, Conative
  • Lack of Ego Mastery, Defective Inhibition
  • Bizarre Sensory Experiences

☐ Descriptors for extremely high scale 8 scores:
  • Blatantly psychotic behavior
  • Confused, disorganized, and disoriented
  • Unusual thoughts or attitudes, delusions, hallucinations
  • Shows poor judgment

☐ Descriptors for very high scale 8 scores:
  • Schizoid life-style
  • Does not feel a part of social environment; feels isolated, alienated, and misunderstood
  • Unaccepted by peers, withdrawn, seclusive, and secretive
  • Emotionally inaccessible
  • Avoids dealing with people and new situations
  • Shy, aloof, and uninvolved
  • Experiences generalized anxiety
  • Resentful, hostile, and aggressive
  • Unable to express feelings; reacts to stress by withdrawing into fantasy and daydreaming
  • Difficulty separating reality and fantasy
  • Many self-doubts, feels inferior, incompetent, and dissatisfied
  • Shows considerable sexual preoccupation and sex-role confusion
  • Nonconforming, unusual, unconventional, and eccentric
  • May present long-standing physical complaints
  • Often seen as stubborn, moody, and opinionated
  • Immature and impulsive
  • Lacks basic information for problem-solving
  • Shows a poor prognosis for therapy, but may stay in therapy longer than most patients

☐ Descriptors for high elevations:
  • Unconventional life-style
  • Nonconforming
  • Somewhat alienated from others
  • Distant and feels different from others
  • Feelings of inferiority
  • Aloof and uninterested
  • Uses fantasy as a defensive mechanism
  • Daydreams frequently
  • Immature and self-preoccupied
  • May be impulsive, aggressive, or anxious

Content

Harris and Lingoes found four rational categories summarizing the item content on Ma:

Ma₁—Amorality (6 items)

High scorers may see others as selfish and dishonest, which provides justification for their behaving this way as well. They derive vicarious satisfaction from the manipulative exploits of others.

Ma₂—Psychomotor Acceleration (11 items)

High scorers show accelerated speech, overactive thought processes, and excessive motor activity. They may be tense, restless, excited, and elated without cause. They are easily bored and tend to seek out excitement. They can be impulsive and do harmful or shocking things.

Ma₃—Imperturbability (8 items)

High scorers deny social anxiety. They are not especially sensitive about what others think. They are often impatient and irritable toward others.

Ma₄—Ego Inflation (9 items)

High scorers appraise themselves unrealistically. They are resentful of demands made by others.

Illustrative Empirical Research

Research on scale 9 has shown it to be related to pathological behavioral and symptomatic correlates. Gilberstadt and Duker (1965) found that patients with high Ma elevation were hyperactive, alcoholic, grandiose, and talkative. They were most frequently diagnosed as manic-depressive, manic type, and tended to have work adjustment problems. Graham and Butcher (1988) found that psychiatric inpatients with high scores on the MMPI-2 Ma scale were rated by clinicians as having an elevated mood, being hostile, and having conceptual disorganization.

Normal individuals with elevations on this scale have been shown to be ebullient, overactive, and guileful (Gough, McKee, & Yandell, 1955). The traditional correlates for Ma scores from normal individuals received considerable empirical support from the couples rating study in the MMPI Restandardization Project (Butcher et al., 1989). High Ma wives were rated by their husbands as wearing strange or unusual clothes, talking too much, making big plans, getting very excited or happy for little reason, stirring up excitement, taking many risks, and telling people off. High Ma men were viewed by their wives as acting bossy, talking back to others without thinking, talking too much, whining and demanding attention, and taking drugs other than those prescribed by a doctor.

Descriptors

Since many individuals from normal samples obtain high scores on this scale and some patients with affective disorder do not, it is important to keep the level of elevation in mind when interpreting this scale.

Very high scorers (T > 75) are viewed as hyperactive, have accelerated speech, and may have hallucinations or delusions of grandeur. They may express a wide range of interests, but do not use energy wisely and tend not to complete projects. They may be viewed as somewhat disorganized. Many very high Ma people are viewed as creative, enterprising, and ingenious; however, they show little interest in routine or detail. They become easily bored and restless, have a low frustration tolerance, and may have difficulty in inhibiting expression of impulses. Episodes of irritability, hostility, and aggressive outbursts may occur. They are usually viewed as unrealistic, possessing unqualified optimism, having grandiose aspirations, and exaggerating self-worth and self-importance. Individuals who score very high on Ma are unable to see their own limitations. They are viewed by others as outgoing, sociable, and gregarious. They like to be around other people and may create a good first impression because they are friendly, pleasant, and enthusiastic. Their relationships tend to be superficial. They tend to be highly manipulative, deceptive, and unreliable, and they experience relationship problems as a result. They may have periods of agitation and periodic episodes of depression. Difficulties at school or work are common. They tend to be resistant to interpretations. They attend therapy sessions irregularly and may terminate therapy prematurely.

Individuals who score high on scale 9 (T scores of 65-74, inclusive) are viewed as energetic, active, talkative, and as having a broad range of interests. They seem to prefer action to thought, but may not use their energies wisely or see projects through to completion. Individuals with elevated Ma scores are usually sociable, manipulative, persuasive, glib, and somewhat impulsive.

Although some normals score in this range of Ma, most high scorers on this scale encounter interpersonal problems as a result of their manipulativeness and lack of follow-through. They tend to experience mood problems, such as elation or euphoria without cause, extreme self-orientation, or impulsivity.

Low scorers (T ≤ 35) report having low energy and activity levels, lethargy, listlessness, apathy, and are difficult to motivate. They report chronic fatigue, physical exhaustion, depression, anxiety, and tension. Low scorers approach problems in conventional, practical ways. They tend to lack self-confidence and are sincere, quiet, modest, withdrawn, seclusive, unpopular, and overcontrolled.

Interpretive guidelines for scale 9 are provided in Table 4-9.

Scale 0: Social Introversion (Si)

Development Procedures

The Si scale was originally published as a separate measure of social introver-

Table 4-9. Scale 9 interpretive guidelines for the MMPI-2

☐ There are four levels of elevation on scale 9: very high (T scores ⩾ 75), high (T scores of 65-74, inclusive), moderate (T scores of 60-64, inclusive), and low scores (T scores < 35). Interpretive statements vary for each of these levels.

☐ Elevations on scale 9 can be more fully understood by examining the item content, as assessed by the Harris-Lingoes subscales, contributing to the scale elevation. The Harris-Lingoes subscales for scale 9 are:
- Amorality
- Psychomotor Acceleration
- Imperturbability
- Ego Inflation

☐ Descriptors for very high scale 9 scores:
- Overactive and may have accelerated speech
- May have hallucinations or delusions of grandeur
- May be experiencing a mood disorder
- Energetic and talkative
- May be extremely narcissistic
- Prefers action to reflection
- Shows a wide range of interests and activities
- Does not utilize energy wisely; does not see projects through to completion
- Has little interest in routine or detail
- Becomes easily bored and restless
- Low frustration tolerance
- Difficulty in inhibiting expression of impulses
- Episodes of irritability, hostility, and aggressive outbursts
- Often has unrealistic, unqualified optimism
- Has grandiose aspirations
- Exaggerates self-worth and self-importance
- Unable to see own limitations
- Outgoing, sociable, and gregarious
- May have periods of agitation
- May have periodic episodes of depression
- Resistant to interpretations in therapy
- Attends therapy irregularly; may terminate therapy prematurely

☐ Descriptors for high scale 9 scores:
- Overactive
- Exaggerated sense of self-worth, narcisstic
- Energetic, talkative, prefers action to reflection
- Shows a wide range of interests
- Does not utilize energy wisely and does not complete projects
- May be viewed as enterprising and ingenious
- Shows inattention to routine matters
- Becomes bored and restless easily
- Low frustration tolerance
- May be impulsive
- May have episodes of irritability, hostility, and aggressive outbursts
- May be overly optimistic at times
- May show some grandiosity and be unable to see own limitations
- Outgoing, sociable, and gregarious
- Socially manipulative
- Repeat problems
- Usually considers therapy unnecessary and is resistant to interpretations in therapy
- Attends sessions irregularly and may terminate therapy prematurely

Table 4-9. Scale 9 interpretive guidelines for the MMPI-2, continued

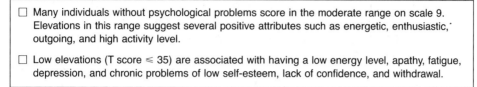

☐ Many individuals without psychological problems score in the moderate range on scale 9. Elevations in this range suggest several positive attributes such as energetic, enthusiastic, outgoing, and high activity level.

☐ Low elevations (T score ≤ 35) are associated with having a low energy level, apathy, fatigue, depression, and chronic problems of low self-esteem, lack of confidence, and withdrawal.

sion-extroversion by Drake (1946). The scale was developed by contrasting groups of college students who scored high and low on another measure of introversion-extroversion. The original scale 0 contained 70 items dealing with social discomfort, inferiority, low affiliation, interpersonal sensitivity, lack of trust, and physical complaints. One item was deleted in the MMPI restandardization owing to its objectionable content, leaving a total of 69 items on the MMPI-2. A total of 8 items was deleted from this long scale to shorten the MMPI-A.

Content

The items on the Si scale have been classified into three subscales using a combined statistical-rational scale construction strategy (Ben-Porath et al., 1989). The subscales were developed to provide high internal consistencies and were validated against external criteria. These subscales can be used to clarify elevations on Si. The Si subscales are:

Si_1 — *Shyness* (14 items)
>High scorers are shy in interpersonal situations. They show discomfort around others and are reluctant to begin relationships. They deny being sociable.

Si_2 — *Social Avoidance* (8 items)
>High scorers tend to avoid groups, are unfriendly, socially withdrawn, and eschew participation with others. They dislike parties and dances.

Si_3 — *Self-Other Alienation* (17 items)
>High scorers report feeling alienated from others and from themselves. They feel estranged from people and are apprehensive and mistrustful of others, while at the same time they possess a very poor self-image. They feel disappointed by others.

Illustrative Empirical Research

Gough, McKee, and Yandell (1955) provided a clear picture of high-scoring Si individuals as slow paced, lacking in originality, insecure, indecisive, inflexible, and socially overcontrolled and inhibited. Low-scoring Si subjects were viewed by Hathaway and Meehl (1952) as outgoing, sociable, talkative, assertive, and adventurous. The interpretation of elevated Si scale scores for nonclinical subjects received substantial empirical support from the couples rating study in the

MMPI Restandardization Project (Butcher et al., 1989). Spouses indicated that high-scoring subjects act very shy, lack self-confidence, avoid contact with people, are unwilling to try new things, and put themselves down a lot.

Sieber and Meyers (1992) conducted a cross-validation study of the MMPI-2 Social Introversion subscales on a sample of 410 college students. They found that persons with elevations on Si_1 were more socially anxious, less social, and had lower self-esteem. Those with elevations on Si_2 were viewed as more shy and less social. Persons with elevated Si_3 showed less self-esteem and had an external locus of control.

Descriptors

The Si scale measures a bipolar personality dimension in which high scores assess social introversion and low scores reflect social extroversion. Unlike other MMPI-2 standard scales, low, as well as high, Si scale elevations can be clinically interpreted.

High scorers (T $\geq$ 65) are socially introverted, more comfortable alone or with a few close friends and reserved, shy, and retiring. They tend to be uncomfortable around members of the opposite sex, are hard to get to know, and are sensitive to what others think. However, they are troubled by lack of involvement with other people. They tend to be overcontrolled and are not likely to display feelings openly. They are typically submissive and compliant in relationships and are overly accepting of authority. Others see high Si individuals as serious, slow paced, reliable, dependable, cautious, conventional, unoriginal in approach to problems, rigid, inflexible in attitudes and opinions, and indecisive. High Si scorers tend to worry a great deal, are irritable and anxious, moody, guilt-prone, and have episodes of depression or low mood.

Low Si scorers (T $\leq$ 45) are sociable, extroverted, outgoing, gregarious, friendly, and talkative. They have a strong need to be around other people. They are usually expressive, verbally fluent, active, energetic, vigorous, interested in status, power, and recognition, and seek out competitive situations. Many low Si individuals have problems with impulse control and may act without considering the consequences of their actions. They may be immature, self-indulgent, superficial, insincere in relationships, manipulative, opportunistic, and arouse resentment and hostility in others.

Table 4-10 provides interpretive guidelines for scale 0.

Case Example of the Standard Scales and Their Subscales

As we have seen, there are several possible descriptors that can be associated with elevated scores on the standard scales. The interpretation of a standard scale can sometimes be complicated by the scale's heterogeneous content. On some standard scales, an individual can obtain an elevated score by endorsing a smaller grouping of more homogeneous items. This has relevance for the selection of potential descriptors for the elevated standard scale score. The Harris-

Table 4-10. Scale 0 interpretive guidelines for the MMPI-2

☐ Scale 0 assesses a bipolar personality dimension that includes introversion at the high and extroversion at the low end of the continuum. Both high and low scale 0 scores are considered to have valuable personality information.

☐ High elevations on scale 0 are T scores ≥ 65. The probability that the descriptors listed below for high elevations apply to a given individual increases with higher scale elevations.

☐ Moderate elevations on scale 0 are T scores of 60-64, inclusive. Elevations in this range may be associated with many of the descriptors listed for elevated scores.

☐ Low elevations on scale 0 are T scores ≤ 45.

☐ Elevations on scale 0 can be more fully understood by examining the item content, as assessed by the scale 0 subscales, contributing to scale elevation. The content subscales for scale 0 are:
  ● Shyness
  ● Social Avoidance
  ● Self-Other Alienation

☐ Descriptors for elevated Si scores:
  ● Socially introverted
  ● More comfortable alone or with a few close friends
  ● Reserved, shy, and retiring
  ● Uncomfortable around members of opposite sex
  ● Hard to get to know
  ● Sensitive to what others think of them
  ● Troubled by lack of involvement with other people
  ● Overcontrolled
  ● Not likely to display feelings openly
  ● Tends to be submissive and compliant
  ● Compliant toward authority
  ● Serious, reliable, dependable, cautious, conventional
  ● Slow personal tempo
  ● Rigid, inflexible in attitudes and opinions
  ● Having difficulty making even minor decisions
  ● Tends to worry and feels guilty easily

☐ Descriptors for low Si scores:
  ● Sociable and extroverted
  ● Outgoing, gregarious, friendly, and talkative
  ● Strong need to be around other people
  ● Mixes well in groups
  ● Socially expressive, verbally fluent, active, energetic
  ● Interested in status, power, and recognition
  ● Seeks out competitive situations
  ● May have problems with impulse control
  ● May act without considering the consequences of actions
  ● May be immature and self-indulgent
  ● May be superficial and insincere in relationships
  ● May be manipulative and opportunistic in relationships

Lingoes subscales and the Si subscales are valuable for selecting the most relevant standard scale descriptors from the large pool of potential descriptors.

The most effective approach to incorporating the Harris-Lingoes MMPI-2 subscales into clinical profile interpretation is to use them to clarify or substantiate

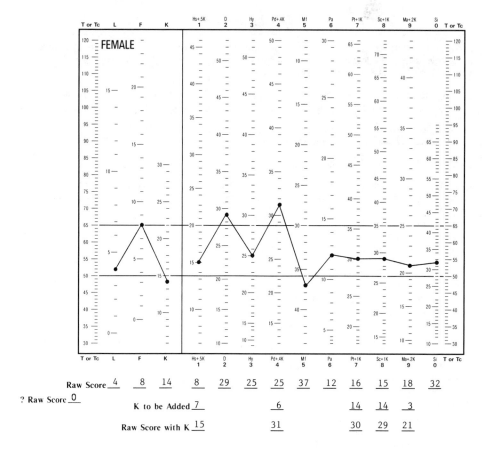

				Hs+.5K 1	D 2	Hy 3	Pd+.4K 4	Mf 5	Pa 6	Pt+1K 7	Sc+1K 8	Ma+2K 9	Si 0	
Raw Score	4	8	14	8	29	25	25	37	12	16	15	18	32	
? Raw Score	0													
			K to be Added	7			6			14	14	3		
			Raw Score with K	15			31			30	29	21		

Figure 4-4. Ann. MMPI-2 basic scales profile

particular interpretations of the parent scale. That is, they should be used to clarify or refine the scale correlates relevant for the interpretation of the scale on which they are contained. This approach will be illustrated with a case, Ann, shown in Figure 4-4.

Ann's MMPI-2 profile would generate a considerable number of possible descriptors or correlates from her elevations on scales 2 and 4. However, by examining the relative elevations on the Harris-Lingoes subscales for scales 2 and 4, we can narrow down this large list of potential descriptors. Inspection of Table 4-11 shows that the elevation on Pd comes predominantly from responses to items in the Pd_1—Familial Discord cluster, suggesting an unpleasant home situation that is viewed as lacking in love, support, and understanding. Ann feels that her family is very critical and controlling. She reports little of the authority problems, social alienation, or self-alienation item content measured by the other Pd subscales. Her scale elevation on the D scale comes predominantly from the D_1—Subjective Depression subscale, suggesting that she feels depressed, unhappy, and nervous. She lacks energy and interest and is not coping

Table 4-11. Harris-Lingoes D and Pd subscale scores for Ann

Scale 2	(Depression)	
	D_1—Subjective Depression	85 T
	D_2—Psychomotor Retardation	60 T
	D_3—Physical Malfunctioning	55 T
	D_4—Mental Dullness	45 T
	D_5—Brooding	55 T
Scale 4	(Psychopathic Deviate)	
	Pd_1—Familial Discord	80 T
	Pd_2—Authority Problems	55 T
	Pd_3—Social Imperturbability	56 T
	Pd_4—Social Alienation	50 T
	Pd_5—Self-Alienation	55 T

well. She has problems in concentration and attention. She reports feeling inferior, lacks self-confidence, and is shy and uneasy in social situations. Response to the content on other subscales of the D scale is negligible. Consequently, we can surmise that Ann's elevations on the Pd and D scales were largely produced by her family problems and depression over them. We would thus minimize the other possible scale 4 correlates suggesting more severe character pathology.

Limitations of the Harris-Lingoes
Content Interpretation Approach

As valuable as they are for understanding the correlates for particular MMPI-2 standard scales, the Harris-Lingoes subscales have clear limitations as content measures.

First, they only assess content factors on a particular MMPI-2 scale. Consequently, they do not sufficiently assess the full range of content in the MMPI-2. They do not, for example, incorporate any of the new MMPI-2 content dimensions because they are limited to the original MMPI-2 scales, which include only original items. Second, many of the Harris-Lingoes subscales are very short, some with as few as six items. The reliability of a scale depends, in part, on its length. Thus, many of the Harris-Lingoes subscales have low reliabilities and should not be relied upon as independent psychometric measures.

The Harris-Lingoes subscales provide a basis for understanding the items that comprise a particular elevation on a standard scale. That is, the relative contribution of the subscales to the total score can help the clinician order the empirical correlates for the scale better by suggesting what scale content best summarizes the individual's problems. Broader content coverage is assessed by the MMPI-2 Content Scales (Chapter 5) and the MMPI-A Content Scales (Chapter 11).

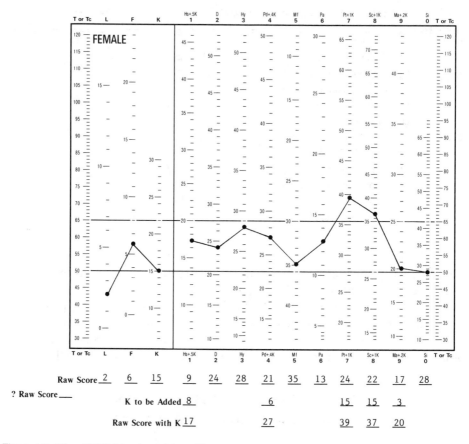

	T or Tc	L	F	K	Hs+.5K 1	D 2	Hy 3	Pd+.4K 4	Mf 5	Pa 6	Pt+1K 7	Sc+1K 8	Ma+.2K 9	Si 0	
Raw Score	2	6	15		9	24	28	21	35	13	24	22	17	28	
? Raw Score ___															
K to be Added				8					6		15	15	3		
Raw Score with K				17					27		39	37	20		

Figure 4-5. Alice. MMPI-2 basic scales profile

Highlight Summary: Alice's Standard Scale Profile

In interpreting the MMPI-2 standard scales, a client's scores are compared with those of people in the normative sample using the T-score distribution on the MMPI-2 profile sheet. Interpretation of the standard scales involves assessing the elevation of the highest scales and applying the appropriate scale descriptors. In our continuing case analysis of Alice's MMPI-2 profile, we will refer to her standard scale elevations to obtain information about her current symptomatic behavior and personality functioning (Figure 4-5).

Alice's elevated Pt score indicates that she is likely to be experiencing considerable anxiety, tension, and perhaps agitation. She has reported a great deal of discomfort, worry, and feelings of apprehension. She would likely be considered high-strung, depressed, and jumpy, and may show concentration difficulties. Personality features associated with scale 7 elevations include being introspective, ruminative, indecisive, obsessive, and compulsive. She responds to MMPI-2 items in a manner suggesting that she feels insecure and inferior, and lacking self-confidence. She is likely to be overly self-conscious and self-derogatory. Many individuals with this prominent pattern are viewed as rigid, moralistic, overly perfectionistic, conscientious, and guilt-prone. She is likely to be interested in entering therapy since she is probably experiencing considerable discomfort.

Her moderate elevation on scale 8 is likely to reflect feelings of alienation and distance from others. Individuals with elevated Sc tend to feel inferior and socially different from others. They may appear aloof and uninterested in others. They tend to employ fantasy as a defense against unpleasant situations and may daydream a great deal. High Sc individuals, such as Alice, are somewhat immature and self-preoccupied. They may be non-conforming and reluctant to go along with the majority. Some high Sc individuals are impulsive, aggressive, or anxious. Alice's Harris-Lingoes subscales for the Sc scale are useful to the interpreter in deciding what her Sc scale elevation represents. The two most prominent subscale elevations were on Lack of Ego Mastery, Cognitive (Sc$_3$, T = 74) and Lack of Ego Mastery, Conative (Sc$_4$, T = 70), indicating that she fears losing her mind and feels unable to cope with her problems. She endorses less content dealing with feelings of social and emotional alienation, indicating that she is less likely to be withdrawn and isolated from others. This is confirmed by her average score on Si. Alice probably does not have extreme problems with interpersonal relationships, which is a strength that can be used during therapy.

Analyzing MMPI-2 profiles by examining the correlates of prominent scale elevations a scale at a time can provide valuable clues to the individual's problems and personality. However, a scale-by-scale analysis can also be somewhat problematic in that numerous, sometimes even contradictory, correlates may be obtained if several scales are elevated. As we will soon see, scale relationships are also viewed as important considerations in profile interpretation. For example, analysis of scales 8 and 7 together or in configuration provides additional information. The relationship between scales 8 and 7 provides clues to whether the individual's problems are acute or chronic. If scale 7 is higher in elevation than scale 8 (as is the case with Alice), then the individual's problems are likely to be acute. If scale 8 is higher in elevation than scale 7, the problems are considered to be chronic.

In the next chapter we will consider interpretation of MMPI-2 profiles from a somewhat different perspective—by considering all of the prominently elevated scores as a single index or profile code (often referred to as a code type). The profile configuration or code-type approach is often considered to be the most efficient, systematic way of analyzing the multiple scale elevations that are commonly found in MMPI-2 profiles. However, as we will see in Chapter 9, this code-type approach remains to be validated for adolescents.

Chapter 5

Interpreting MMPI-2 Profile Types (Code Types)

This chapter explains the definition, structure, and use of MMPI-2 profile types, often referred to as code types. Code types are MMPI-2 clinical-scale summary indexes that include the most prominent scale elevations in a configuration of the standard MMPI-2 scales. Code-type interpretation was developed early in the MMPI's history when it was recognized that, in many cases, more than one standard scale was usually elevated. Psychologists observed that scale patterns occurred with great frequency in some settings and began to develop empirical descriptions of individuals who matched these MMPI patterns. In this chapter we will examine factors important to understanding and using MMPI-2 code types and will summarize the well-established behavioral correlates for the most frequently occurring MMPI-2 profile codes. We will also explore the congruence of MMPI-2 and MMPI codes. In Chapters 9 and 10 we will explain why the code-type approach is not recommended for interpretation of the MMPI-A. Keep in mind that unlike other chapters, the material in the present chapter relates only to MMPI and MMPI-2 use with adults.

A code type is defined by the highest elevated scale or scales in the standard profile and their rank order in terms of elevation. Most of the empirical research on MMPI code types has included only scales Hs, D, Hy, Pd, Pa, Pt, Sc, and Ma. However, some research on special populations, college students, for example, has included other scales, such as Mf and Si (Kelly & King, 1978). As was true of the standard scales, it is important to have a high degree of familiarity with the behavioral correlates for each of the frequently occurring code types. The behavioral descriptions associated with code types can be confidently applied to individuals whose profile matches the code type.

Several code types have been described in the empirical literature. The single-point-code, or "profile spike," occurs when a single standard scale is elevated in the critical range. The two-point code type, one of the more frequently researched profile codes, occurs when two clinical scales, such as scales 2 and 7, are elevated in the critical range, that is, greater than or equal to T of 65. This code type would be defined as a two-point code of 2-7/7-2. The three-point code, prominent in several research populations, occurs when three clinical scales are elevated in the profile. For example, clinical elevations on scales 2, 4, and 7 produce a three-point code of 2-4-7, a profile type often found in drug- and alcohol-treatment programs. The four-point code is somewhat rare, though several have been researched extensively, for example, the 1-2-3-4 code type in medical settings. No research exists on profile codes having greater than four-point elevations.

When and Why to Use Code Types

There are two general rules for determining when to use the MMPI-2 code-type approach instead of the scale-by-scale approach described in Chapter 4:

1.) The profile should be clearly defined (i.e., two or more scales reach interpretive significance using the definitions discussed below).

2.) There has been sufficient research on the behavioral descriptions for the code. For some code types, such as the 2-6-9, there are too few empirical descriptors to provide much information about the client. If a code type is an infrequent one, the scale-by-scale interpretation strategy should be followed.

Why use a simple technique like code-type analysis when more sophisticated statistical approaches to profile analysis (such as cluster analysis, discriminant analysis, and other profile similarity measures) are available? In general, these multivariate research strategies, while providing a statistical means of evaluating research data for stringently classifying diverse subjects, have not provided a practical means of grouping MMPI profiles for clinical practice. They are somewhat cumbersome to use in applied settings and research has not demonstrated that they provide a more accurate classification schema than simple code types.

Code types are more practical, easier to apply, and seemingly no less valid than more complex statistical analyses in most settings. In general, the code type may not only be more efficient to use than multivariate techniques but may actually better summarize the most important elements of a given profile.

Code Type Definitions and Stability

Much of the early literature on the established behavioral correlates of code types used research designs producing codes that were less refined than they might have been. Typically, a large number of cases is required to obtain a sufficient number of subjects with a particular code. For example, from a sample of 556 women and 270 men, Marks and Seeman (1963) found only 20 patients who met the criteria for the 1-3 code type. To have a large enough sample, most researchers studying code types have followed the practice of combining similar code groups, for example, 2-7 and 7-2, ignoring the score level and relative elevation of scales within a code type. However, both elevation level and rank order of elevated scales in the code type have been found to have important differentiating characteristics.

The order of the scales within the code type might make an important difference regarding the relative importance of empirical descriptors that applied to a case. For example, the 3-4 code type has been found to have rather different behavioral features than the 4-3 code type (Persons & Marks, 1971). If scale 4 is higher than scale 3, the individual is considered to act out rather than control emotions. In general, it is best to emphasize the correlates of the higher elevated scale of the code type. Similarly, the elevation range of the code type might also make an important difference in the type, quality, and number of symptoms or descriptions that are applied to the case. The ordering of scales within the code suggests the relative saliency of the empirical correlates and gives clues to the interpreter about which should be given most prominence in the report. The elevation of the scales in the code type provides a confidence estimate of the likelihood that the empirical correlates apply in the case. The higher the scale elevation, the more confident one can be that the prototype pattern matches the client.

As a general rule, MMPI scales have high test-retest stability (Dahlstrom, Welsh, & Dahlstrom, 1975). Test-retest correlations for various groups have been reported to range from moderate to high, depending upon the population studied and the retest interval (Dahlstrom, Welsh, & Dahlstrom, 1975). However, the stability of code types depends upon how well the code type is defined. Graham, Smith, and Schwartz (1986) reported that the percentages of people with the same high-point, low-point, and two-point code showed only modest congruence on retest (43%, 44%, and 28%, respectively). They noted, however, that code types with more extreme scores (i.e., those that were well-defined by a substantial point separation between the scale scores in the code type and those not included in the code) tended to be similar at retest. The greatest code-type agreement at retest was obtained for profiles having a 10-point T-score spread between the code type and the rest of the profile code. However, high congruence was obtained at retest if the code type was even 5 points higher than the next scale in the profile.

Several rules of thumb have been suggested by Graham et al. (1986) for assessing the stability of a profile code:

1. Profile code types that are 10 points or more above the next highest score are very likely to be found on retest.

2. Profile code types that are 5 to 9 points above the next score are likely to remain constant on retest.

3. Profile code types that are 4 or fewer points higher than the next score may shift on later retest, but future profiles will probably maintain some elements (and correlates) of the initial code types.

In general, Graham et al. (1986) recommend exercising caution in applying traditional MMPI behavioral correlates for a given code type if the MMPI profile does not possess clear code-type definition, a clear elevation above the next scale in the profile.

Similarity between MMPI and MMPI-2 Code Types

The standard scale scores are quite consistent between the MMPI and MMPI-2, despite the T-score distributions being based on responses of different subjects. However, the need to make the T scores fall at equivalent percentile values across scales has affected some code types slightly, especially those cases with less clear profile definition. For example, in a three-point code, if the three scale scores are Hs at 77, D at 76, and Hy at 75, the profile will be more likely to shift (i.e., change from a 1-2/2-1 to a 1-3/3-1 or 2-3/3-2) than if the first three scale scores are Hs at 77, Hy at 76, and D at 71. Actually, in this example it would be better to use the three-point code (1-2-3). Graham, Timbrook, Ben-Porath, and Butcher (1991) demonstrated that MMPI-2 code types were quite congruent with MMPI code types when code-type definition was maintained. Over 90% of the profiles with a five-point profile code definition will have the same code type on MMPI-2 as on the original MMPI. In a recent evaluation of the MMPI-2, Vincent (1990) concluded that "we can be reasonably confident that its compatibility with the original is as good as the original to itself and the well-known adaptations" (p. 802). Thus, if the profile code is at least 5 points greater than the next scale in the profile, the code type is likely to be the same on MMPI or MMPI-2 norms.

There are several limitations to using MMPI-2 code types that the clinician needs to keep in mind when using the empirical research literature on code types to interpret profiles. First, although the MMPI Restandardization Committee maintained continuity between the MMPI-2 and the original MMPI standard scales, there may be some shifting of scales within the profile code between the two forms because different standardization samples and T-score transformation procedures were used. This requires some adaptation on the part of the test interpreter. However, Graham et al. (1991) found that when code types differed (completely different profile codes are rare), the MMPI-2 code type had an external validity equal to or greater than the MMPI code type.

With the MMPI-2, as with the original MMPI, empirical descriptors are scarce for some code types. Not enough code types have been empirically studied and described to classify the range of profiles that clinicians obtain. In addition, some settings where the MMPI-2 is widely used are underrepresented in the research literature defining and describing MMPI-2 code types.

While code types have been valuable in interpreting the MMPI and MMPI-2, a considerable amount of additional valuable information can be found in the MMPI profile, for example from Si, MAC-R, APS, or the MMPI-2 Content Scales. Consequently, rather than limiting interpretation to information from the MMPI code-type literature, one might wish to use the available code-type descriptions as an "outline" that can be supplemented with other MMPI-2 based information. This interpretive strategy for MMPI-2 profiles will be discussed more fully in Chapter 8.

Research on MMPI/MMPI-2 Code Types

Interpreting MMPI profiles using actuarial tables was initially shown by Meehl (1954) to be more a powerful strategy than clinical interpretation. He convincingly demonstrated that clinical predictions based on automatic combination of actuarial data for MMPI code types were more accurate than those based on "clinical" or intuitive interpretation of psychological test data. A number of empirical studies followed Meehl's recommendations for developing an actuarial "cookbook" as an aid to stringent test interpretation. One of Meehl's students, Halbower (1955), empirically demonstrated that behavioral correlates for test scores could be accurately and objectively applied to new cases meeting the established test criteria. Meehl's compelling argument on the strength of the actuarial method and the empirical demonstration that such mechanically generated predictions were highly accurate (Halbower, 1955) influenced a number of investigators to develop "actuarial tables" for personality description using MMPI scales and profile codes (e.g., Altman et al., 1973; Arnold, 1970; Boerger, Graham, & Lilly, 1974; Drake & Oetting, 1959; Fowler & Athey, 1971; Gilberstadt & Duker, 1965; Graham, 1973; Gynther, 1972a; Gynther, Altman, & Sletten, 1973; Gynther, Altman, & Warbin, 1972; Gynther, Altman, & Warbin, 1973a; Gynther, Altman, & Warbin, 1973b; Gynther, Altman, & Warbin, 1973c; Gynther, Altman, Warbin, & Sletten, 1972; Halbower, 1955; Kelly & King, 1978; Lewandowski & Graham, 1972; Marks & Seeman, 1963; Marks, Seeman, & Haller, 1974; Meikle & Gerritse, 1970; Persons & Marks, 1971; Sines, 1966; Warbin, Altman, Gynther, & Sletten, 1972).

The empirical research on MMPI profile patterns that followed during the 1960s and 1970s has established a broad interpretive base for many of the common MMPI code types found in clinical settings. The MMPI code-type research literature is widely scattered and not conveniently organized for clinical use. Clinicians might find it helpful to develop a format for their particular setting and catalog appropriate personality and symptomatic descriptors for the various code types. The outline that we will follow in this chapter illustrates one approach to organizing code-type information by putting correlate data into three categories:

Symptoms and Behaviors

Symptomatic behaviors the client reports along with an estimate, if available, of the severity of the individual's problems or behaviors are included in this section.

Personality Characteristics

Information related to the individual's personality adjustment or personality characteristics is provided.

Predictions or Dispositions

Hypotheses or predictions about the individual's behavior, such as diagnoses, likely outcomes, treatment amenability, and so forth are indicated.

Other approaches to organizing correlates have been published. Most MMPI computer interpretation systems incorporate descriptive and diagnostic information into client reports by organizing the narratives into categories or problem considerations. For example, Butcher (1987, 1989a, 1989b) developed the computer interpretation system published by the University of Minnesota (The Minnesota Report) which organizes empirical correlate information pertinent to different settings and profile codes according to a number of hypothesized clinically meaningful topics: Profile Validity, Symptomatic Behavior, Interper-

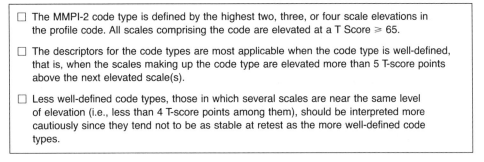

Table 5-1. General guidelines for code-type interpretation

☐ The MMPI-2 code type is defined by the highest two, three, or four scale elevations in the profile code. All scales comprising the code are elevated at a T Score ⩾ 65.

☐ The descriptors for the code types are most applicable when the code type is well-defined, that is, when the scales making up the code type are elevated more than 5 T-score points above the next elevated scale(s).

☐ Less well-defined code types, those in which several scales are near the same level of elevation (i.e., less than 4 T-score points among them), should be interpreted more cautiously since they tend not to be as stable at retest as the more well-defined code types.

sonal Relationships, Behavior Stability, Diagnostic Considerations, and Treatment Considerations. Chapter 12 provides a more detailed description of the Minnesota Report Computer Interpretation System.

Two-Point Code Type Descriptors

Correlates for the two-point code types described in this section typically were obtained by collecting groups of patients who had similar code types and studying their behavioral characteristics by the use of Q-sort ratings, history, or other assessment methods. These empirical descriptions can be applied to other cases who meet the code-type classification rules. The remainder of this chapter highlights empirical correlates for many of the two-point and three-point code types. Table 5-1 provides the general defining characteristics for code types. For a more extensive discussion of MMPI-2 codetypes see Graham (1990).

1-2/2-1 Code Type

Symptoms and Behaviors

Patients are likely to present with extreme somatic problems or chronic pain and to complain of being physically ill. They become overly concerned about health and bodily functions, overreact to minor physical dysfunction. Somatic symptoms in the digestive system are common as are reports of weakness, fatigue, and dizziness. They appear anxious, tense, nervous, restless, irritable, dysphoric, brooding, and unhappy. They show loss of initiative. They may report depressed mood, withdrawal, and reclusiveness. Doubts about their own ability are common, as is vacillation and indecision about even minor matters. They are likely to be hypersensitive.

Personality Characteristics

Individuals with this profile code are viewed as self-conscious, introverted, and shy in social situations. They may be passive-dependent and harbor hostility toward those who are perceived as not offering enough attention and emotional support.

Table 5-2. Descriptors for the 1-2/2-1 code type

☐ Extreme somatic problems or chronic pain

☐ Complaints of being physically ill

☐ Overly concerned about health and bodily functions

☐ Overreacts to minor physical dysfunction

☐ Weakness, fatigue, and dizziness

☐ Anxious, tense, nervous, restless

☐ Irritable, dysphoric, brooding, unhappy

☐ Low initiative

☐ Depressed mood, withdrawn, and reclusive

☐ Doubts about ability

☐ Vacillation and indecision about even minor matters

☐ Hypersensitive

☐ Self-conscious in social situations

☐ Introverted and shy

☐ Passive-dependent in relationships

☐ Hostile toward others

☐ Uses repression as a defense

☐ May use alcohol or prescription drugs to reduce tension

☐ Resists psychological interpretations of symptoms

☐ Lacks insight and self-understanding

Predictions or Dispositions

Excessive use of alcohol or prescription drugs may occur as a tension-reduction mechanism. Individuals with this profile type are usually diagnosed as neurotic (hypochondriacal, anxious, or depressive). They are thought to have a poor prognosis for traditional psychotherapy. They usually can tolerate high levels of discomfort before becoming motivated to change. They resist psychological interpretations of symptoms. They tend to use repression and somatization. They lack insight, self-understanding, and resist accepting responsibility for their own behavior. Treatment gains, if they occur, are typically short-lived symptomatic changes. Table 5-2 summarizes the characteristics associated with the 1-2/2-1 code type.

1-3/3-1 Code Type

Symptoms and Behaviors

Individuals with this pattern tend to report vague physical complaints, which might increase under stress and often disappear when stress subsides. Severe anxiety and depression are usually absent. Clients are likely to function at a reduced level of efficiency. They prefer medical explanations of symptoms and tend to resist psychological interpretations. They tend to deny and rationalize, and they are seen as uninsightful. They view themselves as normal, responsible, and without fault. They lack appropriate concern about their symptoms and problems and are overly optimistic and Pollyannish in manner.

Personality Characteristics

Clients with this code type tend to be seen as immature, egocentric, and selfish. They may be viewed as passive and dependent, and may become insecure when their strong needs for attention, affection, and sympathy are not met. They are viewed as outgoing and socially extroverted, but their relationships are typically superficial. They appear to be self-preoccupied and lack genuine involvement with people. They are manipulative in social relationships, lack skills in dealing with the opposite sex, and tend to be low in heterosexual drive.

Individuals with this clinical profile may show resentment and hostility toward those who are viewed as not offering enough attention and support. They are seen as overcontrolled and passive-aggressive in relationships. They may have occasional angry outbursts. They are usually conventional and conforming in attitudes and beliefs.

Predictions or Dispositions

Clients with this pattern are usually diagnosed as having a psychophysiologic disorder or anxiety disorder, such as conversion or psychogenic pain disorders. They are not likely to be motivated for psychotherapy. They usually expect definite or simple answers and solutions to problems. They may terminate therapy prematurely when the therapist fails to respond to their demands. Interpretive guidelines for the 1-3/3-1 code type are highlighted in Table 5-3.

1-4/4-1 Code Type

Symptoms and Behaviors

Severe hypochondriacal symptoms are probably present with this profile type, especially nonspecific headaches and stomach distress. Individuals fitting this pattern are viewed as indecisive and anxious. They may be socially extroverted but lack skills with the opposite sex. They may be rebellious toward home and parents but do not express these feelings openly. They are likely to be dissatisfied, pessimistic, demanding, and grouchy.

Personality Characteristics

Personality problems are likely to be central in his or her problem expression. Acting-out behavior and poor judgment are likely to be factors in his or her maladjustment.

Table 5-3. Descriptors for the 1-3/3-1 code type

☐ Vague physical complaints

☐ Reacts to stress with physical symptoms

☐ Anxiety and depression are usually absent

☐ Functions at reduced level of efficiency

☐ Prefers medical explanations of symptoms

☐ Resists psychological interpretations

☐ Denies and rationalizes faults

☐ Lacks appropriate concern about their symptoms

☐ Overly optimistic and like Pollyanna in manner

☐ Immature, egocentric, and selfish

☐ Passive-dependent

☐ Becomes insecure when their strong needs for attention, affection, and sympathy are not met

☐ Viewed as outgoing and socially extroverted

☐ Superficial relationships

☐ Self-preoccupied and lacks genuine involvement with others

☐ Manipulative in social relationships

☐ Coquettish, flirtatious

☐ Lacks skills in dealing with opposite sex and tends to be low in heterosexual drive

☐ Shows resentment and hostility toward those who are viewed as not offering enough attention and support

☐ Overcontrolled and passive-aggressive in relationships

☐ Occasional angry outbursts

☐ Usually conventional and conforming in attitudes and beliefs

☐ Uninsightful and unmotivated for therapy

Predictions or Dispositions

Excessive use of alcohol is likely. Individuals with this clinical profile are likely to lack drive and may encounter problems in sustaining work or productive activity. They often have poorly defined goals and motivations. They are often seen as resistant to traditional psychotherapy. The descriptors for the 1-4/4-1 code type are provided in Table 5-4.

1-8/8-1 Code Type

Symptoms and Behaviors

Individuals with the 1-8/8-1 code type tend to have long-term psychological problems. They tend to harbor feelings of hostility and aggression but cannot

Table 5-4. Descriptors for the 1-4/4-1 code type

☐ Hypochondriacal symptoms
☐ Indecisive and anxious
☐ Socially extroverted
☐ Lacks skills with the opposite sex
☐ Rebellious toward home and parents, but does not express these feelings openly
☐ Dissatisfied, pessimistic, demanding, and grouchy
☐ Personality problems are likely
☐ Acting-out behaviors and poor judgment are possible
☐ Excessive use of alcohol is likely
☐ Lacks drive and may encounter problems in sustaining work
☐ Poorly defined goals and motivations
☐ Resistant to traditional psychotherapy

express them in a modulated, adaptive manner. They are often either inhibited and "bottled-up" or overly belligerent and abrasive. They are characterized by feeling unhappy, depressed, confused, and distractible. Many individuals with this profile configuration show flat affect.

Personality Characteristics

Long-term personality characteristics are likely to be a factor in the present symptom pattern for these individuals. They report feeling socially inadequate and lack trust in other people. They are isolated and alienated, and may report having a nomadic life-style.

Predictions or Dispositions

Some individuals with this pattern are diagnosed as schizophrenic. Bizarre somatic complaints may make treatment difficult. Some medical patients with this profile are not schizophrenic but present with severe, chronic, unusual, intractable symptoms. Table 5-5 summarizes the 1-8/8-1 descriptors.

1-9/9-1 Code Type

Symptoms and Behaviors

Extreme distress is usually present in individuals with this profile. They are likely to be anxious, tense, restless, and to have somatic complaints. They may be aggressive and belligerent if their somatic problems are minimized. Some individuals with this pattern can be ambitious and have high drive level, but they tend to lack clear goals, becoming frustrated by an inability to achieve at a high level.

Table 5-5. Descriptors for the 1-8/8-1 code type

☐ Long-term psychological problems

☐ Feelings of hostility and aggression

☐ Either inhibited or overly belligerent and abrasive

☐ Unhappy, depressed, confused, and distractible

☐ Flat affect

☐ Long-standing adjustment problems

☐ Feels socially inadequate

☐ Lacks trust in other people

☐ Isolated and alienated

☐ Bizarre somatic complaints or intractable symptoms

Table 5-6. Descriptors for the 1-9/9-1 code type

☐ Extreme somatic distress

☐ Anxious, tense, restless

☐ Aggressive and belligerent if somatic problems are minimized

☐ Frustrated by an inability to achieve

☐ Passive-dependent or passive-aggressive personality style

☐ Denies personality problems

☐ Reluctant to accept psychological explanations for problems

☐ Determine if a neuropsychological assessment is appropriate

Personality Characteristics

There is some indication that these clients have a passive-dependent personality style but try to deny personality problems.

Predictions or Dispositions

Individuals with this code type are likely to be reluctant to accept psychological explanations for their perceived medical problems. This code type can be found in brain-damaged persons who are experiencing difficulty in coping with organic deficits. Table 5-6 provides a summary of the descriptors for the 1-9/9-1 code type.

2-3/3-2 Code Type

Symptoms and Behaviors

Individuals with the 2-3/3-2 code type do not usually experience disabling anxiety, but report feeling nervous, tense, worried, sad, and depressed. They usually express somatic symptoms such as fatigue, exhaustion, physical weakness, or gastrointestinal complaints. Individuals with this pattern tend to lack interest and involvement in life. They report being unable to "get started." They show decreased physical activity.

Personality Characteristics

Individuals with this pattern appear passive, docile, and dependent. They have a history of self-doubt, inadequacy, insecurity, and helplessness. They engage in behavior that elicits nurturance from others, but do not get what they consider adequate recognition for accomplishments. They are hurt by even minor criticism. They tend to be overcontrolled, unable to express feelings, are "bottled-up," deny unacceptable impulses, avoid social involvement, and feel especially uncomfortable around the opposite sex. Sexual maladjustment, including frigidity and impotence, may be present.

Predictions or Dispositions

Individuals with this code type are usually diagnosed as having a depressive disorder. They tend not to be very responsive to psychotherapy and seem to lack introspective ability. They lack insight and resist psychological formulations of problems. Such people tend to function at a lower level of efficiency for long periods and appear to tolerate a great deal of unhappiness without seeking behavior change. They may seem driven to succeed, but are afraid to place themselves in directly competitive situations. They feel the need to increase their responsibility in life, but dread the pressure associated with this. Descriptors associated with the 2-3/3-2 code type are summarized in Table 5-7.

2-4/4-2 Code Type

Symptoms and Behaviors

Clients with the 2-4/4-2 code type have a history of legal problems and an impulsive behavioral history. They tend to be unable to delay gratification of impulses and they get into difficulty with others. They show little respect for social standards and values, and tend to act out, perhaps by excessive drinking. They may appear to be frustrated by their lack of accomplishments and may be resentful of demands placed by others. After acting-out, they may express guilt and remorse, but are not sincere about changing.

Personality Characteristics

Individuals with this code type may appear sociable and outgoing, and may make a favorable first impression. They tend to manipulate others and show some long-term maladaptive personality characteristics. They cause resentment in long-term relationships. Beneath a facade of competence and self-assurance, these individuals may actually be overly self-conscious and dissatisfied with themselves. Characteristically, they are passive-dependent persons.

Table 5-7. Descriptors for the 2-3/3-2 code type

☐ Feels nervous, tense, worried, sad, and depressed

☐ Expresses somatic symptoms such as fatigue, exhaustion, or physical weakness

☐ Gastrointestinal complaints

☐ Lacks interest and involvement in life situations

☐ Has difficulty getting started on things

☐ Shows decreased physical activity

☐ Appears passive, docile, and dependent

☐ Has a history of self-doubt, inadequacy, insecurity, and helplessness

☐ Seeks excessive nurturance from others

☐ Feels accomplishments are not adequately recognized

☐ Feels hurt by even minor criticism

☐ Overcontrolled

☐ Denies unacceptable impulses

☐ Functions at lower level of efficiency for long periods

☐ Avoids social involvement and feels especially uncomfortable around the opposite sex

☐ Sexual maladjustment, including frigidity and/or impotence, may be present

☐ Depressive disorder likely

☐ Not very responsive to psychotherapy

☐ Lacks introspective ability

☐ Resists psychological formulations of problems

Predictions or Dispositions

Suicidal ideation and attempts are possible (especially if both scales are grossly elevated). Individuals with this clinical profile may express the need for help and desire to change, but prognosis for psychotherapeutic change is poor. They are likely to terminate therapy prematurely when the outside stress subsides or when their environmental pressures or legal difficulties subside. Table 5-8 highlights the descriptors for the 2-4/4-2 code type.

2-7/7-2 Code Type

Symptoms and Behaviors

Individuals with this code type appear anxious, tense, nervous, and depressed. They report feeling unhappy and sad, and tend to worry excessively. They feel vulnerable to real and imagined threats, and typically anticipate problems before they occur—often overreacting to minor stress as though it is a ma-

Table 5-8. Descriptors for the 2-4/4-2 code type

☐ History of impulsive behaviors

☐ May have legal difficulties

☐ Unable to delay gratification of impulses

☐ Interpersonal difficulties

☐ Shows little respect for social standards and values

☐ Acts out, perhaps accompanied by excessive drinking

☐ Frustrated with lack of accomplishments

☐ Resentful of demands placed by others

☐ After episodes of acting-out, may express guilt and remorse but is not sincere about changing

☐ Appears sociable and outgoing, and may make a favorable first impression

☐ Manipulates others

☐ Possesses long-term maladaptive personality characteristics

☐ Depressed

☐ Causes resentment in long-term relationships

☐ Appears competent and self-assured, but may be overly self-conscious and self-dissatisfied

☐ Passive-dependent

☐ Suicidal ideations and attempts may be present

☐ Expresses the need for help and desire to change, but prognosis for psychotherapeutic change is poor

☐ Terminates therapy prematurely when stress subsides

jor catastrophe. They usually report somatic complaints, fatigue, exhaustion, tiredness, weight loss, slow personal tempo, slowed speech, and retarded thought processes. They tend to brood and ruminate a great deal.

These persons may show a strong need for achievement and recognition, and have high expectations for themselves and others. They may feel guilty when their goals are not met. These individuals typically have perfectionistic attitudes and a history of being conscientious. They may be excessively religious and extremely moralistic.

Personality Characteristics

Individuals with this pattern appear docile and passive-dependent in relationships. They report problems in being assertive. They usually show a capacity for forming deep, emotional ties and tend to lean on people to an excessive degree. They tend to solicit nurturance from others. Feelings of inadequacy, insecurity, and inferiority are long-term issues. They tend to be intropunitive in dealing with feelings of aggression.

Table 5-9. Descriptors for the 2-7/7-2 code type

☐ Anxious, tense, nervous, and depressed

☐ Unhappy, sad, and tends to worry excessively

☐ Feels vulnerable to real and imagined threats

☐ Anticipates problems before they occur and may overreact to minor stress

☐ Reports somatic symptoms such as fatigue, exhaustion, weight loss, slowed speech, and retarded thinking

☐ Broods and ruminates a great deal

☐ Feels guilty when personal goals are not met

☐ Perfectionistic and conscientious

☐ Excessively religious or extremely moralistic

☐ Appears docile and passive-dependent in relationships

☐ Non-assertive

☐ Shows a capacity for forming deep emotional ties, but tends to lean on people to an excessive degree

☐ Seeks excessive nurturance from others

☐ Feelings of inadequacy, insecurity, and inferiority

☐ Intropunitive

☐ May be diagnosed as depressive, obsessive-compulsive, or anxiety disordered

☐ Pessimistic about overcoming problems and indecisive and rigid in their thinking

☐ Usually motivated for psychotherapy

Predictions or Dispositions

Individuals with the 2-7/7-2 code type are usually diagnosed as depressive, obsessive-compulsive, or anxiety disordered. They are usually motivated for psychotherapy and tend to remain in therapy longer than other patients. They tend to be somewhat pessimistic about overcoming problems and are indecisive and rigid in their thinking. This negative mindset is likely to interfere with their problem-solving ability. However, they usually improve in treatment (Meresman, 1992). Table 5-9 summarizes the descriptors for the 2-7/7-2 code type.

2-8/8-2 Code Type

Symptoms and Behaviors

Individuals with this pattern appear anxious, agitated, tense, and jumpy. They often report having a sleep disturbance and are unable to concentrate. Disturbed affect and somatic symptoms usually characterize their clinical picture. They are often seen as clinically depressed, have soft and slowed speech, and thought. In interview they may be tearful and emotional, yet are more charac-

teristically viewed as apathetic and indifferent. Problems with anger and interpersonal relationships are usually noted. They indicate that they are often forgetful, confused, and inefficient in carrying out responsibilities. Others may
view them as unoriginal and stereotyped in their thinking and problem-solving.
They tend to underestimate the seriousness of problems and engage in unrealistic self-appraisal. They are overly sensitive to the reactions of others, suspicious of others' motivations, and may have a history of being hurt emotionally.
They fear being hurt more and avoid close interpersonal relationships. Feelings
of despair and worthlessness are common.

Personality Characteristics

Personality features include being dependent, unassertive, irritable, and
resentful. They often fear losing control over their emotions. They may deny
impulses, but dissociative periods of acting-out may occur. Chronic, incapacitating symptoms are usually present. They tend to be guilt-ridden and self-
punitive.

Predictions or Dispositions

Serious maladjustment is likely to be present among individuals with this profile code. The most common diagnoses are manic-depressive psychosis, schizophrenia, schizo-affective type, or severe personality disorder. They are often
preoccupied with suicidal thoughts, and may have specific plans for doing away
with themselves. Interpretive guidelines for the 2-8/8-2 code type are provided
in Table 5-10.

2-9/9-2 Code Type

Symptoms and Behaviors

Patients are likely to be self-centered and narcissistic, and tend to ruminate a
great deal about their self-worth. They are likely to express concern about
achieving at a high level but appear to set themselves up for failure. Younger
persons with this pattern may be experiencing an identity crisis. Symptomati-
cally, clients may be anxious, tense, and have somatic complaints, particularly
concerning the gastrointestinal tract. Some individuals with this pattern are not
currently depressed, but may have a history of serious depression.

Personality Characteristics

A pattern of denial may cover feelings of inadequacy and worthlessness.
Some individuals with this profile tend to be defending against depression
through excessive activity.

Predictions or Dispositions

Alternating periods of increased activity and fatigue are possible. The most
common diagnosis is bipolar disorder. This profile is sometimes found among
brain-damaged patients who have lost control or who are trying to cope with

Table 5-10. Descriptors for the 2-8/8-2 code type

☐ Anxious, agitated, tense, and jumpy

☐ Sleeping disturbance

☐ Unable to concentrate

☐ Somatic symptoms

☐ Clinically depressed

☐ Tearful and emotional, yet viewed as apathetic and indifferent

☐ Anger problems

☐ Relationship problems are usually noted

☐ Forgetful, confused, and inefficient

☐ Engages in unrealistic self-appraisal

☐ Oversensitive to reactions of others

☐ Suspicious of others' motivations, and may have a history of being hurt emotionally

☐ Fearful of being hurt

☐ Avoids close relationships

☐ Feelings of despair and worthlessness

☐ Dependent and unassertive

☐ Irritable and resentful

☐ Fears losing control over emotions

☐ Has chronic, incapacitating symptoms

☐ Guilt-ridden and self-punitive

☐ Serious maladjustment is likely to be present

☐ Preoccupied with suicidal thoughts

deficits through excessive activity. Many individuals with this profile use alcohol as an escape from stress and pressure. The 2-9/9-2 descriptors are highlighted in Table 5-11.

3-4/4-3 Code Type

Symptoms and Behaviors

Chronic and intense anger may be present. Individuals with this clinical profile may harbor hostile and aggressive impulses but cannot express them appropriately. Individuals with this pattern of MMPI scores have problems of self-control. Usually somewhat overcontrolled, they tend to experience occasional brief episodes of assaultive, violent acting-out. They tend to lack insight into the origins and consequences of their aggressive behavior. They tend to be extrapunitive but do not see their own behavior as problematic.

Table 5-11. Descriptors for the 2-9/9-2 code type

☐ Self-centered and narcissistic

☐ Ruminates a great deal about self-worth

☐ Concerned about achieving at a high level

☐ Sets self up for failure

☐ Experiencing an identity crisis

☐ Anxious and tense

☐ Somatic complaints

☐ May not appear depressed, but has a history of serious depression

☐ May cover up feelings of inadequacy and worthlessness by denial

☐ May be defending against depression through excessive activity

☐ May have alternating periods of increased activity and fatigue

☐ May have a history of a bipolar disorder

☐ May have a history of brain-damage

☐ May use alcohol as an escape from stress and pressure

Individuals with this clinical profile are likely to be free of disabling anxiety and depression, but may have somatic complaints. Occasional upset does not seem to be related directly to external stress. Sexual maladjustment and promiscuity are common among clients with this pattern.

Personality Characteristics

Individuals with this code type show long-term and ingrained feelings of hostility toward family members. They tend to demand attention and approval from others. They are overly sensitive to rejection and are usually hostile when criticized. They may be outwardly conforming but inwardly rebellious.

Predictions or Dispositions

Suicidal thoughts and attempts may follow acting-out episodes. The most common diagnoses for this code type are passive-aggressive personality or emotionally unstable personality. Table 5-12 summarizes the correlates for the 3-4/4-3 code type.

3-6/6-3 Code Type

Symptoms and Behaviors

Presenting problems may not seem incapacitating, though moderate tension, anxiety, and physical complaints may occur. Individuals with a 3-6/6-3 code type may not recognize their hostile feelings, but they may appear defiant, uncooperative, hard to get along with. They appear suspicious and resentful at times.

Table 5-12. Descriptors for the 3-4/4-3 code type

- ☐ Chronic and intense anger-control problems
- ☐ Hostile and aggressive
- ☐ Experiences occasional brief episodes of assaultive, violent acting-out
- ☐ Lacks insight into the origins and consequences of aggressive behavior
- ☐ Tends to be extrapunitive, but does not see own behavior as problematic
- ☐ Free of disabling anxiety and depression, but may have somatic complaints
- ☐ Frustration does not seem to be related directly to external stress
- ☐ Sexual maladjustment and promiscuity are common
- ☐ Shows long-term and ingrained feelings of hostility toward family members
- ☐ Demands attention and approval from others
- ☐ Overly sensitive to rejection and usually hostile when criticized
- ☐ May be outwardly conforming, but is inwardly rebellious

Clients with this pattern may be self-centered and narcissistic. They tend to deny serious psychological problems.

Personality Characteristics

These individuals tend to harbor deep and chronic feelings of hostility toward family members and others close to them. They are not likely to express negative feelings directly.

Predictions or Dispositions

Individuals with this profile configuration tend to have naïve attitudes toward others and may be gullible at times. Descriptors for the 3-6/6-3 code type are listed in Table 5-13.

3-8/8-3 Code Type

Symptoms and Behaviors

Individuals with this code typically show intense psychological turmoil, including anxiousness, tension, nervousness, and fearfulness. Phobias may be present. Some symptomatic depression and feelings of hopelessness may occur behind a smiling facade. Indecisiveness, even with regard to minor decisions, is characteristic. A wide variety of physical complaints may occur. Individuals may be vague and evasive when talking about complaints and difficulties. They may show disturbed thinking, concentration problems, lapses of memory, unusual or unconventional ideas, loose ideational associations and obsessive ruminations, delusions, hallucinations, and irrelevant and incoherent speech.

Table 5-13. Descriptors for the 3-6/6-3 code type

☐ Experiences moderate tension, anxiety, and physical complaints

☐ May not recognize his/her own hostile feelings, but may appear defiant and uncooperative

☐ Hard to get along with, suspicious and resentful at times

☐ Self-centered and narcissistic

☐ Denies serious psychological problems

☐ Chronic feelings of hostility toward family members and others close to him or her

☐ Not likely to express negative feelings directly

☐ Naïve attitudes toward others and may be gullible at times

Table 5-14. Descriptors for the 3-8/8-3 code type

☐ Shows intense psychological turmoil, including anxiousness, tension, nervousness, and fearfulness

☐ Phobias may be present

☐ Depression and hopelessness may occur behind a smiling facade

☐ Indecisive, even over minor decisions

☐ Vague physical complaints

☐ Disturbed thinking possible (e.g., concentration problems, lapses of memory, unusual or unconventional ideas, loose ideational associations, obsessive ruminations, delusions, hallucinations, and irrelevant or incoherent speech)

☐ Immature and dependent

☐ May show strong needs for attention and affection

☐ May show intropunitive interpersonal behavior

☐ Apathetic, pessimistic, and not very actively involved or interested in life

☐ Insight-oriented therapy may not be very effective

Personality Characteristics

Individuals with this pattern are likely to be immature and dependent. They may show strong needs for attention and affection. They may show intropunitive interpersonal behavior.

Predictions or Dispositions

Persons fitting this pattern may be seen as apathetic, pessimistic, and not very actively involved or interested in life activities. This apathy tends to limit rehabilitation efforts. Insight-oriented therapy may not be very effective. They may seem unoriginal and stereotyped in their approach to problems. The most common diagnosis is schizophrenia. They tend to be responsive to supportive therapy. Table 5-14 describes the correlates for this code type.

4-6/6-4 Code Type

Symptoms and Behaviors

Individuals with this code type are likely to be immature, narcissistic, and self-indulgent. They typically make excessive and unrealistic demands on relationships. Individuals with this pattern are attention- and sympathy-seekers. They are usually suspicious of others and resentful of demands made on them. Relationship problems are characteristic of their psychological conflicts, especially those involving members of the opposite sex. They are mistrustful of the motives of others and tend to avoid deep emotional involvement. They are often viewed as irritable, sullen, argumentative, generally obnoxious, and resentful of authority.

Personality Characteristics

Personality adjustment problems are common among individuals with this profile type. Some individuals with this pattern are viewed as passive-dependent. They are often characterized by repressed hostility and anger.

Predictions or Dispositions

Individuals with this profile configuration probably deny serious psychological problems through rationalization and transfer of blame to others. They cannot accept responsibility for their own behavior and are unrealistic and grandiose in their self-appraisals. They are viewed as unreceptive to psychotherapy. The typical personality disorder diagnosis for individuals with this personality pattern is passive-aggressive or paranoid personality. They may also receive a diagnosis of paranoid schizophrenia. The descriptors for the 4-6/6-4 code type are provided in Table 5-15.

4-7/7-4 Code Type

Symptoms and Behaviors

Individuals with this code type may alternate between periods of gross insensitivity to the consequences of their own actions and excessive concern about the effects of their behavior. They engage in episodes of acting-out followed by temporary guilt and self-condemnation. Vague somatic complaints, tension, and fatigue are also common. They often report feeling exhausted and being unable to face their pressing environmental problems.

Personality Characteristics

Pervasive feelings of dependency and personal insecurity plague their adjustment.

Predictions or Dispositions

In therapy, these individuals may respond to support and reassurance, but permanent personality changes are difficult for them to make. These individuals

Table 5-15. Descriptors for the 4-6/6-4 code type

☐ Immature, narcissistic, and self-indulgent

☐ Makes excessive and unrealistic demands on relationships

☐ Seeks attention and sympathy to excess

☐ Suspicious of others and resentful of demands made by others

☐ Relationship problems

☐ Mistrustful of the motivation of others and tends to avoid deep emotional involvement

☐ Irritable, sullen, argumentative, and obnoxious

☐ Resentful of authority

☐ Personality adjustment problems

☐ Hostile and angry

☐ Denies serious psychological problems through rationalization and transfer of blame to others

☐ Cannot accept responsibility for own behavior

☐ Unrealistic and grandiose in self-appraisals

☐ Unreceptive to psychotherapy

Table 5-16. Descriptors for the 4-7/7-4 code type

☐ Alternates between periods of acting-out and excessive concern about the effects of his/her behavior

☐ Temporary guilt and self-condemnation possible

☐ Vague somatic complaints, tension, and fatigue

☐ Frequently reports being exhausted and unable to face pressing environmental demands

☐ Feelings of dependency and insecurity plague adjustment

☐ Permanent personality changes are difficult to make

☐ Typically very insecure, requiring frequent reassurances of self-worth

are typically so insecure that they require frequent reassurance of their self-worth. Table 5-16 lists the descriptors for the 4-7/7-4 code type.

4-8/8-4 Code Type

Symptoms and Behaviors

Serious psychological problems are characteristic of individuals with this code type. They do not seem to fit into society very well. They are viewed as odd, peculiar, nonconforming, and resentful of authority. They may espouse unusual religious or political views and behave in erratic, unpredictable ways. Some individuals with this pattern withdraw into fantasy or strike out in anger as a defense against being hurt. Problems with impulse control are likely. They are viewed as angry, irritable, and resentful. They typically act-out in asocial ways. Delinquency, criminal acts, or sexual deviation may be present. Excessive drinking and drug abuse are characteristic. Many individuals with this profile type are obsessed with sexual thoughts. They may be afraid of being unable to perform sexually or may indulge in antisocial sexual acts in an attempt to demonstrate sexual adequacy. They may be withdrawn and isolated socially.

Some individuals with this pattern have periods of suicidal obsessions. They are often distrustful of others and avoid close relationships. They are seen as being impaired in empathic ability and as lacking in basic social skills.

Personality Characteristics

A poor self-concept is central to the problems of these individuals. They set themselves up for rejection and failure, and have deep feelings of insecurity. They tend to have exaggerated needs for attention and affection.

Predictions or Dispositions

Usually, individuals with this profile have a history of underachievement and marginal adjustment. The most common diagnoses are severe personality disorders such as antisocial, paranoid, schizoid, or even schizophrenic disorder.

Since these individuals accept little responsibility for their own behavior, they tend not to respond well to psychological treatment. They tend to rationalize and blame others for their own difficulties. They typically see the world as threatening and rejecting, and thus may encounter some problems in developing a treatment relationship. Table 5-17 presents 4-8/8-4 descriptors.

4-9/9-4 Code Type

Symptoms and Behaviors

Individuals with the 4-9/9-4 code type show a marked disregard for social standards and values, exhibit antisocial behavior, have poorly developed consciences, demonstrate loose morals and fluctuating ethical values. A wide array of antisocial acts (e.g., alcoholism, fighting, stealing, and sexual acting-out) may be characteristic.

They are seen as selfish, self-indulgent, and impulsive. They typically cannot delay gratification of impulses. They show poor judgment and may act without considering the consequences of their actions. They seemingly fail to learn from punishing experiences. They typically manifest low frustration tolerance, moodiness, irritability, and a caustic manner. They show intense feelings of anger and hostility, which are expressed in negative emotional outbursts.

They may be viewed as energetic, restless, overactive, and needing to seek out emotional stimulation and excitement. They are seen as uninhibited, extroverted, and talkative. They tend to create a good first impression, but their relationships are superficial and tend to wear thin over time.

Table 5-17. Descriptors for the 4-8/8-4 code type

☐ Serious psychological problems

☐ May not fit into society very well

☐ Viewed as odd, peculiar, and nonconforming

☐ Resentful of authority

☐ Espouses unusual religious or political views, and behaves in erratic and unpredictable ways

☐ Withdraws into fantasy or strikes out in anger as a defense against being hurt

☐ Impulse-control problems

☐ Angry, irritable, and resentful

☐ Acts-out in asocial ways

☐ Delinquency, criminal acts, or sexual deviation possible

☐ Excessive drinking and drug abuse possible

☐ Obsessed with sexual thoughts

☐ May indulge in antisocial sexual acts

☐ Withdrawn and socially isolated

☐ Suicidal obsessions

☐ Distrustful of others

☐ Avoids close relationships

☐ Impaired in empathic ability and lacking in basic social skills

☐ Poor self-concept is central

☐ Prone to rejection and failure

☐ Deep feelings of insecurity

☐ Sees the world as threatening and rejecting place

☐ Accepts little responsibility for own behavior

☐ May not to respond well to psychological treatment

Personality Characteristics

Individuals with this profile configuration are likely to be narcissistic and incapable of deep emotional ties. They tend to keep others at a distance emotionally. Their social facade may hide a lack of self-confidence and security. Features of an immature, insecure, and dependent personality structure may be present. The typical diagnosis is antisocial personality disorder.

Predictions or Dispositions

Individuals with the 4-9/9-4 code type typically do not accept responsibility for own behavior and tend not to seek treatment unless others pressure them to do

Table 5-18. Descriptors for the 4-9/9-4 code type

☐ Marked disregard for social standards and values

☐ Exhibits antisocial behavior, has poorly developed conscience, and demonstrates loose morals and fluctuating ethical values

☐ Alcoholism possible

☐ Fighting and sexual acting-out possible

☐ Selfish, self-indulgent, and impulsive

☐ Cannot delay gratification of impulses

☐ Poor judgment

☐ Fails to learn from punishing experiences

☐ Manifests low frustration tolerance, moodiness, irritability, and a caustic manner

☐ Shows intense feelings of anger and hostility, which are expressed in negative emotional outbursts

☐ Energetic, restless, overactive, and needing emotional stimulation and excitement

☐ Uninhibited, extroverted, and talkative

☐ May create a good first impression but relationships are superficial

☐ Narcissistic and incapable of deep emotional ties

☐ Keeps others at emotional distance

☐ Immature, insecure, and dependent

☐ Rationalizes own shortcomings and failures, and blames difficulties on others

☐ Has legal, work, or relationship problems

☐ Does not accept responsibility for own behavior

☐ Tends not to seek treatment unless by external pressure

so. They rationalize their own shortcomings and failures, and blame their difficulties on others. Their legal, work, or relationship problems tend to persist over time. Table 5-18 lists the descriptors for the 4-9/9-4 code type.

6-8/8-6 Code Type

Symptoms and Behaviors

Feelings of inferiority and insecurity, low self-confidence and poor self-esteem are prominent. Individuals with this profile configuration may feel guilty about their perceived failures. Withdrawal from activity and emotional apathy are likely. They are not usually very involved with other people. They are viewed as suspicious and distrustful of others. They tend to avoid deep emotional ties and are thought to be deficient in social skills. These people tend to be most comfortable when alone. They resent demands placed on them. They are moody, irritable, unfriendly, and negativistic. Clearly psychotic behavior may be present. Their thinking is likely to be autistic, fragmented, tangential, and circumstantial. They manifest bizarre thought content, difficulties in concentrating, attention deficit and memory problems. They are likely to have poor judgment. They may exhibit severe confusion, delusions of persecution and/or grandeur, feelings of unreality, and preoccupation with abstract or obscure matters. Blunted affect may be present. In addition, they may show rapid and incoherent speech, withdrawal into fantasy, daydreaming, and may have difficulty differentiating fantasy from reality. They seemingly lack effective defenses and tend to react to stress and pressure by regressing.

Personality Characteristics

Severe long-term psychological problems are indicated. A schizoid life-style is likely to be present.

Predictions or Dispositions

Individuals with the 6-8/8-6 code type are usually diagnosed as schizophrenic. Treatment often involves psychotropic medication and placement in a supportive, structured environment if they are viewed as being dangerous to themselves or others. Table 5-19 lists the correlates for the 6-8/8-6 code type.

6-9/9-6 Code Type

Symptoms and Behaviors

Individuals with this profile configuration are likely to be overly sensitive and mistrustful. They are likely to feel vulnerable to real or imagined threat, feel anxious much of the time, and may be tearful and trembling. They tend to overreact to minor stress and may respond to severe setbacks by withdrawing into fantasy.

Individuals with this profile type may show signs of thought disorder, complain of difficulties in thinking, and have concentration problems. They may have delusions and hallucinations, irrelevant and incoherent speech, and appear disoriented and perplexed.

Personality Characteristics

Individuals with this profile pattern may show a strong need for affection and are passive-dependent in relationships.

Predictions or Dispositions

Psychiatric inpatients with the 6-9/9-6 code type may be diagnosed as schizophrenic (paranoid type) or as having a mood disorder. Psychological treatment may be difficult to implement since patients may be plagued by disorganized, unproductive, and ruminative thinking. Implementation of behavior change programs may be hampered by their tendency to be overideational and obsessional. They tend to have problems expressing emotions in adaptive, modulated ways. They may alternate between overcontrol and more direct, uncontrolled

Table 5-19. Descriptors for the 6-8/8-6 code type

☐ Feelings of inferiority and insecurity

☐ Low self-confidence and poor self-esteem

☐ Feels guilty about perceived failures

☐ Withdraws from activity

☐ Emotional apathy

☐ Not usually very involved with others

☐ Suspicious and distrustful of others

☐ Avoids deep emotional ties

☐ Deficient in social skills

☐ Feels most comfortable when alone

☐ Resents demands placed by others

☐ Moody, irritable, unfriendly, and negativistic

☐ Psychotic behavior may be present

☐ Thinking is likely to be autistic, fragmented, tangential, and circumstantial

☐ Manifests bizarre thought content, difficulties in concentrating, attention deficit, and memory problems

☐ Has poor judgment

☐ Exhibits severe confusion, delusions of persecution and/or grandeur, feelings of unreality

☐ Preoccupied with abstract or obscure matters

☐ Blunted affect may be present

☐ Shows rapid and incoherent speech, withdraws into fantasy and daydreaming

☐ Has difficulty differentiating between fantasy and reality

☐ Lacks effective defenses and tends to react to stress and pressure by regressing

☐ Severe long-term psychological problems

☐ Schizoid life-style

☐ Schizophrenic diagnosis possible

☐ Treatment often involves psychotropic medication and placement in a supportive, structured environment

emotional outbursts. The descriptors for individuals with the 6-9/9-6 code type are listed in Table 5-20.

7-8/8-7 Code Type

Symptoms and Behaviors

Patients with this profile code typically show a great deal of turmoil. They are not usually hesitant to admit to psychological problems. They tend to lack de-

Table 5-20. Descriptors for the 6-9/9-6 code type

☐ Overly sensitive and mistrustful

☐ Feels vulnerable to real or imagined threats

☐ Anxious much of the time

☐ Tearful and trembling

☐ Overreacts to minor stress and may respond to severe setbacks by withdrawing into fantasy

☐ May show a strong need for affection, but passive-dependent in relationships

☐ Has problems expressing emotions in adaptive, modulated ways

☐ May alternate between overcontrol and direct, uncontrolled emotional outbursts

☐ Complains of difficulties in thinking and concentration problems

☐ May show signs of thought disorder

☐ May have delusions and hallucinations, irrelevant or incoherent speech, and appears disoriented and perplexed

☐ Psychological treatment may be difficult to implement since patients may be plagued by disorganized, unproductive, and ruminative thinking

fenses to keep themselves comfortable or anxiety-free. They report feeling depressed, worried, tense, and nervous. They may be confused and in a state of panic, show indecisiveness and poor judgment. They do not seem to profit from experience. They tend to be overly introspective, ruminative, and ideational.

Personality Characteristics

Chronic feelings of insecurity, inadequacy, inferiority, and indecisiveness are likely. Individuals with this profile are not socially poised or confident and tend to withdraw from social interactions. They are passive-dependent and cannot take a dominant role in relationships. They tend to have difficulties with mature heterosexual relationships and tend to feel inadequate in traditional gender roles. They tend to engage in extreme or unusual sexual fantasies.

Predictions or Dispositions

Patients with this profile may be diagnosed as anxiety disordered; however, the likelihood of psychotic and personality disorder diagnoses increases with elevation on Sc. Even when diagnosed as psychotic, individuals with this pattern may not show blatant psychotic symptoms. Medications to control intense anxiety and thinking problems are likely to be considered. Table 5-21 summarizes the descriptors for the 7-8/8-7 code type.

8-9/9-8 Code Type

Symptoms and Behaviors

Serious psychological disturbance is likely with this profile. Individuals may

Table 5-21. Descriptors for the 7-8/8-7 code type

☐ Shows a great deal of turmoil

☐ Admits to psychological problems

☐ Lacks defenses to feel comfortable or anxiety-free

☐ Feels depressed, worried, tense, and nervous

☐ Confused and in a state of panic

☐ Shows indecisiveness and poor judgment

☐ Does not seem to learn from experience

☐ Tends to be overly introspective, ruminative, and ideational

☐ Chronic feelings of insecurity, inadequacy, inferiority, indecisiveness are likely

☐ Not socially poised or confident and tends to withdraw from social interactions

☐ Passive-dependent

☐ Non-dominant in relationships

☐ Has difficulties with mature heterosexual relationships

☐ Feels inadequate in traditional gender roles

☐ Engages in extreme or unusual sexual fantasies

☐ May be diagnosed as anxiety disordered; however, the likelihood of psychotic and personality disorder diagnoses increases with elevations on scale 8

☐ Intense anxiety and thinking problems need to be considered in treatment

show social withdrawal and isolation. They may be especially uncomfortable in heterosexual relationships and show poor sexual adjustment. They often are seen as hyperactive, emotionally labile, agitated, and excited. They may be loud and excessively talkative. They typically are unrealistic in their self-appraisals, grandiose, boastful, and fickle. Their behavior is characterized by denial of problems. They may be vague and circumstantial. They report feeling inferior and inadequate, having low self-esteem and limited involvement in competitive or achievement-oriented situations.

Personality Characteristics

Individuals with this profile code are viewed as self-centered and infantile in their expectations of others. They tend to demand much attention and become resentful and hostile when their demands are not met. They appear to resist and even fear close emotional involvement. They avoid close relationships. They are typically unable to focus on issues and are viewed as odd, unusual, and autistic. Circumstantial thinking, bizarre speech (clang associations, neologisms, echolalia), delusions, and hallucinations are sometimes present.

Predictions or Dispositions

The most common diagnosis is schizophrenic disorder or severe personality

Table 5-22. Descriptors for the 8-9/9-8 code type

☐ Serious psychological disturbance is likely

☐ May show social withdrawal and isolation

☐ Uncomfortable in heterosexual relationships and has poor sexual adjustment

☐ Hyperactive, emotionally labile, agitated, and excited

☐ Loud and excessively talkative

☐ Unrealistic in self-appraisal, grandiose, boastful, and fickle

☐ Characterized by denying problems

☐ Vague and circumstantial speech

☐ Feels inferior and inadequate

☐ Has low self-esteem

☐ Limited involvement in competitive or achievement-oriented situations

☐ Self-centered and infantile in expectations of others

☐ Demands much attention and becomes resentful and hostile when the demands are not met

☐ Resists and even fears close emotional involvement

☐ Confused, perplexed, disoriented

☐ Shows feelings of unreality, and difficulties in thinking and concentrating

☐ Unable to focus on issues and viewed as odd, unusual, and autistic

☐ Circumstantial thinking, bizarre speech (clang associations, neologisms, echolalia), delusions, and hallucinations are sometimes found

☐ Severe thought disturbance may be present

☐ Possible schizophrenic disorder or severe personality disorder

disorder. A severe thought disturbance may be present, for example, and they may be confused, perplexed, disoriented, show feelings of unreality, and have difficulty in thinking and concentrating. Individuals with this profile code may state no need for professional help and may not enter willingly into psychological treatment. Although some need to achieve and feel pressure to perform, their actual performance tends to be mediocre. Table 5-22 lists the 8-9/9-8 descriptors.

Three-Point Code-Type Descriptors

1-2-3 Code Type

Symptoms and Behaviors

Individuals with this clinical profile report much physiological distress and difficulty adjusting psychologically. They seem to lack stamina, may feel weak, fatigued, tense, and nervous much of the time. They tend to react to stress by developing physical symptoms. They often overreact to minor or even normal physical changes with extreme concern and complaints. Although physical symptoms may be the primary problems reported, the individual also feels dysphoric and worried. Many individuals with this profile type develop physical symptoms centered around abdominal pain or headaches.

Personality Characteristics

Clients with this code type are rather passive in interpersonal relationships and may interact with others by whining and complaining. Individuals with this profile configuration are usually somewhat dependent and often feel the need to be taken care of. They are likely to become irritable and hostile if their needs are not met.

Predictions or Dispositions

These individuals are likely to experience low sexual drive and may have problems in heterosexual adjustment because of this. There are likely to be long-standing personality factors predisposing them to develop physical symptoms under stress. Individuals with this profile are often viewed as having psychophysiological disorders. The diagnosis of somatoform disorder in a passive-aggressive or dependent personality is probable. These individuals may view their problems as physical and probably do not recognize that psychological factors contribute to their symptoms. They tend to be uninsightful and are not likely to feel that they have any control over their symptoms. They are, therefore, poor candidates for insight-oriented psychotherapy. However, they might need to be confronted with the possible psychological origin of their symptoms. Stress management approaches might help them develop more effective problem-solving skills to better cope with stressful situations. Individuals with this clinical profile often have a hostile manner of interacting with others, which might carry over into the treatment situation, reducing the likelihood of therapeutic gain. Individuals with this personality style are not very receptive to suggestions from others. Descriptors for the 1-2-3 code type are provided in Table 5-23.

2-7-8 Code Type

Symptoms and Behaviors

A pattern of chronic psychological maladjustment characterizes individuals with this MMPI-2 profile. Individuals with this clinical profile are probably feeling overwhelmed by anxiety, tension, and depression. Individuals with the 2-7-8 code type feel helpless, alone, inadequate, insecure, and believe that life is hopeless and that nothing is working out. They attempt to control their worries through intellectualization and unproductive self-analyses, but they have difficulty concentrating and making decisions. They are functioning at a very low level of efficiency. They tend to overreact to even minor stress, and may show rapid behavioral deterioration. They also tend to blame themselves for problems. Their life-style is typically chaotic and disorganized, and they have a his-

Table 5-23. Descriptors for the 1-2-3 code type

☐ Physiological distress and difficulty in adjusting psychologically

☐ Lacks stamina, may feel weak, fatigued, tense, and nervous much of the time

☐ Reacts to stress by developing physical symptoms and frequently overreacts to minor or normal physical changes with extreme concern and complaints

☐ Feels dysphoric and worried

☐ Physical symptoms often center around abdominal pain or headaches

☐ Passive in interpersonal relationships and may interact with others by whining and complaining

☐ Dependent and often feels the need to be taken care of

☐ Becomes irritable and hostile if needs are frustrated

☐ Experiences low sexual drive and may have problems in heterosexual adjustment

☐ Long-standing personality characteristics that predispose to development of physical symptoms under stress

☐ Viewed as having psychophysiological disorders

☐ Sees problems as physical and probably does not recognize that psychological factors contribute to the symptoms

☐ Tends to be uninsightful and not likely to feel any control over symptoms

tory of poor work and achievement. They may be preoccupied with obscure religious ideas.

Personality Characteristics

Problematic interpersonal relationships are also characteristic of such clients. Individuals with this profile configuration seem to lack basic social skills and are often behaviorally withdrawn. They may relate to others ambivalently, never fully trusting or loving anyone. Many 2-7-8 individuals never establish lasting, intimate relationships. Their interpersonal relationships are likely to be unrewarding and impoverished owing, in part, to their feelings of inadequacy and insecurity.

Predictions or Dispositions

This is a rather chronic behavioral pattern. Individuals with this profile usually live a disorganized and pervasively unhappy existence. They may have episodes of more intense and disturbed behavior resulting from an elevated stress level. Individuals with this profile show a severe psychological disorder and would probably be diagnosed as severely neurotic with an anxiety disorder or dysthymic disorder in a schizoid personality. However, the possibility of a more severe psychotic disorder, such as schizophrenic disorder, should also be considered. Many individuals with this profile seek and require psychological treatment for their problems. Since many of their problems tend to be chronic, an intensive therapeutic effort might be required to bring about any significant change. Patients with this profile typically have many psychological and situational concerns; thus, it is often difficult to maintain a focus in treatment. They probably need a great deal of emotional support at this time.

Individuals with this profile configuration usually have low self-esteem and feelings of inadequacy, which make it difficult for them to get energized toward therapeutic action. Their expectation for positive change in therapy may be low. Therapists need to promote a positive, optimistic attitude if treatment is to be successful.

These individuals tend to be overideational and given to unproductive rumination. They tend not to do well in unstructured, insight-oriented therapy and may actually deteriorate in functioning if they are asked to be introspective. They might respond more to supportive treatment of a directive, goal-oriented type. Individuals with this profile present a clear suicide risk, and precautions should be taken. Table 5-24 summarizes the 2-7-8 code-type correlates.

Highlight Summary: Analysis of Alice's Code Type

Following the interpretive procedures suggested in this chapter, we will examine the possible descriptive information from the MMPI code-type literature for Alice's profile that was presented in Chapter 2 on p. 40. We will organize the potential behavioral descriptions of Alice's case into the same three categories used throughout this chapter: Symptoms and Behaviors, Personality Characteristics, and Predictions or Dispositions.

Alice's MMPI-2 code type is not a well-defined 7-8/8-7. The code-type definition tells us how confident we can be that the available code-type descriptors apply to her and increases the likelihood that her pattern will remain stable over time. Alice's scale elevations indicate that she has two standard scales with elevations greater than a T score of 65, scale 7 (T = 72) and scale 8 (T = 67). Because this code type is the same on both the MMPI-2 and the original MMPI norms, the accumulated information on this profile code could be confidently applied in her case. Since the next closest scale, scale 3, is 4 T-score points below at a T score of 63, we can be somewhat assured that this code type may be similar on retest, although it does not reach the recommended 5-point level.

Symptoms and Behaviors

How would Alice be described on the basis of the MMPI-2 profile code? Patients with the 7-8/8-7 code type usually show a great deal of emotional turmoil and an essentially psychoneurotic pattern. They openly report many psychological problems. They tend to lack defenses to keep themselves comfortable or anxiety-free. They report feeling depressed, worried, tense, and nervous. They may be confused, in a state of panic, show indecisiveness, and have poor judgment. They do not seem to learn from experience. They tend to be overly introspective, ruminative, and overideational.

Personality Characteristics

Chronic feelings of insecurity, inadequacy, inferiority, and indecisiveness are

Table 5-24. Descriptors for the 2-7-8 code type

- ☐ Chronic psychological maladjustment
- ☐ Overwhelmed by anxiety, tension, and depression
- ☐ Feels helpless, alone, inadequate, and insecure
- ☐ Believes that life is hopeless and that nothing is working out right
- ☐ Uses intellectualization as a defense
- ☐ Engages in unproductive self-analyses, but has difficulty concentrating and making decisions
- ☐ Functions at a very low level of efficiency
- ☐ Overreacts to even minor stress, and may show rapid behavioral deterioration
- ☐ Blames self for problems
- ☐ Has low self-esteem and feelings of inadequacy
- ☐ Tends to be overideational and given to unproductive rumination
- ☐ Chaotic and disorganized, with a history of poor work and achievement
- ☐ May be preoccupied with obscure religious ideas
- ☐ Has problematic interpersonal relationships
- ☐ Lacks basic social skills and is often withdrawn
- ☐ Relates to others ambivalently, never fully trusting or loving anyone
- ☐ Never establishes lasting, intimate relationships
- ☐ Interpersonal relationships are likely to be unrewarding and impoverished
- ☐ Feels inadequate and insecure
- ☐ Chronic behavioral problems
- ☐ Lives a disorganized and pervasively unhappy existence
- ☐ Has episodes of more intense and disturbed behavior
- ☐ Has a severe psychological disorder
- ☐ Possibly diagnosed as a severe anxiety disorder or dysthymic disorder in a schizoid personality
- ☐ Possibility of a more severe psychotic disorder, such as schizophrenic disorder
- ☐ Tends not to do well in unstructured, insight-oriented therapy and may actually deteriorate in functioning if encouraged to be introspective

likely. Individuals with this code type are not socially poised or confident and tend to withdraw from social interactions. Alice is likely to be passive-dependent and unable to take a dominant role in relationships. She probably has difficulties with mature heterosexual relationships and tends to feel inadequate in her sex-role attitudes. She may engage in excessive sexual fantasies.

Predictions or Dispositions

Patients with this profile may be diagnosed as anxiety disordered. Medications or behavioral interventions to control intense anxiety can be considered as treatment options.

The descriptive information obtained from Alice's MMPI-2 code type resembles the information we obtained in the scale-by-scale review described in the last chapter. In Alice's case, the code-type interpretation (i.e., taking both scales into consideration simultaneously) provides a diagnostic picture that emphasizes the central role of acute anxiety and a psychoneurotic, rather than a schizophrenic, process. A psychotic process might have been considered more likely in a scale-by-scale analysis that placed equal emphasis on scales 7 and 8.

Chapter 6

Interpreting the MMPI-2 Content Scales

If an individual is responding in a cooperative manner, what that person says about himself or herself in a clinical situation should be given considerable weight in the assessment process. The traditional approach to interpreting the empirically derived clinical scales of the MMPI-2 does not directly consider item responses as personal information. Rather, it assumes that answers to MMPI-2 items are simply signs of problem types without regard to specific response content. What matters is the way an item is endorsed, not its content. The meaning of an empirical scale is based not on the make-up of the constituent items, but on the empirical relationships that have been established for the scale. Interpretation of the traditional clinical scales and code types thus requires that an extensive network of empirical correlates be established for each scale or index before meaning can be attached to particular scores.

Content interpretation, on the other hand, is based on the view that responses to items are communications about one's feelings, personality style, and past or current problems. A major assumption of content interpretation is that the subject wishes to reveal his or her ideas, attitudes, beliefs, and problems, and then cooperates with the testing by truthfully acknowledging them. Most people taking the MMPI-2 under clinical conditions provide accurate personality information. However, subjects taking the MMPI under pressure, court order, or in employment-selection situations may distort their responses to create a particular impression. In these cases the scores on the Content Scales may be suppressed somewhat, reflecting a problem-free picture, and thus may not be as accurate as the scale scores of a cooperative subject.

Several approaches to assessing content themes have been explored with the MMPI. In Chapter 4, we discussed one important way in which item content, through the use of subscales, is used to refine interpretation of the standard scales. These rationally derived subscales provide a very useful, though somewhat limited, view of what an individual is communicating through item endorsement.

A more comprehensive and psychometrically sound approach to assessing item content dimensions in the original MMPI was developed by Wiggins (1966; 1969). Nichols (1987) provides a useful summary of content interpretive strategies for the Wiggins scales. Wiggins published a set of content homogeneous scales that represented the major dimensions in the item pool. Each dimension had high internal consistency and strong predictive validity. However, a number of the Wiggins Content Scales contained items with objectionable content, which were deleted in the revision of the MMPI. Moreover, a number of new

items were added to the MMPI-2 to address additional content areas. Consequently, although some of the Wiggins scales are intact and can be scored, a new
set of MMPI-2 Content Scales was developed (Butcher, Graham, Williams, &
Ben-Porath, 1990) to assess the major content dimensions in the MMPI-2 and to
provide new measures of the expanded item content in the inventory.

MMPI-2 Content Scale Development

The MMPI-2 Content Scales were developed following a multistage, multimethod scale-construction strategy. Initially, content dimensions were derived
from the 704-item MMPI (Form AX). These item groups were then purified statistically using item-scale correlations on normal (college students and military
personnel) and clinical samples. The MMPI-2 restandardization sample (N =
2,600) was employed only for developing norms in the final stages of scale development. The item dimensions were purified by eliminating items that were
uncorrelated with the total score of the scale. Additional items were obtained by
evaluating item-scale correlations of the 704 items with the total score of the defined dimensions. The revised dimensions (content scales) were then rationally
reviewed to ensure that the additional items met the criterion of content homogeneity. Alpha coefficients were computed to ensure that all the items on a particular scale actually added to the scale homogeneity, that is, that they increased
the scale's alpha level. The last psychometric stage involved reducing, and in
most cases eliminating, item overlap by dropping items from the scales on which
their correlation was lower. In other words, an item was kept on a scale only if it
was most highly correlated with that scale. Some item overlap was allowed on
scales that measured general problems such as WRK and TRT. Finally, norms
were constructed using the MMPI-2 community normative sample. The uni-
form-T-score approach adopted in the MMPI-2 restandardization was also employed in the development of T scores for the Content Scales so that the two
types of scales would be comparable.

Psychometric Properties of the
MMPI-2 Content Scales

Internal Consistency

The MMPI-2 Content Scales, having been developed in part following an internal consistency strategy, have internal consistency coefficients ranging from .68
to .86 in the normative sample (Butcher et al., 1990). These internal consistency
coefficients compare quite favorably to the Wiggins Content Scales in the original MMPI. The internally consistent scale properties allow the interpreter to consider the scale as having a single dimension readily interpretable by rational or
intuitive strategies.

Validity

Although the MMPI-2 Content Scales were derived rationally and refined by item-scale statistical analyses, the empirically based descriptors have proven to be an important characteristic of the scales as well. Butcher et al. (1990) report acceptable external correlates for many of the scales based on the behavior ratings of the couples in the MMPI-2 restandardization study. In particular, the ANX, DEP, HEA, ANG, ASP, LSE, SOD, and TPA scales showed strong external relationships to behavior as rated by the individual's spouse. The TPA scale for men also showed strong external correlates. The validity coefficients for the MMPI-2 Content Scales obtained in the normative study were equal to or higher than those obtained for the MMPI-2 clinical scales using the same external correlate ratings.

Several more recent studies have found strong external correlates for some of the Content Scales, particularly FAM and ASP. In a study of marital couples in distress, Hjemboe and Butcher (1991) found that the FAM scale was associated with marital and family problems. ASP has been found to predict antisocial personality characteristics and behavior. Lilienfeld (1991) reported that scores on the MMPI-2 ASP scale were significantly related to DSM III-R-based antisocial personality. Egeland, Erickson, Butcher, and Ben-Porath (1991) found that scores on the ASP scale differentiated mothers who had been identified as being at high risk for abusing their children from other women taking the test.

The Content Scales provide the clinician with as valid a psychometric comparison of the client as other MMPI-2 scales do. A study by Keller and Butcher (1991) showed that chronic pain patients can be empirically distinguished from the MMPI-2 normative sample by using the HEA scale. Schill and Wang (1990) found that the ANG scale correlated significantly with other measures of anger. The role of the MMPI-2 Content Scales in discriminant diagnosis has been evaluated in two recent investigations. One study using inpatient psychiatric profiles (Ben-Porath, Butcher, & Graham, 1991) showed that the BIZ and DEP scales separated inpatient depressed patients from schizophrenic patients more effectively than did the MMPI-2 clinical scales D and Sc. In another study, Walsh et al. (1991) found that the MMPI-2 Content Scales outperformed the clinical scales in differentiating between alcohol-abusing groups.

An Interpretive Strategy for the
MMPI-2 Content Scales

Clinical interpretation of the MMPI-2 Content Scales, unlike interpretation of the empirically derived clinical scales, is relatively straightforward and requires few assumptions. Endorsement of the items comprising a particular scale indicates admission of symptoms and attitudes contained in the items—assuming, of course, that the protocol is valid. The Content Scales are interpretable as summaries of the extent to which clients admit to particular problem areas. As noted earlier, they provide psychometric comparisons that are as reliable and valid as those of other MMPI-2 scales. However, interpreting these scales is not limited to predicting membership in a clinical group. More important, because the Content Scales contain homogeneous item content, the clinician is able to employ the descriptive qualitative characteristics reflected in the scale's items to describe the behavioral features the client acknowledges. For example, a client with an elevated score on HEA (T = 65) could accurately be described as endorsing excessive somatic complaints across several body systems, including gastrointestinal symptoms (e.g., constipation, nausea and vomiting, stomach trouble), neurological problems (e.g., convulsions, dizzy and fainting spells, paralysis), sensory problems such as poor hearing or eyesight, cardiovascular symptoms (e.g., heart or chest pains), and respiratory troubles (e.g., coughs, hay fever, or asthma). Such a client is likely to worry about his or her health, report feeling sicker more often than the average person, report experiencing a great deal of pain (e.g., headaches, neck pains), and seek attention for his or her complaints.

The interpreter should be aware of several ways in which the MMPI-2 Content Scales can add to interpretation. First, the Content Scales can often help clinicians understand clinical-scale elevations by allowing them to confirm or eliminate certain behavioral features represented in the scale. For example, if an individual has a high Pd score but a low ASP score and a high elevation on FAM, the elevation on scale 4 is likely due to family problems rather than antisocial features. Or, if the individual has a high elevation on the Pt scale but a low elevation on OBS, then one would conclude that the client does not appear to be plagued with excessive rumination and obsessive behavior, but may be experiencing more generalized anxiety without obsessive features.

The MMPI-2 Content Scales can also provide information that is not available through the clinical scales because they contain new items in the MMPI-2 item pool. The MMPI-2 Content Scales are grouped to provide information in several areas.

1. The Internal Symptom Cluster

The six scales comprising this group (ANX, FRS, OBS, DEP, HEA, and BIZ) address symptoms and maladaptive cognitions the individual might be experiencing. Clues to internal symptomatic behavior, maladaptive cognitive beliefs, and disabling thoughts are found in elevations on this cluster.

Anxiety

The ANX scale of 23 items addresses problems of generalized anxiety. Individuals who score high on ANX report symptoms including tension, somatic problems such as heart pounding and shortness of breath, sleep difficulties, excessive worries, and concentration problems. High scorers fear they are losing their mind, find life a strain, and have difficulties making decisions, even minor ones. They appear to be very aware of these symptoms and problems, and are willing to admit to them.

Table 6-1. ANX interpretive guidelines for the MMPI-2

☐ High elevations on ANX are T scores ⩾ 65. High scores indicate the endorsement of many of the anxiety symptoms included in the scale.

☐ Moderate elevations on ANX are T scores of 60-64, inclusive. Elevations in this range suggest that the individual has endorsed several symptoms of anxiety.

☐ High scorers on ANX report:
- Symptoms of anxiety, worry, and tension
- Somatic problems such as heart pounding and shortness of breath
- Sleep difficulties
- Decision-making difficulties
- Poor concentration
- Being fearful of losing their mind
- Indecision
- Finding life a strain
- An awareness of these symptoms and problems
- A willingness to admit to anxiety-related symptoms

Table 6-2. FRS interpretive guidelines for the MMPI-2

☐ High elevations on FRS are T scores ⩾ 65. High scores indicate the endorsement of many of the fears included in the scale.

☐ Moderate elevations on FRS are T scores of 60-64, inclusive. Elevations in this range suggest that the subject has endorsed several different fears.

☐ High scorers on FRS report:
- Having many specific fears (e.g., blood, high places, money, animals, leaving home, fire, storms, natural disasters, water, the dark, being indoors, and dirt)

Fears

The FRS scale, containing 23 items, focuses on specific fears or phobias. Individuals who score high on FRS report an inordinate number of fears or phobias of many different situations or things. These include blood, high places, money, animals (such as snakes, mice, or spiders), leaving home, fire, storms and natural disasters, water, the dark, being indoors, and dirt. This scale does not contain general symptoms of anxiety, which are addressed by the ANX scale.

Obsessiveness

The OBS scale of 16 items addresses the cognitive processes of maladaptive rumination and obsessive thinking. Individuals who score high on OBS have tremendous difficulties making decisions and are likely to ruminate excessively about issues and problems, causing others to become impatient. Having to make changes distresses them, and they may report some compulsive behaviors like counting or saving unimportant things. They are excessive worriers who frequently become overwhelmed by their own thoughts and appear unable to function in a practical manner.

Table 6-3. OBS interpretive guidelines for the MMPI-2

☐ High elevations on OBS are T scores ≥ 65. High scores indicate the endorsement of many obsessional behaviors assessed by the scale.

☐ Moderate elevations on OBS are T scores of 60-64, inclusive. Elevations in this range suggest that several of the obsessive behaviors are endorsed.

☐ High scorers on OBS report:
  ● Tremendous difficulties making decisions
  ● Being likely to ruminate excessively about issues and problems
  ● Fearing that they cause others to become impatient with them
  ● Being distressed by having to make changes
  ● Compulsive behaviors like counting or saving unimportant things
  ● Worrying excessively
  ● Feeling overwhelmed by their own thoughts

Table 6-4. DEP interpretive guidelines for the MMPI-2

☐ High elevations on DEP are T scores ≥ 65. High scores indicate the endorsement of many of the mood problems included in the scale.

☐ Moderate elevations on DEP are T scores of 60-64, inclusive. Elevations in this range suggest that several of the depressive symptoms are endorsed.

☐ High scorers on DEP report:
  ● Significant depressive thoughts
  ● Feeling blue and uncertain about their future
  ● Being uninterested in their life
  ● Being likely to brood, being unhappy, and crying easily
  ● Feeling hopeless and empty much of the time
  ● Possible thoughts of suicide or wishes that they were dead
  ● Beliefs that they are condemned or have committed unpardonable sins
  ● Feeling that other people are not supportive

Depression

The DEP scale, containing 33 items, assesses symptomatic depression. Individuals who score high on this scale are characterized as having significant depressive thoughts. They report feeling blue and uncertain about their future, and seem uninterested in their lives. They are likely to brood, be unhappy, cry easily, and feel hopeless about the future. They report feeling empty and may have thoughts of suicide or wish they were dead. They may believe they are condemned or have committed unpardonable sins. They tend to consider other people unsupportive.

Health Concerns

The HEA scale of 36 items addresses health symptoms and concerns. Individuals with high scores on HEA report many physical symptoms across several body systems, including gastro-intestinal symptoms (e.g., constipation, nausea and vomiting, stomach trouble), neurological problems (e.g., convulsions, dizzy and fainting spells, paralysis), sensory problems (e.g., poor hearing or eye-

Table 6-5. HEA interpretive guidelines for the MMPI-2

☐ High elevations on HEA are T scores ≥ 65. High scores indicate the endorsement of many of the health concerns included in the scale.

☐ Moderate elevations on HEA are T scores of 60-64, inclusive. Elevations in this range suggest that several somatic symptoms are endorsed.

☐ High scores on HEA report:
- Many physical symptoms across several body systems, including gastro-intestinal symptoms, neurological problems, sensory problems, cardiovascular symptoms, skin problems, pain, and respiratory troubles
- Worries about their health
- Feeling sicker than the average person

Table 6-6. BIZ interpretive guidelines for the MMPI-2

☐ High elevations on BIZ are T scores ≥ 65. High scores indicate the endorsement of many of the unusual thinking problems included in the scale.

☐ Moderate elevations on BIZ are T scores of 60-64, inclusive. Elevations in this range suggest that several of the problem behaviors are endorsed.

☐ High scorers on BIZ report:
- Possible auditory, visual, or olfactory hallucinations
- Recognizing that their thoughts are strange and peculiar
- Paranoid ideations (e.g., being plotted against or someone trying to poison them)
- Unrealistic feelings that they have a special mission or powers in life

---

sight), cardiovascular symptoms (e.g., heart or chest pains), skin problems, pain (e.g., headaches, neck pains), and respiratory troubles (e.g., coughs, hay fever or asthma). Individuals who score high on HEA tend to worry about their health and report feeling sicker more often than does the average person.

Bizarre Mentation

The BIZ scale, containing 24 items, addresses severe symptoms of thought disorder. Individuals who respond to items on this scale are likely to manifest psychotic thought processes. They may report auditory, visual, or olfactory hallucinations and may recognize that their thoughts are strange and peculiar. Paranoid ideation (e.g., the belief that they are being plotted against or that someone is trying to poison them) may be reported as well. These individuals may feel they have a special mission or powers. Elevations greater than 65 on this scale suggest severe and unusual thinking problems.

2. The External Aggressive Tendencies Cluster

The four scales in this cluster (ANG, CYN, ASP, and TPA) center around behavior control and outward expression of emotions. Scores on these scales indicate how the individual is dealing with others—high elevations on these scales sug-

Table 6-7. ANG interpretive guidelines for the MMPI-2

☐ High elevations on ANG are T scores ≥ 65. High scores indicate the endorsement of many of the anger-control problems included in the scale.

☐ Moderate elevations on ANG are T scores of 60-64, inclusive. Elevations in this range suggest that several of the anger behaviors are endorsed.

☐ High scorers on the ANG scale report:
  • Anger-control problems
  • Feeling irritable, grouchy, and impatient
  • Being hotheaded, annoyed, and stubborn
  • Sometimes feeling like swearing or smashing things
  • Concern over losing self-control
  • Having been physically abusive toward people and objects

Table 6-8. CYN interpretive guidelines for the MMPI-2

☐ High elevations on CYN are T scores ≥ 65. High scores indicate extensive endorsement of the cynical attitudes and behaviors included in the scale.

☐ Moderate elevations on CYN are T scores of 60-64, inclusive. Elevations in this range suggest that many of the cynical attitudes and behaviors are endorsed.

☐ High scorers on the CYN scale report:
  • Many misanthropic beliefs
  • Expecting hidden, negative motives behind the actions of others
  • Believing that most people are honest simply because they fear being caught
  • Distrusting other people
  • Believing that people use others and are friendly only for selfish reasons
  • Negative attitudes about those close to them, including fellow workers, family, and friends

gest that the individual has maladaptive attitudes about the way he or she attempts to deal with demands of their life-situation.

Anger

The ANG scale of 16 items assesses loss of control while angry. Individuals who score high on ANG are likely to have anger control problems. These individuals report being irritable, grouchy, impatient, hotheaded, annoyed, and stubborn. They feel like swearing or smashing things at times. They may lose self-control and report having been physically abusive of people and objects.

Cynicism

The CYN scale, measuring cynical beliefs and misanthropic attitudes, contains 23 items, 20 of which were initially developed through item factor analysis of the MMPI in a study by Johnson et al. (1984). Three new MMPI-2 items were added to the scale through item analysis procedures. Individuals who score high on this scale have negative attitudes toward others and seem to expect hidden, negative motives behind the actions of others. For example, they believe that most people are honest simply because they fear being caught; other people are to be distrusted; other people use each other and are friendly only for selfish

Table 6-9. ASP interpretive guidelines for the MMPI-2

☐ High elevations on ASP are T scores ≥ 65. High scores indicate extensive endorsement of the antisocial problems included in the scale.

☐ Moderate elevations on ASP are T scores of 60-64, inclusive. Elevations in this range suggest that many of the antisocial behaviors are endorsed.

☐ High scorers on the ASP scale report:
- Misanthropic attitudes similar to high CYN scorers
- Problem behaviors during their school years
- Antisocial practices like being in trouble with the law, stealing, or shoplifting
- Enjoying the antics of criminals
- Believing that it is all right to get around the law, as long as it is not broken

Table 6-10. TPA interpretive guidelines for the MMPI-2

☐ High elevations on TPA are T scores ≥ 65. High scores indicate extensive endorsement of the behaviors found in Type A personalities.

☐ Moderate elevations on TPA are T scores of 60-64, inclusive. Elevations in this range suggest that many of the Type A behaviors are endorsed.

☐ High scorers on TPA report:
- Being hard-driving, fast-moving, and work-oriented
- Frequently becoming impatient, irritable, and annoyed
- Not liking to wait or being interrupted at a task
- Never having enough time in a day to complete their tasks
- Being direct and overbearing in their relationships with others

reasons. High scorers are likely to hold negative attitudes about those close to them, including fellow workers, family, and friends.

Antisocial Practices

The ASP scale of 22 items addresses antisocial personality characteristics. High scorers, in addition to holding misanthropic attitudes similar to high scorers on the CYN scale, are likely to report problem behaviors during their school years and other antisocial practices such as being in trouble with the law, stealing or shoplifting. They admit to enjoying the antics of criminals and believe that it is all right to get around the law, as long as it is not broken.

Type A

The 19 items of the TPA scale, most of them new with the MMPI-2, address a driven, competitive, and hostile personality style. High scorers on TPA are hard-driving, fast-moving, and work-oriented individuals, who frequently become impatient, irritable, and annoyed when they are interrupted. They do not like to wait or be delayed in tasks they are attempting. They report that there is never enough time in a day for them to complete their tasks. They tend to be direct, blunt, and overbearing in their relationships with others. Others view them as aggressive, overbearing and petty about minor details.

Table 6-11. LSE interpretive guidelines for the MMPI-2

☐ High elevations on LSE are T scores ≥ 65. High scores indicate extensive endorsement of low self-esteem problems.
☐ Moderate elevations on LSE are T scores of 60-64, inclusive. Elevations in this range suggest that many of the negative self-views are endorsed.
☐ High scorers on LSE report: • Low opinions of themselves • Not believing that they are liked by others • Feeling they are unimportant • Holding many negative attitudes about themselves, including beliefs that they are unattractive, awkward and clumsy, useless, and a burden to others • Lacking self-confidence • Finding it hard to accept compliments from others • Feeling overwhelmed by all the faults they see in themselves

3. Negative Self-View

The LSE scale provides clues to how the individual views himself or herself. This scale measures feelings of self-efficacy and of security about being able to function in life—it provides information about how confidently the individual deals with the demands of his or her life.

Low Self-Esteem

The LSE scale of 24 items addresses negative self-views. It was developed to provide a relatively "symptom-free" measure of negative attitudes toward the self. That is, an effort was made to exclude items related to depression and anxiousness. Individuals who score high on LSE tend to characterize themselves in negative terms and have low opinions of themselves. They do not believe that they are liked by others or that they are important. They hold many negative attitudes about themselves including beliefs that they are unattractive, awkward, clumsy, useless, and a burden to others. They report that they lack self-confidence and find it hard to accept compliments. They tend to feel overwhelmed by all the faults they see in themselves. Others view them as too hard on themselves.

4. General Problem Areas Cluster

The scales included in this interpretive cluster (SOD, FAM, WRK, and TRT) are more complex problem areas, not simply personality traits or attitudinal dispositions, as in the previous three groups of scales. These scales summarize problems in social relationships, perceptions and concerns over family problems, maladaptive attitudes and activities related to work adjustment, and clues as to whether the individual holds negative views about the change process that would interfere with a psychological intervention.

Table 6-12. SOD interpretive guidelines for the MMPI-2

☐ High elevations on SOD are T scores ≥ 65. High scores indicate extensive endorsement of social discomfort behaviors.

☐ Moderate elevations on SOD are T scores of 60-64, inclusive. Elevations in this range suggest that many of the social discomfort items are endorsed.

☐ High scorers on SOD are:
  - Very introverted and distant from others
  - Very uneasy around others, preferring to be by themselves
  - Likely to sit alone, rather than joining in the group
  - Shy and dislike parties and other group events

Table 6-13. FAM interpretive guidelines for the MMPI-2

☐ High elevations on FAM are T scores ≥ 65. High scores indicate extensive endorsement of family problems included in the scale.

☐ Moderate elevations on FAM are T scores of 60-64, inclusive. Elevations in this range suggest that the individual has endorsed many problems centering around family relationships.

☐ High scorers on FAM report:
  - Considerable family discord
  - Their families are lacking in love, quarrelsome, and unpleasant
  - Hatred of members of their families
  - Their childhood may have been abusive
  - Their marriages are unhappy and lacking in affection

Social Discomfort

The SOD scale, containing 24 items, assesses uneasiness in social situations. Individuals who score high on SOD tend to be very uneasy around others and prefer to be by themselves. In social situations, they are likely to sit alone rather than join in the group. They view themselves as shy and dislike parties and other group events.

Family Problems

The FAM scale of 25 items centers around family relationship problems. Individuals who score high on FAM experience considerable family discord. Their families are described as lacking in love, quarrelsome, and unpleasant. High scorers may report hating members of their families. Their childhood is usually portrayed as abusive, and their marriages may be seen as unhappy and lacking in affection. Individuals in marital distress have significantly more elevation on FAM than the normative MMPI-2 sample (Hjemboe & Butcher, 1991).

Work Interference

The WRK scale, containing 33 items, addresses problems and negative attitudes related to work or achievement. Individuals who score high on WRK are likely to possess negative work attitudes or personal problems that contribute to

Table 6-14. WRK interpretive guidelines for the MMPI-2

☐ High elevations on WRK are T scores ≥ 65. High scores indicate extensive endorsement of the problems likely to interfere with job performance.

☐ Moderate elevations on WRK are T scores of 60-64, inclusive. Elevations in this range suggest that many negative work items are endorsed.

☐ High scorers on WRK report:
- Behaviors or attitudes that are likely to contribute to poor work performance
- Low self-confidence
- Concentration difficulties, obsessiveness, tension, and pressure
- Difficulty getting started on things
- Giving up quickly when difficulties mount
- Decision-making problems
- Lack of family support for their career choice
- Personal questioning of career choice
- Negative attitudes toward co-workers and supervisors

Table 6-15. TRT interpretive guidelines for the MMPI-2

☐ High elevations on TRT are T scores ≥ 65. High scores indicate extensive endorsement of the negative attitudes toward mental-health treatment.

☐ Moderate elevations on TRT are T scores of 60-64, inclusive. Elevations in this range suggest that many of the negative treatment indicators are endorsed.

☐ High scorers on TRT report:
- Having negative attitudes toward physicians and mental health-treatment professionals
- Nobody can understand or help them
- Having issues or problems they are not comfortable discussing with anyone
- Not wanting to change anything in their lives
- Not believing that change is possible
- Preferring to give up, rather than face a crisis or difficulty

poor work performance. Some of the problems relate to low self-confidence, concentration difficulties, obsessiveness, tension and pressure, and indecision. Others suggest lack of family support for their career choice, their own questioning of career choice, and negative attitudes toward co-workers.

Negative Treatment Indicators

The TRT scale of 26 items focuses on attitudes or problems in accepting help or in changing behavior. Individuals who score high on TRT possess negative attitudes toward doctors and mental-health treatment. High-scoring individuals don't believe that anyone can understand or help them with their problems. They acknowledge that they have problems they are not comfortable discussing with anyone. They may not want to change anything in their lives, and they feel that changing their present situation is not possible. They prefer giving up, rather than facing a crisis or difficulty.

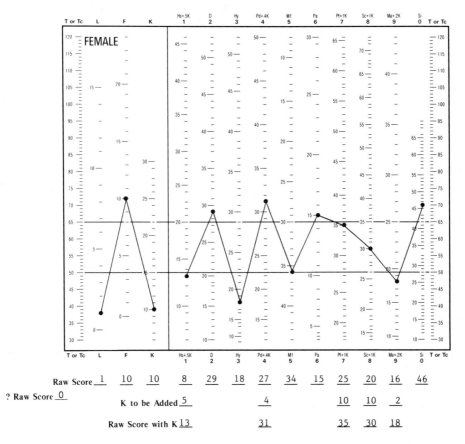

	T or Tc	L	F	K	Hs+.5K 1	D 2	Hy 3	Pd+.4K 4	Mf 5	Pa 6	Pt+1K 7	Sc+1K 8	Ma+.2K 9	Si 0	T or Tc
Raw Score	1	10	10		8	29	18	27	34	15	25	20	16	46	
? Raw Score 0															
K to be Added				5				4			10	10	2		
Raw Score with K				13				31			35	30	18		

Figure 6-1. Rena. MMPI-2 basic scales profile

Case of a Binge Eater

The case shown in Figures 6-1 and 6-2 provides a clear example of how the MMPI-2 Content Scales can aid in understanding clinical-scale elevations, as well as providing useful hypotheses about how the client has described herself through MMPI-2 content. This woman, who is quite emotionally unstable, sought psychological treatment for depression, relationship problems, and an eating disorder. She has had a substantial and lengthy history of psychological treatment over the past five years. This history, along with her MMPI-2 performance, was valuable in obtaining an appropriate referral for her.

Presenting Problems

Rena, an overweight, single 37-year-old woman, has a long history of psychological problems involving intense anger conflicts and relationship problems. She is being seen in an outpatient private practice and presently reports severe

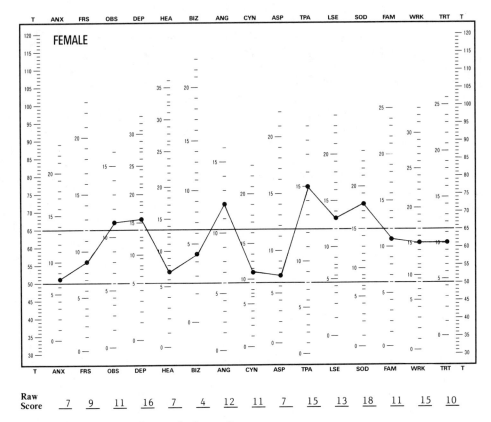

Raw Score	ANX	FRS	OBS	DEP	HEA	BIZ	ANG	CYN	ASP	TPA	LSE	SOD	FAM	WRK	TRT
	7	9	11	16	7	4	12	11	7	15	13	18	11	15	10

Figure 6-2. Rena. MMPI-2 Content Scales profile

depression, intense mood fluctuation, work difficulties, and continued eating problems.

Treatment History

The client has a substantial history of mental health treatment:

1984 (spring). She reportedly had a psychiatric breakdown (depression) and could not function at work. She was hospitalized and received treatment in an open psychiatric unit. She left the hospital, after only a short time, against medical advice.

1984 (fall). She was hospitalized in an inpatient eating disorders facility for severe bulimia for about three weeks. She reportedly has always been overweight and tended to binge eat. Before being hospitalized, she was eating about $25 worth of candy at a sitting. She binges mostly in the evenings and uses laxatives (often as many as 100 daily). During her initial period in the program, she alienated most of the staff and other patients. She was very verbally aggressive toward others and did not cooperate fully with the treatment. She remained for the course of the treatment and participated in the group treatment, although it was traumatic for her and for others. Her intense anger toward her parents and toward men was the focus of many sessions. She was discharged "improved." Her discharge diagnoses were bulimia and borderline personality.

1985. Rena entered outpatient psychological treatment but became angry with the therapist and terminated therapy after only two sessions.

1986. After an intense argument with her mother, she entered therapy again, this time with a social worker. She remained in treatment for five sessions before leaving "disappointed" with the results.

1987. After experiencing a break-up in a relationship, having an abortion, and making a serious suicide attempt, she entered treatment again. She became angry over the therapist's questioning and stormed out of the initial session.

1988. She was treated by a psychiatrist for her depression and was placed on antidepressant medication. She has been taking medication regularly ever since.

1989. The present referral for depression and eating problems was self-initiated.

Family and Personal History

Rena lives alone but spends most of her time with her mother, age 60, who is somewhat dominating. Rena works as a lower-level manager with a large corporation, but has been having considerable difficulty getting along with others. Her position has recently been "downgraded" (because of her interpersonal problems), and she is no longer supervising other employees.

Rena's personal relationships have been quite estranged in recent years. She does not, at present, have any stable relationships. She broke up with her fiancé about four years ago and has not been dating anyone on a regular basis. She has had a number of "one-night stands" over the past few years. She views herself as sexually promiscuous; she usually meets men in bars and has sex with them, but they seldom call her after that.

MMPI-2 Basic Scales Interpretation

Rena's validity-scale configuration suggests that she approached the MMPI-2 items in a frank, open manner, producing a valid clinical profile. She cooperated fully with the evaluation, endorsing a number of psychological problems she appears concerned about.

Her MMPI-2 clinical profile (elevations on scales 2, 4, 6, and 0) shows a high degree of psychological distress. She appears to have a mixed pattern of symptoms, including tension, depression, and agitation over problems she is having in her life-situation. She appears to be socially alienated and distant from others, and is likely to be overly sensitive to rejection. She is likely to be very suspicious of other people's motives and may have great difficulty trusting anyone.

Longstanding personality problems are likely to be central to her clinical picture. She appears to be angry over her present situation and feels that others are responsible for her problems. She tends to show poor impulse control and appears not to accept societal values. She may be seeking a temporary respite from intense situational problems she is encountering. Drug use or alcohol abuse are probably central to her problem situation, given her elevations on D and Pd.

Rena's interpersonal relationships appear to be strained. She is likely to be a manipulative individual who views others as a means to her own gratification. She appears to be somewhat hedonistic and may attempt to control people. She is likely to view her home life as very unpleasant and feels that she is being dominated by her family.

Individuals with this MMPI-2 pattern may express a great need for treatment, but they tend to be marginal candidates for psychological treatment because their difficulty in forming positive personal relationships could impair the development of a treatment alliance. Her longstanding personality problems are probably resistant to behavioral change. Individuals with this profile tend to have problems with anger control and often become enraged and aggressive toward others. Many individuals with this clinical pattern tend to be experiencing extensive family problems that need to be addressed in treatment.

MMPI-2 Content Scale Interpretation

Rena's MMPI-2 Content Scale performance is very useful in clarifying her clinical-scale elevations, as well as in providing information not available through the clinical-scale scores. Her high elevation on the Pd scale raises the possibility that she has an antisocial personality disorder. However, the Content Scale ASP is not elevated, suggesting that her Pd elevation does not represent purely antisocial features, but, rather, self-and social-alienation, anger, and family relationship problems. Consequently, our interpretation of her clinical profile should minimize discussion of antisocial personality features or criminal behavior and, instead, stress her negative alienation, lack of anger control, and family problems.

The aggressiveness suggested by her Pd-scale elevation is further clarified by her high scores on ANG. People who score high on ANG, as she does, are likely to have anger-control problems. These individuals report being irritable, grouchy, impatient, hotheaded, annoyed, and stubborn. They feel like swearing or smashing things at times. Rena acknowledges that she loses self-control in interactions with others and may be abusive toward people.

She appears to be feeling quite depressed at this time, as reflected in her high score on the DEP scale. She reports feeling blue and uncertain about her future. She broods a lot and is unhappy, and feels hopeless about the future. She feels empty and may have thoughts of suicide. She reports feeling that she has committed unpardonable sins. She feels that other people are not supportive of her. Perhaps central to her problems is her indication of low self-esteem as measured by the LSE scale. People who have elevations on this scale tend to characterize themselves in negative terms and have low opinions of themselves. Apparently, Rena has many negative attitudes about herself, including beliefs that she is unattractive, useless, and a burden to others. She lacks self-confidence. She seems to be overwhelmed by all the faults she sees in herself.

The difficulties she encounters in relationships and in continuing in therapy may be explained somewhat by her high score on OBS. She appears to have tremendous difficulties making decisions and is likely to ruminate excessively about issues and problems, causing others to become impatient with her. She apparently has difficulty making changes in her life and is distressed by change. She seems to be an excessive worrier who frequently becomes overwhelmed by her own thoughts and is at times unable to function in a practical manner.

Treatment Referral

Because of Rena's extensive interpersonal relationship problems and her history of having been moderately successful in group treatment in the past, it was recommended that she enter a group-therapy treatment program to work on her interpersonal problems. In addition, she was also seen in individual psychological treatment for a period of time.

Any treatment program should consider the following features of Rena's personality and address them early in treatment if progress (including her remaining in treatment) is to occur:

She tends to mistrust others and overreacts to minor problems as though great injustices have been done to her.

She tends to obsess and ruminate over minor irritations to the point that she makes great problems of them.

She manifests low self-esteem and is likely to be prone to feeling rejected.

She has many personality features of aggressiveness, alienation, and interpersonal hostility.

She has a low tolerance for frustration and is likely to react to minor problems with considerable rage.

She is socially ineffective and withdrawn from others.

Treatment Progress

Rena's individual sessions were described as usually stormy and somewhat unproductive since she tended to focus blame for her problems on others and was not open to viewing her own contribution to them. Her experiences in group treatment were initially quite traumatic for her. She reportedly began to attack others in the group in a highly aggressive manner. In one very dramatic session, the group retaliated against her persistent attacks by providing her extensive feedback on her behavior without rejecting her. Although she was hurt by their criticisms, she remained in the group, participating in a less aggressive manner.

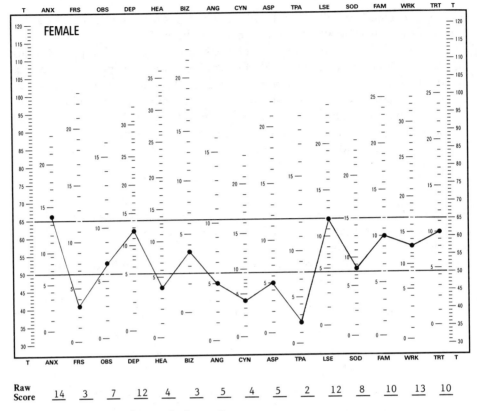

Raw Score	ANX	FRS	OBS	DEP	HEA	BIZ	ANG	CYN	ASP	TPA	LSE	SOD	FAM	WRK	TRT
	14	3	7	12	4	3	5	4	5	2	12	8	10	13	10

Figure 6-3. Alice. MMPI-2 Content Scales profile

Highlight Summary: The Case of Alice

The MMPI-2 standard scales are based on the assumption that they are diagnostic signs without regard to specific item content. Thus, the traditional clinical scales and code types require an extensive network of empirical correlates for interpretation. Content interpretation, on the other hand, is based on the view that responses to items are communications between the client and the clinician.

The MMPI-2 Content Scales provide a summary, in a psychometric framework, of the major content themes as viewed by the client. Through these measures, the specific problems or characteristics in the client's themes are compared with others in a standardized manner.

The interpretive hypotheses derived from Alice's Content Scale elevations provide information about her that was not available through the standard scales. As noted in Chapter 3, Alice's approach to the validity scales suggests that her content endorsement is likely to be an accurate reflection of her view of her problems. Figure 6-3 presents her Content Scale profile.

In Alice's case, we are able to learn more about the focus of her anxiety by evaluating the elevations on the three MMPI-2 Content Scales that assess Anxiety (ANX), Fears (FRS), and Obsessiveness (OBS). Her anxiety appears to be quite generalized, as shown by the high score she obtained on ANX, rather than empha-sizing specific fears or phobias, as shown by her lower score on FRS. She appears to have some obsessive qualities as well, as shown by the score on OBS. The general rather than specific forms of her anxiousness can assist us in pre-treatment planning, as we will see in Chapter 8.

Her elevation on the LSE scale warrants particular attention. Perhaps basic to her tendency to become anxious is her low self-confidence and feelings of ineffectiveness. She appears to be very uncertain about her ability to function. Her high score on LSE indicates an extremely negative self-appraisal. Her negative self-views might create a vulnerability to self-defeating behavior, which could, of course, trigger further experience of anxiety.

Chapter 7

Interpreting the MMPI-2 Supplementary Measures

The standard scales, with their focus on psychopathology, do not address all personality characteristics or problems of interest to practitioners and researchers. A number of additional scales, often referred to as supplementary or special scales, can be used to augment the standard MMPI-2 measures. Hundreds of special scales were developed for the original MMPI; several of the most valuable measures will be described in this chapter.[1] Most of the special or supplementary scales for the MMPI were developed with fairly specific purposes in mind (e.g., to assess over-controlled hostility, alcohol-abuse problems, or college maladjustment). Their application is usually more narrow and more limited than the standard scales or the MMPI-2 Content Scales.

We find the most clinically useful supplementary scales available on the MMPI-2 to be the MacAndrew Alcoholism Scale (MAC-R), the Addiction Proneness Scale (APS), the Addiction Acknowledgment Scale (AAS), the Marital Distress Scale (MDS), and the Overcontrolled-Hostility Scale (O-H). Our discussion of each of these will be followed by illustrative cases. Several other special scales, including Dominance (Do), Responsibility (Re), Post-Traumatic Disorder (PTSD), Anxiety (A), Repression (R), and several indexes or combinations of scales will be briefly described. Finally, we also provide a discussion of the "critical items" (i.e., items that are thought to serve as useful problem indicators).

The Primary MMPI-2 Supplementary Scales

MacAndrew Alcoholism Scale

The MacAndrew Alcoholism Scale (MAC) was originally developed to assess alcohol-abuse problems in clinical settings (MacAndrew, 1965). It was constructed by selecting items that statistically differentiated individuals with alcohol-abuse problems from individuals experiencing psychiatric problems that were not alcohol-related. The MAC scale originally contained 51 items, but MacAndrew recommended using a 49-item version that eliminated two items with obvious alcohol-abuse content: "I have used alcohol excessively" and "I have used alcohol

---

[1]Other scales from the original MMPI might also be scorable on the MMPI-2. The user interested in them should refer to Dahlstrom, Welsh, and Dahlstrom (1975) to determine item-scale membership then refer to Appendix J of the MMPI-2 manual (Butcher et al., 1989) to determine whether the items needed to score the scale are available in the MMPI-2. However, it is unlikely that norms based on the MMPI-2 standardization sample will be available for the scale.

moderately or not at all." MacAndrew surmised that many alcoholics would not admit to abusing alcohol, and viewed these two items as nonproductive in many assessments because alcoholics would recognize their content and distort responses to them.

MacAndrew originally recommended employing a raw-score cut-off of 24 for men and 22 for women as suggestive of alcohol-abuse potential. However, practitioners typically find a raw score cut-off of 26 for men and 24 for women (about one standard deviation above the mean) more effective. Empirical research with the MAC scale has generally been supportive of its use in the assessment of addiction problems (Graham & Strenger, 1988). However, the scale is likely to be less effective when the lower cut-off scores (i.e., 24 for men and 22 for women) are used (Gottesman & Prescott, 1989).

Research suggests that a high MacAndrew score is associated with addiction problems such as drug abuse and pathological gambling (Graham & Strenger, 1988) but is not useful for differentiating between alcohol abuse and abuse of other drugs. The MAC scale is best thought of as a measure of addiction-proneness, rather than as an alcohol-use or -abuse scale.

In the revision of the MMPI, several MAC items containing objectionable content, particularly of a religious nature, were deleted from the booklet. Since many practitioners use raw scores rather than T scores, the item deletions were considered problematic. Therefore, these deleted items were replaced with four items from the new MMPI-2 item pool on the MAC-R. The criteria for selecting replacement items on MAC-R were essentially the same as those used by MacAndrew (1965) in his original scale development. That is, items were selected that significantly separated alcoholics from non-alcohol-abusing psychiatric patients (McKenna & Butcher, 1987).

Two studies of the MAC-R for detecting possible substance-abuse problems have been reported. Levenson et al. (1990) studied alcohol abuse and other problem behaviors in a large normal population (1,117 men in the Normative Aging Study) and found support for MacAndrew's interpretation of the meaning of the MAC scale. They found that heavy drinkers and problem drinkers had higher MAC-R scores than lighter drinkers or non-problem drinkers. Moreover, men who had higher arrest records (possibly related to substance use or abuse) had MAC-R scores nearly identical to those of men who were problem drinkers. In another study, Graham (1989) reported that MAC-R scores were significantly associated with the following problems as rated by spouses in the MMPI-2 restandardization study:

> For men: *According to their wives, the high MAC-R husband has been arrested or in trouble with the law, swears and curses, drinks alcohol to excess (gets sick and passes out), has temper tantrums, takes drugs other than those prescribed by a doctor, does not show sound judgment, drives fast and recklessly, takes too many risks, laughs and jokes with people, and tells lies for no apparent reason.*

> For women: *Wives with high MAC-R scores were rated by their husbands as drinking alcohol excessively (gets sick and passes out), taking too many risks, extroverted, giving advice too freely, having been arrested or in trouble with the law, and not seeming to care about other people's feelings.*

Table 7-1. MAC-R interpretive guidelines for the MMPI-2

☐ T scores of ≥ 65 on MAC-R suggest strongly the presence of life-style characteristics associated with developing an addictive disorder.

☐ T scores of 60-64, inclusive, on MAC-R suggest that characteristics of the individual's lifestyle could lead to an alcohol- or drug-abuse problem.

☐ Current use or abuse of addictive substances is not assessed by MAC-R. Only the potential for developing an alcohol- or drug-abuse problem is suggested by elevations on MAC-R.

☐ Use or abuse of particular substances, such as alcohol or drugs, cannot be determined by scores on the MAC-R scale.

☐ Low MAC-R T scores (≤ 59) in a known alcohol or drug abuser can be valuable information for treatment planning. This situation suggests the possibility that the substance abuse is based more upon psychological maladjustment than the typical addictive behavior pattern.

These behavioral correlates suggest that the MAC-R scale, for both men and women, assesses behaviors that are relevant to determining alcohol- or drug-abuse problems. Interpretive guidelines for elevations on MAC-R are included in Table 7-1. Because it is widely used in clinical assessment and research, we have included an illustrative case (Figure 7-1).

Background Information

For the past two years, Mr. Gabriel has been employed as a security guard in a nuclear power facility, where he has had free access to the nuclear control room. Previously, for about 10 years, he had been employed by the same corporation in a fossil fuel plant and had been a loyal, effective employee. Since transferring to the corporation's nuclear division, he has had some difficulty with his immediate supervisor and has complained to fellow workers about his supervisor's "lack of knowledge." About three months before the referral, Mr. Gabriel began writing letters to the corporate vice president in charge of personnel. He wrote three different letters about two weeks apart. They were extremely difficult to read, contained unusual, obscure references, and appeared to become increasingly hostile and aggressive. Fearing that Mr. Gabriel was deteriorating and potentially dangerous to the plant's operation, the vice president recommended a psychological evaluation to determine his fitness for duty.

When Mr. Gabriel came to the psychological evaluation he was very friendly, extroverted, articulate, and outgoing. He cooperated with the evaluation in a generally non-defensive manner. He voiced some pleasure over the attention that his complaints had received. During the three-hour interview, he showed no bitterness or anger toward the company, although he acknowledged having some problems with his supervisor. In the two weeks before the evaluation, he was especially pleased that the supervisor was drawing a great deal of negative attention from his own superior for some problems he had created a few days before. During the evaluation, Mr. Gabriel showed no signs of depression, anxiety, antisocial features, or psychotic thinking.

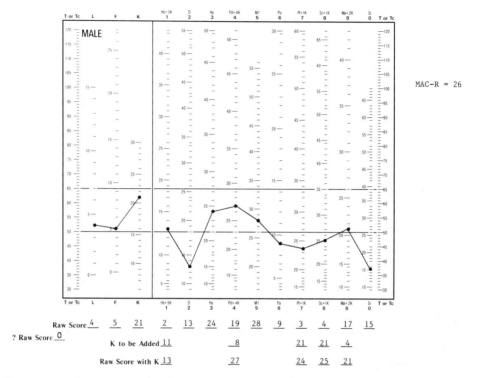

MAC−R = 26

Raw Score 4   5   21   2   13   24   19 28   9   3   4   17   15
? Raw Score 0
K to be Added 11   8   21   21   4
Raw Score with K 13   27   24   25   21

Figure 7-1. Mr. Gabriel. MMPI-2 basic scales profile

Interpretation of the MMPI-2 Basic and Content Scales Profiles

Mr. Gabriel's performance on the validity scales of the MMPI-2 indicated that his approach to the items was generally open and valid. Scores on the MMPI-2 L, F, and K scales were within the normal range, suggesting that he cooperated sufficiently with the evaluation to produce an interpretable profile. The range of elevations on the standard scales and the Content Scales (not shown) indicates that Mr. Gabriel is not reporting any symptoms of psychological distress such as depression, anxiety, or thought disorder. The generally low scores suggest that he has no extreme symptoms of psychological disturbance at this time.

Interpretation of MAC-R

Mr. Gabriel's score of 26 on MAC-R is much more revealing of problems than is his basic scale profile. It suggests the possibility that alcohol or other drug abuse might be related to his difficulties at work. His elevation on MAC-R can be used as a beginning point for further assessment in this area.

Follow-up Interview and Referral

Mr. Gabriel was seen in a follow-up session in which behavior leading to the referral, his MMPI-2 profiles, and his possible substance abuse were discussed. He was generally open and cooperative in the interview, though somewhat con-

Table 7-2. APS interpretive guidelines for the MMPI-2

☐ Individuals with T scores ≥ 65 on APS possess a great many of the life-style characteristics associated with developing an addictive disorder.

☐ T scores of 60-64, inclusive, on APS suggest that the individual endorses many life-style characteristics found among individuals with an alcohol- or drug-abuse problem.

☐ Current use or abuse of addictive substances is not assessed by APS. Only the potential for developing an alcohol- or drug-abuse problem is suggested by high scores on APS.

☐ Use or abuse of particular substances, such as alcohol or drugs, cannot be determined by scores on APS.

☐ Low APS T scores (≤ 59) in a known alcohol or drug abuser can be valuable information for treatment planning. This situation reflects the possibility that the substance-abuse disorder is based more upon psychological maladjustment than the typical addictive behavior pattern.

cerned about having been referred. He explained that he had written the letters to the vice president because he had considered the vice president to be open, considerate, and interested in the company's problems. Mr. Gabriel recalled meeting the vice president at an employee orientation during which the vice president, in a somewhat casual manner, had seemingly promoted the idea of letter-writing by inviting any employee to "let him know if problems occur."

Although Mr. Gabriel's motivation for the letters was explained, their unusual content and somewhat disconnected quality needed further exploration. Mr. Gabriel confessed that the letters were written during drinking episodes that usually followed an altercation with his supervisor. He acknowledged, after considerable probing, which included discussion of MAC-R and his score, that he was drinking too much and at times things "got out of hand." The remainder of the session was devoted to exploring an alcohol treatment program to help him deal with his alcohol-control problems.

Addiction Potential Scale

The Addiction Potential Scale (APS) was designed as a measure of the personality factors underlying the development of addictive disorders (Weed et al., 1992). The scale was empirically derived by selecting items that differentiated alcoholics and drug abusers from psychiatric patients and normals. Scale development procedures followed those used by MacAndrew (1965) in developing the MAC scale except that the MMPI-2 item pool, which incorporated additional relevant item content, was used. The APS contains 39 items, nine of which overlap with MAC.

The APS has been cross-validated in two recent studies. Weed et al. (1992) and Greene et al. (1992) found that the APS outperformed the MAC-R scale and another MMPI addiction scale (Substance Abuse Proneness Scale [MacAndrew, 1986]) in discriminating groups of substance abusers from psychiatric patients and normals. Table 7-2 presents interpretive guidelines for the APS.

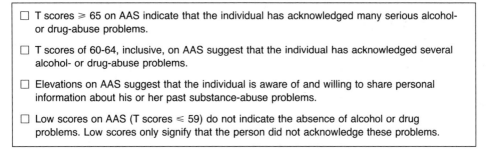

Table 7-3. AAS interpretive guidelines for the MMPI-2

☐ T scores ≥ 65 on AAS indicate that the individual has acknowledged many serious alcohol- or drug-abuse problems.

☐ T scores of 60-64, inclusive, on AAS suggest that the individual has acknowledged several alcohol- or drug-abuse problems.

☐ Elevations on AAS suggest that the individual is aware of and willing to share personal information about his or her past substance-abuse problems.

☐ Low scores on AAS (T scores ≤ 59) do not indicate the absence of alcohol or drug problems. Low scores only signify that the person did not acknowledge these problems.

Addiction Acknowledgment Scale

The Addiction Acknowledgment Scale (AAS) was developed as a measure of willingness to acknowledge problems with alcohol or drugs (Weed et al., 1992). The scale provides a psychometric comparison of acknowledged alcohol or drug problems. This 13-item scale was developed using a combined rational-statistical scale construction strategy. Initially, items that clearly addressed substance-abuse problems were selected from the MMPI-2 item pool. This provisional scale was then correlated with the other MMPI-2 items to determine if any other items in the pool were significantly associated with it. Then the scale was purified by examining the alpha coefficients, keeping items that improved scale homogeneity. The AAS assesses the extent to which the individual has acknowledged having problems in using or abusing drugs or alcohol.

The AAS has been cross-validated in two recent studies. Weed et al. (1992) and Greene et al. (1992) reported that the AAS significantly discriminated individuals in alcohol or drug treatment from normals and psychiatric patients better than either the MAC scale or the Substance Abuse Proneness Scale. Interpretive guidelines for AAS are provided in Table 7-3.

The case presented in Figures 7-2a and b illustrates the joint use of APS and AAS in evaluating drug or alcohol problems. Mr. Jenkins, a 42-year-old salesman, had been experiencing substantial life problems in recent years. Along with his marital problems, financial difficulties, and work problems, he was arrested recently for driving under the influence of alcohol (a charge that was reduced to careless and reckless operation of a motor vehicle). Following an incident in which a bottle of bourbon was found in his office, his employer referred him for a substance-abuse evaluation as a condition of further employment. Initially quite incensed about being asked to undergo psychological evaluation, he finally agreed, although he denied having a problem with alcohol. Mr. Jenkins's MMPI-2 basic profile is given in Figure 7-2a, his supplementary-scale profile in Figure 7-2b. His relative performance on the APS and the AAS is informative. He obtained a very high score (T = 76) on APS, suggesting that he possesses many of the life-style characteristics associated with developing a drug or alcohol problem. However, his relatively low score on AAS (a T score of 36) indicates that he has not been willing to directly endorse having a substance-abuse prob-

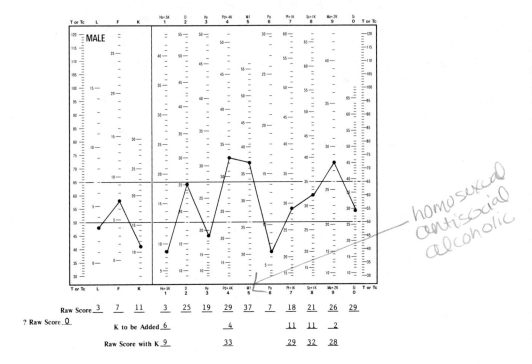

Raw Score 3   7   11   3   25   19   29   37   7   18   21   26   29

? Raw Score 0   K to be Added 6   4   11   11   2

Raw Score with K 9   33   29   32   28

Figure 7-2a. Mr. Jenkins. MMPI-2 basic scales profile

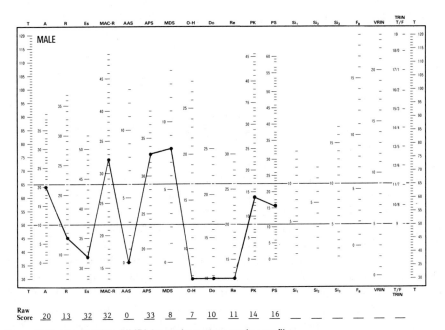

Raw Score 20   13   32   32   0   33   8   7   10   11   14   16   _   _   _   _   _   _

Figure 7-2b. Mr. Jenkins. MMPI-2 supplementary scales profile

Table 7-4. MDS interpretive guidelines for the MMPI-2

☐ The MDS is interpreted only for clients who are married, separated, or (if appropriate) divorced.

☐ Some indication of marital relationship problems is noted for MDS T scores of 60-64, inclusive.

☐ Strong indication of marital distress is found with clients who obtain T scores ≥ 65 on MDS.

lem. His reluctance to admit having alcohol or drug problems suggests that any effort to confront him with his abuse may be met with great resistance. In addition, his seemingly high potential for abuse along with his unwillingness or lack of recognition of problems with substance abuse suggests that he may not be willing to cooperate in a treatment program if one is proposed. This case is further discussed and a computerized MMPI-2 report is presented in Chapter 12.

Marital Distress Scale

Many marital therapists have sought to understand marital maladjustment by examining the personality profiles of husbands and wives. Early studies of MMPI profiles of couples in marital distress focussed on clinical scale and profile differences between distressed and "normal" couples (Arnold, 1970; Barrett, 1973; Snyder & Regts, 1990). The Pd scale typically has been found to be associated with marital disturbance. More recently, Hjemboe and Butcher (1991) also found the MMPI-2 Content Scale FAM to be significantly related to marital distress. Neither of these scales was developed for nor specifically related to marital distress. They tend to be associated with family problems in general.

Hjemboe, Almagor, and Butcher (in press) recently developed a specific scale for assessing marital distress, a 14-item empirically derived scale called the Marital Distress Scale (MDS). MDS was developed by selecting items that were strongly associated with a measure of marital distress, the Spanier Dyadic Adjustment Scale. The scale contains items with content related to marital problems or relationship difficulties. MDS shows a higher degree of association with measured marital distress than does either the Pd or the FAM scale (Hjemboe et al., in press). MDS interpretive guidelines are presented in Table 7-4.

Figures 7-3a-d present the MMPI-2 profiles from a couple with elevated scores on the MDS (Mr. Levin had a T score of 71; Ms. Levin a T score of 73) illustrating the potential usefulness of MDS in detecting marital relationship problems. Both Mr. and Ms. Levin reported a substantial degree of marital distress on the MMPI-2 MDS. We will examine their history and MMPI-2 profiles to highlight the usefulness of the MMPI-2 in the assessment of marital distress. Their marital problems are likely to be a central concern in their psychological evaluation.

Referral Problems

The Levins have known each other for 11 years. Mr. Levin is a 43-year-old Jewish self-employed professional. Ms. Levin is a 39-year-old Catholic who

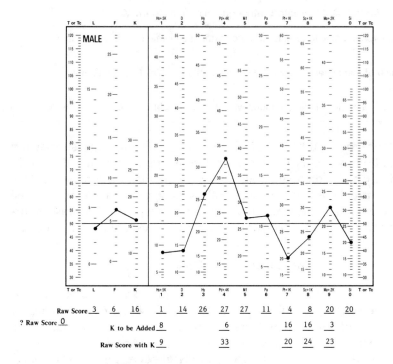

Raw Score	3	6	16	1	14	26	27	27	11	4	8	20	20
? Raw Score 0													
K to be Added			8				6			16	16	3	
Raw Score with K			9				33			20	24	23	

Figure 7-3a. Mr. Levin. MMPI-2 basic scales profile

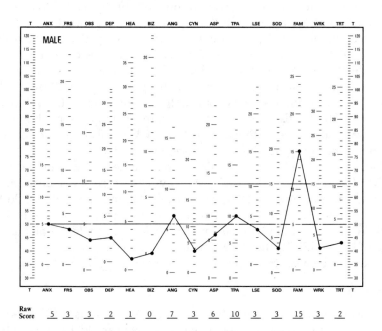

Raw Score	5	3	3	2	1	0	7	3	6	10	3	3	15	3	2

Figure 7-3b. Mr. Levin. MMPI-2 Content Scales profile

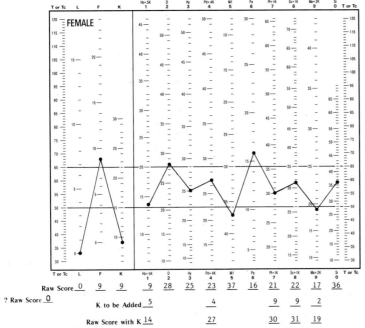

Raw Score	L 0	F 9	K 9	Hs+.5K 1 9	D 2 28	Hy 3 25	Pd+.4K 4 23	Mf 5 37	Pa 6 16	Pt+1K 7 21	Sc+1K 8 22	Ma+.2K 9 17	Si 0 36

? Raw Score 0

K to be Added 5   4   9   9   2

Raw Score with K 14   27   30   31   19

Figure 7-3c. Ms. Levin. MMPI-2 basic scales profile

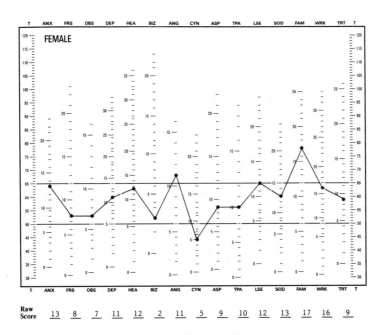

ANX	FRS	OBS	DEP	HEA	BIZ	ANG	CYN	ASP	TPA	LSE	SOD	FAM	WRK	TRT
13	8	7	11	12	2	11	5	9	10	12	13	17	16	9

Raw Score

Figure 7-3d. Ms. Levin. MMPI-2 Content Scales profile

works part-time. The Levins have one child, a boy of 9. Ms. Levin has a 19-year-old child from a previous marriage, who is presently in college. Although the Levins currently live together, Mr. Levin has been threatening to move out, claiming that he can no longer tolerate living with her severe drinking episodes.

Ms. Levin reports serious problems, both personal and marital. She acknowledges that she has a severe drinking problem, but feels that she is now getting it under control.

She reportedly is quite anxious and depressed over recent financial setbacks, problems with her older son, and with the deterioration in her marital relationship. She is having problems sleeping at night and reports problems in concentration. She considers her marital problems to be quite significant, including lack of communication, absence of love, her failure in family roles, and her work responsibilities. She has recently reduced her work to half-time in order to solve some of her personal problems.

Mr. Levin also reports significant problems in the marriage but attributes most of them to Ms. Levin. He considers her addiction one of the more serious problems but also believes their verbal abuse of each other and their poor money management contribute substantially to their marital problems. He reports that he sometimes drinks to the point of feeling high but does not consider himself a problem drinker. He has one brother who has been treated for emotional problems.

Interpretation of Ms. Levin's MMPI-2

Ms. Levin's performance on the MMPI-2 suggests that she approached the test openly and acknowledged a considerable number of psychological problems. Her standard profile reveals a number of psychological maladjustment problems, including a tendency to feel mistreated or picked on, to feel anger and resentment toward others, to harbor grudges, to be overly sensitive to interpersonal relationships, to bear hostility and resentment toward others and to express this in an argumentative manner, and to having difficulty in establishing rapport with others. Ms. Levin tends to use projection as a defense mechanism by attributing negative qualities to other people when she feels stressed. She tends to be rather suspicious and guarded in interpersonal situations and overly self-protective. Ms. Levin appears at this time to be somewhat depressed, tense, and angry, and hostile toward other people around her. Her score on MDS confirms that her marital relationship is a major focus of her problems.

On the MMPI-2 Content Scales, Ms. Levin reports a considerable number of family problems. She indicates that her family situation is lacking in love and is unpleasant. Quarrelsome relationships and abusive interactions are likely to be characteristic of her marriage at this point. In addition, Ms. Levin's high score on ANG suggests that she is having a great deal of difficulty with anger control. She reports being quite irritable, grouchy, impatient with others, hotheaded, and annoyed. She indicates that she sometimes swears and curses, and feels like smashing things or being abusive toward members of her family. She often loses self-control. Ms. Levin also has considerable problems with self-esteem, as shown by a high score on the LSE. She has a low opinion of herself, does not believe she is liked by others, and does not feel she is very important to other people. She holds many negative attitudes about herself including feelings that she is unattractive, awkward, and useless. She at times feels she is a burden to others and expresses a great deal of self-pity. She is lacking in self-confidence and at times feels overwhelmed by the faults she sees in herself.

Interpretation of Mr. Levin's MMPI-2

On the validity scales, Mr. Levin performed well within the normal range. His performance indicates that his MMPI-2 profile is valid, interpretable, and probably a good indication of his present personality functioning. The only prominent clinical-scale elevation is on scale 4. This high elevation is usually interpreted as reflecting problems in incorporating the values and standards of society. Individuals with Pd elevations engage in somewhat antisocial acts, are rebellious toward authority figures, and have other antisocial personality characteristics.

However, on closer evaluation and especially considering Mr. Levin's performance on the MDS and MMPI-2 Content Scales, we would want to modify our interpretation of these antisocial attributes of the Pd elevation. The only significant content theme he presents throughout the entire MMPI-2 protocol is that of intense family and marital problems. He reported no other antisocial features or emotional problems. Consequently, our interpretation of his MMPI-2 performance would focus more clearly on stormy relationships within his family, his tendency to blame other family members for his difficulties, his experience of extreme marital problems at this time, his anger and frustration over his family situation, and reports of his immaturity and childishness, and poor judgment. We might also consider the possibility that he is not feeling emotionally responsive toward his wife, tends to be resentful and aggressive toward her, is unable to maintain a warm attachment to her, and his relationships in general tend to be somewhat shallow and superficial. He seems insensitive to the needs and feelings of others at this time, and seems only interested in others in terms of how they can be used.

The Levins' MDS scores showed a clear problem with marital distress, which they both reported in interviews. In this case, the MDS was confirmatory and did not provide new information. However, the MDS may serve a discovery role in other cases—for example, where the major complaint is a mental-health problem such as depression, not relationship problems. A high MDS score might serve as a screening aid or as a clue to an unexpressed problem for the clinician to follow up in the clinical interview.

Over-Controlled Hostility Scale

The Over-Controlled Hostility scale (O-H) was developed by Megargee, Cook, and Mendelsohn (1967) to identify individuals who appeared to have difficulty expressing anger openly and usually behaved in an overcontrolled manner, yet who had actually engaged in hostile, assaultive behavior. Individuals who score high on the O-H scale (T ≥ 65) tend to guard rigidly against the open expression

Table 7-5. O-H interpretive guidelines for the MMPI-2

☐ Elevated O-H scores are T scores ≥ 65. Elevated O-H scores are not direct indicators of potential acting-out behavior.

☐ The O-H scale is more valuable as a post-diction indicator (that, is to explain behavior that has occurred in the past) than as a predictor of future behavior. Elevated O-H scores can be valuable indicators when they occur in individuals who are known to have engaged in explosive behavior. Elevations on O-H in individuals who have committed violent crimes suggest the possibility that they are emotionally constricted individuals who tend to deal ineffectively with their emotions then explode with over-determined affect when their defenses are overtaxed and they fail to control their anger.

☐ Many individuals with elevated O-H scores (e.g., airline pilot applicants in a personnel-screening setting) are simply highly socialized and well-controlled, and are not struggling with tenuous control over hostile impulses.

of aggression, often in the face of extreme provocation, until, unexpectedly, they act-out—often in a very violent manner. Many individuals who appear to be passive and who have committed violent, impulsive crimes of aggressiveness have been found to have high O-H scores. The O-H scale contains 28 items on the MMPI-2.

The O-H scale can be quite valuable to a clinician trying to understand possible personality factors leading up to the commission of violent acts (e.g., the so-called passion murder). Through post hoc evaluation, the clinician might be able to develop hypotheses about the individual's likely pre-incident conflict management personality style. However, the O-H scale is less valuable as a predictive measure, because many individuals obtain high scores in the 65+ range, but most will not lose control in an extreme manner. Although the O-H scale is not particularly useful as a predictor of repressed hostility, it can serve as a useful measure in understanding personality factors that may have influenced the commission of a violent act. The guidelines for interpreting O-H are summarized in Table 7-5.

Figures 7-4a and b present the profile of Juan Olmedos, age 38, who was married and had one adult child not living at home. Mr. Olmedos co-owned, with his cousin, a small retail store in a large metropolitan area in the eastern United States. He moved to the United States about 15 years ago from Mexico, but had not obtained citizenship. Although his store had never been robbed, in recent months he became quite concerned over this possibility since reading in the newspaper about robberies in his neighborhood. He talked to his partner about the terrible people in the neighborhood and the possibility of a hold-up. He recently decided to purchase a handgun, which he kept in the store for protection.

One evening, after closing the store, he noticed some people walking down the street, and he accidently brushed up against one of them as they passed. They were talking loudly and laughing (he thought at him). He reported later that he became quite afraid of them and angry because, as they passed him, they were disrespectful toward him, making an obscene gesture. As he watched them walk away, he found himself becoming even more angry over their lack of respect. He began to follow them, holding onto the handgun that he had in his

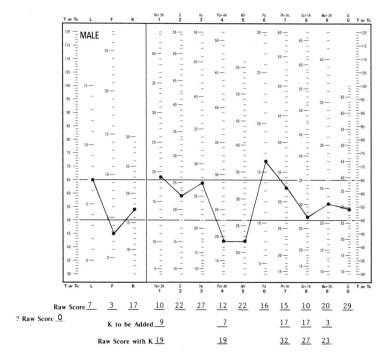

Figure 7-4a. Mr. Olmedos. MMPI-2 basic scales profile

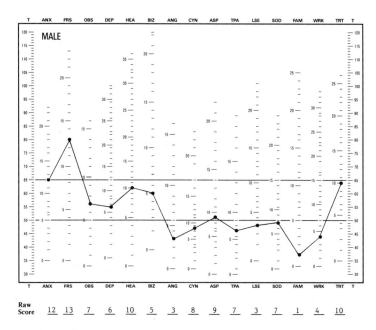

Figure 7-4b. Mr. Olmedos. MMPI-2 Content Scales profile

pocket. He planned to talk to them and make them apologize to him for their disrespect. After a few blocks, the young people noticed him following and sped up. He quickened his pace in pursuit. After a few more blocks, one of the young men decided to scare him away and started making aggressive motions toward him with his arms. Mr. Olmedos "felt intimidated," took out the handgun, shot and killed the youth while the others looked on in shock. Mr. Olmedos ran away and went into hiding for several weeks, finally turning himself in to the authorities. He was tried for murder in the first degree. His defense attorneys, however, pleaded that it was a case of self-defense since, in his psychological state, he saw himself as threatened by the teenagers.

He was administered the English language version of the MMPI-2 since his reading skills and cultural experience suggested that this version was appropriate. Because he was not tested before the crime, it is not possible to know with confidence exactly what his mental state was at the time of the murder. However, his MMPI-2 profile might be helpful in determining his psychological condition after his arrest and might provide some clues about long-term personality features that could have accounted for his actions.

Profile Validity

Mr. Olmedos's approach to the MMPI-2 items was defensive, consistent with his being evaluated in a court setting. He attempted to present himself as a morally virtuous and highly responsible person who would do nothing wrong. Individuals with his validity configuration tend to be rigid and moralistic, presenting themselves as somewhat righteous in their thinking about moral issues.

Standard Profile and Content Scales

The extreme elevation on the Pa scale suggests that Mr. Olmedos is very concerned about what others think of him. He tends to be highly suspicious, mistrustful, and is likely to project blame for his own shortcomings onto others. His attribution of negative motives to others is consistent with the finding that he may have strong feelings of persecution, as reflected in his highly elevated score on the Harris-Lingoes subscale (Pa_1). Many individuals with this elevation on the clinical scales are diagnosed as having delusional disorder or paranoid personality disorder.

In addition to the paranoid thinking reflected in the high elevation on Pa, he appears to be experiencing some somatic problems, shown by his elevation on the Hs scale. It is likely that he is feeling some vulnerability as a result of being incarcerated. His somatic complaints may result, in part, from his being unable to deal effectively with the stress he is experiencing.

Two content themes appear to be important in Mr. Olmedos's responses to the MMPI-2 Content Scales. He appears to be expressing a great deal of specific fears and generalized anxiety. He acknowledges being fearful of a number of circumstances, things, or situations. He appears to be a very tense individual who is uncertain about the future and his ability to deal with circumstances.

The O-H Scale

Mr. Olmedos's score on the O-H scale, elevated at a T of 65, suggests that he tends to be a rigid individual who overcontrols his emotions and does not deal effectively with emotional stimuli. Those who score in this range tend to be passive individuals who act aggressively and uncontrollably in circumstances in which their overcontrolling defenses do not effectively control their aggressive tendencies.

Case Conclusions

The MMPI-2 suggests that Mr. Olmedos is characteristically a rigid, suspicious, and somewhat paranoid individual who tends to see danger in many situations, even when there is none. He is likely to be overideational, may engage in unproductive thinking, and may not adequately "check out" his thoughts with others before acting on them. There is a strong possibility that he was operating on the basis of delusional beliefs at the time of the incident. He is likely to be a fearful person who becomes oversensitized to possible harm to himself. Individuals with his personality pattern may attribute negative motives to others without sufficient cause. He tends to deal with uncertainty and emotional turmoil in his life by repressing his aggressive motives. Individuals with this pattern typically deal with anger and other emotional situations in an overcontrolling manner and cannot effectively manage emotions when extreme situations present themselves. He could act in a violent, uncontrollable manner when he feels threatened.

What was the outcome of the trial? As often happens, a plea bargain allowed Mr. Olmedos to plead guilty to a lesser charge (manslaughter), and he was sentenced to three years in prison. Some sentencing leniency was granted in his case owing to extenuating circumstances and his lack of a prior record of violent crimes.

Other Supplementary Scales

Clinicians should be familiar with several additional supplementary scales since they are often available in computer-scoring programs or discussed in research articles on the MMPI and MMPI-2.

Dominance

The Dominance scale (Do) was developed by Gough, McClosky, and Meehl (1951) to assess personality characteristics of social dominance. The authors defined high and low dominant individuals by asking their peers to identify the subjects as either passive or dominant in social relationships. The authors then performed an item analysis using the MMPI to separate the two groups. The Do scale measures personality attributes such as comfort in social relationships, self-confidence, possessing strong opinions, persevering at tasks, and having the

Table 7-6. Do interpretive guidelines for the MMPI-2

☐ T scores ≥ 65 on Do are associated with:
- Being dominant in social situations
- Feeling poised and self-assured in groups
- Having self-confidence
- Appearing optimistic to others
- Being task-oriented and realistic
- Feeling adequate to handle problems
- Having dutiful attitudes toward others

☐ T scores of 60-64, inclusive, on Do are associated with having self-confidence and showing initiative in interpersonal situations.

---

ability to concentrate. Individuals who score high on the Do scale are generally viewed as dominant in social situations. This scale is widely used in personnel-screening applications, such as police officer selection, to assess whether the individual might have personality characteristics such as passivity, that could interfere with job performance. Do interpretive guidelines are provided in Table 7-6.

Social Responsibility

The Social Responsibility scale (Re) was developed by Gough, McClosky, and Meehl (1952) as an assessment of an individual's sense of responsibility toward others. Individuals who were high and low "responsible," as identified by peer nominations or teacher ratings, served as criterion groups. Originally, 32 MMPI items that separated individuals into the two groups comprised the Social Responsibility scale. High scores on this scale suggest that an individual is dependable and willing to accept the consequences of his or her behavior. High scorers (above 60 T) are thought to have a strong sense of justice and high standards, to be self-confident, trustworthy, and dependable, and to possess a sense of social obligation. Low scorers (below 40 T) are thought to be unwilling to assume responsibility and may not have accepted societal values or conduct. This scale has been widely used as an index of positive personality characteristics in personnel screening. The Re scale contains 30 items on the MMPI-2; two items were deleted in the revision. Re interpretive guidelines are provided in Table 7-7.

Post-Traumatic Stress Disorder Scale

The Post-Traumatic Stress Disorder Scale (PTSD) was developed by Keane, Malloy, and Fairbank in 1984 to assess the presence of Post-Traumatic Stress Disorder symptoms in military veterans. The authors employed a group of 100 veterans who had been diagnosed as having PTSD and contrasted their MMPI responses with those of 100 veterans having other psychiatric problems. The PTSD scale contains 49 items with a broad range of somatic and psychological symptoms. The scale was found to have an 82% rate in classifying the disorder among veterans.

Table 7-7. Re interpretive guidelines for the MMPI-2

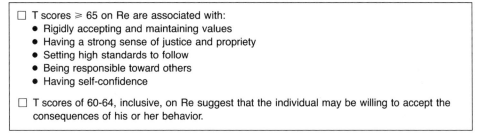

☐ T scores ⩾ 65 on Re are associated with:
- Rigidly accepting and maintaining values
- Having a strong sense of justice and propriety
- Setting high standards to follow
- Being responsible toward others
- Having self-confidence

☐ T scores of 60-64, inclusive, on Re suggest that the individual may be willing to accept the consequences of his or her behavior.

Table 7-8. PTSD interpretive guidelines for the MMPI-2

☐ T scores ⩾ 65 on PTSD are associated with:
- Feelings of intense emotional distress
- Experiencing anxiety and sleep disturbances
- Feeling guilty
- Depression
- Having disturbed, intrusive thoughts
- Experiencing loss of control over thinking
- Believing they are misunderstood or mistreated

☐ High scores on PTSD do not indicate the experience of recent trauma. Trauma must be established by other assessment procedures before a diagnosis of post-traumatic stress disorder is indicated.

The PTSD scale was developed on the original MMPI and has been continued for the MMPI-2. Research by Litz et al. (1991) has shown the scale to operate in the same manner in the MMPI-2 as it did in the original MMPI since most of the items on the scale are also found in MMPI-2. The PTSD scale appears to be highly related to other MMPI indices of anxiety such as the Pt scale and the A scale. The Keane, Malloy, and Fairbank scale appears as PK on the Supplementary Scales profile; also reported is a score for PS, an experimental PTSD scale developed by Schlenger and his colleagues (Schlenger et al., 1987, 1989).

Combat veterans and others who have experienced a catastrophic event who score high on this scale are likely to have PTSD symptoms including anxiety, depression, emotional turmoil, sleep disturbance, intrusive thoughts, and feelings of being misunderstood or mistreated. Table 7-8 summarizes the interpretive guidelines for the PTSD scale.

Ego Strength

The Ego Strength scale (Es) was developed as a potential measure of the ability to benefit from a psychotherapeutic experience (Barron, 1953). The scale was developed by contrasting groups of successful and unsuccessful patients in psychotherapy. Much of the research on Es suggests that it actually measures "ability to withstand stress" more than potential for therapeutic success. The scale originally contained 68 items; however, 12 were deleted during the MMPI revision. The extent to which the MMPI-2 version of the Es scale assesses the char-

Table 7-9. Es interpretive guidelines for the MMPI-2

☐ T scores ⩾ 65 on the Es scale suggest:
- Great ability to withstand stress
- Absence of chronic psychological problems
- Being emotionally stable
- Having tolerance and lack of prejudice
- Possessing self-confidence
- Having intelligence and resourcefulness
- Being accepted by others
- Having well-developed interests
- Being determined and persistent
- Responding well to verbal psychotherapy
- Tolerance of confrontation in therapy

---

acteristics measured by the original scale has not been determined. Consequently, the use of the scale in the MMPI-2 should be considered experimental until empirical research has further documented its predictive power. Table 7-9 summarizes the Es interpretive guidelines.

Anxiety

The Anxiety scale (A) was developed as a measure of the first, and largest, factor dimension in the original MMPI (Welsh, 1956), which also defines the first factor of the MMPI-2 (Butcher et al., 1989). All but one of the 39 items on the scale are endorsed true. The scale contains items that assess general maladjustment or emotional upset, for example, "I wish I could be as happy as others seem to be" and "Criticism or scolding hurts me terribly." A and the second factor, R, are not widely used as clinical assessment measures, but they are valuable in research as marker variables of the first two MMPI factors. The information provided by the A scale is available through other MMPI-2 measures, especially the Pt scale, which is highly correlated with A (.75).

Researchers and practitioners can evaluate proposed new measures by determining their relationship to the A factor. Many scales that have been developed for the MMPI in the past have turned out to be simply redundant measures or markers of the Anxiety factor (i.e., they correlated highly enough with the A scale to be considered an alternative measure of the first MMPI factor). For example, Stein (1968) proposed that several cluster scales (the Tryon, Stein, and Chu or TSC scales) represented the MMPI item domain. However, all seven of the TSC scales were found to be highly correlated with the A and Pt scales. Thus, they actually provided little additional information beyond their association with anxiousness.

Individuals who score high on the Anxiety scale are endorsing symptoms of anxiety, tension, inability to function, lack of efficiency in managing everyday affairs, and admitting numerous psychological symptoms. These features are summarized in Table 7-10.

Table 7-10. A interpretive guidelines for the MMPI-2

☐ The A scale is a marker of the first factor dimension (Anxiety) of the MMPI-2. The scale is highly correlated with scales 7 and 8.

☐ T scores ≥ 65 are elevated and are associated with individuals who are:
- Anxious
- Disorganized and maladaptive under stress
- Lacking in self-confidence
- Pessimistic
- Shy and retiring
- Insecure
- Slow in personal tempo

Table 7-11. R interpretive guidelines for the MMPI-2

☐ The R scale is a marker of the second major factor of the MMPI-2, often referred to as Repression or overcontrol. This scale is correlated with scales 2, L, and K.

☐ T scores ≥ 65 on R are elevated and associated with individuals who are viewed as:
- Overcontrolled
- Having a tendency to deny and rationalize
- Submissive
- Conventional and formal
- Exhibiting caution in their approach to life

Repression

Like the A scale, the Repression (R) scale was derived through factor analysis and marks the second major factor in the MMPI item pool, overcontrol or denial of conflict. The Repression scale is composed of 37 items that assess the tendency to deny problems, such as "I believe my sins are unpardonable-False." However, the scale also measures the general tendency of some subjects to respond false to everything—even to somewhat neutral items, such as "I think I would like the work of a forest ranger" or "I like science." The scale content addresses overcontrol and defensive reliance on denial and repression (Welsh, 1956).

Individuals who score high on R appear to be uninsightful, overcontrolled, and socially inhibited. High scorers are considered emotionally constricted, bland, and nonspontaneous. They tend to deal with conflict by avoidance rather than direct action. Others view them as overly conservative in actions and behavior. People who score high on the R scale generally report few psychological problems, tending rather to view themselves as problem-free compared to other people. They tend to see themselves as conventional and reserved in relationships. These features are summarized in Table 7-11.

Useful Indexes for the MMPI-2

A number of indexes that combine MMPI scales have been developed for special interpretive purposes. These indexes are either clinically or actuarially devised measures and serve to give the interpreter a valuable perspective on scale relationships. Among the more useful indexes are the Goldberg Index, the Megargee Felon Classification System, and the chronic pain classification system (PAIN).

Goldberg Index

Goldberg (1965), who was interested in exploring objective classification procedures, developed a linear regression model for discriminating neurotic from psychotic MMPI profiles. Goldberg's extensive research indicated that a simple linear combination of five MMPI scores produced an objective prediction formula that, when applied to neurotics and psychotics, classified the cases with greater success than most clinicians interpreting the profile. The Goldberg Index is computed by adding and subtracting the T scores of the following scales: L + Pa + Sc − Hy − Pt. If the resulting sum is greater than 45, a psychotic diagnosis is suggested. If the sum is 44 or less, a neurotic diagnosis is indicated. The Goldberg Index was considered to be a useful rule of thumb for discriminating psychotics from neurotics within inpatient mental-health settings. However, it is not recommended for use in other settings. Its utility with the MMPI-2 has not been widely explored. Thus, interpretation of the Goldberg Index with MMPI-2 scores should be considered experimental, and caution should be used in making clinical decisions based on it. It has not been studied for adolescents on the MMPI-A.

Megargee Classification System for Criminal Offenders

Megargee and Bohn (1977) identified 10 types of criminal offenders in the Florida State Correctional System by using their MMPI test patterns and related a number of demographic variables and prison behaviors to these profile groupings. The Megargee Inmate Classification System has been widely used since it was first published. (For an informative review, see Kennedy, 1986.) A number of articles have provided empirical tests of the Megargee System (Bohn, 1979; Booth & Howell, 1980; Dahlstrom et al., 1986; Edinger, 1979; Edinger, Reuterfors, & Logue, 1982; Hanson et al., 1983; Johnson, Simmons, & Gordon, 1983; Louscher, Hosford, & Moss, 1983; Megargee, 1984; Moss, Johnson, & Hosford, 1984; Motiuk, Bonta, & Andrews, 1986; Mrad, Kabacoff, & Duckro, 1983; Simmons et al., 1981; Walters, 1986; Zager, 1983). The 10 Megargee types appear to replicate across different inmate samples. For example, the same types are found in similar proportions in maximum-security prisons, medium-security facilities, and halfway houses (Dahlstrom et al., 1986; Edinger, 1979; Edinger, Reuterfors, & Logue, 1982; Johnson, Simmons, & Gordon, 1983; Mrad, Kabacoff, & Duckro, 1983; Walters, 1986). No well-defined demographic characteristics are typically associated with the different types. Research with female inmates does not justify applying the classification system to them (cf. Edinger, 1979), and the system may not apply with older male inmates.

Although the Megargee classification types can be found across many settings, correlates of the types have not been consistently found to generalize across settings. Several studies reported no history, psychiatric, demographic, prison adjustment, or outcome variables to be differentially associated with any of the types. The CHARLIE type seems to be the class of inmate that has most consistently been associated with psychological maladjustment and poor adjustment to prison. The HOW type also seems to be fairly consistently related to adjustment problems.

Research to date does not support the stability of the types over time. Some studies have questioned the stability of any of the Megargee types, finding that 60% to 90% change after as little as four months (Dahlstrom et al., 1986; Johnson, Simmons, & Gordon, 1983; Simmons et al., 1981). However, whether these changes reflect unreliable typology or actual changes in inmate personality, coping style, behavior, and so forth, remains an open question (Zager, 1983). One study reported that a sample of death-row inmates who had their sentences commuted shifted away from the pathological types of CHARLIE and HOW into less pathological ITEM, EASY, or GEORGE types (Dahlstrom et al., 1986). This finding might reflect a valid change in mental state after the sentence change. In general, caution should be exercised in making administrative or clinical decisions based on the Megargee typology; however, the system could provide useful hypotheses when supplemented with other information. The Megargee system is currently being validated with MMPI-2 norms (Megargee, 1991).

The Chronic Pain Typology

The MMPI has been the most widely used personality measure for investigating the personality characteristics and symptomatic behaviors of chronic pain patients (Armentrout et al., 1982; Bernstein & Garbin, 1983; Bradley et al., 1978; Bradley & Van der Heide, 1984; Fordyce, 1987; Hart, 1984; McCreary, 1985; McGill et al., 1983; and Prokop, Bradley, Margolis, & Gentry, 1980). Recently, to systematize the MMPI factors associated with chronic pain, Costello et al. (1987) summarized the extensive MMPI chronic pain research literature, demonstrating that four main clusters of MMPI types account for a significant percentage of pain patients. They found that pain patients from a wide variety of treatment settings appeared to fall into the four groups, which they referred to as P, A, I, or N subtypes (i.e., the PAIN typology). Preliminary research has supported the view that these profile types represent distinctly different problem and personality types in terms of symptoms, treatment amenability, and outcome.

Keller and Butcher (1991), using the MMPI-2, found the Costello et al. (1987) PAIN subtypes in a large sample of chronic pain patients. Their study demonstrated that the Chronic Pain Typology can be useful in assessing individuals in pain treatment programs. However, the PAIN classification rules identified only about half of their total sample, suggesting that the guidelines are overly conservative in assigning patients to a cluster type.

Critical Items

The critical item approach involves using individual MMPI items as signs or pathognomic indicators of pathology, specific content themes, or special problems the patient is experiencing. This approach has a long history in personality assessment. The first formal personality inventory, the *Personal Data Sheet* (Woodworth, 1920), incorporated critical items or pathognomic indicators to highlight special problems the individual might be experiencing.

For the MMPI, early critical item approaches such as the Grayson Critical Items (Grayson, 1951), were largely developed through purely rational means by simply selecting those items believed to reflect particular problems of interest to the clinician. The first effort to develop an empirically valid MMPI critical set was conducted by Koss and Butcher (1973), Koss, Butcher, and Hoffmann (1976), and Koss (1979). They developed and validated a set of critical items by differentiating patients who were experiencing a crisis requiring hospitalization from other patients not experiencing that particular crisis. The items that empirically differentiated the crisis groups from other patients or crisis groups were shown to have both empirical and content validity (i.e., they directly assessed symptoms, themes, and attitudes related to the actual crisis and reported them accurately through the MMPI booklet). These critical items were shown to have considerable clinical utility when used as clues to special problems. They have been maintained with some revisions in the MMPI-2 booklet. Four items each were added to the alcohol-drug crisis set and to the depressed-suicidal item set through further empirical analysis with MMPI-2 research groups (Butcher et al., 1989).

Another critical item set was published by Lachar and Wrobel (1979) to address several different crisis-problem areas. About two-thirds of the Koss-Butcher items were replicated in the Lachar-Wrobel study. However, several additional item groups were constructed to focus upon different areas of concern. Both the Koss-Butcher critical items and items from the Lachar-Wrobel set that are not redundant with the Koss-Butcher are listed in Table 7-12.

How Are Critical Items Used in Clinical Assessment?

Critical items are used clinically or impressionistically to suggest possible interpretive hypotheses about the individual's current problems, beliefs, or attitudes. For example, the clinician assessing an individual who is depressed might examine the client's responses to the following items to determine what the individual reported their thoughts about suicide to be:

506.   I have recently considered killing myself. (T)

520.   Lately I have thought a lot about killing myself. (T)

524.   No one knows it but I have tried to kill myself. (T)

Table 7-12. MMPI-2 critical item sets

Koss-Butcher Critical Items, Revised

Acute Anxiety State

2. I have a good appetite. (F)
3. I wake up fresh and rested most mornings. (F)
5. I am easily awakened by noise. (T)
10. I am about as able to work as I ever was. (F)
15. I work under a great deal of tension. (T)
28. I am bothered by an upset stomach several times a week. (T)
39. My sleep is fitful and disturbed. (T)
59. I am troubled by discomfort in the pit of my stomach every few days or oftener. (T)
140. Most nights I go to sleep without thoughts or ideas bothering me. (F)
172. I frequently notice my hand shakes when I try to do something. (T)
208. I hardly ever notice my heart pounding and I am seldom short of breath. (F)
218. I have periods of such great restlessness that I cannot sit long in a chair. (T)
223. I believe I am no more nervous than most others. (F)
301. I feel anxiety about something or someone almost all the time. (T)
444. I am a high-strung person. (T)
463. Several times a week I feel as if something dreadful is about to happen. (T)
469. I sometimes feel that I am about to go to pieces. (T)

Depressed Suicidal Ideation

9. My daily life is full of things that keep me interested. (F)
38. I have had periods of days, weeks, or months when I couldn't take care of things because I couldn't "get going." (T)
65. Most of the time I feel blue. (T)
71. These days I find it hard not to give up hope of amounting to something. (T)
75. I usually feel that life is worthwhile. (F)
92. I don't seem to care what happens to me. (T)
95. I am happy most of the time. (F)
130. I certainly feel useless at times (T)
146. I cry easily. (T)
215. I brood a great deal. (T)
233. I have difficulty in starting to do things. (T)
273. Life is a strain for me much of the time. (T)
303. Most of the time I wish I were dead. (T)
306. No one cares much what happens to you. (T)
388. I very seldom have spells of the blues. (F)
411. At times I think I am no good at all. (T)
454. The future seems hopeless to me. (T)
485. I often feel that I'm not as good as other people. (T)
506. I have recently considered killing myself. (T)
518. I have made lots of bad mistakes in my life. (T)
520. Lately I have thought a lot about killing myself. (T)
524. No one knows it but I have tried to kill myself. (T)

Threatened Assault

37. At times I feel like smashing things. (T)
85. At times I have a strong urge to do something harmful or shocking. (T)

Table 7-12. MMPI-2 critical item sets, continued

134.   At times I feel like picking a fist fight with someone. (T)
213.   I get mad easily and then get over it soon. (T)
389.   I am often said to be hotheaded. (T)

Situational Stress Due to Alcoholism

125.   I believe that my home life is as pleasant as that of most people I know. (F)
264.   I have used alcohol excessively. (T)
487.   I have enjoyed using marijuana. (T)
489.   I have a drug or alcohol problem (T)
502.   I have some habits that are really harmful. (T)
511.   Once a week or more I get high or drunk. (T)
518.   I have made lots of bad mistakes in my life. (T)

Mental Confusion

24.   Evil spirits possess me at times. (T)
31.   I find it hard to keep my mind on a task or a job. (T)
32.   I have had very peculiar and strange experiences. (T)
72.   My soul sometimes leaves my body. (T)
96.   I see things or animals or people around me that others do not see. (T)
180.   There is something wrong with my mind. (T)
198.   I often hear voices without knowing where they come from. (T)
299.   I cannot keep my mind on one thing. (T)
311.   I often feel as if things are not real. (T)
316.   I have strange and peculiar thoughts. (T)
325.   I have more trouble concentrating than others seem to have. (T)

Persecutory Ideas

17.   I am sure I get a raw deal from life. (T)
42.   If people had not had it in for me, I would have been much more successful. (T)
99.   Someone has it in for me. (T)
124.   I often wonder what hidden reason another person may have for doing something nice for me. (T)
138.   I believe I am being plotted against. (T)
144.   I believe I am being followed. (T)
145.   I feel that I have often been punished without cause. (T)
162.   Someone has been trying to poison me. (T)
216.   Someone has been trying to rob me. (T)
228.   There are persons who are trying to steal my thoughts and ideas. (T)
241.   It is safer to trust to nobody. (T)
251.   I have often felt that strangers were looking at me critically. (T)
259.   I am sure I am being talked about. (T)
314.   I have no enemies who really wish to harm me. (F)
333.   People say insulting and vulgar things about me. (T)
361.   Someone has been trying to influence my mind. (T)

Lachar-Wrobel Critical Items

Characterological Adjustment (Antisocial Attitude)

27.   When people do me a wrong I feel I should pay them back if I can, just for the principle of the thing. (T)

Table 7-12. MMPI-2 critical item sets, continued

35.	Sometimes when I was young I stole things. (T)
84.	I was suspended from school one or more times for bad behavior. (T)
105.	In school I was sometimes sent to the principal for bad behavior. (T)
227.	I don't blame people for trying to grab everything they can get in this world. (T)
240.	At times it has been impossible for me to keep from stealing or shoplifting something. (T)
254.	Most people make friends because friends are likely to be useful to them. (T)
266.	I have never been in trouble with the law. (F)
324.	I can easily make other people afraid of me, and sometimes do for the fun of it. (T)

Characterological Adjustment (Family Conflict)

21.	At times I have very much wanted to leave home. (T)
83.	I have very few quarrels with members of my family. (F)
125.	I believe that my home life is as pleasant as that of most people I know. (F)
288.	My parents and family find more fault with me than they should. (T)

Somatic Symptoms

18.	I am troubled by attacks of nausea and vomiting. (T)
28.	I am bothered by an upset stomach several times a week. (T)
33.	I seldom worry about my health. (F)
40.	Much of the time my head seems to hurt all over. (T)
44.	Once a week or oftener I feel suddenly hot all over, for no real reason. (T)
47.	I am almost never bothered by pains over the heart or in my chest. (F)
53.	Parts of my body often have feelings like burning, tingling, crawling, or like "going to sleep." (T)
57.	I hardly ever feel pain in the back of my neck. (F)
59.	I am troubled by discomfort in the pit of my stomach every few days or oftener. (T)
101.	Often I feel as if there is a tight band around my head. (T)
111.	I have a great deal of stomach trouble. (T)
142.	I have never had a fit or convulsion. (F)
159.	I have never had a fainting spell. (F)
164.	I seldom or never have dizzy spells. (F)
175.	I feel weak all over much of the time. (T)
176.	I have very few headaches. (F)
182.	I have had attacks in which I could not control my movements or speech but in which I knew what was going on around me. (T)
224.	I have few or no pains. (F)
229.	I have had blank spells in which my activities were interrupted and I did not know what was going on around me. (T)
247.	I have numbness in one or more places on my skin. (T)
255.	I do not often notice my ears ringing or buzzing. (F)
295.	I have never been paralyzed or had any unusual weakness of any of my muscles. (F)
464.	I feel tired a good deal of the time. (T)

Sexual Concern and Deviation

12.	My sex life is satisfactory. (F)
34.	I have never been in trouble because of my sex behavior. (F)
62.	I have often wished I were a girl. (Or if you are a girl) I have never been sorry that I am a girl. (T-males, F-females)
121.	I have never indulged in any unusual sex practices. (F)
166.	I am worried about sex. (T-males, F-females)
268.	I wish I were not bothered by thoughts about sex. (T)

Critical items should not be used as psychometric indicators or scales since single item responses tend to be much less reliable as psychometric predictors than are groups of items or scales. The critical item has its greatest value as a suggested hypothesis to follow up in clinical interview or in further scrutiny of the assessment data.

Cautions about Supplementary Scales

Over the first 50 years of the MMPI's development, many scales were published for particular applications and special populations. In fact, there were actually more scales available for the MMPI than there were items on the inventory. Scales proliferated, in part, because empirical scale-construction methodology encouraged the development of new scales, and any number of scales is possible—limited only by the imagination of the researcher. A new empirical scale could be developed by simply compiling cases fitting an interesting group and then performing an item analysis between that group and another group, such as normal subjects. Consequently, "blind empiricism," as this approach is usually called, promoted the development of hundreds of scales—many based on samples of convenience that had little underlying conceptual rationale. Many, if not the majority, of these scales were not sufficiently cross-validated (or even initially validated) before being used.

Some experimental MMPI scales, developed to study particular problems and meant for somewhat limited application, have been expanded and used for very different purposes than their original developers intended. In all fairness, it should be pointed out that the scale originators often had little to do with the scale after its initial development. For example, when Hal Williams, who developed the Ca scale for his doctoral dissertation (Williams, 1952), was told that many people were using his scale to assess organic damage and were widely disseminating the scores in computerized reports, he exclaimed in embarrassment: "That's ridiculous, that was only my doctoral research . . . [it was] not intended to be used for any practical purposes!" Another example is the scale called "Success in Baseball" (LaPlace, 1952). The original author was attempting to appraise cooperative teamwork, yet some mistakenly thought it assessed the ability or mindset to succeed in baseball!

This section is not intended to discourage the development of new empirical scales, but to caution users that the development and naming of a scale does not necessarily imply that it satisfactorily assesses the behaviors it purports to measure. Many MMPI scales have been developed that do not actually or consistently perform as proposed, and they are probably quite misleading. We caution users of the MMPI-2 and MMPI-A to be wary consumers before using any new scale to make predictions about an individual.

The "Subtle Keys"

One of the most widespread misconceptions about the MMPI is that several clinical scales contain "subtle" items that allow the clinician to assess individuals without their being consciously aware that they are providing important personal information in the assessment. Wiener (1948) believed that all items on a scale were equally valid as predictors of the characteristics involved. Since some of the items are not obviously related to the criterion characteristics (e.g., "I am happy most of the time" is not obviously related to paranoid thinking on the Pa scale) then these items are "subtle" predictors and have special properties. Wiener and Harmon (Wiener, 1948) developed subtle and obvious subscales for several scales (i.e., D, Hy, Pd, Pa, and Ma).

There are several points to consider when evaluating the utility of subtle items as predictors of psychopathology and as validity indicators. One likely explanation for the lack of content relevance in the subtle items is that they are imperfectly related to the criterion and were actually selected by chance as a result of incomplete validation procedures. As we saw in Chapter 4, Hathaway and McKinley used relatively small samples in their original scale development and in some cases no cross-validation procedures. In developing a scale to assess characteristic "x" using 550 items, chance alone would place 27 items on the scale. We assume that cross-validation would have eliminated the chance items, leaving only those items that are valid indicators of the characteristic being assessed. A second major point to consider in evaluating the subtle subscales is that they have not been shown to be valid measures of the types of psychopathology they purportedly measure. Several studies have shown that the subtle scales do not predict behaviors as clearly as the obvious items on the scales do (Herkov, Archer, & Gordon, 1991; Nelson, 1987; Nelson & Cicchetti, 1991; Grossman et al., 1990; Timbrook et al., 1991). In fact, Weed, Ben-Porath, and Butcher (1990) found that the subtle items actually lower the validities of the full scale score. Greene (1991) suggests that the subtle items give the interpreter a way to evaluate invalid or unusual response attitudes. In his view, the differences in responses to obvious, as opposed to subtle, items on a scale can be used as an indicator of test invalidity. However, empirical support for this view is lacking (Timbrook, Graham, Keiller, & Watts, 1991). The subtle items are not able to correct for intentional deception on the part of the test-taker. The MMPI-2, like the original MMPI, is an instrument for people who want to be assessed and are cooperative with the psychological evaluation.

Developing and Evaluating New Scales for the MMPI-2

It is likely that new scales will be developed for the MMPI-2 as they were for the original instrument. New scales and improved versions of the original scales are desirable since the MMPI-2 contains some new items that would allow for an expanded assessment and could improve the existing clinical scales. The following guidelines are suggested for appraising the value and suitability of proposed new measures.

A scale should be used because it performs a particular assessment better or more efficiently than other scales or provides valuable information not accessible through another assessment approach. For example, to determine an individual's "social facility," one could observe the subject in several situations and record his or her behavior, or perhaps more efficiently have someone who knows the person well observe him or her and rate the person's social facility. Another way of obtaining social skills information is to ask the person to rate himself or herself. The MMPI-2 Si scale does just that, and does it quite well. The Si scale performs as well as behavioral ratings in predicting sociability (Williams, 1981).

It seems desirable that standards be established for the construction of MMPI-2 scales to aid both scale developers and scale users in evaluating psychometric characteristics and clinical utility. Following are some suggested guidelines that could serve as a "checklist" for the practitioner and researcher in evaluating a potential MMPI-2 scale:

1. *The construct under study is well defined.* The variable in question should not simply be the result of interesting group differences in convenience samples. The construct should be related to personality or symptomatic variables. The dimension or set of characteristics should be a personality variable and not non-personality factors such as abilities, intellectual qualities, and so forth.

2. *The item pool is relevant for the construct being assessed.* The MMPI-2 item pool has limitations. It is not possible, for example, to develop a scale measuring language ability or successful performance as a business manager. Scale developers should ascertain whether the item content of the MMPI-2 is relevant to the question studied.

3. *The research design includes cross-validation.* This is most necessary for empirically derived scales, to eliminate items that would be selected on the basis of chance or specific sample characteristics. The sample sizes for both the developmental and the cross-validated samples should be sufficient to provide stable test scores and to reduce error.

4. *The scale has appropriate statistical properties including*:

    a) Adequate internal consistency (e.g., an alpha coefficient of .70 or greater) if the scale is desirable as a measure of a single dimension.

    b) A meaningful factor structure if the scale is multifaceted and made up of several discrete content groups. The scale's factor structure should be reported.

    c) If the proposed measure is an empirical scale, it is not required that the scale possess split-half reliability. However, it should possess other relevant psychometric properties, such as test-retest reliability.

5. *All scales, even those developed by rational or internal consistency methods, have demonstrable validities.* It is important for any scale to measure what it is supposed to measure, regardless of the method of scale construction. That is, all personality measures should predict,

describe, or detect the psychological characteristics they purport to measure.

6. *Uses are explored and demonstrated.* Does the scale possess sensitivity and specificity in predicting the quality it is supposed to assess? How well the scale classifies relevant cases should be reported.

7. *Correlations between the proposed scale and other, well established, MMPI-2 measures are presented.* This will enable users to compare the new measures with existing ones. For example, the correlations between the proposed scale and the factor dimensions *A* and *R* are important to establish the new scale's independence.

Highlight Summary: The Case of Alice

As described in Chapters 4, 5, and 6, Alice's high elevations on scales 7, 8, and the MMPI-2 Content Scales, focus attention on her extreme anxiousness, insecurity, lack of self-confidence, and low cognitive problem-solving skills. The special or supplementary measures that have been developed for the MMPI provide some elaboration for Alice's problems or personality. Several of her supplementary scale scores support the results of the standard scales. Other scales, such as MDS, are not relevant to her case. Her relatively high score on A (T = 61) and the PTSD scale (T = 61) indicate that she has some tendency to become anxious under stressful conditions. However, she does not have a history of a recent catastrophic stressor to support a PTSD diagnostic hypothesis. Her relatively low score on Es (T = 35) supports the interpretation that Alice has little ability to withstand stress and meet challenges in her life-situation.

Alice's low score on the Dominance (Do) scale adds further support to the interpretation, based on her standard scale scores, that she is lacking in self-confidence and is not assertive in relationships. Her low Re score also suggests a lack of self-confidence and an unwillingness to assume responsibility.

Alice's low scores on MAC-R (T = 42) and APS (T = 50) suggest that she is not likely to develop addiction problems, and her low score on AAS (40) indicates that she has not reported problems with drugs or alcohol. This suggests that if psychotropic medication is considered, medications abuse is not likely to become a problem. Given Alice's willingness to admit to other problems, addiction proneness is unlikely.

Chapter 8

Integrating MMPI-2 Inferences into an Interpretive Report

Thus far we have discussed a number of diverse sources of information available in the MMPI-2. These measures range from indicators of response attitudes to empirically derived symptom scales to content-based descriptions to specially focused problem scales. As we have seen, these measures differ in their purpose, their value as predictors, and their psychometric basis. In interpreting a client's MMPI-2, the practitioner faces a wide array of inferences about personality and symptomatic characteristics from varying sources that may, at first examination, appear difficult to integrate.

In this chapter, we will consider an approach to organizing MMPI-2–based inferences into an integrated interpretation. We will provide a framework for establishing interpretive priorities and for incorporating hypotheses into an internally consistent report. The interpretive approach in this chapter will be organized by formulating particular questions or issues that a clinician might encounter in interpreting a profile, then examining the elements in the MMPI-2 profile that can provide clues to help resolve the questions. We will point to MMPI-2–based information that might confirm the existence of a problem or elucidate a behavior pattern. We will explore the information that might help the clinician set priorities for the diverse inferences and integrate them into a meaningful, organized report. Finally, Alice's case will again be used to illustrate the process by which information can be integrated into a personality study. A similar process is covered in Chapter 11 for the MMPI-A.

A Strategy for Integrating MMPI-2 Information

A purposeful strategy for organizing psychological test information can most effectively follow from a structured inquiry into what is needed to resolve particular questions that bear on the dispositions of a case. The shape of our conclusions and the form the clinical report will take depend as much upon how well we are able to formulate questions as upon the data available in the clinical evaluation. The strategy we suggest for interpreting the MMPI-2 is much the same whether it is the only instrument being employed or whether it is used as part of a test battery.

In initially approaching an MMPI-2 interpretation, it is desirable to pose a series of questions or issues that can be addressed regardless of the reason for referral. Several general issues that are pertinent to most MMPI-2 interpretations

Table 8-1. Questions for MMPI-2 interpretations

1. Are there any extra-test factors that can explain the MMPI-2 results?
2. What are the individual's response attitudes?
3. What are the individual's reported symptoms and behaviors? Is the client experiencing any acute mood states?
4. Is the individual experiencing problems in self control? If so, how might they be manifested?
5. Are there any trait-based hypotheses about the individual's personality characteristics?
6. Does the individual show a potential for developing a problem with alcohol or other drugs? Has he or she acknowledged excessive alcohol or other drug use?
7. What are the individual's interpersonal relationships like? Is he or she able to deal effectively with others?
8. How stable is the individual's profile likely to be over time?
9. How severely disturbed is the individual compared to others?
10. What are the diagnostic considerations in the case?

Table 8-2. MMPI-2 treatment planning questions

1. Is the individual in need of psychological treatment at this time?
2. How aware is the individual of his or her problems?
3. How credible is the individual's self-report?
4. Is the individual willing to disclose personal information to the therapist?
5. How motivated is the individual for treatment?
6. Is the individual capable of gaining insight into his or her problems?
7. Is he or she amenable to treatment? Is the individual willing to change his or her behavior?
8. Are there specific treatment needs suggested by the MMPI-2?
9. Are there any strengths or assets that can be built upon in treatment?
10. Are there negative personality features that could interfere with the treatment relationship?

are listed in Table 8-1. In seeking answers to these questions, the interpreter is likely to obtain a fairly good picture of the client's personality and problem situation from the perspective of the MMPI-2. We provide a similar strategy and list of questions in Chapter 11, Table 11-17, for the MMPI-A.

After these general issues, consider referral problems or issues that are more specific to the setting in which the individual is being evaluated (Butcher, 1990a). For example, if the individual is being seen in a pre-treatment psychological evaluation, as in the case we will be discussing, a number of additional questions present themselves. For example, "Is this individual in need of psychological treatment at this time?" "Is he or she able to form a treatment relationship?" "Is he or she amenable to change?" "Are there negative personality characteristics that could interfere with treatment?" These specific treatment-oriented questions are listed in Table 8-2. Similar issues are addressed in Chapter 11, Table 11-18, for the MMPI-A.

Extra-Test Information

Basic demographic and setting characteristics are important considerations because they set the stage for test interpretation by providing clear expectations by which to judge the client's MMPI-2. One can gauge the believability of a personality study by considering the individual's performance in light of the background factors. For example, consider the background factors in the following cases:

— A 37-year-old, middle-class client with a high-school education took the MMPI-2 in the context of a psychological evaluation. She is being evaluated for outpatient psychotherapy.

— An 81-year-old former mechanic with a sixth-grade reading level is being evaluated to determine his competency at a commitment hearing.

— The 19-year-old son of a Vietnamese refugee is being assessed for an insanity defense in pre-trial investigation for a capital crime he allegedly committed.

In the case of the 37-year-old woman we would not expect reading problems, cultural factors, or an uncooperative attitude toward testing to interfere with the information-gathering process. With the 81-year-old man, we would need to consider the possibility that reading skills, comprehension difficulties, fatigue, or sensory impairment might interfere with his responses to MMPI-2 items. In assessing the 19-year-old Vietnamese man, we would wish to consider further the possibility of cultural or language problems influencing the evaluation. Additionally, we might consider the possibility that the evaluation's setting, as part of an insanity defense, could compromise profile validity.

Although much can be said about an MMPI-2 or MMPI-A profile without information about the client, the more one knows about the individual's life circumstances, the more specific the test interpretation can be. Several demographic or situational variables might influence an individual's performance on personality scales. Some that should be taken into account in MMPI-2 and MMPI-A interpretations are described in the following sections.

Gender

Clear gender differences are apparent in responses to personality inventory items. Consequently, most personality scales, including scales on the MMPI-2 and the MMPI-A, incorporate separate norms for men and women. Thus, it is important that the appropriate norms (T-score tables) are used for the two genders. Most of the descriptors for the MMPI-2 standard and Content Scales appear to work equally well for men and women. However, some adjustment might be needed for certain scales. As we have seen, for example, interpretive rules differ by gender for the Mf scale. Another example is the MMPI-2 Content Scale TPA, which appears to be a better scale (and construct) for men than for women.

Age

Age can influence responses to personality items. Research with the MMPI indicated that people below age 18 responded to the MMPI items differently than did adults (see Chapter 9). This influenced the decision to develop a different version of the instrument for adolescents, which included new item content and age-specific adolescent norms. Individuals younger than 18 years should be tested with the MMPI-A.

Research with the original MMPI also suggested that older individuals perform somewhat differently on MMPI scales than do younger adults. For example, older persons tend to endorse more frequently items dealing with somatic changes, low mood, reduced risk taking, and introverted thinking. These differences influence scoring on several standard scales such as D, Pd, and Si. Although some mean scale score differences between older individuals and the normative populations on the MMPI and MMPI-2 have been noted (Butcher et al., 1991), these group differences are typically small and not powerful enough to be used for individual prediction. In fact, the general conclusion from most MMPI/MMPI-2 aging research is that there are few differences between individuals at various age or cohort levels. Separate norms for older adults are not provided (Butcher et al., 1989), nor do they appear to be needed (Butcher et al., 1991).

Social Class

Social-class factors, except in the case of very low socioeconomic level on two of the standard scales, have not proven to be of much importance in interpreting MMPI profiles—at least not sufficiently important to recommend the development of special norms for various socioeconomic groups. On the original MMPI, lower social-status individuals showed some tendency to report more symptoms than higher social-class individuals. On the original norms, higher social-class individuals are viewed as more "defensive," at least as measured by higher scores on K (Dahlstrom, Welsh, & Dahlstrom, 1975). These individuals also tended to score higher on Mf. These scale relationships probably reflect the higher education level usually accompanying higher social class. The original MMPI normative sample was relatively uneducated compared to most people today, which perhaps accounts for elevations on K and Mf in more contemporary samples using the older norms.

As we saw in Chapter 1, the new MMPI-2 norms are based on a more representative sample of middle and higher SES subjects. Interpretive adjustments do not appear to be needed for MMPI-2 profiles from most socioeconomic strata. However, the K and Mf scores from very low SES individuals, who often have a lower education level, should be interpreted with care, as noted in the next section. These socioeconomic differences have not been studied with adolescents, thus their relevance for those younger is unknown at present.

Education

In the original MMPI, educational factors were considered to influence, to some extent, performance on two MMPI basic scales, K and Mf. Interpretive adjustments had to be made when interpreting profiles of more educated individuals (college education) because the original MMPI normative group had only a ninth-grade education, on average. This contrasts with the projected average education for the United States in the 1990s as more than two years of college (Bogue, 1985).

The MMPI-2 normative sample has an average education level that is closer to the contemporary subjects taking the test (15.0 years for men and 14.4 for women). All educational levels but the lowest produce mean profiles that match the full MMPI-2 normative sample, indicating that for most people the new norms can be applied without adjustments.

For individuals with very low education levels (6th through 11th grades) some adjustment might be needed, since the new MMPI-2 norms contain somewhat fewer subjects with this level of education. Some scales, such as K and Mf, may need to be cautiously interpreted for individuals of lower education levels. Reading comprehension is also an issue. The examiner should ensure that the individual's F and VRIN scores are within the interpretable range (below a T score of 90 for F and 80 for VRIN) before interpretive statements are applied to the profile.

Ethnic and Cultural Factors

The criticism that the original MMPI needed special norms for blacks and other minorities (Gynther, 1972b) arose from the absence of minority subjects in the original MMPI normative sample. The possible influence of ethnic background on MMPI scores was the subject of considerable empirical research and debate. A major question was whether separate norms for minorities were needed. Dahlstrom, Lachar, and Dahlstrom (1986), after reviewing the extensive empirical research, concluded that:

> When all the background factors introduced in these analyses are considered, it is apparent that they do not account for the major portion of the variance in the component scales of the MMPI (p. 202).

> At this stage in the development of the knowledge of how to use the MMPI in personnel and psychiatric assessments with various minority subjects or clients, the best procedure would seem to be to accept the pattern of results generated by the standard scales on the basic MMPI profile (p. 204).

The MMPI-2 is likely to be less controversial to use with members of ethnic minority groups than the original MMPI because approximately representative samples of minority subjects were included in the new norms. The ethnic group membership of the MMPI-2 normative samples is shown in Tables 8-3 for men and 8-4 for women. All of the ethnic group samples fall very near the general normative sample mean on the MMPI-2 validity and standard scales. These data indicate that the MMPI-2 norms apply equally well, regardless of ethnic group background, and that no special interpretive considerations need to be made with regard to race.

Table 8-3. Means and standard deviations by ethnic origin for 1,138 community adult men

Scale	White (N = 933)		Black (N = 126)		Native American (N = 38)		Hispanic (N = 35)		Asian (N = 6)	
	Mean	S.D.	Mean	S.D.	Mean	S.D.	Mean	S.D.	Mean	S.D.
L	3.36	2.13	4.26	2.77	4.26	2.78	4.51	2.63	4.50	3.27
F	4.29	2.98	5.18	3.76	6.42	4.46	6.17	4.07	7.33	5.61
K	15.45	4.74	15.08	4.88	13.55	4.64	14.29	4.50	13.83	5.08
Hs	4.69	3.78	5.58	3.91	6.92	4.48	6.17	4.11	6.50	5.28
D	18.16	4.59	19.02	4.24	19.08	4.98	19.06	5.00	16.83	3.97
Hy	21.06	4.60	20.03	5.06	20.42	5.49	19.77	5.56	17.50	4.89
Pd	16.25	4.49	17.57	4.40	19.50	5.23	18.29	5.62	16.67	4.13
Mf	26.21	5.13	25.84	4.20	23.39	6.07	24.43	4.60	24.17	6.18
Pa	10.09	2.82	9.87	3.09	10.70	3.21	10.51	3.07	10.33	2.16
Pt	11.04	6.53	11.60	6.75	12.79	7.34	13.00	6.81	14.33	7.15
Sc	10.75	6.86	12.79	7.38	13.82	9.01	13.89	8.20	16.50	10.05
Ma	16.58	4.46	18.33	4.31	17.84	4.59	18.77	4.88	15.83	5.98
Si	25.80	8.70	25.56	7.43	28.32	8.63	24.77	8.26	32.17	9.45

Table 8-4. Means and standard deviations by ethnic origin for 1,462 community adult women

Scale	White (N = 1184)		Black (N = 188)		Native American (N = 39)		Hispanic (N = 38)		Asian (N = 13)	
	Mean	S.D.	Mean	S.D.	Mean	S.D.	Mean	S.D.	Mean	S.D.
L	3.47	1.98	3.95	2.32	4.64	2.68	2.92	2.16	4.85	3.31
F	3.89	2.64	4.43	3.38	5.69	3.99	6.32	4.35	3.54	2.07
K	15.34	4.47	14.13	4.56	12.41	5.67	12.37	4.88	14.85	4.04
Hs	5.49	4.24	7.50	5.16	8.74	4.63	8.92	5.50	6.38	2.84
D	19.93	4.97	21.00	4.99	21.33	4.84	21.55	4.69	19.23	4.28
Hy	22.05	4.55	22.17	5.38	22.59	5.39	22.53	6.00	20.62	4.09
Pd	15.68	4.48	18.30	4.42	19.08	4.74	19.89	5.34	14.31	4.89
Mf	36.31	3.91	34.60	4.22	33.23	4.85	34.05	4.76	35.62	4.39
Pa	10.13	2.91	10.40	3.11	11.51	3.62	11.34	3.15	9.54	2.88
Pt	12.27	6.89	13.55	7.68	17.64	8.76	17.21	8.92	10.00	5.03
Sc	10.39	6.88	14.10	8.63	17.00	9.93	18.42	10.63	8.92	4.01
Ma	15.61	4.29	17.85	4.62	17.90	5.29	20.00	4.91	15.31	3.84
Si	27.78	9.36	28.37	8.54	32.26	7.25	27.45	7.79	28.77	7.67

Setting

The setting in which the MMPI-2 or MMPI-A is administered is an important determinant of responses to test items. The MMPI-2 or MMPI-A interpreter should be aware of factors that might distort responses in a particular setting and attempt to either alleviate their influence or compensate for them in the interpretation. Settings that can produce distortion include personnel screening and domestic court (child-custody) assessments, in which subjects may try to present an overly favorable view of themselves. Other settings can produce an opposite, but equally troublesome distortion, the exaggerated or feigned mental-illness stance. Exaggerated profiles of this type typically are produced in settings like court referrals involving personal injury litigation or an insanity defense following a capital crime. In these cases, the individual attempts to claim a severe mental disorder needing attention or special services.

The MMPI-2 validity scales are important interpretive elements when considering the possibility that individuals in some settings may be trying to create a certain image. Psychologists working in settings that tend to elicit distorted profiles should be aware of the typical or base-rate validity pattern for that setting. For example, clients being seen in child-custody evaluations typically produce profiles with high elevations on L (T $\geq$ 60), low elevations on F (T $\leq$ 50), and high elevations on K (T $\geq$ 60). The absence of profile elevations in settings that generate defensive profiles does not necessarily indicate that the individual is psychologically healthy. On the other hand, when elevated profiles are obtained in these settings and validity scores are acceptable, the profile is likely to be interpretable.

Response Attitudes

As noted in Chapters 3 and 10, it is extremely important to assess the individual's view of the test situation and how he or she deals with its demands. The MMPI-2 and MMPI-A validity-scale patterns provide important clues to the subject's cooperativeness, ability to understand the items, literacy level, and willingness to follow instructions. The Cannot Say score, for example, indicates whether the individual has answered all or most of the items. The F scale indicates whether the individual is responding in a frank and open manner or is exaggerating symptoms to convince the examiner that he or she is more disturbed than is actually the case. Other validity scales, such as L and K, indicate whether the individual is willing to admit relevant problems. L and K scores below a T of 65, for example, show a non-defensive symptom pattern. The TRIN and VRIN scales provide information about response inconsistency. It is important to assess the individual's approach to the test situation in order to determine the amount of credibility to place on his or her scores when interpreting the standard and Content Scale profiles.

Assessing Symptoms and Behaviors

The MMPI-2 standard scales and profile configurations described in Chapters 4 and 5 have been related to descriptions of presenting problems, typical symptoms, unusual beliefs, and characteristic problems that patients with similar scores have. Evaluation of a client's personality and behavioral problems should proceed from appraising the most significantly elevated scale scores or profile configurations.

In profile interpretation, we must first decide which of the prototype (scale or code-type) MMPI-2 descriptors to use as the empirical structure of the report, that is, which scale or code-type correlates would most likely apply to a particular case. For example, if the individual has a T score of 75 on D and 68 on Pd, we would consider this profile a 2-4 and search through the relevant code-type descriptors and organize the correlates as they apply to our case and the referral problem. With a profile that has a significant elevation on Pt (T=69) and no other scales elevated above a T score of 64, we would use correlate literature on scale 7.

With many profiles it is relatively easy to choose the proper correlate data set to use in the interpretation. We simply take the highest clinical profile point, two-point pair, or three-or four-point code type as our prototype. However, in a number of cases, several scales will be elevated above a T score of 65, and it may be difficult to determine what scale or code type should be used as the correlate prototype. In these more complicated cases, it is best to determine the prototype that includes the greatest number of scales in the profile code. For example, if scales 1, 2, 3, 4, and 7 are elevated, the 1-2-3-4 code type is employed. Since scale 7 was also elevated above a T score of 65, we would want to incorporate major features of the Pt scale (i.e., indications the individual is anxious, tense, ruminative, perfectionistic, etc.) into our report. The interpreter should keep profile definition (discussed in Chapter 5) in mind when determining the extent to which the traditional scale correlates fit the client.

Once we have determined the most suitable profile prototype to follow and have chosen the correlates to serve as the empirical outline of our report, we can search other scale elevations, for example, the Harris-Lingoes subscales or the supplementary scales, for additional hypotheses about the individual's problems and behavior. Next, we would consult scores on the MMPI-2 Content Scales to confirm previously generated hypotheses or to develop new ones. In evaluating other scales, a T score of 65 will yield the likely correlate to incorporate in the evaluation; however, for many scales a T score of 60 might be used for hypotheses about the client's behavior.

In using correlates or personality descriptions from many scales or code types, it is possible that contradictory hypotheses will be suggested. To use an extreme example, if an individual obtained an elevated D score, we would consider the scale correlate "fatigued and low energy." If this same individual had a high elevation on Ma, a possible correlate would be "energetic, talkative, preferring action to reflection." How does the interpreter resolve the apparent contradiction to prevent the report from appearing internally inconsistent? Actually, internal contradictions in the test data can provide the interpreter with more interesting and fruitful assessment data. Resolving apparent internal inconsistencies may provide important clues to understanding the patient. The case of the individual with elevations on both D and Ma is quite unusual and raises the question of a bipolar disorder, which would require additional assessment to confirm. The Harris-Lingoes subscales should be consulted to see if they can resolve the discrepancy. For example, if the elevated D score was accompanied by elevations on D_1-Subjective Depression and D_5-Brooding, but not with elevations on D_1-Psychomotor Retardation or D_4-Mental Dullness, fatigue and lack of energy might not be highlighted as a prominent descriptor for the individual. Similarly, if Ma_1-Amorality and Ma_3-Imperturbability were the only elevated Ma subscales, then a high energy level would not be highlighted. We provide other examples of resolving conflicting descriptors in Chapter 11 on the MMPI-A.

As Table 8-1 indicates, assessing the presence of an acute mood state is an important question in the interpretive process. These acute states, such as periods of anxiousness or depressed mood, are reflected in MMPI-2 profile elevations. The presence of several possible scale elevations or profile relationships should alert the interpreter to the possibility that the individual is experiencing acute mood states. Several clinical states have been recognized in MMPI-2 profiles:

Anxiety:	Pt 65-79; Pt greater than Sc (Moderate)
	Pt 80-89; Pt greater than Sc (Marked)
	Pt 90+; Pt greater than Sc (Severe)
Depressive State:	D 65-79; Ma less than 40 (Moderate)
	D 80-89; Ma less than 40 (Marked)
	D 90+; Ma less than 40 (Severe)
Manic State:	Ma greater than 80; Ma highest score; D less than 55
Psychosis:	Sc greater than 80; Sc the highest score; Sc greater than Pt by 10 points
Suspicion-Mistrust:	Pa greater than 70; Pa highest score
Acting-Out:	Pd greater than 65 or Ma greater than 70 and Si lower than 40 ANG greater than 65
Confused, Disoriented:	F greater than 80 Sc greater than 80 or Pt greater than 80 or Mean Profile Elevation greater than 70
Crisis States:	Koss-Butcher and Lachar-Wrobel critical items serve as clues to significant problems

Assessing Self-Control or Acting-Out

There are a number of indicators of self-control and acting-out potential in the MMPI-2 to answer the fourth set of questions in Table 8-1. These indicators should be evaluated to appraise the possibility of control problems or disabling overcontrol. The following factors are assessed by MMPI-2 scales:

Inhibition (Constriction):	Indicated by scores greater than 65 on the Si scale
Overcontrol (Repression):	Suggested by elevated scores greater than 65 on the Hy scale or the O-H scale
Acting-Out (Impulsivity):	Suggested by scores greater than 65 on the Pd and Ma scales; or low Si scores (below a T score of 40)
Anger (Loss of Control):	Suggested by scores greater than 65 on the ANG scale

Generating Trait-Based Hypotheses

The MMPI-2, like its predecessor, contains several indicators that address long-term personality characteristics or traits. Various MMPI-2 scales are trait-based measures that contain many items that assess personality characteristics. Some of these measures and the traits they reflect are:

Impulsivity: Indicated by Pd greater than 65 or Ma greater than 70 with Si below 40
Introversion: Si greater than 65
Obsessiveness: Pt greater than 65; Pt highest point in the profile; OBS greater than 65
Dominance: Do greater than 65
Cynicism: CYN greater than 65

Problems with Alcohol or Other Drugs

Several MMPI-2 scales provide useful information about possible difficulties with alcohol or drug abuse. Substantial research on MMPI-2 clinical scales Pd, D, and Pt in the assessment of substance-abuse problems has shown these scales are prominent in individuals with addictive disorders. In addition, the APS and MAC-R scales, described in Chapter 6, have been developed to assess alcohol- and drug-problem potential. The AAS scale addresses the individual's willingness to acknowledge problems with alcohol or drug use.

The MMPI-2 scale patterns most commonly associated with disorders of substance use or abuse are:

High elevations (T greater than 65) on Pd

High elevations (T greater than 65) on D and Pd

High elevations (T greater than 65) on D, Pd, and Pt

Moderate to high elevations (T greater than 60) on MAC-R, APS, or AAS

Assessing Quality of Interpersonal Relations

The MMPI-2 can provide hypotheses about how an individual interacts with others and whether social factors might influence the individual's psychological adjustment in order to answer the seventh set of interpretive questions in Table 8-1. Information about the client's social skills and interpersonal problems is available from several sources in the MMPI-2. Most directly, the Si scale addresses social introversion and social maladjustment. The Si scale provides a reliable evaluation of the individual's basic sociability and comfort in social situations. Moreover, the Si subscales allow the interpreter to determine the relative contribution of the subscale components (shyness, avoidance, or self-alienation) to the individual's self-reported interpersonal attitudes. However, there are other social adjustment and relationship indicators in the MMPI-2; the scale and code-type descriptors provide additional clues about how the individual interacts with others. Following are examples:

—High scorers on scale 1 are viewed by others as passive, self-preoccupied, dissatisfied, and unhappy. They tend to make others feel miserable with their complaining, whining, demanding, and critical behavior, but they may express hostility indirectly.

—High scorers on scale 4 tend to have considerable social adjustment problems. Although they may be seen as extroverted, outgoing, talkative, active, energetic, spontaneous, and self-confident, they are also viewed as ostentatious, exhibitionistic, insensitive, and manipulative. They tend to be interested in others only in terms of how they can be used to satisfy their own needs. Although they tend to make good first impressions, their relationships tend to be shallow and superficial. They seem unable to form lasting, warm attachments. Their interpersonal and family relationships tend to be stormy.

—High scores on Dominance (Do) suggest that individuals tend to view themselves as the dominant person in interpersonal interaction. They are quite assertive in interpersonal situations.

—High scorers on scale 6 appear to others as hypersensitive, moralistic, and overly responsive to reactions of others. They feel they are picked on and become resentful and angry. They typically harbor grudges against others and are often suspicious and guarded in relationships.

—High scorers on scale 8 typically do not feel a part of the social environment. They are isolated and alienated from other people and feel misunderstood. They are unaccepted by their peers and are often seen as withdrawn, seclusive, secretive, and emotionally inaccessible. They usually avoid dealing with people and new situations.

—High scores on MDS for married or separated clients indicate the possibility of marital distress.

—High scores on the MMPI-2 Content Scale SOD can provide clues about how the individual feels in interpersonal situations.

Stability of the Profile

The stability of MMPI-2 profiles over time is an important interpretive question (Table 8-1). Clinicians need to be able to appraise whether a client's behavior will change over time or persist regardless of treatment. The MMPI-2 profile can aid in assessing whether change is likely. Some MMPI-2 indicators have quite stable test-retest characteristics. For example, Leon et al. (1979) found the test-retest correlation for the Si scale to be .73 over 30 years with a sample of normals. The Si scale measures personality characteristics that are not likely to change very much. Other scales, such as D and Pt, are likely to reflect a situational problem that could alter with a change in circumstances.

As noted earlier, an important factor in assessing profile stability is determining how well defined the profile is. For example, if the two highest scales are 10 T-score points above the next scale in the code, the profile is considered to have very high profile definition. These profiles tend to be quite stable over time.

Moreover, profiles with a 5 to 9 T-score gap between them and the next highest scale or code type (high profile definition) also tend to be very stable. Those profiles with fewer T scores separating the code from the next scale or code type (low profile definition) tend to be relatively unstable over time (Graham, Smith, & Schwartz, 1986).

Severity of Disorder

Level of psychological adjustment, and a disorder's severity, are other questions that can be addressed by an individual's scores on MMPI-2 scales and patterns (Table 8-1). An evaluation of the individual's standard and Content Scale profiles and performance on the supplementary scales provides some general guidelines to how severely disturbed the individual is. For example, an individual having a profile within normal limits, with all scales and indicators below a T score of 60, would be viewed as well adjusted, provided his or her validity scales did not indicate a defensive response attitude. Similarly, if an individual has several clinical and content scale scores ranging in the 80+ T-score range, severe psychological maladjustment is suggested. A number of indexes and configural patterns, described in Chapter 6, have been developed to aid the interpreter in appraising adjustment.

Diagnostic Considerations

Although the MMPI was originally constructed with the idea that clinical-scale elevations would correspond to diagnostic groups, clinical diagnosis has not been the primary focus in using the instrument. The MMPI is used most extensively for descriptive diagnosis, that is, providing behavioral and personality descriptions of an individual based upon the empirical scale and code-type literature. In descriptive diagnosis of clients with the MMPI-2 several sources of information are used:

standard-scale elevations

slope of profile

code-type information

Content Scale scores

Many MMPI scales and code types have been shown to have good correspondence with clinical diagnostic groups, especially with the latest categories provided in the *Diagnostic and Statistical Manual of the American Psychiatric Association*, which are based upon clearer diagnostic criteria than were earlier versions (Savacir & Erol, 1990; Thatte, Manos, & Butcher, 1987; Moldin et al., 1991). The MMPI-2 Content Scales have recently been found to make a contribution to differential diagnosis (Ben-Porath, Butcher, & Graham, 1991; Walsh et al., 1991) as well as providing content-based assessment information. When preparing a clinical report, the interpreter may find the correspondence between scale information and clinical diagnosis useful, although it should not be the primary consideration in reaching a clinical diagnosis.

Treatment Considerations

An important use of the MMPI-2 in clinical assessment involves evaluation of relevant personal characteristics in treatment planning (see Butcher, 1990a for an extended discussion of the use of the MMPI-2 in treatment planning). The MMPI-2 profiles and supplementary scores provide several sources of information that assist in treatment planning by addressing the questions listed in Table 8-2. For example, response attitudes provide clues about the individual's willingness to share personal information, awareness of problems, and ability to understand his or her problems. The clinical scales provide clues about the extent of problems and motivation for treatment. The MMPI-2 Content Scales provide information about the nature of the individual's problems, attitudes, self-views, or behaviors that might interfere with treatment progress.

Case Study: Alice

At several points in earlier chapters we discussed specific aspects of Alice's MMPI-2 profile to illustrate how the various scales are interpreted. We now turn to a fuller exploration of her MMPI-2 profiles and will provide an integrated presentation of her important test responses. The case of 18-year-old Alice, being evaluated in a pre-treatment planning assessment, illustrates how the MMPI-2 variables can provide descriptive and predictive information about her before treatment is initiated. Her standard and Content Scale profiles are repeated in Figures 8-1 and 8-2 for convenience. Relevant extra-test information to assist with her MMPI-2 interpretation is presented below summarizing her past history, symptomatic problems, and life-situation demands. Alice's MMPI-2 profile will be interpreted by answering the questions pertinent to understanding her case.

Referral Problem

Alice is an 18-year-old unemployed, Caucasian woman who was referred to an outpatient mental-health center by her parents following an intense episode of extreme anxiety and panic. Alice was accompanied on all clinic visits by her mother. She had been seen by her family physician for physical complaints (nausea, chest pains, shortness of breath, and sweating), but the physician felt that a psychological referral was more appropriate. Alice reportedly had been feeling quite insecure and inadequate, that she let her family down in not being able to keep a job.

Behavioral Observations

In the initial interview, Alice appeared to be quite tense and under considerable strain. She had difficulty sitting still in the waiting room and walked about talk-

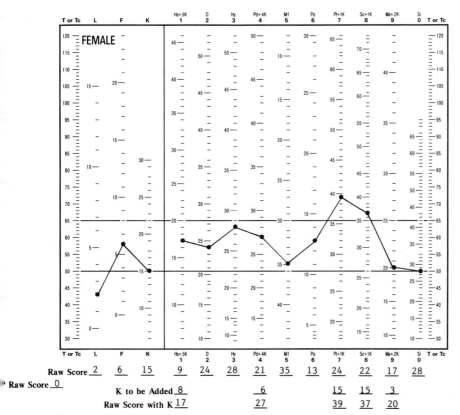

Figure 8-1. Alice. MMPI-2 basic scales profile

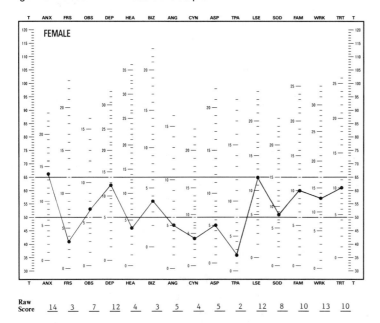

Figure 8-2. Alice. MMPI-2 Content Scales profile

ing with her mother who had accompanied her. Alice was a rather plain woman who was mildly overweight and had a very informal, almost unkempt appearance. She appeared rather disorganized and carried a handbag from which numerous papers were sticking out. She had a very serious manner and appeared preoccupied. She smiled very little, even when it would have been appropriate to do so.

History

Alice completed high school about eight months earlier and had difficulty finding stable employment. Recently, she took a job as a cashier in an all-night convenience store. However, after only a few days of work, she felt she was not learning the job well and she quit. She reportedly felt she was making too many mistakes and was embarrassed to continue working.

Alice presently lived at home with her mother, who was 58-years-old, and her father, who was 55-years-old. She was born when her mother was almost 40-years-old and her three older siblings, all girls, were 15 or more years older than she. All of her siblings were married and living elsewhere in the state. Alice's mother had been a general office worker for an insurance company for the past eight years. Alice's father had not worked since he had a stroke about eight years ago, forcing his early retirement. He spent most of his time at home watching television. None of her sisters was employed outside the home, although one sister completed business school and worked in business for a while.

Alice considered her home situation unpleasant but felt that she was not able to move out of her parents' home at the present time. She reported that her family relationships were not close and that she felt somewhat distant from both her mother and her father ever since she could remember.

Alice reportedly was quite sickly as a child. She was hospitalized when she was four-years-old for a period of about four days with high fever of unknown origin. Alice missed a great deal of school during first and second grades as a result of sickness, and had a great deal of difficulty learning how to read. Her parents obtained special tutors during her third and fourth grades to enable her to keep up with her classmates.

Alice's academic work during high school was marginal and her motivation for school was quite low. She reportedly "couldn't wait 'til graduation." Her grades during high school were mostly Ds and Cs. Alice had very little involvement with extracurricular activities and reportedly did not feel that she was very close to many people at school. Alice reported that she had two close girlfriends with whom she liked to spend time.

Alice dated only occasionally in high school, considering herself not to be very popular. She reportedly stayed at home during school activity nights such as proms, dances, and so forth. Alice reported that she had had three sexual experiences during the past year. Her first experience occurred with a young man in the neighborhood who was home on leave from the navy. This was a difficult experience for her, in part because the situation was interrupted by her parents coming home. Her second sexual experience was with a divorced man for whom she was babysitting. This experience, which she reportedly did not initiate or want, left her "feeling dumb and used." About six months ago, shortly after her high-school graduation, she reported that she had sexual intercourse with one of her former classmates, after which she developed a great concern over AIDS. In the weeks that followed, she was fearful that she had contracted AIDS and eventually went to see a physician to be tested. The medical examination was negative.

Clinical Symptoms

In the initial interview, Alice reported feeling quite anxious and tense much of the time, and reported that she was having difficulties concentrating and making decisions. She had been experiencing shortness of breath, heart palpitations, and chest pains. Alice indicated that she was having a great deal of difficulty falling asleep at night and tended to lie awake much of the night worrying about what she was going to do next. She indicated that she had a tightness in her chest most of the time and had difficulty breathing. She felt these problems interfered at work and she was very slow at learning to work the cash register, which caused her embarrassment.

Alice viewed herself as a very passive person who cannot "stick up for herself." She felt as though she never thought of the right thing to say, particularly when someone made unrealistic demands on her. She became frustrated and angry when people tried to take advantage of her. However, she reported being unable to tell them what she thought or to stand up for herself. Alice was quite self-critical during the interview and stated that she had not lived up to the standards that her mother had set for her. She thought she had let her mother down and felt quite guilty about this.

Goals

At the end of the initial session, Alice indicated that she would like to get relief from the tension and anxiety she was currently experiencing. She also reported that she would like to obtain medication so that she might be able to sleep better. Further, she felt she needed to talk over her feelings of failure and inability to make decisions with a therapist so that she might conquer her concerns about working in public.

MMPI-2 Interpretation

We begin Alice's MMPI-2 interpretation by considering possible extraneous demographic factors that might influence her responses to the MMPI-2. Although Alice still lived at home, the clinician chose to administer the MMPI-2 rather than the MMPI-A. Either instrument can be used with 18-year-olds, but the content of the MMPI-2 related to work, rather than school, was thought to be more relevant to Alice's life circumstances. Alice did not appear to present any problematic demographic or status factors that were likely to adversely affect her

MMPI-2 performance. She was a high-school graduate from a lower middle-class background. No known environmental or cultural factors required consideration. It is, of course, important to determine if the appropriate norms for women were used to plot her profiles.

Since Alice was being administered the MMPI-2 in an outpatient treatment setting in which she was seeking psychological treatment, it is unlikely that she would be uncooperative or defensive in responding to test items. Thus, we would expect that her validity configuration would be problem-oriented and open.

Validity Appraisal

Alice's MMPI-2 validity pattern is clearly in the interpretable range. Her low score on L and average score on K demonstrate that she responded to the MMPI-2 items in an open and non-defensive manner. The slight elevation on F indicates that she has endorsed some psychological problems, but has not exaggerated her symptom picture. Additionally, her scores on TRIN and VRIN show that she has responded to the MMPI-2 items in a consistent manner throughout the booklet. Overall, Alice's approach to the MMPI-2 items was open and cooperative. Her MMPI-2 profile is a valid indication of her present personality functioning and problems.

Symptoms and Behavior

Alice's clinical profile suggests that she is experiencing intense anxiety, considerable ruminations, and self-critical behavior, as reflected in her Pt score. She apparently has great self-doubt and feels she is unworthy. Individuals with high Pt scores like Alice's are prone to worry and are indecisive even when minor decisions need to be made. She is likely experiencing an acute anxiety state of moderate severity. More information about Alice's anxiousness is available by evaluating the relative elevations on the three MMPI-2 Content Scales that assess anxiousness—Anxiety (ANX), Fears (FRS), and Obsessiveness (OBS). We see that her anxiety is generalized, as shown by the high score on ANX, rather than related to specific fears or phobias, as shown by her lower score on FRS. She does appear to have some obsessive qualities as well, as shown by the score on OBS.

Perhaps basic to her tendency to worry and feel uncertain about her ability to function is her very low self-esteem. The feelings of low self-worth are reflected in several MMPI-2 measures. Her high score on the Low Self-Esteem (LSE) scale shows an extremely negative self-appraisal. These negative self-views might create in her a vulnerability to self-defeating behavior that could, of course, trigger further experience of anxiety.

Assessing Alice's Self-Control

On the MMPI-2, Alice appears to be a generally constricted individual who tends to intellectualize and ruminate a great deal. This is suggested by her high elevation on the Pt scale. In addition, she probably overrelies upon denial as a defense mechanism, as noted by her slight Hy and high R elevations; however, at this time she appears to be experiencing more stress than she can manage through her normal defenses. Again, central to her management of conflict appears to be her low self-esteem; she may be nonassertive in interpersonal contexts because of her own feelings of uncertainty and inferiority.

Assessing Problems with Alcohol or Other Drugs

Addiction problems or addiction potential in Alice's case would be considered relatively low. She appears to possess few of the personality factors or "life-style" features, measured by Pd, MAC-R, and APS scale scores, that appear to predispose people to abusing addictive substances.

Although she has a prominent elevation on Pt, a scale that appears elevated among some severe alcohol and drug abusers, this does not present a problem in her case. The role of Pt in the manifestation of alcohol- and drug-abuse problems requires further clarification. The Pt scale alone does not reflect alcohol- or drug-abuse problems; it seldom appears as the single prominent scale in alcohol treatment populations. When the Pt scale is elevated in alcohol- or drug-abusing cases, it indicates the presence of acute anxiety, perhaps associated with the situational problems the individual has caused for himself or herself. The Pt scale also can be associated with *compulsive characteristics* that appear to add an element of extreme urgency to the use of addictive substances. For example, correlates for the 4-7 profile type discussed in Chapter 5 reflect a cyclical pattern of acting-out behavior involving alcohol or drugs. The individual experiences periods of seemingly compulsive excess alternating with periods of guilt and superficial remorse over his or her actions.

Alice appears to be seeking relief for her anxiety and may benefit from anti-anxiety medication for symptom relief. No contraindicating factors (such as high MAC-R, high Pd, or AAS) appear in her personality profile.

Interpersonal Behavior

The MMPI-2 provides useful information about Alice's interpersonal behavior. Her score on Si suggests that she has average social skills, although her relatively higher score on the Si subscale Si_1 suggests some degree of self-consciousness. Individuals with her Si score can, however, function well in interpersonal situations, and she appears not to have any extreme problems interpersonally.

However, individuals with her clinical profile (7-8) typically are somewhat over-ideational, perfectionistic, and nonassertive in relationships. Her nonassertiveness with regard to her own wishes and rights could create frustration if others take advantage of her. Alice's low score on Do, discussed in Chapter 7, also supports the interpretation of passivity in interpersonal situations.

Assessing Alice's MMPI-2 Profile Stability

The major elements in her clinical profile, particularly the high Pt elevation, may have a strong situational component. It is likely that the manifest anxiety this profile reflects could be reduced by treatment or more adaptive efforts on her part. Thus, if retested at a later date or after treatment, her profile is likely to shift somewhat if her ability to deal with anxiety improves.

However, some aspects of her profile are likely not to change much over time, even with intervention. Her generally effective social orientation and ability to deal with others in social situations is not likely to change much. On the positive side, after successful treatment she is not likely to be viewed as extremely introverted or extremely extroverted.

Assessing the Severity of Alice's Disorder

Although she is experiencing troublesome psychological symptoms and anxiety-based physical discomfort, Alice's MMPI-2 profiles suggest that her disorder is mild to moderate in severity. Her problems appear to be somewhat disabling, yet not severe enough to require hospitalization. First, her profile elevations are in the range associated with moderate psychological problems. Moreover, the relative scale elevations suggest that her problems are acute rather than chronic since her Pt elevation is greater than her Sc elevation.

Diagnostic Considerations

Any clinical diagnosis in Alice's case should take into consideration the anxiety-based nature of the problems she is experiencing. Panic disorder is a likely diagnosis, since her score on the Pt scale reflects considerable anxiety. The clinical diagnosis can be further refined by using the MMPI-2 Content Scale scores. Alice produced a high score on the ANX Content Scale but a relatively low score on FRS, suggesting that she is generally anxious but does not report extensive fears or phobias. This possibly rules out agoraphobia in the clinical diagnosis. Thus, the diagnosis of panic disorder without agoraphobia is supported by her performance on the MMPI-2.

Potential Factors in Alice's Response to Treatment

To illustrate the information available to the practitioner in treatment planning, we will evaluate Alice's MMPI-2 profiles and scale scores to determine possible recommendations for treatment and to address the referral questions the clinician encounters in her case. To organize the MMPI-2 information in this case we will address the questions from Table 8-2 about Alice:

—Does she need to be in psychological treatment at this time?

According to Alice's MMPI-2 profile she appears to be a very unhappy individual who is experiencing considerable emotional turmoil at present. In addition, she appears to have strong feelings of insecurity, inferiority, and low self-esteem that make her vulnerable to anxiety states.

—How aware is Alice of the problems she is experiencing?

Alice appears to be intensely aware of her present anxious state, as noted by her willingness to report problems through the MMPI-2. She has endorsed a large number of symptoms related to anxiety and general maladjustment, as shown by her high score on Pt. The intensity of her awareness is shown by her seeming inability to act effectively to resolve her problems at this time.

—How credible is her personality appraisal?

Alice is presenting a valid symptom pattern according to her performance on the F scale. She is not exaggerating her symptoms. Rather, she is selectively responding to the item content. This suggests that she would probably enter into treatment sessions with a problem-oriented approach.

—How willing is Alice to disclose personal information to the therapist?

Alice's approach to the MMPI-2 items, as reflected in her validity-scale pattern, shows her openness to evaluation and her willingness to disclose personal information. She is not defensive and presents an open self-appraisal, which is also reflected in her elevations on the MMPI-A scales.

—How motivated is Alice to become engaged in therapy?

Alice's symptom expression and need for relief of her intense anxiety are likely to be strong motivating factors for psychological treatment.

—Is she capable of gaining insight into her problems?

Individuals with her validity profile configuration appear to have a problem-oriented approach to life's difficulties. Moreover, individuals with high Pt scores tend to be introspective and conscientious.

—Is she amenable to treatment? Will she be able to change her behavior?

With her motivation to get help and her willingness to enter treatment, she is likely to benefit from psychological treatment.

—Are there any specific treatment needs suggested by the MMPI-2?

Anxiety reduction would be an important component in any treatment program with Alice. Whether it be anti-anxiety medication or behavior therapy, her intense anxiety and her tendency to have panic episodes should be primary treatment focuses.

In addition, she appears to have a very poor self-concept and low self-esteem, which might make her prone to further problems. Insight-oriented treatment to reduce her negative self-views and improve her morale would be valuable.

A third factor that might be addressed is her tendency toward passivity in relationships. Alice appears to have little self-confidence and assertiveness. She might benefit from having assertiveness training in order to learn to stand up for herself more effectively.

—Are there any personality strengths that can be used as assets in therapy?

Alice has several areas that can be considered assets in therapy. Her intense discomfort and emotional distress are strong motivating factors for behavioral change. She is responsible, organized, and shows a willingness to discuss her problem areas.

—Are there any persistent personality problems that could interfere with the treatment relationship?

One caution the therapist should keep in mind is that many individuals with elevated Pt scores may ruminate and obsess about their inadequacy, and may be unable to put into practice any behavioral changes. Any treatment program involving high Pt clients should have a clear behavioral component, that is, it should require the client to take practical steps to implement behavioral changes.

Summary

This chapter illustrated the importance of organizing MMPI-2–based inferences into an integrated and internally consistent personality appraisal. In considering information from the various MMPI-2 sources, clinicians need to establish clear interpretive priorities and incorporate hypotheses into an internally consistent, accurate interpretation. By using the suggested interpretive outline, evaluators can organize MMPI-2 inferences from several sources into a cohesive picture. This strategy provides a number of questions to assist the interpreter in formulating a personality evaluation. A number of MMPI-2–based variables help the clinician set priorities within the various inferences and integrate them into a meaningful, organized picture. As we saw in the case of Alice, considered incrementally in previous chapters, this integrated approach using the many information sources available provides the most comprehensive picture of the client and his or her problems to address in psychological treatment. This approach is modified for the MMPI-A in Chapter 11.

Chapter 9

MMPI-A: Extending the Use of the MMPI to Adolescents

The MMPI has been used with adolescents to meet the same practical need for an assessment device that was the impetus for Hathaway and McKinley to develop the original instrument for adults. Much of the early MMPI research with adolescents concentrated on identifying youth prone to juvenile delinquency. This work had a public-health focus, growing out of the mental hygiene movement that began in 1908 and the subsequent child-guidance-clinic movement that started during the 1920s. Unlike the development of the MMPI for adults, work with adolescents was not limited to improving psychiatric diagnosis within clinical or personnel settings.

Starke Hathaway and his collaborator, Elio Monachesi, recognized that underlying many aspects of primary prevention efforts like the child-guidance movement was the assumption that therapeutic work with individual children would decrease the likelihood of later development of delinquency or mental illness. Hathaway and Monachesi (1953a) suggested that there was little experimental evidence supporting this basic assumption:

> But even if we did know that special therapeutic efforts would decrease the later incidence of maladjustment, we have no established, practical, reliable, and valid survey method for identifying the various subgroups of children that are more likely than others to have trouble. We must either blindly do general preventive work on whole populations or wait for children to become deviant in behavior and then offer treatment, depending on the unhappy fact that a person already in trouble is more likely than others to have additional trouble (p. 3).

The earliest studies using the MMPI with adolescents sought to determine whether the instrument could reliably and validly identify subgroups of youth predisposed to delinquency. Although Hathaway and Monachesi (1953a) recognized the etiological significance of the social environment, they also observed that not all children living in stressful environments became delinquent. Rather, they theorized, some personality characteristics might predispose youth toward deviant behavior.

The first extension of MMPI research to adolescents was attributed to Dora Capwell (1945a, 1945b, 1953). She began her work even before the completed instrument was available, using a card-box form that did not include items for scales K, 5, and 0. Capwell sought to determine whether the MMPI would provide useful information about 101 delinquent girls from the Minnesota Home

School for Girls in the small town of Sauk Centre. Because she speculated that adult normative comparisons might not be the most appropriate for adolescents, Capwell included a comparison group of 85 nondelinquents from the Sauk Centre public schools. Her design was longitudinal, with a retesting from four to 15 months after the first examination, and included the MMPI and several other personality tests, as well as intelligence and academic achievement tests. She found that of all the personality measures studied, the MMPI most clearly differentiated the two groups. The delinquent girls had reliably greater mean adult T scores on all the validity and clinical scales, except for L and scale 3. She further demonstrated that this difference in mean scores on the scales did not seem to be related to intelligence.

Shortly after Capwell's pioneering efforts, Elio Monachesi began studies to extend her findings to boys using the published version of the instrument that included scales K, 5, and 0 (Monachesi, 1948, 1950a, 1950b, 1953). Monachesi was able to confirm Capwell's original findings. The scales on which delinquent boys and girls most clearly exceeded control group means were scales 4, 6, 7, 8, and 9. Scale 4 was the most different. In keeping with expectations, scales 1, 2, and 3 were not consistently elevated among the delinquent boys or girls. These studies also presented important differences between the genders. Delinquent girls seemed to have more tendencies toward sensitivity and feelings that they were unduly controlled, indicated by their elevations on scale 6. A subsequent follow-up of Capwell's samples (Hathaway, Hastings, Capwell, & Bell, 1953) found that elevations on scale 6 seemed to be a positive factor in girls' adjustment. The interpersonal sensitivity indicated by scale 6 elevations proved to be beneficial later on.

These earlier studies led to a landmark 15-year prospective study, funded by the National Institute of Mental Health (NIMH) and the University of Minnesota Graduate School (Hathaway & Monachesi, 1963). A total of 15,300 ninth graders from throughout Minnesota were assessed with the MMPI. In addition to MMPIs on each of these subjects, information was collected about them from schools, law-enforcement agencies, and social-service agencies. Subjects included 3,971 Minneapolis public-school ninth graders from the 1947-1948 school year, representing 89% of the total ninth-grade enrollment for that year. The rest of the sample, 11,329 subjects, was collected outside Minneapolis from 92 schools in 86 Minnesota communities during the spring of 1954. This extensive data base was used to investigate the prediction of delinquency and other acting-out behaviors, as well as to describe differences in adult and adolescent personality as measured by the MMPI. In their studies predicting delinquency and other behavior problems, Hathaway and Monachesi demonstrated the utility and validity of the MMPI with adolescents. The studies on adult-adolescent differences helped in understanding how to use the MMPI with adolescents. Williams (1986) summarized their findings about adult-adolescent differences into three main areas: 1) item endorsements, 2) code types and, 3) elevation. Over the years other researchers documented these differences, including our recent work on the development of the MMPI-A (e.g., Butcher et al., 1992; Williams et al., 1992).

Adult-Adolescent Differences on the MMPI

Item Endorsements

Item-level differences are perhaps the most basic distinction between adult and adolescent MMPI responding. These item differences are understandable when viewed from a developmental perspective (Williams, 1986; Williams et al., 1992). The first four items found by Hathaway and Monachesi (1963) to most differentiate boys from men illustrate this:

I am neither gaining nor losing weight.

My relatives are nearly all in sympathy with me.

Sometimes at elections I vote for men about whom I know very little.

I would like to hunt lions in Africa.

Ninth-grade boys, unlike men, are in the adolescent growth spurt, which accounts for their greater likelihood to report fluctuations in weight. Adolescents' increasing needs for autonomy, along with their proclivity for excitement and adventure (illustrated by their greater desire to hunt lions), can account for some increasing tension with family members. Because the elections in which they participate are usually within school settings, they are much more likely to know all the candidates. This contrasts with the dilemma faced by adults in a typical election.

Interestingly, both Hathaway and Monachesi's (1963) data set and the recent data from the MMPI Restandardization Project, reveal that girls differ more from women than boys do from men (Williams et al., 1992). Girls and women have a far greater number of item-endorsement differences than do boys and men. Some of the differences in the earlier samples are related to gender roles, with girls endorsing more stereotypically feminine vocation items and preferring to flirt more than did women. For example, over half the girls, but only 6% of the women, report a preference to work with women in the Hathaway and Monachesi (1963) data set. However, the new samples of girls and women do not differ in expressed preferences for being a nurse, dressmaker, or private secretary, as did the earlier samples (Williams et al., 1992).

Williams et al. (1992) summarized many of these adult-adolescent item differences. Adolescents tended to express greater interest in excitement and loud fun (e.g., "When I get bored I like to stir up some excitement"—True), coupled with greater dislike of intellectual pursuits (e.g., "I like to read about history"—False) relative to adults. Adolescents were more likely to endorse emotionality (e.g., "At times I feel like picking a fist fight with someone"; "At times I have fits of laughing and crying that I cannot control").

Some of the items assessing more pathological problems in adults also demonstrated adult-adolescent response differences. For example, 45% of the normative boys and 46% of the normative girls admitted to having "strange and peculiar thoughts," compared with only 15% of normative men and 10% of normative women (Williams et al., 1992). Adolescents were more likely to report urges to do harmful or shocking things, ideas of reference, feelings of unreality, and peculiar and strange experiences. These items appeared on several of the validity and standard scales originally developed with adult samples. These item-level differences indicate that the items are not psychometrically equivalent with adults and adolescents. This may contribute to differential validity of these scales with adults and adolescents.

Code Types

A "no-high-point" profile type (i.e., one with no scales with a T score greater than 54) was used in early research on the MMPI. Hathaway and Monachesi (1963) were struck by the greater number of no-high-point profiles occurring in adults compared with adolescents. They wondered if this profile type was indicative of normal personality. If so, their results suggested that normal personality was much more frequent among adults than among adolescents. However, subsequent studies did not support this definition of normal personality.

Hathaway and Monachesi's (1963) comparative data showed several other code-type differences as well. Adults, especially women, had more profiles suggestive of neuroses (i.e., elevations on scales 1, 2, and 3). Adolescents, even those in school populations, more often had sociopathic or psychotic profile types (i.e., elevations on scales 4, 8, 9). The 49/94 code type was the most frequently occurring code type among adolescents in clinical settings (Marks et al., 1974; Williams & Butcher, 1989b).

Code types have been the basis of MMPI interpretation for both adults and adolescents (Marks et al., 1974). Surprisingly, however, we were able to demonstrate only limited validity for the code-type approach with adolescents (Williams & Butcher, 1989b). In this study only the 46/64 code type had adequate empirical validity. Adolescents elevated on this code type seemed to have the most serious psychopathology. It is important to note that sample differences between ours and the Marks et al. (1974) study cannot account for our inability to support the validity of code types with adolescents. When using the earlier rules for defining code types, we demonstrated remarkable similarities in the two samples. Although there was good congruence between code types based on the earlier adolescent norms and the new MMPI-A norms, the MMPI-A manual advises clinicians to use caution in following the code-type approach with MMPI-A interpretations, suggesting that further research is needed (Butcher et al., 1992).

Scale Elevations

Hathaway and Monachesi (1963) found that scale elevation is another important dimension differentiating adult and adolescent MMPI responding. This finding has been replicated many times subsequently, including in the large study reported by Marks et al. (1974) and the MMPI Restandardization Project (Butcher et al., 1992; Williams et al., 1992). Figures 9-1 and 9-2 illustrate the scale-eleva-

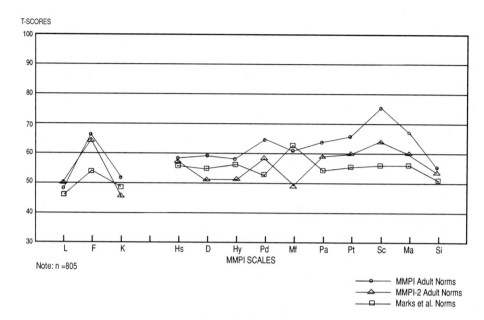

Figure 9-1. Boys normative sample plotted on three different norms (N = 805)

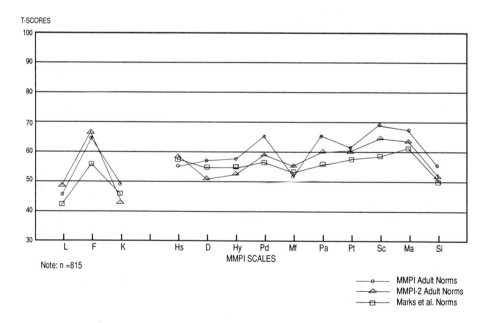

Figure 9-2. Girls normative sample plotted on three different norms (N = 815)

tion differences between adults and adolescents for MMPI-A normative sample boys and girls, respectively. These figures present the normative adolescents' mean scores on two adult norm sets (i.e., original MMPI and MMPI-2) and the adolescent norms presented by Marks et al. (1974). Normal adolescents score at least one standard deviation higher than adults on the original F, Pd, Pa, Pt, Sc, and Ma scales when using the original adult norms (Williams, Butcher, & Graham, 1986). Elevation differences, although somewhat reduced, remain meaningful with the new MMPI-2 adult norms. Scale-elevation differences between adults and adolescents are most directly related to interpretation and led to the development of adolescent norms for the MMPI. However, the adolescent norms presented by Marks et al. (1974) do not yield mean scale T scores of 50 for normal adolescents as is true for normal adults. Figures 9-1 and 9-2 illustrate that most adolescent mean scale scores are elevated at T scores of 55-60 on the Marks et al. (1974) norms. On the other hand, the new MMPI-A norms, produce mean scale scores of 50, which is consistent with the adult MMPI-2 mean scale scores.

The Norm Issue and Adolescents

Elevation differences between adults and adolescents led to the development of a separate norm set for adolescents. This was done despite opposition from Starke Hathaway and Elio Monachesi. They questioned whether it would be fairer to compare adolescents to other young people rather than to the average adult. Hathaway and Monachesi (1953a) argued that even though differences are recognized in adolescents and adults, society still judges the appropriateness of behavior using an adult standard:

> In light of this attitude, the application of adult norms to young people is proper and adjustment of the norms would obscure the very real fact that there is a significant, almost universal, quality in young people that makes them prone to socially unacceptable behavior. We want our scales to show behavior differences that are significant to society even if the implied personalities are "normal" for the age level. Since the core of society is the early adult and middle aged pattern of mores, the use of MMPI norms based chiefly on middle aged married persons can be justified even for young people (p. 25).

Because of emphatic statements like this from the test author, some argued for the exclusive use of adult norms in interpreting adolescents' profiles. Hathaway and Monachesi's (1961) *An Atlas of Juvenile MMPI Profiles* used the adult norms to present information for over 1,000 profiles of adolescents from their extensive sample. However, the atlas approach to MMPI interpretation proved unwieldy and was never widely used.

The first interpretative manual to extend the instrument's use to boys and girls as young as 12 or 13 was presented by Philip Marks and his colleagues (1974). This volume included an adolescent norm set to be used with their actuarial system. These norms were based on the Minnesota data collected by Hathaway and Monachesi (1963), combined with data from six other states. Peter

Briggs worked with Marks et al. (1974) to develop these adolescent norms. Although Marks et al. (1974) developed and presented the most widely used adolescent norm set, they did not advocate its exclusive use. Rather, they indicated that there might be times, particularly for 17- and 18-year-olds, when the adult norm set would produce a more valid profile. Others, however, argued for the exclusive use of adolescent-derived norms when interpreting MMPIs in this age range (e.g., Archer, 1984; 1987).

Unfortunately, use of the adolescent norms in clinical settings frequently produced false negative MMPIs (i.e., normal-limits profiles). Studies of adolescents in treatment for emotional and behavioral problems frequently yielded mean scores within normal limits (e.g., Ehrenworth & Archer, 1985; Klinge, Culbert, & Piggott, 1982; Klinge, Lachar, Grisell, & Berman, 1978; Lachar, Klinge, & Grisell, 1976). Figure 9-3, mean scores of boys in clinical settings, and Figure 9-4, mean scores of girls in clinical settings, highlight this problem. Boys in the clinical sample used in the development of the MMPI-A produced a normal-limits profile on the Marks et al. (1974) adolescent norms (Figure 9-3). A similar pattern is evident for the clinical girls plotted on the adolescent norms, although the elevation on scale 4 approaches the T-score cut-off of 70 (Figure 9-4). By contrast, both sets of adult norms (i.e., MMPI and MMPI-2) produced clinically significant elevations on several scales.

Two recommendations for interpretation evolved to handle the problem of fewer clinically meaningful elevations with the Marks et al. (1974) norms. Some suggested that profiles from both the adult and adolescent norm sets be plotted for each adolescent (Graham, 1987; Williams, 1986). Interpretations would incorporate information from both norm sets. Another suggestion was to use an adolescent T-score cut-off of 65, rather than the traditional T-score cut-off of 70 for adults (Archer, 1987; Ehrenworth & Archer, 1985). However, a T-score cut-off of 65 was used in the code-type study described earlier and yielded only limited evidence of validity for code-type interpretations for adolescents.

Recently, two additional adolescent norm sets have been presented as potential replacements for the Marks et al. (1974) adolescent norms (i.e., Colligan & Offord, 1989; Gottesman, Hanson, Kroeker, & Briggs, 1987). These norm sets were included as appendixes in Archer (1987). Both are limited clinically. Neither has been studied to determine the validity of MMPI interpretations based on its scores, and one study suggested that each of these potential replacements was roughly equivalent to the Marks et al. (1974) norms in discriminating among adolescents in outpatient, inpatient, and normal settings (Klinefelter, Pancoast, Archer, & Pruitt, 1990). The Gottesman et al. (1987) adolescent norms were actually based on a re-analysis of the original Hathaway and Monachesi data set collected in the 1940s and 1950s.

The norms offered by Colligan and Offord (1989) have limited clinical applications for several reasons. Their MMPI profiles were collected from adolescents in three midwestern states near Rochester, Minnesota (Minnesota, Iowa, and Wisconsin), raising questions about the norms' generalizability to youth from other areas. Their design included mailing the instrument to the subjects' homes, which did not ensure the required supervised administration. Another

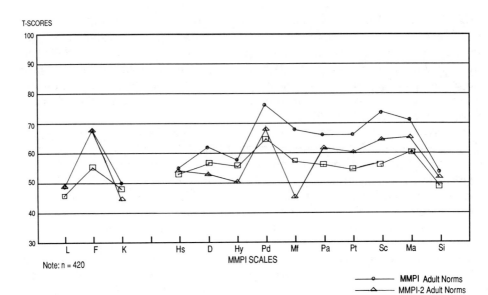

Figure 9-3. Boys clinical sample plotted on three different norms (N = 420)

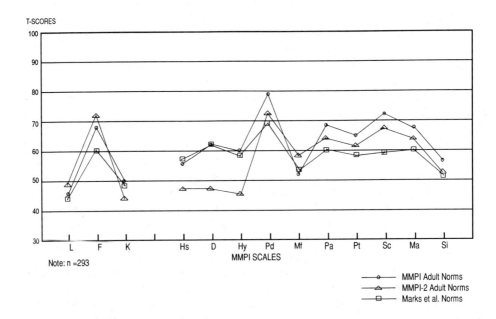

Figure 9-4. Girls clinical sample plotted on three different norms (N = 293)

important limitation was the use of a procedure to generate T scores that yielded results not comparable to traditional MMPI T scores. Rather than using linear T scores, as Hathaway and McKinley (1940) did with the original MMPI norms for adults and Marks et al. (1974) did with the adolescent norms, Colligan and Offord used a normalized T-score approach. Normalizing procedures result in T-score distributions that are artificially restricted in range. The normalizing procedure thus resulted in considerable attenuation of T scores at clinically meaningful levels of scale elevation.

After clinicians using the original MMPI decided upon norms, they next faced the issue of which descriptors to use to derive interpretive statements. Until 1989 there were two primary sources of MMPI descriptors: the adult code-type and scale literature (e.g., Graham, 1977, 1987) or the Marks et al. (1974) adolescent code-type correlates. In 1989 we provided additional information in the form of scale descriptors (Williams & Butcher, 1989a). Many different interpretive strategies evolved for the MMPI and adolescents based on various combinations of norms and descriptors. We will look briefly at: the adult interpretive approach, adolescent interpretive approach, mixed interpretive approach, combined interpretive approach, and scale descriptor interpretive approach (Table 9-1).

Interpretive Strategies for Adolescents' MMPI Profiles

The interpretive strategies described in Table 9-1 evolved over the years as research accumulated on the use of the MMPI with adolescents. As we have seen, one of the test authors, Starke Hathaway, did not believe that special norms were required in interpreting the instrument for adolescents. Instead, he suggested that adolescents' mean scores and two standard deviations above the mean be plotted on any individual adolescent's profile. Hathaway probably agreed with the theory that adolescence was a time of "storm and stress" (Hall, 1904) and preferred not to disguise what he believed to be an essential feature of adolescence. However, the first comprehensive approach to interpreting MMPI profiles for adolescents provided age-appropriate norms and code-type descriptors from samples of adolescents as a source of interpretive statements (Marks et al., 1974). When clinicians discovered problems with the accuracy of interpretations based on either the adult or adolescent interpretive approaches, the next strategy emerged (i.e., the mixed interpretive approach). This approach drew upon both previous methods with its recommendation to use the adolescent norm set (Marks et al., 1974) along with adult descriptors (e.g., Graham, 1987).

Only one empirical study examined the accuracy of these three primary adolescent interpretive strategies (Ehrenworth & Archer, 1985). In it, clinicians rated the accuracy of narrative reports based on the three approaches. Both the adult and mixed interpretive strategies were rated more accurate than the adolescent interpretive approach. Williams (1986) presented a case illustrating how different interpretations can be depending upon which of these three strategies was used.

Table 9-1. Examples of interpretive strategies for using the MMPI with adolescents

---

ADULT INTERPRETIVE APPROACH

This approach is essentially the same as deriving interpretations from adults' MMPI profiles. It is based on the adult norms and adult scale and code-type descriptors. It assumes that no special procedures are required for interpreting adolescents' profiles.

ADOLESCENT INTERPRETIVE APPROACH

The Marks et al. (1974) book is the basis of this strategy. Their age-appropriate norms and code-type descriptors are used to derive interpretive statements. However, Marks et al. suggested that this approach be used in combination with the adult interpretive approach, particularly with older adolescents.

MIXED INTERPRETIVE APPROACH

This strategy uses the adolescent norms (Marks et al., 1974) in combination with the adult code-type descriptors available in interpretive manuals like Graham's (1987). It evolved because of problems with the accuracy of interpretations based on the two previous approaches (i.e., the adult and adolescent interpretive strategies).

COMBINED INTERPRETIVE APPROACH

This strategy was developed by Archer (1987) after a review of the literature. He combined adolescent descriptors found in Marks et al. (1974) with the adult-derived descriptors available in Graham (1977), Greene (1980), and Lachar (1974), providing narrative descriptions for 29 different code types. These descriptors began with statements found to be common in the adolescent and adult sources and concluded with information found in one, but not the other.

SCALE DESCRIPTOR INTERPRETIVE APPROACH

This is the most recent interpretive strategy for the original MMPI. We suggested it as an interim approach to be used until the MMPI-A became available, because of our recent empirical findings (i.e., Williams & Butcher, 1989a, 1989b). It presented raw-score cut-offs and scale-by-scale descriptors.

Two other approaches were developed more recently. The combined interpretive approach was presented by Archer (1987), based on descriptors found in the literature until 1986. Archer (1987) provided clinicians with interpretive summaries for 29 MMPI code types. After our studies on the MMPI standard scales and code types (Williams & Butcher, 1989a, 1989b), we recommended the most recent interpretive approach. Given our findings, it seemed more prudent to rely on scale descriptors, rather than code-type descriptors (Greene, 1991). Because of problems that had earlier been identified with the adolescent norm set described above, raw-score cut-offs, rather than T scores, were provided for generating interpretations. It was presented as an interim strategy to be used until the MMPI-A became available. As described in Chapter 10, interpretations based on the MMPI-A used a variation of the scale elevation approach (Butcher et al., 1992). However, age-appropriate T scores, rather than raw scores, were provided for the MMPI-A.

Problems in Using the Original MMPI with Adolescents

Although, almost from its inception, the MMPI was used with young people for both research and clinical purposes, its use in this age range was controversial in spite of positive findings about its reliability and validity. Despite its wide use and research with adolescents, the test did not have the same extensive research base with this population that it did with adults. Even after Dora Capwell's and Elio Monachesi's careful preliminary studies, Hathaway and Monachesi (1953b) noted concerns about the possible inappropriateness of some of the MMPI items for younger adolescents. Because of this, Hathaway and Monachesi speculated it might be best to use the instrument only at upper grade levels. However, because their research focused on the development of juvenile delinquency, the MMPI was used with younger adolescents.

Hathaway and Monachesi (1953b) recognized an abrupt rise in the incidence of juvenile delinquency at approximately age 14. Therefore, they felt compelled to begin their large prospective study with comparatively younger children in the ninth grade. Because of the possibility that parents or others might object to MMPI item content, Hathaway and Monachesi (1953b) designed a pilot study to determine whether there would be adverse reactions to testing school children with the MMPI. They selected a school with a ninth-grade enrollment of 192 students and solicited the cooperation of the principal, counselors, and teachers. These staff members became actively interested in the project. Two-hour periods were set aside for the testing, and boys and girls were segregated during the testing sessions. (Such segregation did not prove feasible, or particularly necessary, during their later data collection.)

Test instructions addressed the possibility of inappropriate or objectionable item content, and advised use of the Cannot Say response category when necessary. Instructions used with adolescents were:

> This is a test to study personality. The study is being made by the University and your records will be kept by them. No one will look at your answers to individual questions because the grades depend on counting up the marks only. The test has a great many statements about people, what they are like, and what they think. It is used to aid in advising men and women about jobs and other problems. We want to see if it will be a help when taken by persons who are younger. So we are asking you to do it. You may find that some of the statements don't fit you at all, or they won't fit you until you are older. If you find any of these, answer them the best you can or leave them blank, but try to answer every statement. Work quickly, but don't be careless. Some statements will be in the past tense, for example: 'My father was.' Answer as though in the present if your father is still living and you are with him (Hathaway & Monachesi, 1953b, p. 88).

The boys and girls were instructed to read the directions printed on the Hankes answer sheet and to feel free to ask for any other information they needed. Teachers and other supervisors were available to answer questions. Furthermore, the test administrators wandered about the room unobtrusively watching for children who appeared to be "in any way bewildered by the MMPI." It was common for students to inquire about the meaning of a word or whether or not he or she should answer it in a particular way. The examiners were instructed to evade direct responses.

Hathaway and Monachesi (1953b) indicated that these test instructions and administration procedures resulted in very few problems during the testing. Following the pilot test, the teachers and counselors were instructed to be alert to any discussion among the children or others that might be related to the MMPI. Four months were allowed to elapse before large-scale testing proceeded in other schools. No disturbing events or adverse reactions were reported during this four-month period. Researchers were gratified by this because the trial school was more culturally, economically, and socially diverse than most other schools in their sample.

Thus Hathaway and Monachesi (1953a, 1953b) set the precedent for using the MMPI with adolescents. No attempts were made to change the item content, and very few attempts were made to improve the scales for adolescents (Williams et al., 1992). An instrument written and developed for adults was simply adopted for use with adolescents. No structural changes were made. It became widely used with adolescents in spite of recognized problems and criticism of this practice.

Table 9-2 summarizes the problems with using the original MMPI with adolescents. These problems occur at several levels, including item, scale, norm, interpretation, and general criticisms. Many may be related to failure to adapt the instrument for adolescents. The most general problem is the more limited research base on the use of the MMPI with adolescents. As we have seen, this has contributed to the employment of many idiosyncratic procedures for interpreting MMPI profiles for adolescents.

Many of the item-level problems noted in Table 9-1 apply equally as well to adults, although adolescents seem to be even more distracted when encountering them. The out-of-date phrases and awkward wording characteristic of the original instrument, written during the 1930s and not updated until the MMPI Restandardization Project, tended to annoy and confuse adolescents. These stylistic problems exacerbated the comprehension difficulties of younger adolescents, with more limited reading abilities. Early on Hathaway and Monachesi (1953b) noted that the sexual behavior items were not as relevant for adolescents as adults, yet were surprised that they did not pose a major problem during testing sessions. However, as people became more familiar with the MMPI and its content, the sexual behavior items became more associated with the instrument, which sometimes led to difficulties in administering the instrument in school settings, particularly those serving younger adolescents (Butcher et al., 1992; Crewe & Crewe, 1973). Interestingly, Hathaway and Monachesi (1953b) recognized that a shorter version of the MMPI might be better for use with adolescents.

In one normative data collection site for the MMPI Restandardization Project, Regis High School in New York City, we used a brief follow-up questionnaire to survey students' reactions to the MMPI (Williams, Ben-Porath, & Hevern, 1991). The items that bothered the young people most were of a fairly consistent type.

Table 9-2. Problems in using the original MMPI with adolescents

ITEM PROBLEMS	SCALE AND NORM PROBLEMS	INTERPRETATION PROBLEMS	GENERAL CRITICISMS
• The MMPI's content is sometimes confusing to today's adolescents owing to out-of-date phrases, awkward wording, and other stylistic problems. • Some items are not appropriate for young adolescents. • The limited item pool does not have themes specific to adolescents and their problems. • Items do not directly assess important problems that occur more frequently with today's adolescents (e.g., eating problems, suicide, marijuana and other drug use). • The limited item pool does not measure other important areas: personal strengths, motivations for treatment, or change potential. • There are too many items for an adolescent to answer and some adolescents in clinical settings do not have an adequate reading level or the necessary attention and concentration skills to successfully complete the test.	• Scales developed specifically for adolescent populations are not available. • No research data are available from adolescents for the potentially useful content scales, subscales, or other special scales. No adolescent norms are available for these scales. (The one notable exception is the MacAndrew Alcoholism scale). • Scale norms are out-of-date, based on responses from adolescents in the 1940s-1960s. • Results of available research studies are equivocal about which norms (i.e., adolescent or adult) are most appropriate to use with an adolescent patient, although some studies suggest that the adolescent norms may be more appropriate. • Mean profiles of adolescents in clinical settings scored on adolescent norms are in the normal range. • Practice dictates adding a K-correction to scales 1, 4, 7, 8, 9 when using adult norms. The K-correction is not used with adolescent norms, which further contributes to the differences between the two sets of norms. • Several new adolescent norms have recently been proposed, none of which is derived from a contemporary, nationwide, representative sample of adolescents.	• Predictive and descriptive accuracy for adolescents is lower than for adults. • Many interpretive statements are only available from research on adult populations. • Code types, and thus the resulting interpretations, can change dramatically when going from adult to adolescent norms. • Often the interpretations based on the adolescent code-type descriptors provided by Marks et al. (1974) differ from interpretations based on the adult code-type descriptors. • Use of potentially valid content measures is hampered because of limited research with adolescents. • Williams and Butcher (1989a) is the only source of MMPI standard-scale descriptors available from a large adolescent clinical sample. • Williams and Butcher (1989b) found only limited validity for the code-type approach in their large adolescent clinical study.	• There is not one widely used method of interpreting MMPI profiles from adolescents, resulting in several idiosyncratic procedures being used. • Much less research is available about use of the MMPI with adolescents.

These were items without face validity, including questions about "fixing door latches," "liking mannish women," and items about bowel and bladder functioning. This offensive content was eliminated from the MMPI-A.

Very little scale development for adolescents was done using the original MMPI. For example, no age-appropriate norms were ever provided for the Wiggins Content Scales, Harris-Lingoes subscales, and other supplementary MMPI scales. Although the MacAndrew Alcoholism scale is an exception to this generalization, this lack of scale development hampered the interpretation process. Until the development of the MMPI-A, use of content measures to enhance interpretation had limited research support, including the lack of a set of adolescent norms.

The different strategies described in Table 9-1 highlight many of the interpretation problems. A basic issue is that predictive and descriptive accuracy for adolescents appears to be lower than for adults. This may, in part, be attributed to the fact that many interpretive statements are available only from research on adult populations. The code-type approach has been shown to have limited validity with adolescents, and code types can change dramatically when going from adult to adolescent norms. When the code type changes, the resulting interpretation also changes (Williams, 1986). Despite all these problems, there are clear advantages in using the MMPI with adolescents and even greater advantages associated with the MMPI-A.

Advantages of the MMPI-A

Table 9-3 describes the advantages of the new MMPI-A. The general advantages apply equally well to the original instrument and its newest version, the MMPI-A (see also Chapter 1, Table 1-1). Practitioners and researchers choose the MMPI over other personality measures because of its ability to assess many different psychological problems using limited professional time. Its objective nature makes it easy to administer in settings like schools. Students are used to true-false responding and are willing to disclose psychological problems by responding to MMPI items.

Ease of scoring the MMPI increased with the advent of computer scoring. This scoring method allowed many different scales, including content scales, subscales, and special scales, to be scored quickly and accurately. The computer-administered adaptation of the test seemed to be preferred by adolescents.

A clear advantage of the MMPI-A and the original instrument is that they can be used with other family members, including parents and adolescent siblings. This reduces the frequently occurring tendency in treatment settings to single out the referred adolescent as the only family member with problems. Adolescent clients are more willing to complete the MMPI-A knowing that their parents and/or siblings will be completing a similar instrument.

A major advantage in using the MMPI with adolescents (and adults as well) is the use of a feedback session. In a feedback session the clinician provides interpretive statements based on MMPI-A scale elevations. However, these are not presented to the young person as the "absolute truth." Rather, the young per-

Table 9-3. Advantages of using the MMPI-A

GENERAL	ITEM	SCALE	NORM/ DESCRIPTOR	INTERPRETATION
• A wide variety of psychological problems is assessed with the MMPI-A, which requires little professional time for administration. • Many adolescents who are reluctant to admit to problems in clinical interviews will respond less defensively to the MMPI-A. • Most adolescents like the true-false format of the MMPI-A. • The MMPI-A can be scored quickly and accurately by computer. A number of content scales, subscales, and special scales are available through computer scoring. The test can be adapted for computer administration, a format that many adolescents prefer. • The MMPI-2 can be used with parents and the MMPI-A with adolescent siblings of clients, thus reducing the tendency to single out the referred adolescent as the only family member with problems. • A feedback session with the adolescent can be used for relationship-building and gathering further information. The MMPI-A interpretation is presented to the adolescent as a series of hypotheses or guesses that the patient and therapist explore for accuracy.	• 70 items with problematic wording were rewritten for the MMPI-A booklet. • Offensive items that were eliminated from the MMPI-2 booklet were also deleted from the MMPI-A. In addition, some items assuming sexual activities were eliminated because they were objectionable for youth and did not necessarily have the same psychological meaning. • Unique items with adolescent-specific themes, including peer-group influences, family relations, and issues about school and teachers, were added to MMPI-A. • Items were added to assess problems more commonly seen in contemporary treatment settings serving adolescents, including eating problems, suicidal behavior, and alcohol and other drug problems. • MMPI-2 items used to develop the Negative Treatment Indicators Content Scale were also included in the MMPI-A.	• Continuity between the original MMPI and the MMPI-A was maintained for several validity scales, the clinical scales, and MAC, A, and R. • Scales 5 and 0, two rather long scales on the MMPI and MMPI-2, were shortened on the MMPI-A without significant psychometric cost. • MMPI-2 scales were not simply assumed to work with adolescents. Rather, statistical analyses using adolescent samples and rational procedures that included a developmental perspective were used in refining or developing the F scale (including F_1 and F_2), VRIN, TRIN, and the MMPI-A Content Scales. • Some of the MMPI-A Content Scales were developed from the adolescent-specific items, and thus are unique on the MMPI-A. Other MMPI-A Content Scales like A-fam were revised with the addition of adolescent-specific content.	• MMPI-A scale norms were based on a contemporary sample, selected from several regions of the U.S., and including minority youth. • MMPI-A norms, like the MMPI-2 norms, were based on a uniform T-score transformation that ensured percentile equivalence across the different MMPI scale scores. • Both the MMPI-A and MMPI-2 norms were developed using the same target distribution, ensuring percentile equivalence across the two forms. Thus, as a person ages, his or her MMPI-A and MMPI-2 T scores can be compared directly. • Descriptors were derived from the normative sample and a large clinical sample of boys and girls. Thus, with the MMPI-A, scale descriptors based on adolescent responding (not adult responding) were presented separately by gender and by normative or treatment settings.	• The MMPI-A manual presents one norm set to use with adolescents. This eliminates the number of idiosyncratic interpretive strategies for adolescents. • The same cut-off for clinical interpretations (i.e., T score of 65) is recommended for MMPI-A and MMPI-2. However, for adolescents, clinicians are advised to consider scales elevated in the 60-64 T-score range as yielding potentially significant descriptors. • Interpretation can be based on scales and descriptors derived from studies of adolescents. • Code-type congruence between the MMPI-A and original adolescent norms is substantial, allowing for use of the original Marks et al. (1974) adolescent code-type descriptors. However, the contemporary MMPI-A samples do not provide evidence for the validity of the code-type descriptors. Future studies are needed to demonstrate the validity of code-type descriptors.

son is encouraged by the therapist to begin problem-solving by deciding whether the interpretation applies to him or her. The MMPI-A interpretation is presented as a series of hypotheses or guesses that the patient and therapist explore for accuracy. This strategy can be used at the beginning of therapy to build a relationship with the young person (e.g., Williams, 1982). Adolescents enjoy MMPI feedback sessions, perhaps partly because of the process of identity formation.

The feedback session can be extended to other family members as well. After providing individual interpretations for each family member, the therapist can meet with the family as a group. It is important in the individual interpretation sessions to determine if there is anything that the adolescent or parent would prefer not be discussed in the general family session. Some areas, like possible marital problems or the sexual behavior of the adolescent (or parent), are probably best not interpreted in a family feedback session held relatively early in the therapeutic process. However, a number of MMPI-2 and MMPI-A correlates describe personality features of importance to other family members. For example, one could describe potential conflicts between individuals who are high on Si and those low on Si. The Family Problems Content Scale would be another interesting source for discussions.

Often the feedback session provides even richer information for the clinician to use in formulating a treatment plan. Some clinicians use information from the MMPI throughout the course of treatment when examples of personality descriptors occur. For example, an overly sensitive person, indicated by a high Pa elevation, may, in the process of therapy, report interpersonal difficulties stemming from suspicion of other people's behavior. Going back to the MMPI interpretation may be a less threatening way to introduce the individual's possible contribution to these problems.

Although the general advantages listed in Table 9-3 apply to both versions of the instrument with adolescents, the more specific ones apply only to the MMPI-A. These advantages resulted from changes made in the original instrument. As indicated above, the item-level problems were originally handled through instructions given to the subjects. However, the MMPI Restandardization Committee actually changed the item content to make the instrument more appropriate for young people. Some of the item-level changes were common to both the MMPI-2 and MMPI-A (i.e., rewording awkward items, eliminating offensive items, and including items to assess amenability to treatment). Other item-level changes were implemented to make the instrument more appropriate for adolescents. Items with adolescent-specific themes, including peer-group influences, family relations, and school issues, were added to the MMPI-A. Items that are objectionable for youth and do not have the same psychological meaning as they have for adults were eliminated. Hathaway and Monachesi's (1953b) suggestion to shorten the instrument for adolescents was accomplished with the 478-item MMPI-A booklet (in contrast to the 567-item MMPI-2 booklet).

Most of the previous work on the original instrument with adolescents focussed on the norm and descriptor levels. The new instrument offers improvements in these areas as well (Table 9-2). MMPI-A scale norms are based on a contemporary sample of adolescents selected from schools in several regions of the

United States and including minority youth (Butcher et al., 1992). The uniform T-score transformation (Tellegen & Ben-Porath, in press), which ensured percentile equivalence across the different MMPI scale scores, was used on the MMPI-A norms, as it was for the MMPI-2. Both the MMPI-A and MMPI-2 norms were developed using the same target distribution, which ensured percentile equivalence across the two forms. This means that as a person ages, his or her MMPI-A and MMPI-2 T scores can be compared directly.

Several scale-level advantages are apparent on the new MMPI-A. Like the MMPI-2, continuity between the original instrument and the MMPI-A was maintained for the original validity scales, the standard scales, MAC-R, and supplementary scales Anxiety (A) and Repression (R). Scales 5 and 0, which were quite long on the original instrument and on the MMPI-2, were shortened on the MMPI-A without significant psychometric cost. Whereas continuity was maintained with the original scales of the MMPI, the new features of the MMPI-2 were not simply assumed to work with adolescents. More specifically, the MMPI-2 Content Scales were reexamined to determine their appropriateness for adolescents and then submitted to similar rational and statistical procedures using adolescent samples (Williams et al., 1992). Similarly, the MMPI-A contains VRIN and TRIN scales developed specifically by Tellegen and his colleagues for adolescents. The concluding section of this chapter describes these scales.

Finally, descriptors for the MMPI-A scales are based on data from adolescent normative and clinical samples (Butcher et al., 1992; Williams et al., 1992). These descriptors are presented separately by gender, because, like Hathaway and Monachesi (1963), we found some differences between the genders. Clinicians, for the first time, will have available clinically relevant scale descriptors based on adolescent responding (not adult responding) presented separately by gender and by normative and clinical settings. These descriptors are presented in Chapter 10 for the validity, standard, and supplementary scales, and in Chapter 11 for the Content Scales.

The MMPI-A has several other substantive interpretation advantages, as indicated in Table 9-3. One norm set is provided, which will greatly reduce the number of idiosyncratic strategies for adolescents. The same cut-off score for clinical interpretations (i.e., T score of 65) is recommended for the MMPI-A and MMPI-2. Clinicians with expertise in MMPI-2 interpretation will be able to use their skills with the new instrument. Clinicians are also advised to consider moderately elevated scales in the 60-64 T-score range on the MMPI-A as possibly yielding significant descriptors. More precise interpretive guidelines are presented in the following two chapters.

Highlight Summary: The MMPI-A Scales

From its inception, the MMPI has been used with both adults and adolescents. It is essentially an adult-derived instrument, adopted without modifications in its basic structure (i.e., item content or scales), for younger test-takers. Problems in using the MMPI with adolescents have been apparent over the years, leading to different interpretive strategies. However, even given the problems that have been identified over the years, the MMPI's reliability, validity, and utility in assessing psychopathology in adolescents have been demonstrated.

Many of the difficulties in using the instrument with adolescents were addressed during the restandardization of the MMPI. In addition to obtaining contemporary normative and clinical samples, improvements were made in the items and scales to make it more relevant for younger people. This concluding summary describes the primary scales from the MMPI-A used to interpret an adolescent's profile. Included are descriptions of changes made in the original MMPI versions of these scales and comparisons with the MMPI-2 version.

MMPI-A Validity Indicators

MMPI validity scales and indicators have long been recognized as a unique advantage of the MMPI over many other measures of psychopathology and personality. Because the MMPI, MMPI-A, and MMPI-2 are based on self-report, it is crucial to first know the attitude of the person completing these inventories before interpreting his or her other scores. The accuracy of an MMPI interpretation is dependent upon the degree to which the individual responds honestly to the MMPI item pool in providing a self-description. If an individual distorts his or her answers to MMPI items, the precision of the interpretation can be compromised.

While many see a person's willingness to be honest as imperative in interpreting content-based measures, individuals who distort their answers also constrain the validity of the empirically derived standard scales. Because of this, Hathaway and his colleagues included validity indicators in the original instrument that were maintained in the MMPI-A and MMPI-2. These indicators address whether the individual is overly defensive and unwilling to admit to having psychological problems, responds inconsistently, misunderstands items, or exaggerates psychological symptoms and problems.

Proper administration and instructions are effective in controlling response sets that can compromise the accuracy of an MMPI-A interpretation (see Chapter 2). However, even after ensuring that a young person has the necessary reading level for the instrument (sixth grade), understands the purpose of the testing, and knows that he or she will be given feedback about the MMPI-A interpretation, there are times when adolescents distort their responses. The MMPI-A validity indicators are useful in detecting those individuals. Table 9-4 describes the MMPI-A validity indicators, including comparisons with MMPI and MMPI-2.

Scales L, F, K, and the Cannot Say validity indicator were included on the original instrument. They were developed in studies using adult subjects and used without any change when the original MMPI was administered to adolescents. On the MMPI-A some revisions were made, most notably in the F scale. In addition to its different item content for the MMPI-A, the F scale was divided into two subscales so that the validity of the entire booklet could be assessed. The changes in F are described in more detail in the following chapter. The MMPI-2 also introduced two other measures of MMPI profile validity (Chapter 3) that were included on the MMPI-A, the inconsistency measures VRIN and TRIN. Use of each of these measures on the MMPI-A is described in Chapter 10.

Table 9-4. The MMPI validity indicators

Name	Abbreviation	Number of Items		
		MMPI	**MMPI-A**	**MMPI-2**
Cannot Say indicator	? or Cs	Varies	Varies	Varies
Lie scale	L	15	14	*
Defensiveness scale	K	30	*	*
True Response Inconsistency scale	TRIN	NA	21 item pairs	20 item pairs
Infrequency scale	F	64	66	60
Infrequency subscale 1	F_1	NA	33	NA
Infrequency subscale 2	F_2	NA	33	NA
Variable Response Inconsistency scale	VRIN	NA	42 item pairs	45 item pairs

*Indicates item content identical with original MMPI.

NA Not available on this version of the instrument.

MMPI-A Standard Scales

For almost 50 years the MMPI standard scales have been the basis of interpretations for both adults and adolescents. These scales were empirically developed using samples of adult psychiatric patients contrasted with adult control subjects who were visitors to the University of Minnesota hospitals (see Chapter 4). They were never adapted or adjusted when used with adolescents. For the most part, the standard scales were included in the MMPI-A without substantial revisions to maintain continuity with the original instrument.

There were a few exceptions to the general rule of maintaining continuity between the MMPI and MMPI-A standard scales, including the item deletions and wording improvements described above. Table 9-5 summarizes the item-level differences on the MMPI, MMPI-A, and MMPI-2 for the standard scales. The general exceptions to the continuity rule for the standard scales included the deletion of the items that were deleted from the MMPI-2 because of their objectionable content, the inclusion of 70 rewritten items, as well as several item/scale changes that are unique to the MMPI-A (i.e., stating youthful activities and behaviors in the present tense, not in the past tense as in the MMPI and MMPI-2; shortening the instrument by deleting items from longer scales; and deleting developmentally inappropriate or objectionable content).

Even with these changes, most of the MMPI-A standard scales have either very minor or no changes. Scales 3, 6, 7, and 9 have the same item content on all three versions of the instrument. Two MMPI-A standard scales have the same content as the MMPI-2 (scales 1 and 2). Scale 1 lost one objectionable item, "I have no difficulty in starting or holding my bowel movements," on the newer versions of the instrument. Scale 2 lost three items about religious practices and beliefs on the restandardized versions. Two MMPI-A standard scales (4 and 8) differ from the MMPI-2 standard scales by only one item. "My sex life is satisfactory" was

Table 9-5. The MMPI standard scales

Scale	Original Name	Abbreviation	Number of Items		
			MMPI	MMPI-A	MMPI-2
1	Hypochondriasis	Hs	33	32	*
2	Depression	D	60	57	*
3	Hysteria	Hy	60	**	**
4	Psychopathic Deviate	Pd	50	49	**
5	Masculinity-Femininity	Mf	60	44	56
6	Paranoia	Pa	40	**	**
7	Psychasthenia	Pt	48	**	**
8	Schizophrenia	Sc	78	77	**
9	Hypomania	Ma	46	**	**
0	Social Introversion	Si	70	62	69

*Indicates items identical with MMPI-A.

**Indicates item content identical with original MMPI.

dropped from both scales 4 and 8 because of its objectionable content for adolescents and because it did not have the same psychological meaning for adults and adolescents.

Only two of the MMPI-A basic scales (5 and 0) changed by more than one or two item deletions, which was done to shorten the instrument. These scales were rather long on the original MMPI at 60 items for Mf and 70 items for Si. They were shortened without reducing their reliability or validity. Examples of scale 5 item deletions included those with limited face or content validity (e.g., "I used to like drop-the-handkerchief;" "I liked 'Alice in Wonderland' by Lewis Carroll"); those with objectionable content (e.g., "I believe there is a Devil and a Hell in afterlife"); developmentally inappropriate content (e.g., "I have never had any breaking out on my skin that has worried me"); and developmentally objectionable content (e.g., "I am strongly attracted by members of my own sex;" "I have never indulged in any unusual sex practices"). Examples of scale 0 item deletions include those with limited face or content validity (e.g., "I would like to be a singer;" "I am embarrassed by dirty stories") and those with objectionable content (e.g., "I have had no difficulty starting or holding my urine"). Interpretive guidelines for these scales, including use of their subscales (i.e., the Harris-Lingoes and Si subscales), are provided in Chapter 10.

MMPI-A Supplementary Scales

Over the years a number of additional scales were developed for the MMPI. Very few of these supplementary scales were studied adequately to recommend their use in interpreting adolescents' profiles. In fact, only three of the original supplementary scales were among the "protected scales" when the MMPI Adolescent Project Committee took on the task of reducing the Form TX booklet from 704 items to the 478-item MMPI-A booklet (Butcher et al., 1992). Those three scales included the MacAndrew Alcoholism scale (MAC-R), and two of the factor scales (Anxiety and Repression). Many of the other MMPI scales and indexes have not been adequately studied with adolescent samples to recommend their use in adolescent clinical interpretations. A new supplementary scale, Immaturity (Imm), was introduced in the MMPI-A. Research on its validity will be helpful in establishing the contribution it makes to interpretation.

The MAC-R includes 49 items, the same total on the MMPI and MMPI-2 versions of this scale. However, four of the MAC-R items do not overlap with either the MMPI or MMPI-2 versions. The MMPI-A Anxiety Scale retains 35 of the 39 items in the two adult versions. The Repression scale has 40 items on the MMPI and MMPI-2 and 33 items on the MMPI-A. Chapter 10 describes how to use these scales in interpreting an adolescent's profile, as well as introducing two new alcohol-and drug-problem scales (the Alcohol and Drug Problem Acknowledgment Scale [ACK] and the Alcohol and Drug Problem Proneness Scale [PRO]) that are unique to the MMPI-A.

MMPI-A Content Scales

The MMPI-A and MMPI-2 Content Scales were developed using similar procedures and theoretical perspectives, although with different age-appropriate samples. They have many similarities, but do not overlap exactly. Table 9-6 compares the two sets of content scales. Some of these scales differ by very few items (A-anx and ANX; A-cyn and CYN), whereas others have much less overlapping content (A-fam and FAM). One MMPI-2 scale changed substantially on the MMPI-A and was renamed (ASP became A-con). Three scales are unique to the MMPI-A because their content is not developmentally relevant for adults (A-las, A-sch, A-aln). Likewise, three MMPI-2 scales are not included on the MMPI-A (FRS, WRK, TPA). Many of the items used to develop the MMPI-2 WRK and TPA scales were not included in the adolescent experimental booklet because of limited relevance. Although most of the FRS items were available to develop this scale for adolescents, several of its items appeared only on FRS. Since there were other anxiety measures available on the MMPI-A, FRS was dropped from the booklet to help achieve the goal of shortening the MMPI-A.

The MMPI-2 and MMPI-A Content Scales contribute to the uniqueness of these new versions of the MMPI. This is particularly true of the adolescent scales since this is the first time a full set of scales has been developed and normed for adolescents. Chapter 11 provides interpretive rules for these new Content Scales, illustrates how to integrate MMPI-A information into an interpretive report, and concludes with an integrated MMPI-A case example.

Table 9-6. Comparison of the MMPI-A and MMPI-2 Content Scales

MMPI-A Scale	MMPI-A Abbreviation	MMPI-2 Scale	MMPI-2 Abbreviation	Number of Items		
				MMPI-A	MMPI-2	Overlap
Adolescent-Anxiety	A-anx	Anxiety	ANX	21	23	20
Adolescent-Obsessive-ness	A-obs	Obsessiveness	OBS	15	16	12
Adolescent-Health Concerns	A-hea	Health Concerns	HEA	37	36	34
Adolescent-Depression	A-dep	Depression	DEP	26	33	25
Adolescent-Bizarre Mentation	A-biz	Bizarre Mentation	BIZ	19	23	17
Adolescent-Anger	A-ang	Anger	ANG	17	16	11
Adolescent-Cynicism	A-cyn	Cynicism	CYN	22	23	21
Adolescent-Alienation	A-aln	NA	NA	20	NA	NA
Adolescent-Conduct Problems	A-con	Anti-Social Practices	ASP	23	22	7
Adolescent-Low Self-Esteem	A-lse	Low Self-Esteem	LSE	18	24	18
Adolescent-Low Aspirations	A-las	NA	NA	16	NA	NA
Adolescent-Social Discomfort	A-sod	Social Discomfort	SOD	24	24	21
Adolescent-Family Problems	A-fam	Family Problems	FAM	35	25	15
Adolescent-School Problems	A-sch	NA	NA	20	NA	NA
Adolescent-Negative Treatment Indicators	A-trt	Negative Treatment Indicators	TRT	26	26	21
NA	NA	Fears	FRS	NA	23	NA
NA	NA	Type A	TPA	NA	19	NA
NA	NA	Work Interference	WRK	NA	33	NA

Note: NA indicates the scale is not available on this version.

Chapter 10

Interpreting the MMPI-A Validity, Standard, and Supplementary Scales

There are many similarities between the new MMPI-A, its predecessor, the MMPI, and its counterpart for adults, the MMPI-2. These similarities will allow those already familiar with the original MMPI and the restandardized MMPI-2 to adapt readily to the newest version of the instrument. Those with less familiarity with the MMPI and MMPI-2 can gain an understanding of these instruments in the earlier chapters of this book. This understanding is important because the MMPI-A is a modification of the MMPI and MMPI-2 for younger test-takers.

This chapter and the one following highlight the features of the MMPI-A used in generating clinical interpretations of young people's MMPI-A profiles. Chapters 1 and 9 provide additional background on the development of the MMPI-A, brief summaries of the use of the MMPI with adolescents, research from the MMPI Restandardization Project used in developing the MMPI-A, and an overview of the MMPI-A scales. Readers interested in more detail than is provided in those chapters can consult other publications from the MMPI Restandardization Project's work with adolescents (e.g., Butcher et al., 1992; Williams et al., 1992; Williams & Butcher, 1989a, 1989b) and earlier reports about the use of the original MMPI with adolescents (e.g., Archer, 1984, 1987; Hathaway & Monachesi, 1963; Marks et al., 1974; Williams, 1986). The present chapter focuses on the validity, standard, and supplementary scales. Of the MMPI-A scales these overlap the most with the original MMPI. Chapter 11 presents interpretive guidelines for the MMPI-A Content Scales and describes an interpretive strategy for the MMPI-A.

MMPI-A Validity Indicators

There are six primary measures on the MMPI-A designed to evaluate whether a response style was used that would compromise the validity of an adolescent's self-report. In some cases, as in extremely inconsistent responding (e.g., an all-false pattern), the response style is so problematic that the entire profile is declared invalid. The individual simply did not comply with the test instructions by providing an accurate self-description using the MMPI-A items. In other examples (e.g., a defensive attitude), the profile can be interpreted with adjustments, taking into consideration the response style used by the young person.

MMPI-A validity measures can be grouped into two primary categories: 1) measures of defensiveness and inconsistent "yea/nay-saying"; and 2) mea-

Table 10-1. Cs interpretative guidelines for the MMPI-A

☐ Cs scores ≥ 30 are significant and indicative of profile invalidity. MMPI-A profiles with ≥ 30 omissions should not be used to generate interpretive statements, except in the circumstances described below or if the adolescent can be encouraged to complete the omitted items.

☐ If Cs omissions occur after item 350, the validity and standard scales can be interpreted. The supplementary and MMPI-A Content Scales should not be interpreted with significant omissions after item 350.

☐ Possible reasons for high Cs responding:

Limited understanding of items or reading difficulty
Irrelevant item content
Defensiveness
Carelessness
Indecisiveness
Depression, fatigue

sures of random or inconsistent responding. These measures were described earlier for the MMPI-2 in Chapter 3. We will consider their use with adolescents in this section and include case illustrations.

Measures of Defensiveness and Inconsistent "Yea/Nay-Saying"

Cannot Say Score

The Cannot Say score (abbreviated by either ? or Cs) is not a scale, but simply a count of items either left unanswered or marked both true and false by the young person. Because Cs items are not scored (i.e., they are omitted from the test), a large number of them can lead to lower scores on the MMPI-A scales. Cs raw scores greater than 30 are interpreted as indicating profile invalidity.

The number of Cs items can be decreased by encouraging the individual to answer previously omitted items. If it is not possible to have the young person complete the omitted items, the psychologist should determine where on the answer sheet the items were omitted. If the omissions occurred after the first 350 items on the MMPI-A, the validity and standard scales can be interpreted because all their items appear in items 1-350. However, the MMPI-A Content Scales and the supplementary scales will be missing items and should not be interpreted.

A young person may have a number of reasons for omitting items on the MMPI-A. The test interpreter should attempt to evaluate which reasons are likely to apply to the particular individual. One of the best ways to determine this is in an interview with the young person about his or her opinion of the MMPI-A and how she or he responded to the items. Some adolescents will indicate they left out a few items because they did not understand the meaning or because they considered them irrelevant to their life experiences. Carelessness, poor reading skills, or indecision also account for omitted items. Very depressed individuals may not have the energy to complete an MMPI-A. An overly defensive test-taking attitude is also related to high Cs responding. The interpretive report should address which of these reasons likely accounts for the individual's score. Guidelines for Cs interpretations are provided in Table 10-1.

Lie Scale

Hathaway and Monachesi (1953a) indicated that the 15 MMPI Lie scale (L) items detected any naïve attempt by a young person to put himself or herself in a favorable light, particularly with reference to personal ethics and social behavior. Individuals with high L scores were thought to be trying, sometimes unconsciously, to answer all the MMPI items in ways that denied even relatively minor flaws or weaknesses. Individuals who scored high on L were seen as fairly naïve and claiming excessive virtue. One L item, about voting in elections, was dropped from the MMPI-A because it did not function as intended with adolescents (see Chapter 9, p. 207).

The L scale, rationally developed to detect a naïve and virtuous presentation of self using the MMPI item pool, alerts the interpreter to the presence of this response set. A T-score elevation in the shaded area on the profile (60-64) suggests a moderate elevation on L requiring a cautionary statement in the interpretive report. Greater certainty of a problematic response set is indicated with higher elevations (i.e., T scores $\geq$ 65). An MMPI-A L score in these ranges, coupled with flat MMPI-A profiles (i.e., no standard, content, or supplementary scale T scores $\geq$ 60) should be interpreted as a defensive profile, not as the absence of significant psychopathology. However, when adolescents with this defensive test-taking attitude also achieve clinical elevations on the standard, content, or supplementary scales, problems are presented. The interpretation of elevated L scores (T score $\geq$ 65) can be enhanced by using the TRIN scale (see below).

The validity data presented in the MMPI-A manual (Butcher et al., 1992) support interpreting the L scale as a measure of naïve defensiveness in adolescents. The higher their L score, the less likely the MMPI-A normative subjects were to be doing well in school. High L adolescents in clinical samples were less likely to act-out, in keeping with responses indicating a high moral or ethical code. Table 10-2 provides the interpretive rules for L-scale elevations.

K Scale

The K scale was also developed to identify attempts to deny psychopathology and present an overly favorable picture by individuals with non-test evidence of significant psychopathology (i.e., those in clinical settings). It is similar to L in its purpose of identifying individuals who are defensive and not candid. The utility of K is setting-dependent, having been developed with clinical, not normal samples. Hathaway and Monachesi (1953a) indicated that K was developed as a correction for scores on five of the clinical scales (i.e., scales 1, 4, 7, 8, 9). However, the K correction was not routinely employed when the test was used with adolescents, since its use as a correction factor had not been validated in this age range. The original adolescent norms presented by Marks et al. (1974) did not include the K correction. Nor is the K correction included in the new MMPI-A norms.

Table 10-2. L interpretive guidelines for the MMPI-A

☐ T scores ≥ 65 signify a high elevation on L indicative of a potentially problematic and defensive response set.

☐ T scores of 60-64, inclusive, on L are moderately elevated, suggestive of a possibly defensive response set.

☐ Absence of psychological problems should not be assumed with an elevated L score and normal-limits scale scores.

☐ Elevated MMPI-A scales should be interpreted in the presence of elevated L scores.

☐ The TRIN scale can be used to determine if indiscriminate "nay-saying" accounts for the elevated L score.

☐ Descriptive statements:
  • Naïve and virtuous presentation of self
  • Unwilling to admit to relatively minor flaws
  • Claiming high moral and ethical code
  • Somewhat unlikely to act-out
  • Possible "nay-saying" response set (use TRIN to rule out)

Table 10-3. K interpretive guidelines for the MMPI-A

☐ T scores ≥ 65 signify a high elevation on K indicative of the presence of a potentially problematic defensive response set.

☐ T scores of 60-64, inclusive, on K are moderately elevated, suggestive of a possible defensive response set.

☐ The TRIN scale can be used to determine if indiscriminate "nay-saying," or false responding, accounts for the elevated K score, or alternatively if indiscriminate "yea-saying," or true responding, accounts for a very low K score.

☐ MMPI-A profiles should not be declared uninterpretable based solely on elevated K scores.

☐ The K correction is *not* used for any MMPI-A scale.

☐ Absence of psychological problems should not be assumed with an elevated K score and normal-limits scale scores.

Little research is available about K-responding in adolescents. As we mentioned before, it is not used as a correction for defensiveness on the MMPI-A. Its validity for adolescents remains to be demonstrated. Few descriptors were found for the adolescent normative or clinical samples (Butcher et al., 1992). Elevated T scores (i.e., in the shaded range of the profile or those ≥ 65) should include a cautionary statement about the possibility of a defensive test-taking attitude. The TRIN scale should be used to clarify elevations on K (see below). However, an adolescent's MMPI-A profile should not be invalidated solely on the basis of K. Table 10-3 summarizes the interpretive guidelines for K.

True Response Inconsistency Scale

The True Response Inconsistency scale (TRIN) is a measure of inconsistent responding developed by Tellegen (1988) for the MMPI-2 and adapted for the

Table 10-4. TRIN interpretive guidelines for the MMPI-A

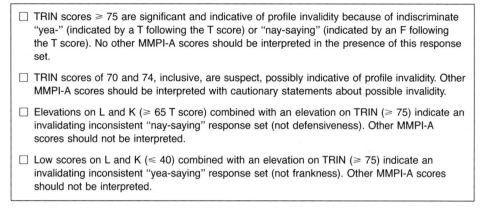

☐ TRIN scores ≥ 75 are significant and indicative of profile invalidity because of indiscriminate "yea-" (indicated by a T following the T score) or "nay-saying" (indicated by an F following the T score). No other MMPI-A scores should be interpreted in the presence of this response set.

☐ TRIN scores of 70 and 74, inclusive, are suspect, possibly indicative of profile invalidity. Other MMPI-A scores should be interpreted with cautionary statements about possible invalidity.

☐ Elevations on L and K (≥ 65 T score) combined with an elevation on TRIN (≥ 75) indicate an invalidating inconsistent "nay-saying" response set (not defensiveness). Other MMPI-A scores should not be interpreted.

☐ Low scores on L and K (≤ 40) combined with an elevation on TRIN (≥ 75) indicate an invalidating inconsistent "yea-saying" response set (not frankness). Other MMPI-A scores should not be interpreted.

MMPI-A. Like its companion VRIN, the MMPI-A TRIN was developed from the MMPI-A item pool and with adolescent samples (Tellegen, 1991). The MMPI-2 TRIN scale was not simply transferred to the MMPI-A, although there are some overlapping items on the two versions.

TRIN assesses the tendencies toward indiscriminate "yea-saying" (true-response inconsistency) or "nay-saying" (false-response inconsistency). All TRIN T scores are equal to or greater than 50. T scores above 50 are followed by a T or F (e.g., 61T, 72F), indicating a true or false pattern of inconsistencies. The TRIN scale can be used for two purposes. First, elevations on TRIN clearly distinguish indiscriminate "yea-" or "nay-saying" from the patterns obtained by adolescents seen in clinical settings. Tellegen (1991) indicates that MMPI-A TRIN elevations ≥ 75 T score are more common among randomly generated true- or false-response biased protocols than in a sample of adolescents tested in clinical settings and should be considered highly suspect. T-score elevations of 70-74 on TRIN are also quite unusual in clinical settings with adolescents and may indicate an invalidating, indiscriminate "yea-" or "nay-saying" tendency. Although future studies may lead to revisions of these cut-off scores, our current recommendation is to invalidate an adolescent's MMPI-A profile if TRIN ≥ 75 T score and to treat TRIN elevations between 70-74 as possibly indicative of an invalid record. A feedback interview with the adolescent respondent may help the psychologist determine if "yea-" or "nay-saying" was used, particularly for scores in the 70-74 range.

TRIN can also be helpful in refining the interpretation of elevations on L or K. Since all the L items and all but one K item are keyed false, a tendency toward "nay-saying" may cause elevations on L and K that do not reflect a defensive test-taking attitude. Instead, elevations on L and K coupled with an elevation on TRIN indicate an inconsistent "false" response pattern, not necessarily defensiveness.

Traditionally, low scores on L and K are interpreted as indicating openness and a willingness to admit to problems or difficulties. For example, low K scores are seen as similar to high F scores, indicating a degree of frankness and self-criticism. We did not include these descriptors of low scores in the interpretive

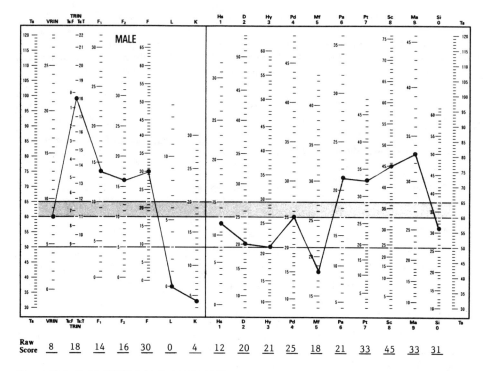

Figure 10-1. Russ. MMPI-A basic scales profile

rules for the MMPI-A L and K scales because the meaning of low scores on these scales for adolescents has not been adequately investigated. However, those whose interpretation of low L and K scores on the MMPI-A follows the traditional interpretations used with adults must rule out indiscriminate "yea-saying" on the basis of the TRIN score before interpreting a low score on L or K as indicative of openness and a self-critical attitude. Likewise, indiscriminate true responding ("yea-saying") may cause a lowering of scores on L and K. Table 10-4 presents a summary of the TRIN interpretive guidelines.

Case Examples

Russ, a 15-year-old white adolescent, produced the MMPI-A validity and standard scale profile seen in Figure 10-1. Russ's profile illustrates the use of the validity indicators covered to this point. His Cs raw score was 0, indicating that he omitted no items (i.e., there are no concerns about profile validity from this measure). L and K are quite low, possibly indicating a willingness to describe problems, which is reflected in high elevations on several standard scales. If one looks only at the original MMPI validity scales (Cs, L, K, as well as F, which is described in the next section), no validity problems are indicated. The rest of Russ's MMPI-A could be interpreted according to the original validity scales. However, Russ's extreme score on TRIN (T score = 99T) indicates an invalid response pattern of inconsistent "yea-saying." Given this TRIN score, his other MMPI-A scale scores are highly suspect and should not be interpreted.

The psychologist working with Russ provided feedback about his MMPI-A profile and was able to verify that Russ used this invalid response style. The psychologist began the feedback session in the following manner:

"Do you remember the MMPI-A? What did you think of it?"

"How could I forget? Where did you get all those dumb questions? I didn't think I'd ever finish it!" (Suggests boredom or impatience as possible contributors to his invalid response set.)

"We ask so many questions to be sure to cover all the areas where kids may be having trouble. Did you have any problems understanding the questions?"

"Nope." (Suggests his inconsistent "yea-saying" was not due to reading comprehension problems.)

After explaining a little background about the MMPI-A validity and standard scales, the psychologist continued the interview:

"So, we use these scales on this side of the profile to tell whether there are any problems with how you responded to the items. On your profile, all these scales look pretty good, no problems—except this one (pointing to TRIN). Do you have any idea what problem this scale might be measuring?"

"Not a clue."

"Well, sometimes people get a little bored with the test and begin answering the items true without even reading them. That's what this high score says might have happened to you."

"Wow! How did it do that? How do you know that?"

Feedback sessions like Russ's can be useful in providing additional confirmation of information obtained from the MMPI-A. It is important to maintain respect for the young person and present the information in a non-accusatory fashion. In the above example, although Russ is told that his profile is invalid, he is not demeaned for responding inconsistently. Instead, the psychologist appears to be trying to understand him using an instrument that has several features that interest Russ. Now that he has a greater understanding of the MMPI-A, Russ may agree to a retest and respond more consistently.

Figure 10-2, 16-year-old Lisa's MMPI-A profile, illustrates how TRIN can confirm the interpretation of elevated L and K scores as indicative of a defensive testing attitude. Although Lisa had 0 Cs responses, her L score of 64 is a moderately high elevation, along with a very high elevation on K at 78. However, before calling her profile defensive, inconsistent "nay-saying" should be ruled out. Her TRIN score of 54T indicates that she did not inconsistently endorse items as false. Her interpretation should include statements about her unwillingness to admit to even minor flaws, that she responded to MMPI-A items somewhat naïvely, and presented herself as highly virtuous. She subscribes to a high moral standard or ethical code and may, in fact, be less likely than other adolescents to act-out, although this cannot be assumed. Her defensive test-taking attitude is evident in what is an unusually submerged standard-scale

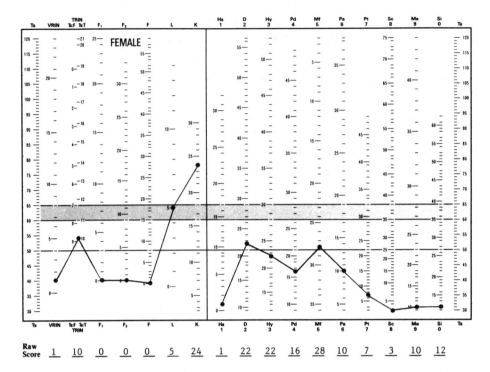

Figure 10-2. Lisa. MMPI-A basic scales profile

profile for an adolescent. Because of her defensive test-taking attitude, this sub-merged profile should not be interpreted as "normal." Lisa did not produce el-evations on any of the other MMPI-A supplementary or Content Scales. This is a result of her defensiveness, not an indication of psychological health.

Measures of Random or Inconsistent Responding

F Scale

The Infrequency scale (F) was described by Hathaway and Monachesi (1953a) as somewhat the opposite of the L scale. Unlike high L scores with their sugges-tion of faking good, persons with high F scores seem to be attempting to present themselves in a bad light or "faking bad" (perhaps unconsciously). As with high L scores, there were several reasons for elevated F scores. Hathaway and Monachesi (1953a) suggested that some adolescents simply could be overly can-did. The F score could be elevated if the young person, for any reason, failed to answer carefully or consistently, as for those who cannot read well enough. Reading comprehension problems were particularly relevant in using the inven-tory with adolescents. The F score could also be high if the young person an-swered carelessly or made random or facetious responses to the items. A final hypothesis for elevated F scores was general maladjustment of a severe nature.

Interpretation of the F scale with adolescents has been difficult over the years. It consistently appears as one of the more elevated scales in adolescent clinical settings. Archer (1987) reports that using the conservative adult standard to define MMPI profile invalidity (i.e., F $\geq$ 16 raw score) seems unwarranted with adolescents, given the large number of cases that would be defined as invalid (i.e., between 34% to 44% in clinical settings) and the meaningful descriptors found associated with high F responding in adolescents (e.g., acting-out behaviors, psychotic symptoms). Gallucci (1987) suggests that the F scale does not measure motivation to exaggerate symptoms or a "plea for help" in adolescents; rather, elevated F scores are a feature of the modal adolescent MMPI profile.

Williams et al. (1992) noted that despite the straightforward development of F (i.e., items were selected on the basis of endorsement frequencies, see Chapter 3), no attempts were made before the MMPI Restandardization Project to refine the F scale for adolescents. When the endorsement percentages of F scale items were examined for the adolescent normative sample (Butcher et al., 1992) many of the items did not act as infrequency indicators with adolescents. Because of this, a new version of the F scale was developed for the MMPI-A.

F is the only basic scale with items substantially different on the MMPI-A from those on the MMPI and MMPI-2. Items were selected for the adolescent version of F if they were endorsed in the deviant direction by no more than 20% of the adolescent normative sample. As with adults, high F responding in adolescents can be due to inconsistent responding, reading problems, faking bad, exaggeration, or serious psychopathology. Its external correlates from both normative and clinical samples and across genders, reported in the MMPI-A manual, provide support for this interpretation (Butcher et al., 1992). F is divided into two subscales on the MMPI-A, F_1 assessing the first half of the booklet (up to item 236) and F_2 assessing the second half (beginning with item 242).

For the original MMPI, T scores on F greater than 90 or 100 were frequently used to declare adolescent profiles invalid. Data used in developing the MMPI-A indicated the need for a different interpretive strategy, partly because of the availability of the new VRIN inconsistency measure (Tellegen, 1991). On the MMPI-A, suspicions about a problematic response pattern begin with elevations in the 80-89 T-score range for F and its subscales. Greater likelihood of a potential problematic response set occurs with elevations of 90 or greater, and profiles elevated above 110 on F should be considered invalid.

The test interpreter must determine which of several possible reasons for elevations on F apply to a given adolescent. Again, an MMPI-A feedback session can assist, along with a review of the adolescent's records or information from school about potential reading problems. Reasons for exaggeration of symptoms or malingering can also be examined by interview with the young person and parents. Extra-test evidence of severe psychopathology (e.g., observations of hallucinations) would suggest that severe symptoms likely account for the elevated F. Careless or inconsistent responding should be ruled out as an explanation of an elevated F score using the VRIN scale described below.

An elevation on F_2 affects the Content Scales and supplementary scales because their item content continues into the second half of the booklet. An elevation on F_2, but not F_1, suggests that boredom may have occurred during the administration of the second half of the booklet, perhaps resulting in random responding. Since all the items for the standard scales occur in the first half of

Table 10-5. F interpretive guidelines for the MMPI-A

☐ T scores ≥ 110 indicate an invalid MMPI-A that should not be interpreted.

☐ T scores ≥ 90 on F, F_1, or F_2 signify very high elevations indicative of a potentially problematic response set. Possible reasons for this elevation have to be determined using the list of interpretive statements provided below.

☐ T scores of 80-89, inclusive, on F, F_1, and F_2 indicate high elevations suggestive of a potentially problematic response set. The interpreter should determine the probable reasons for this moderate elevation.

☐ T scores between 60-79, inclusive, on F, F_1, or F_2 indicate moderate elevations reflecting endorsement of a variety of symptoms.

☐ Elevated T scores on F should be carefully evaluated using VRIN to determine if significant inconsistency invalidates the record.

☐ Elevations on F_2, but not F_1, indicate that the potentially problematic response set occurred in the second half of the booklet, not the first. In this instance, the Content Scales and supplementary scales will be affected more than the standard scales.

☐ Interpretive statements for elevated F scores:
- Possible random responding
- Possible reading problems
- Possible faking bad
- Possible exaggeration of symptoms
- Possible serious psychopathology

---

the booklet, an F_2 elevation in the absence of an F_1 elevation does not signify potential problems for interpreting these scales. VRIN cannot be used to resolve score discrepancies between F_1 and F_2. Interpretive rules for F and its subscales are summarized in Table 10-5.

Variable Response Inconsistency Scale

The Variable Response Inconsistency scale (VRIN), like TRIN, is a new validity scale (Tellegen, 1988), also developed for the MMPI-2, for assessing inconsistent responding. Inconsistency occurs if an adolescent responds carelessly or randomly. Because the content of the F scale includes symptoms of severe psychopathology, an elevated F could indicate severe psychopathology. However, an elevated F can also reflect carelessness. The VRIN scale, unlike F, is not confounded with severe psychopathology; it is elevated only in the case of carelessness.

The MMPI-A VRIN scale was developed from the MMPI-A item content and with adolescent samples using the same procedures that resulted in the MMPI-2 VRIN scale (see Chapter 3 for further discussion of its development). Although there is item overlap, the MMPI-2 and MMPI-A VRIN scales are not identical. Elevations on VRIN are defined similarly as for TRIN (Tellegen, 1991). MMPI-A VRIN T-score elevations equal to or greater than 75 are highly suspect and far more common in a sample of randomly generated records than in adolescent clinical samples. VRIN T-score elevations of 70-74 are also quite unusual in clinical adolescents and may indicate random inconsistent responding. We recommend using a VRIN elevation of 75 to declare a profile invalid because of incon-

Table 10-6. VRIN interpretive guidelines for the MMPI-A

☐ VRIN scores ≥ 75 are significant and indicative of profile invalidity because of marked inconsistency. No other MMPI-A scales should be interpreted in the presence of this response set.

☐ VRIN scores of 70-74, inclusive, are suspect, possibly indicative of profile invalidity. Other MMPI-A scores should be interpreted with cautionary statements about the possibility of significant response inconsistency.

☐ Interpretation of moderate to high elevations on F can be refined by using VRIN scores to rule in (VRIN ≥ 75) or rule out (VRIN ≤ 69) inconsistent responding.

sistent responding. A VRIN score between 70-74 is suspect and its interpretation should include a cautionary statement about potentially invalidating inconsistency. It is possible that future research on VRIN may indicate a need to revise these provisional cut-off values.

VRIN can also be used to refine the interpretation of elevated F scores. An elevated F score paired with a VRIN score of 75 or higher indicates a degree of inconsistency that invalidates the MMPI-A profile. Such a profile should not be interpreted. A VRIN score of 70-74, along with an elevated F score, raises the possibility that the adolescent was responding inconsistently to the MMPI-A. Appropriate cautionary statements should be included in the interpretive report. VRIN guidelines are provided in Table 10-6.

Case Examples

Jodi's MMPI-A profile presented in Figure 10-3 illustrates the use of VRIN to detect inconsistent responding. Jodi, a 14-year-old white girl, had no significant elevations on F, F_1, and F_2. This level of elevation on F in a clinical setting is not at all unusual and would not invalidate the protocol under the guidelines for interpreting the MMPI for adolescents. However, her extremely elevated VRIN score of 93 indicates that she responded highly inconsistently to the MMPI-A item content. Her scores on the MMPI-A scales would not provide an accurate interpretation of her problems.

On the other hand, 16-year-old Elizabeth's profile (Figure 10-4) does not provide evidence of inconsistency, even in the presence of fairly extreme elevations on F and its subscales (i.e., F of 82, F_1 of 95, F_2 of 90). With a VRIN score of 40, the test interpreter can rule out inconsistency as contributing to the F elevations. Likewise, her low scores on L (38) and K (33) cannot be attributed to inconsistent yea-saying with her average TRIN score. It is likely that Elizabeth has significant symptomatology given her scores on the validity and standard scales. Although there is a possibility of some exaggeration of symptoms or even faking bad, the likelihood of severe psychopathology is great.

All-True Response Set

Figure 10-5 shows the pattern of MMPI-A validity- and standard-scale scores that is obtained when an individual endorses all the items on the MMPI-A true. Note that the all-true response set produces an average VRIN score. However,

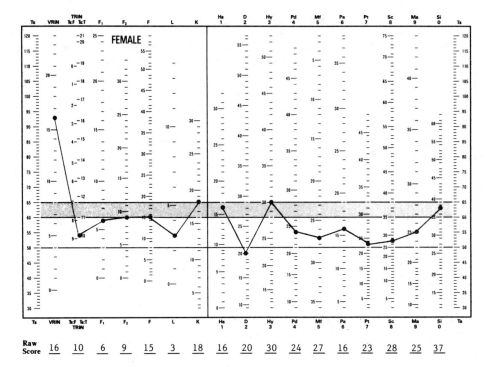

Figure 10-3. Jodi. MMPI-A basic scales profile

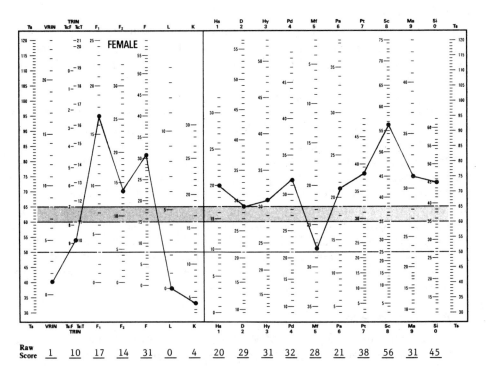

Figure 10-4. Elizabeth. MMPI-A basic scales profile

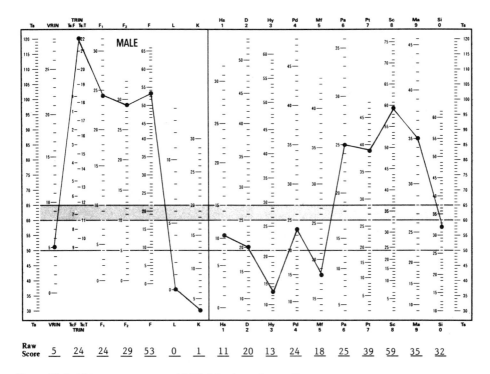

Raw Score	Ts	VRIN	TₑF TₑT TRIN	F₁	F₂	F	L	K	Hs 1	D 2	Hy 3	Pd 4	Mf 5	Pa 6	Pt 7	Sc 8	Ma 9	Si 0	Ts
	5	24	24	29	53	0	1	11	20	13	24	18	25	39	59	35	32		

Figure 10-5. All-true response set. MMPI-A basic scales profile

TRIN, F, F₁, and F₂ are extremely elevated under this condition. The TRIN T score of 120T and raw score of 24 indicate that all of the TRIN items were endorsed as true, regardless of their content. Because many of the items on the F scale and its subscales (F₁, F₂) are keyed in the true direction, these scores are also highly elevated. L and K produce very low scores in this condition, since their items are keyed in the false direction (i.e., all L items are keyed false; all but one K item are keyed false). The standard-scale profile does show some variation in scale scores. Only scales on the right side of the profile (i.e., those measuring more psychotic-like disturbances) are extremely elevated. Scales on the left side of the profile (i.e., the neurotic and acting-out scales) are not elevated under this response condition.

All-False Response Set

Figure 10-6 presents the profile that would emerge if an individual endorses all MMPI-A items as false. Again, the VRIN score produced under this condition is average. However, the TRIN score is highly elevated, as are L and K. The F scores themselves do not suggest a problematic response set. The opposite pattern occurs for the standard scales compared with the all-true response seen in Figure 10-5. Here, the neurotic scales (scales 1, 2, and 3) are extremely elevated, with all other scales below a T score of 60.

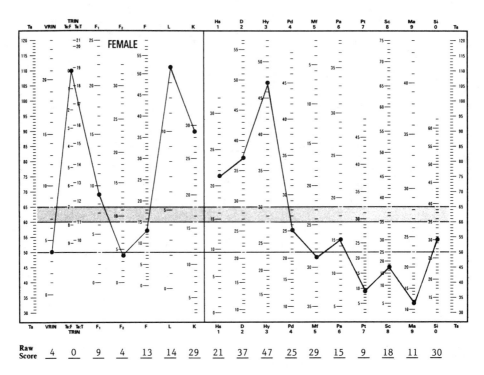

Raw Score	4	0	9	4	13	14	29	21	37	47	25	29	15	9	18	11	30

Figure 10-6. All-false response set. MMPI-A basic scales profile

MMPI-A Standard Scales

The MMPI-A clinical scales, Hs, D, Hy, Pd, Pa, Pt, Sc, and Ma, are interpreted using uniform T scores generated from the adolescent normative sample (Butcher et al., 1992), similar to the process described in Chapter 4 for interpretations of the MMPI-2. However, it is important to note that MMPI-2 uniform T scores generated from the adult normative sample are never used with MMPI-A interpretations. The MMPI-A Mf and Si scales, like their MMPI-2 counterparts, use linear T scores, which, for the MMPI-A, are generated from the adolescent normative samples. MMPI-A interpretation will be much more straightforward than interpretation of the original instrument, which required integrating information from both adult and adolescent norm sets (see Chapter 9). The MMPI-A profile has a shaded area between T scores of 60-64 to indicate moderate elevations. Interpretations can be made for scale scores in this range, although less confidence is placed in interpretations of scores in these lower ranges. A T score of 65 is the cut-off for determining clinically significant elevations. Standard scale scores above a T score of 65 indicate a greater probability that the scale descriptors apply to the individual.

Elevations on the standard scales can vary across scales, settings, and gender. Table 10-7 highlights this variability. The MMPI-A normative and clinical samples were used to describe these differences. The MMPI-A normative sample was selected from school settings and the percentages in Table 10-7 for

Table 10-7. Percentages of elevated standard scale scores in the MMPI-A normative and clinical samples

| | | Scales | | | | | | | | | |
		1	2	3	4	5	6	7	8	9	0
Normative	Boys	9.4	10.2	7.2	11.3	6.0	9.4	8.8	8.4	10.1	6.8
	Girls	9.3	9.7	10.3	8.0	7.4	10.7	10.1	9.4	7.2	7.5
Clinical	Boys	5.2	8.8	3.8	33.8	3.1	11.4	14.0	11.0	18.3	5.7
	Girls	11.9	19.8	19.5	33.8	4.8	18.8	19.1	15.0	10.2	9.9

Note: Elevations are defined as T scores $\geqslant$ 65. Normative boys = 805 subjects, normative girls = 815 subjects, clinical boys = 420 subjects, clinical girls = 293 subjects.

the normative boys and girls estimate the frequency of the standard-scale elevations in general population school settings. The MMPI-A clinical samples were drawn from alcohol-and other drug-problem treatment units, psychiatric inpatient units, day treatment centers, and a special school for emotionally or behaviorally disturbed adolescents. The percentages in Table 10-7 estimate the frequency of standard-scale elevations in these types of treatment facilities for boys and girls. These percentages can be used to determine how unusual a given adolescent's standard-scale elevations are. For example, a boy seen in a treatment setting with elevations on scales 1, 3, and 0 would be unlike most boys in these facilities and might not respond to a standard treatment protocol designed for boys with elevations on the more frequently occurring scales 4 and 9.

As we indicated in Chapter 4, because the standard scales are empirically derived, their scores do not tell whether a given individual has more or less of the construct being assessed. For example, a higher elevation on scale 8 does not indicate that the person is more "schizophrenic" than those with lower scores. Rather, an elevated score indicates a higher probability that the given individual is more like the criterion group of schizophrenic adult patients than those with lower scores. Over the years, descriptors have been found to be associated with the various scale elevations and code types. Again, an elevated T score on these scales indicates the greater probability that an individual has the characteristics associated with scale elevations. This meaning of scale elevation should be kept in mind when writing interpretive statements based on the elevations from the standard scales. As we will see in the next chapter, the MMPI-A Content Scales are based on somewhat different meanings of scale elevations.

Because the MMPI-A standard scales parallel the MMPI-2 standard scales, information presented in Chapter 4 about scale-development procedures and the content of each scale remains relevant for the MMPI-A. This information will not be repeated in this chapter. Rather, the reader is referred to Chapter 4 for a description of the development and content of each scale. The same Harris-Lingoes subscales described in Chapter 4 for the MMPI-2 are relevant in interpreting the MMPI-A standard scales. The MMPI-A manual presents T scores based on the adolescent normative sample to facilitate use of the Harris-Lingoes subscales. In the original MMPI, adolescent-based T scores were not available for subscales.

Table 10-8. General guidelines for interpreting the MMPI-A standard scales

☐ Use only the age-appropriate MMPI-A T scores for generating interpretive statements. A clinically significant elevation is defined as an MMPI-A T score ≥ 65. Scores in this range indicate a high probability that the scale correlates or descriptors apply to the individual. However, recognize that not all scale correlates are likely to apply to any given young person.

☐ Moderately elevated scores are indicated in the shaded area of the profile, 60-64, inclusive. Interpretations can be made for scores in this range, although less confidence should be placed on interpretations based on these scores.

☐ Use the Harris-Lingoes and Si subscales to select which descriptors to highlight for standard scales with elevations ≥ 60. Only subscales that are elevated ≥ 65 should be interpreted.

☐ Place the most confidence in descriptors that replicate across scales and come from scales with the highest elevations. See Chapter 11 for suggestions for resolving possible inconsistencies in scale correlates.

Another set of useful subscales, developed by Ben-Porath et al. (1989), facilitate interpretation of Si elevations and are also described in Chapter 4.

The Harris-Lingoes and Si subscales are used to refine interpretations on elevated standard scales (i.e., T scores ≥ 60). Subscales, perhaps because of their length, are less reliable measures than the standard scales, and only those Harris-Lingoes or Si subscales with elevations above a T score of 65 should be used to generate hypotheses. Because many of the standard scales have quite heterogeneous item content, these subscales can be used to determine which of the many possible descriptors to emphasize in the interpretation (see the description of Ann's interpretation in Chapter 4 p. 96 for an example). As indicated in Chapter 4, problems with item overlap in the Harris-Lingoes subscales can detract from their usefulness. Table 10-8 summarizes the general guidelines for interpreting the MMPI-A standard scales.

Although the development and content are similar on the standard scales for the MMPI, MMPI-2, and MMPI-A, new empirical descriptors are available for these scales derived from adolescent samples. This information, taken from the MMPI-A manual and combined with correlates derived from earlier studies of adolescents, particularly those of Hathaway and Monachesi, is used to develop the following interpretive guidelines for use of the standard scales with adolescents. Integrating information from the standard scales with other MMPI-A scales will be covered in the next chapter.

Scale 1—Hypochondriasis (Hs)

Consistent with research on the original MMPI (e.g., Wrobel & Lachar, in press), moderate to high adolescent scorers on Hs have a wide variety of physical complaints across several body systems. Because Hs is a very homogeneous scale, no subscales were needed to facilitate its interpretation. Although moderate scores could occur in individuals with known physical illness, more extreme scores suggest a greater preoccupation with health than occurred in patients with known illnesses. In addition to its association with numerous physical complaints, several personality and behavioral descriptors are associated with eleva-

Table 10-9. Scale 1 interpretive guidelines for the MMPI-A

☐ Elevated Hs scores suggest a greater preoccupation with health than occurs in patients with known illnesses. However, adolescents with chronic illnesses sometimes score in the moderately elevated range.

☐ Elevations are unusual for boys in clinical settings and although also somewhat uncommon in girls, they are more likely than in boys. Because these young people are unlike others in treatment settings, program modifications may be necessary to accommodate their differences.

☐ Boys and girls in school settings with elevated scores are unlikely to be doing well, and may report increasing problems, particularly academic. Girls are also likely to report more family problems, including marital discord and financial difficulties.

☐ Parents of clinical boys describe their sons as having many internalizing problems in addition to their physical complaints, including being fearful, guilt-prone, withdrawn, perfectionistic, clinging, and worrying.

☐ Clinical girls may have eating problems in addition to their numerous physical complaints.

tions on scale 1. Boys and girls in school settings who scored high on scale 1 were unlikely to be doing well in school and reported increasing problems, particularly academic. Girls were also likely to report more family problems, including parental marital disagreements and financial difficulties. It was an unusual elevation for boys in clinical settings. Although also somewhat uncommon in girls, scale 1 elevations were more likely for girls than for boys (see Table 10-7). Parents of high-scoring boys seen in clinical settings described their sons as having many internalizing problems in addition to their physical complaints, including being fearful, guilt prone, withdrawn, perfectionistic, clinging, and worrying. Girls seen in clinical settings might have eating problems along with their numerous physical complaints. Interpretive guidelines are summarized in Table 10-9.

Scale 2—Depression (D)

Scale 2 is a measure of depression for both adolescents and adults. Hathaway and Monachesi (1953a) reported that high scorers were likely to feel unsure of themselves and the future, often saying they were sad and blue. They suggested that high scores normally occurred when individuals were in trouble so that the absence of a higher score from someone in trouble was an unexpected sign indicating that the person was not responding in the modal way. Because high D scores indicated personal unhappiness and dissatisfaction, elevations on D were seen to be a good prognostic indicator for psychotherapy and their absence indicative of a person not particularly motivated for change. Archer, Gordon, Giannetti, and Singles (1988) replicated the prognostic significance of elevated D scores in adolescents (i.e., therapists rated high D adolescents as being more willing to seek advice, open in discussing feelings, and more motivated to make change than other adolescents).

The validity of scale 2 as a measure of depression on the MMPI-A was confirmed, its correlates including an association with suicidal ideations and gestures and indications of depression in hospital records (Butcher et al., 1992). More significant correlates were found for girls on scale 2 than for boys (Butcher et al., 1992). Wrobel and Lachar (in press) also found more D correlates for girls than boys with an outpatient sample using the original MMPI. Although this could indicate differential validity for measuring depression with this scale in girls and boys, it is also possible that the relatively lower prevalence of high elevations for boys could account for this as well (Table 10-7). Girls in school settings with high scale 2 scores are unlikely to be doing well in school and more likely to report that their parents' arguments have worsened. The parents of clinical boys described their sons as guilt-prone, fearful, withdrawn, perfectionistic, clinging, and worrying. Similar correlates were found by Archer et al. (1988) with a combined gender sample using the original MMPI D Scale. High-scoring girls in clinical settings were less likely to engage in acting-out behaviors, including sexual promiscuity, and much more likely to be socially withdrawn, with few or no friends, have eating problems, somatic concerns, and low self-esteem (Butcher et al., 1992). Social withdrawal and limited friendships were also characteristic of girls in Wrobel and Lachar's (in press) study. Earlier research established D as an inhibitory scale in both boys and girls (Hathaway & Monachesi, 1963). Adolescents in Archer et al.'s combined gender samples were likely to have low self-esteem, eating problems, somatic complaints, and sleep difficulties.

The Harris-Lingoes subscales can be used to clarify scale 2 elevated scores in adolescents. The MMPI-A provides age-appropriate T scores for D_1—Subjective Depression, D_2—Psychomotor Retardation, D_3—Physical Malfunction, D_4—Mental Dullness, and D_5—Brooding. Only those Harris-Lingoes scores greater than or equal to 65 should be interpreted in the presence of an elevated D score. Table 10-10 summarizes the interpretive guidelines for scale 2.

Scale 3—Hysteria (Hy)

Scale 3's validity with adolescents was more limited than some of the other standard scales in the MMPI-A clinical sample (Butcher et al., 1992). Hathaway and Monachesi (1963), in their general population sample, found that adolescents with scale 3 as the highest point in their profile were more likely to come from an upper socioeconomic level and more likely to be above average in intelligence. Their study did not include somatic complaints as possible correlates. Only elevated Hy scores in girls were shown to be associated with somatic complaints in the MMPI-A clinical sample, again perhaps owing to its low prevalence in boys (Table 10-7). Normative boys were more likely to have problems in school, and boys in the clinical sample were likely to have a history of suicidal ideas and/or gestures. However, in a smaller, combined-gender clinical sample tested with the original MMPI, Archer et al. (1988) found evidence that elevated Hy adolescents were likely to react to stress with somatic complaints, be seen as passive-dependent, unpredictable, and having limited friendships. Wrobel and Lachar (in press) found parent-reported paralysis associated with high scores in outpatient boys. The Harris-Lingoes subscales (i.e., Hy_1—Denial of Social Anxiety,

Table 10-10. Scale 2 interpretive guidelines for the MMPI-A

☐ Elevations on D indicate depression and possible suicidal ideations and gestures in both boys and girls in clinical settings.

☐ Girls in school settings with elevated scores are unlikely to be doing well in school and are more likely to report a worsening in parents' arguments.

☐ Parents of clinical boys describe their sons as guilt-prone, fearful, withdrawn, perfectionistic, clinging, and worrying.

☐ High-scoring clinical girls are less likely to engage in acting-out behaviors (including sexual promiscuity) and much more likely to be socially withdrawn, with few or no friends, to have eating problems, somatic concerns, and low self-esteem.

☐ Somatic complaints and sleep difficulties are possible correlates, based on research from the original MMPI.

☐ Because high scale 2 scores indicate personal unhappiness and dissatisfaction, they are seen to be a good prognostic indicator for psychotherapy and their absence indicative of a person not particularly motivated for change. Research on the original MMPI suggests high D adolescents may be more willing to seek advice, more open in discussing feelings, and more motivated for change.

☐ Several Harris-Lingoes subscales can be used to clarify elevated scale 2 scores. Only Harris-Lingoes T scores ⩾ 65 should be interpreted. The following are content-based hypotheses for each of the D subscales:

D_1—Subjective Depression (29 items)

- Worried, nervous, brooding
- Feelings of inadequacy, low self-esteem
- Lassitude, listlessness, fatigue
- Dysphoric, unhappy
- Sleep difficulties
- Concentration problems
- Social withdrawal
- Apathetic
- Denial of feeling contentment
- Other symptoms of depression like crying spells and poor appetite

D_2—Psychomotor Retardation (14 items)

- Denial of strong affect
- Apathetic
- Lassitude, listlessness, low energy
- Social withdrawal
- Fear of losing his or her mind
- Denial of persistence on a task

D_3—Physical Malfunction (11 items)

- Denial of good health
- Multiple somatic complaints like nausea, vomiting, hay fever, convulsions
- Weakness
- Poor appetite, fluctuating weight

Table 10-10. Scale 2 interpretive guidelines for the MMPI-A, continued

---

D_4—Mental Dullness (15 items)

- Concentration, memory problems
- Limited self-confidence
- Lassitude, listlessness
- Apathetic
- Denial of ability to work as well as before
- Feels tension

D_5—Brooding (10 items)

- Desires to be as happy as others, denies feeling happy
- Denial of concern about what happens to him or her
- Denies that life is worthwhile
- Broods, is hurt by criticisms
- Fears losing mind
- Crying spells
- Feels useless

Hy_2—Need for Affection, Hy_3—Lassitude-Malaise, Hy_4—Somatic Complaints, Hy_5—Inhibition of Aggression) can be consulted to refine interpretations of elevated scores on scale 3. Table 10-11 provides a summary of scale 3 interpretive rules.

Scale 4—Psychopathic Deviate (Pd)

Scale 4 is one of the more prominent scales on adolescents' profiles (e.g., Archer, 1987; Marks et al., 1974; Williams & Butcher, 1989b). It is by far the most frequently elevated scale in the MMPI-A clinical sample, with over one-third of the boys and girls scoring greater than or equal to a T score of 65 (Table 10-7). Hathaway and Monachesi (1953a) indicated that high scorers are often young, delinquent, affected little by remorse, and not particularly responsive to censure or punishment. They are more likely to commit asocial acts, be in conflict with their families, and have more extensive social problems.

Numerous descriptors have been found to be associated with high scale 4 responding in adolescents. Even in general population samples (e.g., Hathaway & Monachesi, 1963), many behavior problems are associated with high Pd responding (e.g., family problems, poor school adjustment, poor school conduct, school dropout, teacher-predicted delinquency, and emotional problems). More recent studies demonstrate that high scale 4 adolescents are more likely to be involved with the use of alcohol or other drugs (e.g., Archer et al., 1988; Butcher et al., 1992). The problems become more severe when one is sampling from clinical settings where elevated Pd responding is also associated with school, family, and legal problems (Butcher et al., 1992; Wrobel & Lachar, in press). Parents of these young people describe numerous externalizing behavior problems including lying, cheating, stealing, temper outbursts, and aggression. In the MMPI-A clinical samples, high scale 4 responding also is associated with having been physically abused and a run-away (boys) or sexually abused and active (girls).

Table 10-11. Scale 3 interpretive guidelines for the MMPI-A

☐ Elevations on Hy may be associated with somatic complaints, particularly in girls.

☐ Boys in school settings are more likely to have problems in school; clinical boys could be assessed for a history of suicidal ideation and/or gestures.

☐ Previous research on the MMPI with adolescents suggests that elevations may be associated with the tendency to develop physical problems as a reaction to stress or paralysis in outpatient boys.

☐ The Harris-Lingoes subscales with elevations ≥ 65 can be consulted to refine interpretations of scale 3 elevations. The following are content-based interpretive statements:

Hy_1—Denial of Social Anxiety (6 items)

- Denies concerns about shyness
- Denies difficulties in meeting or talking to others
- Denies his or her behavior is influenced by others
- Denies not speaking unless spoken to

Hy_2—Need for Affection (12 items)

- Denies negative feelings or thoughts about others or concerns about his or her motivations
- Denies that others exaggerate problems to elicit sympathy or use unfair means
- Denies that others lie or that it's best to trust no one
- Denies getting mad easily or engaging in oppositional behavior
- Indicates being friendly with others even if they do things considered wrong

Hy_3—Lassitude-Malaise (15 items)

- Denial of good health
- Denies feeling fresh and rested in mornings, reports tiring quickly, having fitful and disturbed sleep
- Reports sadness, denies happiness
- Weak
- Restless
- Apathetic
- Poor appetite
- Problems with staying on task
- Denies home life is pleasant

Hy_4—Somatic Complaints (17 items)

- Headaches or tight band around head
- Fainting or dizzy spells, balance problems
- Hand shaking or twitching muscles
- Eye problems
- Cardiovascular symptoms like chest pains, heart pounding, shortness of breath
- Other symptoms like a lump in the throat, nausea, hot flashes, general pains

Hy_5—Inhibition of Aggression (7 items)

- Dislikes crime articles, mystery or detective stories
- Denies irritability or feeling like swearing
- Denies that what others think does not bother him or her
- Denies that seeing blood does not bother him or her
- Denies problems with indecisiveness

Run-away behavior was found for high-scoring outpatient girls by Wrobel and Lachar (in press). Therapists rated adolescents with elevated Pd scores as less motivated and open in therapy sessions (Archer et al., 1988).

A major problem in interpreting high scale 4 responding is determining which of the many possible descriptors apply to a given adolescent. Inspection of the Harris-Lingoes subscales is one way to resolve these questions. The Harris-Lingoes subscales that more clearly specify its content include: Pd_1—Family Discord, Pd_2—Authority Problems, Pd_3—Social Imperturbability, Pd_4—Social Alienation, and Pd_5—Self-Alienation. As we will discover in Chapter 11, use of the MMPI-A Content Scales is also very helpful in further interpreting high Pd responses. Table 10-12 provides a summary of interpretive guidelines for Pd.

Scale 5—Masculinity/Femininity (Mf)

Hathaway and Monachesi (1953a) described scale 5 as a measure of masculinity or femininity of interests. They suggested that high scores in boys or men were indicative of general feminine interests as they appeared in contrast to the average man. According to Hathaway and Monachesi (1953a) high scores in girls and women indicated masculine interests. However, we described several conceptual and methodological problems in the development of the Mf scale which suggest that caution be used in deriving interpretive statements for elevations on Mf. These issues were discussed in Chapter 4 and we will not repeat them here. The interpretation of scale 5 is less straightforward than the interpretation of most of the other MMPI-A scales. We suggested that Mf could be dropped from the MMPI-A without a significant loss of information (Williams & Butcher, 1989a). Perhaps studies will be done which will indicate its usefulness in clinical assessment. Until that time, scale 5 is best considered a general personality measure, not an indicator of psychopathology. Correlates for high-scoring boys and girls differ, and are described separately. Mf elevations are rare in the MMPI-A clinical sample, with only 3% of the clinical boys and 4.8% of the clinical girls elevated at or above a T score of 65 (T scores for Mf are linear, not uniform). Surprisingly, as indicated in Table 10-7, elevated scores (T scores ⩾ 65) are slightly more common, although still unusual, in the MMPI-A normative sample (6% boys; 7% girls).

Boys

High-scoring boys endorse an unusual pattern of stereotypically feminine interests. Hathaway and Monachesi (1963) suggested that high-scoring scale 5 boys were more intelligent, had higher grades, and better school adjustment than those who had lower scores. They also demonstrated scale 5 as an inhibitory scale for acting-out behaviors in both boys and girls. High scale 5 boys were less likely to be engaged in delinquent behavior or to receive predicted delinquency and emotional-problem ratings from teachers. This inhibitory effect of scale 5, although not found in our first descriptor study using contrasting high- and low-scoring groups (Williams & Butcher, 1989a) was weakly demonstrated in the correlation analyses presented in the MMPI-A manual (Butcher et al.,

Table 10-12. Scale 4 interpretive guidelines for the MMPI-A

☐ In both school and clinical settings elevations on scale 4 are associated with numerous behavior problems, including family difficulties, poor school adjustment, poor school conduct, school dropout, suspensions, and failures.

☐ Use of alcohol or other drugs is likely in those with elevated scores. These problems become more extreme in young people seen in clinical settings.

☐ Difficulties with the law and juvenile authorities increase in clinical settings.

☐ Parents of clinical adolescents report many externalizing behavior problems, including lying, cheating, disobedience, impulsivity, stealing, swearing, associating with a bad peer group, poor school work, alcohol and other drug use, being remorseless, secretive, threatening, cruel, argumentative, jealous, moody, demanding of attention, and having temper outbursts and feelings of persecution.

☐ Therapists of clinical boys also report similar, very problematic acting-out behaviors, as well as moodiness, attention-seeking, resentfulness, clinging to adults, and beliefs that they are evil or deserving of severe punishment.

☐ Boys are more likely to have a history of running away from home and could be evaluated for a history of being physically abused. Previous MMPI research suggests that clinical girls may also run away.

☐ Clinical girls could be evaluated for having a history of sexual abuse and are likely to be sexually active.

☐ Based on the original MMPI, adolescents with high Pd may be less motivated and open in therapy sessions.

☐ The Harris-Lingoes subscales ≥ 65 can be used to resolve which of the many descriptors to emphasize in an elevated Pd score:

Pd_1—Family Discord (9 items)

- Quarrelsome, unpleasant family life
- Fault-finding family members
- Little love and companionship
- Desire to leave home
- Parental disapproval of peer group
- Parental disapproval of future career choice

Pd_2—Authority Problems (8 items)

- Admits stealing, problematic sexual behavior, or being in trouble with the law
- Dislikes school or reports school behavior problems
- Denies being influenced by others or giving up easily in arguments
- Denies being disgusted when criminals are freed by smart lawyers

Pd_3—Social Imperturbability (6 items)

- Denies concerns about shyness or difficulties meeting or talking to others
- Denies being easily downed in arguments or that his or her behavior is influenced by others

Table 10-12. Scale 4 interpretive guidelines for the MMPI-A, continued

---

Pd$_4$—Social Alienation (12 items)

- Feels misunderstood by others
- Feels mistreated by others
- Projects blame onto others
- May have been disappointed by love
- Frequently is regretful about his or her behavior
- Denies that his or her behavior is influenced by others
- Denies not being bothered by what others think of him or her

Pd$_5$—Self-Alienation (12 items)

- Self-critical, regretful
- Desires being as happy as others, denies feeling happy
- Hopeless and apathetic
- Problems with concentrating on a task or job
- Admits peculiar and strange experiences
- May report excessive alcohol use

1992). However, given the relatively weak negative association with acting-out behaviors, along with Hathaway and Monachesi's caveat that the inhibitory scales were less salient than the excitatory scales, an inhibitory effect for scale 5 should not be overinterpreted in an adolescent's profile.

Girls

High-scoring girls endorse many unusual stereotypically masculine-oriented or "macho" interests. According to Hathaway and Monachesi's findings (1963), these girls were less likely to be highly intelligent and more likely to have lower grades in school. High-scoring scale 5 girls were also less likely to have poor school conduct or receive teacher-predicted delinquency and emotional-problem ratings. Elevated scores in the MMPI-A normative girls were also related to poor grades, but, inconsistent with Hathaway and Monachesi's (1963) findings, were associated with behavior problems and suspensions from school. Behavior problems were also apparent in the clinical girls including suspensions, history of learning disabilities, and therapists' ratings of acting-out behaviors. The therapists were likely to describe these girls as oppositional, resentful, having poor anger control, easily upset, moody, lying, stealing, and having other problem behaviors. Similar correlates of aggressive behaviors were found by Wrobel and Lachar (in press) for outpatient girls with the original MMPI.

The inconsistencies in the descriptors from Hathaway and Monachesi (1963) and more contemporary studies (Butcher et al., 1992; Wrobel & Lachar, in press) indicate problems with interpreting this scale for adolescent girls. The inconsistencies could be due to differences in the samples and analyses used by each (i.e., the earlier descriptors are derived for normative girls when scale 5 is the highest point in the profile, whereas the MMPI-A descriptors are based on correlational analyses of raw scores across the entire range of elevations from both

Table 10-13. Scale 5 interpretive guidelines for the MMPI-A

☐ Elevated scores suggest an unusual interest pattern in boys compared with their peers. They endorse interests that seem more stereotypically feminine and deny more stereotypically masculine interests. They may be less likely to act-out. However, if other MMPI-A scales associated with externalizing behaviors are elevated, then a tendency to act-out should not be ruled out on the basis of a scale 5 elevation.

☐ Elevated scores in girls are also unusual and suggest a more stereotypically masculine or "macho" interest pattern. Further research is needed to clarify the interpretation of scale 5 with girls.

---

normative and clinical samples of girls). Unless further research clarifies its interpretation for girls, we recommend making only the cautious interpretive statements provided in Table 10-13.

Scale 6—Paranoia (Pa)

Hathaway and Monachesi (1953a) reported an interesting gender difference in the interpretation of scale 6 elevations. Moderate elevations from girls in juvenile delinquency facilities were seen to be a personality asset in that, perhaps because of their greater tendency for interpersonal sensitivity, delinquent girls with Pa elevations made special efforts to be liked and appreciated. On the other hand, Hathaway and Monachesi (1953a) noted that boys with high scores on scale 6 dropped out of school early. Wrobel and Lachar (in press) reported only very limited descriptors for Pa in outpatient adolescents. Pancoast and Archer (1988) found that normal adolescents endorsed more scale 6 items than did normal adults, particularly for Pa_1 (Persecutory Ideas), a Harris-Lingoes subscale. The other Harris-Lingoes subscales for refining interpretations of Pa elevations are Pa_2—Poignancy and Pa_3—Naïveté.

The MMPI-A manual reported a number of school-related problems (behavioral and academic) for both boys and girls in the normative sample with elevations on scale 6 (Butcher et al., 1992). In addition, clinical boys were also described by their parents as being more hostile and withdrawn (i.e., unliked and having poor peer relations, feelings of persecution, immature, destructive, argumentative, and fighting). Their treatment counselors were also likely to describe them as overly dependent, clinging to adults, attention-seeking, resentful, anxious, worried or obsessed, and believing that they were bad and deserving of punishment. The only significant descriptor for clinical girls was a self-reported increase in disagreements with parents. These guidelines are summarized in Table 10-14.

Scale 7—Psychasthenia (Pt)

Although scale 7 as a high point was relatively frequent in Hathaway and Monachesi's (1963) adolescent normative samples, few descriptors were found for Pt elevations, perhaps because their correlates did not include anxiety-based measures. Wrobel and Lachar (in press) indicated that elevated scores in outpa-

Table 10-14. Scale 6 interpretive guidelines for the MMPI-A

☐ Pa elevations are related to both behavioral and academic problems for boys and girls in school settings. They are likely to report more problems than the average young person, including school suspensions and poor grades. Girls may report school failures as well.

☐ Clinical girls are likely to report more disagreements with their parent(s).

☐ Parents of clinical boys describe them as hostile and withdrawn (e.g., being unliked and having poor peer relationships, having feelings of persecution, being immature, destructive, argumentative, and fighting).

☐ Clinical boys' treatment counselors are also likely to describe them as overly dependent, clinging to adults, attention-seeking, resentful, anxious, worried or obsessed, and believing that they are bad and deserving of punishment.

☐ Earlier research with girls in correctional facilities suggests that an elevated Pa may mark a personality asset whereby these girls may have greater interpersonal sensitivity that makes them more likely to make special efforts to be liked and appreciated.

☐ The Harris-Lingoes subscales ≥ 65 can be used to refine elevated Pa interpretations:

Pa_1—Persecutory Ideas (17 items)

- Feels misunderstood by others or punished without cause
- Projects blame onto others
- Feels talked about or that others are trying to control him or her
- Has identified someone who is responsible for his or her problems
- Feels threatened
- May indicate being followed, plotted against, poisoned, or hypnotized

Pa_2—Poignancy (9 items)

- Intensely sensitive
- Feels lonely or misunderstood
- Feels uneasy indoors
- Cries easily
- Denies never having participated in a dangerous, thrill-seeking activity
- Denies that excitement can alleviate "down" feelings

Pa_3—Naïveté (9 items)

- Denies negative feelings or thoughts about others or concerns about their motivations
- Denies that others lie or are honest only because they fear being caught
- Denies oppositional behavior
- May report occasionally thinking about something too bad to discuss

---

tient boys were related to limited self-confidence and to suicidal threats and stealing in girls. Many of the items on scale 7 deal with uncontrollable or obsessive thoughts, feelings of fear and/or anxiety, self-doubts, physical complaints, and concentration difficulties. No subscales were developed for scale 7. The MMPI-A manual indicated that Pt elevations were related to depression and increasing discord with parents in clinical girls and a history of sexual abuse in clinical boys (Butcher et al., 1992). Additional verification of its validity with adolescents would prove useful. Hathaway and Monachesi (1963) speculated that

Table 10-15. Scale 7 interpretive guidelines for the MMPI-A

☐ Correlates have yet to be found for adolescents in school settings with elevated Pt scores. It is possible that the rigid personality style reflective of adult Pt elevations does not become problematic until adulthood.

☐ Clinical girls are likely to be depressed and report more disagreements with parents.

☐ Clinical boys could be evaluated for a history of being sexually abused.

☐ Previous research with the original MMPI suggests that high Pt clinical boys may have limited self-confidence and clinical girls may make suicide threats or steal.

Pt might reflect a rigid personality style that does not become problematic until adulthood, an issue for longitudinal study. Interpretive guidelines are summarized in Table 10-15 for scale 7.

Scale 8—Schizophrenia (Sc)

Hathaway and Monachesi (1963) found several problems associated with high Sc responding in their general population sample. High scorers on scale 8 were more likely to have low intelligence and few achievements in school. They became school drop-outs and had family problems. Similar findings are reported in the MMPI-A manual (Butcher et al., 1992). High 8 normative boys and girls are more likely to have behavior problems in school and lower grades. Normative boys reported school suspensions. Normative girls with high scale 8 scores were less likely to report outstanding personal achievement, and they reported weight gain.

In the MMPI-A clinical samples, elevated Sc scores in both genders were associated with a history of having been sexually abused. Adolescents with elevations on scale 8 could be assessed for the possibility of abuse. Girls, regardless of setting, were quite likely to report an increase in disagreements with parents.

The clinical boys had more correlates than the girls. Their therapists were likely to describe them as exhibiting psychotic behaviors (e.g., hallucinations, delusions, ideas of reference, peculiar speech and mannerisms, grandiose beliefs). Their parents reported many internalizing behavior problems, including fears, withdrawal, being guilt-prone, perfectionism, worries, and clinging behaviors. The parents also reported several somatic complaints (e.g., stomach aches and nausea, headaches, dizziness) in these high 8 boys. Finally, their hospital records were likely to note low self-esteem as a problem. Archer et al. (1988) found similar correlates in combined gender samples for the original MMPI Sc scale. In addition, high 8 adolescents were rated as having a poor prognosis for psychotherapy because they were distrustful of their therapists, less motivated for therapy, reluctant to discuss feelings, and had a poor relationship with their therapist. They were also slow to adjust to treatment routines and expectations. Wrobel and Lachar (in press) reported that both genders were seen as different from their peers; outpatient boys were shy, withdrawn, and had low self-confidence; outpatient girls were aggressive, had temper outbursts, acted-out, and threatened suicide. The six Harris-Lingoes subscales for Sc are Sc_1—Social Alienation; Sc_2—Emotional Alienation; Sc_3—Lack of Ego Mastery, Cognitive; Sc_4—Lack of Ego Mastery, Conative; Sc_5—Lack of Ego Mastery, Defective Inhibition; Sc_6—Bizarre Sensory Experiences. A summary of the Sc interpretive guidelines is provided in Table 10-16.

Scale 9—Mania (Ma)

Hathaway and Monachesi (1953a) indicated that scale 9 was related to enthusiasm and energy. High scorers were quite interested in many things and approached problems with animation. When this became abnormal, the person's activity level could lead to antisocial acts or irrational manic behavior. Hathaway and Monachesi (1953a) indicated that young people were normally characterized by a considerable amount of the construct this scale measures, also confirmed later by Pancoast and Archer (1988). However, when adolescents had too much Ma, they became restless and frequently stirred up excitement for excitement's sake alone.

High scale 9 scorers are reported in the MMPI-A manual to be associated with both school and home problems in normal girls. School behavior problems were apparent in the clinical girls, as was less likelihood of participating in social organizations. Academic underachievement was also found to be a descriptor. The only correlate for clinical boys was a notation in their records of having previous experience with amphetamines. Elevations on the original MMPI Ma were also associated with experience with drugs, and these adolescents were also described as having poor motivation for therapy, being less willing to explore feelings, and insensitive to criticism (Archer et al., 1988). However, Wrobel and Lachar (in press) reported few significant scale 9 correlates in an outpatient sample. Harris-Lingoes identified four subscales for elevated Ma scores (i.e., Ma_1—Amorality, Ma_2—Psychomotor Acceleration, Ma_3—Imperturbability, and Ma_4—Ego Inflation). Table 10-17 summarizes the Ma interpretive guidelines.

Scale 0—Social Introversion (Si)

Si is a very strong measure of problems in social relationships in clinical boys and girls (Butcher et al., 1992; Wrobel & Lachar, in press). Elevated Si scores are associated with social withdrawal and low self-esteem in both genders. There were more correlates found for the MMPI-A clinical girls than clinical boys, possibly a result of the slightly higher prevalence of elevated Si responding in the girls compared with boys (Table 10-7). Interestingly, the opposite pattern of significant correlates by gender was reported by Wrobel and Lachar (in press). Clinical girls with high scale 0 scores were likely to have eating problems and reported weight gain, depression, suicidal ideations and/or gestures, and a history of few or no friends. Their therapists were likely to describe them as withdrawn, timid, shy, physically weak and uncoordinated, fearful, and depressed. Therapists saw these girls as unlikely to have interests in heterosexual relationships or to act sexually provocatively. Scale 0 appeared to be an inhibitory scale for girls (i.e., there is a negative association with alcohol or other drug use, delinquent

Table 10-16. Scale 8 interpretive guidelines for the MMPI-A

☐ Both boys and girls in school settings with elevated Sc scores are more likely to have several behavior problems in school and lower grades. Normative boys may also be suspended from school. Normative girls are less likely to have an outstanding personal achievement and more likely to report weight gain.

☐ Elevated Sc scores in clinical settings are associated with a history of having been sexually abused. Adolescents with Sc elevations could be assessed for the possibility of abuse.

☐ Girls, regardless of setting, are quite likely to report an increase in disagreements with parents.

☐ Clinical boys are likely to exhibit psychotic behaviors which may include hallucinations, delusions, ideas of reference, peculiar speech and mannerisms, or grandiose beliefs.

☐ Parents of boys in clinical settings report many internalizing behavior problems, including fears, withdrawal, being guilt-prone, perfectionistic, worried, and exhibiting clinging behaviors. Parents also report several somatic complaints, including stomachaches, nausea, headaches, and dizziness.

☐ Low self-esteem is likely to be a problem in clinical boys.

☐ Research with the original MMPI suggests adolescents with high Sc elevations may have a poor prognosis for psychotherapy because of being distrustful of their therapists, less motivated for therapy, reluctant to discuss feelings, and having a poor relationship with their therapists. They may also be slow to adapt to treatment-unit routines and expectations.

☐ Previous MMPI research suggests clinical boys may be shy and withdrawn and have low self-confidence. Clinical girls may be aggressive, have temper outbursts, act-out, and threaten suicide.

☐ The six Harris-Lingoes subscales for elevated Sc scores and their content-based hypotheses are:

Sc_1—Social Alienation (21 items)

- Family discord, very negative feelings toward family
- Withdrawal, relationship problems
- Feels mistreated, punished without cause
- Feels misunderstood
- Loneliness
- Fearfulness
- Indicates being plotted against

Sc_2—Emotional Alienation (11 items)

- Unhappy, apathetic
- Feels condemned, life is a strain
- Enjoys hurting others, being hurt by others
- Has a death wish
- Fearfulness

Sc_3—Lack of Ego Mastery, Cognitive (10 items)

- Concentration difficulties, memory problems
- Fears losing mind
- Peculiar and strange experiences or thoughts
- Feels things are not real

Table 10-16. Scale 8 interpretive guidelines for the MMPI-A, continued

---

Sc_4—Lack of Ego Mastery, Conative (14 items)

- Apathetic, difficulty staying on task
- Concentration difficulties
- Unhappy
- Feels condemned, life is a strain
- Withdraws into daydreams
- Has a death wish

Sc_5—Lack of Ego Mastery, Defective Inhibition (11 items)

- Uncontrollable urges
- Blank spells
- Emotional outbursts
- Restlessness, excitement
- Fearfulness
- Being touchy

Sc_6—Bizarre Sensory Experiences (20 items)

- Blank spells
- Auditory or olfactory hallucinations
- Speech problems
- Twitching muscles, clumsiness, balance problems
- Paralysis
- Emotional outbursts
- Peculiar and strange experiences
- Hot flashes
- Feeling unreal or that others are hypnotizing him or her

---

behaviors as reported by parents, and other indicators of acting-out). Clinical boys were very unlikely to participate in school activities. Three subscales, developed by Ben-Porath et al. (1989), are available to refine Si interpretations: Si_1—Shyness/Self-Consciousness, Si_2—Social Avoidance, and Si_3—Alienation—Self and Others. Table 10-18 provides the Si interpretive guidelines.

Caution about Using Code Types with Adolescents

Although considerable congruence was demonstrated between codes based on the MMPI-A and original Marks et al. (1974) adolescent norms with adequate code-type definitions (i.e., at least 5 points of definition), interpretation of the MMPI-A based on code types awaits further validation (Butcher et al., 1992; Greene, 1991; Williams et al., 1992; Williams & Butcher, 1989b). Much larger clinical samples of adolescents than have been used in the past (i.e., several thousand) will be needed to validate code-type descriptors for adolescents. Until such validation work is completed, it is more conservative to use scale descriptors in interpreting an adolescent's profile. There is ample support for interpre-

Table 10-17. Scale 9 interpretive guidelines for the MMPI-A

☐ Elevated Ma scores are associated with both school and home problems in girls from school settings. School behavior problems are also apparent in clinical girls as is less likelihood of participating in social organizations at school. Academic underachievement can also be seen in boys.

☐ Experience with drugs like amphetamines is possible, particularly if the individual is a boy.

☐ Work with the original MMPI suggests scale 9 elevations may be related to enthusiasm, interest in many things, and an animated approach to problems. These descriptors frequently characterize the adolescent years, although in extremes may be associated with antisocial acts or irrational, manic behaviors.

☐ Ma elevations for adolescents using the original MMPI suggest a poor motivation for therapy, little willingness to explore feelings, and insensitivity to criticisms.

☐ The four Harris-Lingoes subscales for evaluating elevated Ma scores are:

Ma_1—Amorality (6 items)

- Believes in taking advantage of others
- Identifies with a peer group, indicates peers should agree on a single story in times of trouble
- Enjoys antics of criminals or having criminals freed by smart lawyers

Ma_2—Psychomotor Acceleration (11 items)

- Enjoys excitement
- Restlessness
- Racing thoughts
- Harmful or shocking urges
- Denies ever having participated in a dangerous, thrill-seeking activity
- Feels tension

Ma_3—Imperturbability (8 items)

- Denies social anxiety or discomfort around others
- Denies being irritable even when ill
- Denies being impatient

Ma_4—Ego Inflation (9 items)

- Believes authority figures often do not know as much as he or she does and that they punish without cause
- Intentionally oppositional at times
- Self-confident
- Others get impatient with him or her

tations based on scale descriptors, in contrast to what is available for using code types.

As we indicated in Chapter 5, the code-type interpretive approach is preferred for interpreting MMPI-2 profiles for adults, particularly when the profile is clearly defined and there is sufficient research providing behavioral descriptors for the code type. The code-type interpretive strategy has the advantage of

Table 10-18. Scale 0 interpretive guidelines for the MMPI-A

☐ Si elevations are a strong indicator of problems in social relationships in clinical boys and girls. They are associated with social withdrawal and low self-esteem.

☐ Clinical girls with elevated Si scores are likely to have eating problems and report weight gain, depression, suicidal ideations and/or gestures, and a history of few or no friends.

☐ Therapists of clinical girls are likely to see them as withdrawn, timid, shy, physically weak and uncoordinated, fearful, and depressed. These girls are unlikely to be seen as having an interest in heterosexual relationships or to act sexually provocative.

☐ Elevated scale 0 scores appear to have an inhibitory effect on girls in that they are unlikely to use alcohol or other drugs, have delinquent behaviors reported by their parents, or other acting-out behaviors.

☐ Clinical boys are unlikely to participate in school activities.

☐ Three subscales, developed by Ben-Porath et al. (1989), are available to refine elevated Si interpretations:

Si_1—Shyness/Self-Consciousness (14 items)

- Difficulties meeting or talking to others
- Shy, bashful
- Social anxiety
- Uncomfortable at parties
- Denies being sociable

Si_2—Social Avoidance (8 items)

- Dislikes parties, socials, or dances
- Dislikes and avoids crowds

Si_3—Alienation—Self and Others (17 items)

- Lacks self-confidence
- Distrusts others' motivation
- Easily overwhelmed by difficulties
- Concentration or memory problems
- Disappointed by others
- Impatient with others
- Ruminates
- Desires to be as happy as others

---

producing fewer contradictory descriptors than does the scale-by-scale analysis recommended for the MMPI-A. In Chapter 11 we will provide guidelines for resolving conflicting correlates that can occur when interpreting the MMPI-A.

MMPI-A Supplementary Scales

Alcohol- and Other Drug-Problem Scales

MAC-R

The MacAndrew Alcoholism Scale was revised for both the MMPI-2 and MMPI-A, with four of the original items deleted because of offensive content. In

Table 10-19. MAC-R interpretive guidelines for the MMPI-A

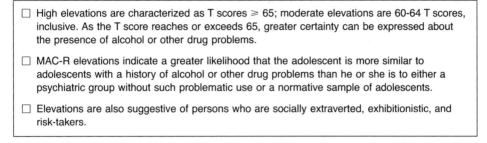

☐ High elevations are characterized as T scores ⩾ 65; moderate elevations are 60-64 T scores, inclusive. As the T score reaches or exceeds 65, greater certainty can be expressed about the presence of alcohol or other drug problems.

☐ MAC-R elevations indicate a greater likelihood that the adolescent is more similar to adolescents with a history of alcohol or other drug problems than he or she is to either a psychiatric group without such problematic use or a normative sample of adolescents.

☐ Elevations are also suggestive of persons who are socially extraverted, exhibitionistic, and risk-takers.

each version the four omitted items were replaced with other items that empirically separated individuals in clinical settings with alcohol- and other drug-use problems from those without a history of such problems. The revised version of the MacAndrew is referred to as the MAC-R. Because normative scores were unavailable for the MacAndrew Scale on the original MMPI, MAC has traditionally been interpreted through the use of raw scores. The same number of items was included on the MAC-R as in the original MAC, to facilitate use of these raw score cut-offs for clinical interpretations. Wolfson and Erbaugh (1984) recommended raw-score cut-offs on the original MacAndrew of 24 for girls and 26 for boys as best distinguishing adolescents in treatment for substance abuse from psychiatric patients and from high-school students. A raw score of 24 for girls equals a linear T score of 60 on the MMPI-A norms, which is the beginning of the shaded area on the profile characterizing a moderately elevated profile. A raw score of 26 for males is the equivalent of a linear T score of 61 on the MMPI-A norms, again indicative of moderate elevation. Both these raw scores are consistent with the interpretation of the possibility of an alcohol- or other drug-use problem. It is likely that clinicians will switch to using linear T scores, rather than raw scores, with the MMPI-A. If the T scores exceed 65, greater certainty can be expressed in the interpretive report about the presence of alcohol or other drug problems.

Elevations on MAC-R indicate a greater likelihood that the young person is more similar to adolescents with a history of alcohol or other drug problems than either a psychiatric sample without such problematic use or a normative sample of adolescents. Over the years, elevations of MAC have been refined to indicate an association with a general tendency toward alcohol or other drug problems, rather than alcoholic tendencies alone. In addition, elevations are suggestive of persons who are socially extraverted, exhibitionistic, and risk-takers. The interpretive guidelines for MAC-R are presented in Table 10-19.

ACK

The Alcohol Drug Problem Acknowledgment scale is a newly developed measure for the MMPI-A (Weed, Butcher, & Williams, in preparation). It is similar to the adult AAS on the MMPI-2 (see Chapter 7). ACK assesses an adolescent's willingness to acknowledge having problematic alcohol or drug use, with its associated symptoms. The scale was developed using a combined rational-empirical scale-construction strategy. Initially items that contained obvious references

Table 10-20. ACK interpretive guidelines for the MMPI-A

☐ High elevations on ACK are T scores ≥ 65; moderate elevations are in the 60-64 T-score range. Elevations on ACK indicate the extent to which the adolescent has admitted to having alcohol or drug problems.

☐ High scores indicate that the young person openly acknowledges using alcohol, marijuana, or other drugs. High scorers report problem use, having harmful habits, and relying on alcohol or other drug use to express true feelings or as a coping strategy. Others may tell them they have a problem with alcohol use, and they may get into fights when drinking.

to alcohol or other drug problems were selected for potential membership. Next, these provisional items were correlated with the remaining MMPI-A items to uncover any other items which, when combined with the provisional problem acknowledgment items, improved discrimination of individuals with known alcohol-drug problem use from those without these problems. Elevations on ACK indicate the extent to which the adolescent has admitted having alcohol or drug problems. Interpretation should begin in the shaded range of the profile (60-64 T scores); increased confidence can be placed on elevations above a T score of 65. These high scores indicate that the young person openly acknowledges having alcohol- and drug-use problems. Table 10-20 summarizes these interpretive guidelines.

PRO

The Alcohol Drug Problem Proneness scale is an empirically derived measure to assess the likelihood of a young person developing an alcohol- or drug-use problem (Weed et al., in preparation). It is similar in construct to the MMPI-2 APS (Chapter 7). PRO was developed by identifying items that significantly differentiated adolescent boys and girls in alcohol and drug inpatient treatment units from adolescents without alcohol or other drug problems who were in psychiatric inpatient treatment or those in the normative sample. The items selected for the final PRO scale were those cross-validating without significant shrinkage. Interestingly, many of the new adolescent-specific items about negative peer-group influences, unavailable on the original MMPI, were related to this construct and are included on PRO. Behavior problems at home and school are also included in PRO's item content. The shaded area indicates moderate elevations, and T scores ≥ 65 indicate high scorers. Elevations suggest a proneness to develop problematic alcohol or drug use. Future studies are needed to examine the relative predictive validity of MAC-R and PRO with adolescents. The interpretive guidelines for PRO can be found in Table 10-21.

Factor Scales

Two scales were derived from a factor analysis of the basic MMPI-A scales. As indicated in Chapter 7, these are the Anxiety (A) and Repression (R) scales. The A scale is based on the first factor that emerges when the MMPI basic scales are factor analyzed. Its 35 items are best characterized as a measure of general maladjustment (the original A scale had 39 items). Individuals with moderately and

Table 10-21. PRO interpretive guidelines for the MMPI-A

☐ High elevations on PRO are T scores ⩾ 65; moderate elevations are 60-64, inclusive.

☐ Elevations suggest a proneness to develop problematic alcohol or drug use.

☐ Item content includes negative peer-group influences, as well as behavior problems at home and school. No obvious items about problematic alcohol or other drug use are included in PRO's content.

☐ Elevations indicate a greater likelihood of belonging to the criterion group of adolescents in alcohol and drug treatment evaluation units than to those in psychiatric inpatient treatment or school settings.

Table 10-22. Factor Scales (A and R) interpretive guidelines for the MMPI-A

☐ High elevations on A and R are T scores ⩾ 65. Moderate elevations are in the 60-64 range, inclusive.

☐ Elevations on A (Anxiety) signify general maladjustment. Individuals with high scores are likely to be in distress, report anxiety, discomfort, and greater emotional upset than most others, although replication of these correlates for adolescents is needed.

☐ High scorers on R (Repression) are characterized as being conventional, submissive, and striving to avoid unpleasantness or disagreeable situations. Again, replication of these correlates for adolescents is needed.

highly elevated scores are likely to be in distress, report anxiety, discomfort, and greater emotional upset, based on studies from adults.

Repression or R is the second factor when the basic MMPI scales are factor analyzed. The original R had 40 items, the MMPI-A version of R has 33 items. Adult high scorers on R are characterized as being conventional, submissive, and striving to avoid unpleasantness or disagreeable situations. Additional research with adolescent samples is needed to determine if these descriptors generalize to those younger.

Highlight Summary: An Adolescent Case

In concluding this chapter, we must turn our attention from Alice. At 18 years of age, Alice could have been administered the MMPI-A, but her psychologist felt her life circumstances would be better assessed with the MMPI-2 item content. The MMPI-A is the only appropriate version of the instrument for our new case, Tony, a 14-year-old black Hispanic eighth grader being evaluated at a special public school for youth with emotional and behavioral problems. Tony's school provided a more structured, therapeutic environment than is available in mainstream schools. The problems leading to Tony's referral included theft (resulting in court-ordered probation), fighting, truancy, and oppositional behavior. He had previously been treated for similar problems in an outpatient mental-health clinic.

Tony's Hispanic ethnicity raises the possibility that English may not be his primary language. Furthermore, his special education placement suggests a greater likelihood of reading comprehension problems. Before administering an MMPI-A in these circumstances, it is important to determine whether the young person has the necessary sixth-grade reading level required by the instrument. In Tony's case, his educational testing records revealed no potential reading difficulties that would preclude administration of the MMPI-A.

MMPI-A interpretations should be made using available diagnostic information, along with any other information known about the young person. However, psychiatric diagnoses were not routinely made for students at Tony's school. Because Tony was part of the MMPI-A clinical sample, he was administered a computerized version of the Diagnostic Interview for Children and Adolescents (DICA, Herjanic & Campbell, 1977). His DICA diagnostic report was consistent with the referral concerns and included the following DSM-III based diagnoses: conduct disorder, socialized, aggressive; oppositional disorder; and marijuana use.

Tony was a bright student, capable of above average work when he applied himself. He reported enjoying his participation in sports and band, and was hoping to participate in a work-study program. However, he had a number of problems in school, including suspension and course and grade failures. His teacher indicated that he frequently did not apply himself and was somewhat inattentive and distractible. He did not like school and was argumentative, disobedient, and disruptive in class. School officials reported that he had a history of gang involvement and assaultive behavior. There were also problems in his family including heavy drinking by his stepfather and possible wife abuse. Tony reported being worried about his mother's safety, along with the safety of himself and his younger sister. Other members of the family also experienced difficulties with the law.

Interpretation of MMPI-A Validity Scales

Tony produced an interpretable MMPI-A profile, with no evidence of an overly defensive response style, indicated by the L and K scales and his zero Cannot Say responses. He was careful and attentive to the task of completing the MMPI-A as revealed by his F and VRIN scores. His F_1 and F_2 scores showed that this cooperative response style was maintained throughout the booklet. His TRIN score provided further support of the validity of his self-report, revealing no tendencies toward inconsistent yea- or nay-saying. This validity pattern indicated that other MMPI-A scores could be used to provide inferences about his behavior and problems.

Interpretation of MMPI-A Standard Scales

Tony's Ma, at a T score of 62, was the only standard scale reaching an interpretable level. Thus, only limited inferences about Tony's behavior can be made based on these scales. His moderate Ma elevation was not unusual for an adolescent, suggesting enthusiasm and possibly higher than average activity level with some tendencies toward acting-out. Academic underachievement and drug use are possible problems. However, the severity of Tony's acting-out problems noted at referral were not reflected in his scores on the standard scales, particularly his low score

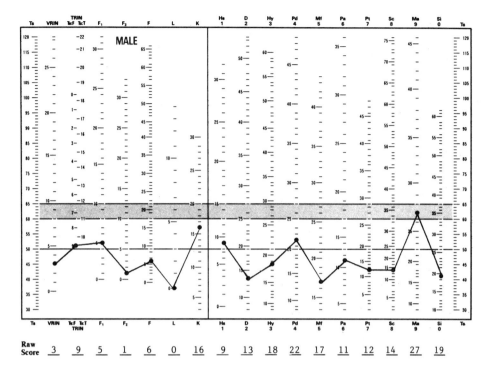

| Raw Score | 3 | 9 | 5 | 1 | 6 | 0 | 16 | 9 | 13 | 18 | 22 | 17 | 11 | 12 | 14 | 27 | 19 |

Figure 10-7. Tony. MMPI-A basic scales profile

on scale 4 (53) and moderate scale 9 elevation. Tony is not likely to be a good candidate for psychotherapy given his moderate Ma score and lack of other indicators of personal distress.

An examination of Tony's scale 9 Harris-Lingoes subscale scores (Ma_1 = 66, Ma_2 = 57, Ma_3 = 62, Ma_4 = 48) (see Figure 10-8) provided another source of inferences about his moderately elevated scale 9 score. This pattern of subscale scores suggests that Tony feels misunderstood by others, possibly subjected to punishment without cause. He likely projects blame onto others and feels that others are trying to control him. He may feel threatened and report being followed or plotted against. These are not uncommon feelings in adolescents. Tony's low score on Si suggests facility in social relationships, with no indication of withdrawal.

Interpretation of Alcohol/Drug Problem Scales

Tony's scores on the three scales measuring alcohol and drug problems identified severe difficulties in this area (see supplementary scale profile, Figure 10-9). Tony readily acknowledged problems associated with the use of alcohol and other drugs, given his ACK elevation. He recognized this as a problem area. His MAC-R and PRO scores suggested a personality style consistent with alcohol and other drug problems. He likely was part of a peer group who used drugs and alcohol and frequently got into trouble.

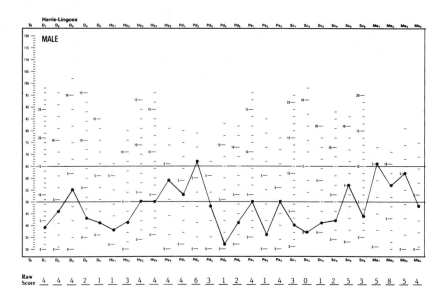

Figure 10-8. Tony. MMPI-A Harris-Lingoes profile

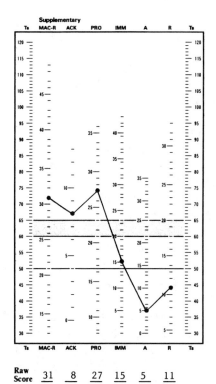

Figure 10-9. Tony. MMPI-A
supplementary scales profile

Interpretation of Factor Scales

Tony produced very low scores on A and R, which was not surprising given his standard and validity scale scores. (The A and R scales were derived from a factor analysis of these scales.) No interpretive statements should be made for such low scores on these scales. That Tony did not evidence significant maladjustment (A) was also inconsistent with the significant problems observed at referral.

Comments

Tony's limited elevations on the MMPI-A standard scales was somewhat surprising given the intensity of his behavior problems and the setting in which he was seen. If his MMPI-A interpretation was limited to the scales covered in this chapter, Tony's problems would not be attributed to significant psychopathology, with the exception of a high probability of the presence of an alcohol- or drug-use disorder. There was only very marginal support for the conduct disorder identified by the DICA and probable given his behavioral problems in school, history of assaultive behavior, and difficulties with the law. However, as we will see in the next chapter, the MMPI-A Content Scales are a new feature of the instrument that can add to an interpretive report. After these new scales are described, we will return to Tony to see if we can resolve some of the inconsistencies noted above.

Chapter 11

Integrating the MMPI-A Content Scales into an Interpretive Strategy

The development of the MMPI-A Content Scales represents a refinement of the instrument for use with adolescents. These scales were created using the multistage, multistep scale-development procedures from our work with the MMPI-2 Content Scales described in Chapter 6. However, for the first time in the use of MMPI scales with adolescents, Content Scales were constructed using adolescent samples combined with rational procedures that ensured consideration of the unique developmental features of this age range. In addition, item content new with the MMPI-A and specifically related to adolescence was used. Williams et al. (1992) described the details of the development of these scales. We begin this chapter with a synopsis of the development of the Content Scales, then summarize the scale descriptions used for interpretations, and conclude with a description of how to integrate information from the MMPI-A Content Scales with descriptors from the other MMPI-A scales described in Chapter 10.

The MMPI-A interpretive strategy presented in the second half of this chapter is very similar to the one described in Chapter 8 for the MMPI-2. A series of 10 questions guides the process of integrating descriptors from the MMPI-A Content Scales presented here with the many other MMPI-A scale descriptors described in Chapter 10. An outline for an MMPI-A interpretive report, as well as worksheets for organizing the many possible scales descriptors, are included to facilitate the process of interpretation. Finally, 14-year-old Tony's MMPI-A interpretation is used at the conclusion of this chapter to highlight the interpretive procedures.

Development of the MMPI-A Content Scales

The first stage in the development of the MMPI-A Content Scales was rational and involved an examination of the appropriateness of the MMPI-2 Content Scales for adolescents. Step 1 within this stage was to determine if any of the constructs measured by the MMPI-2 Content Scales seemed developmentally inappropriate for adolescents. The Work Interference Scale was identified as less relevant for adolescents. Furthermore, its items had not been included in the Form TX experimental booklet. However, many school-related items took the place of the work interference items and allowed for the development of a school problems scale. We next determined how many items from the other 14 MMPI-2 Content Scales were retained on Form TX. All of the items for some of the

MMPI-2 Content Scales were included in Form TX (e.g., Anxiety, Antisocial Practices), whereas other scales lost several items (e.g., Obsessiveness, Type A Behavior). The new adolescent-specific content was examined to determine if any items could be added to the 14 basic MMPI-2 Content Scales. We then went through the provisional content scales to identify any items that seemed developmentally inappropriate as measures of personality or psychopathology in adolescents. There were only a few items that we rationally deleted at this stage. Some examples included a Health Concerns item "I have never had any breaking out on my skin that has worried me", and another example from the Anxiety Scale, "I worry over money and business."

By the last step in the first rational stage we had a list of provisional content scales derived from the MMPI-2 list. However, we also had a substantial number of adolescent-specific items that were not appropriate for any of the MMPI-2 Content Scales. Therefore, we took the next step of having independent raters identify a list of potential adolescent-specific content scales. Three of these provisional scales were developed for the MMPI-A (i.e., Adolescent-School Problems, Adolescent-Alienation, and Adolescent-Low Aspirations).

The last step in Stage 1 was the elimination of most item overlap. We were aware of the problems of the high prevalence of scale 4 responding in adolescents, which has been a source of difficulty in interpreting adolescent MMPIs, described in the previous two chapters. Scale 4 had quite heterogeneous content, and it was difficult to know which of its many descriptors applied in any individual's case. For the Content Scales that assess acting-out problems we developed separate scales with no item overlap: Adolescent-Conduct Problems (A-con), Adolescent-School Problems (A-sch), Adolescent-Family Problems (A-fam), and Adolescent-Alienation (A-aln).

Stage 2 in the development of the MMPI-A Content Scales was very similar to the second stage in the development of the MMPI-2 Content Scales. It involved statistical verification of the provisional content scales. Item/scale correlations were run to determine if the items rationally selected actually belonged on the scales. The internal consistency of these scales was examined, and the validity coefficients of those with low reliability were studied further.

Both the MMPI-2 Type A and the Adolescent-Low Aspirations (A-las) scales had reliability coefficients in the .55 to .65 range. We examined the validity coefficients of these scales before making a decision about whether to drop or retain them. The Type A scale was dropped from the MMPI-A because of both low reliability and validity. There were just too few items on Form TX to develop a reliable and valid Type A measure for adolescents. On the other hand, because A-las demonstrated good validity with measures of poor school performance, it was retained on the MMPI-A.

Stage 3, like the analogous stage in the development of the MMPI-2 Content Scales, was the final rational review of the provisional scales. One of the most significant outcomes of this stage was the development of an alternative Antisocial Practices scale. The Adolescent-Conduct Problems scale (A-con) was developed during Stage 3 because of the relatively poor validity for the Antisocial Practices scale in our adolescent samples.

The final statistical refinement occurred at Stage 4. Items that were more highly correlated with other scales were eliminated from the provisional scales. The final reliability and validity coefficients were calculated, as were uniform T scores. The validity coefficients from Stage 4 indicated that nine of the scales had strong support of their validity (i.e., A-hea, A-biz, A-ang, A-con, A-lse, A-las, A-sod, A-fam, and A-sch). Several other scales showed adequate validity (A-anx, A-dep, and A-aln). Additional validity work is needed for the A-cyn and A-trt scales. Studies using more adequate criterion measures are needed, as are treatment-outcome studies.

The final Stage 5 was rational and involved writing descriptions of the scales. These descriptions, along with the validity coefficients from Stage 4, were the basis of the descriptors presented in the next section. One of the MMPI-2 Content Scales, Fears, survived through Stage 5, but it was dropped from the MMPI-A. It contained approximately 13 items that were unique to it; by dropping the Fears scale, the MMPI-A could be further shortened. Since there were several other anxiety-related measures on the MMPI-A, the decision was made to drop it. All the procedures described in this summary are detailed in Williams et al. (1992).

The two primary sources for interpretive statements for the MMPI-A Content Scales are the item content of the scales and the empirically derived descriptors or correlates of the scales (Williams et al., 1992). The addition of content-based statements in the interpretive process differs from the guidelines for interpreting the empirical or standard scales. Although the Harris-Lingoes and Si subscales allow for some content-based interpretive statements for the standard scales, their interpretation, as we saw in Chapters 4 and 10, relies primarily on empirically established correlates and much less on their heterogeneous content.

Elevations on the MMPI-A Content Scales (T scores of 60-64, inclusive, are moderate elevations, T scores $\geq$ 65 are high elevations) mean that the young person has endorsed more of a particular group of symptoms (e.g., anxiety, bizarre mentation, or school problems) than individuals in the normative sample. The higher the score, the more symptoms endorsed. Average and low scores indicate the converse (i.e., the individual does not acknowledge problems in the area being assessed). Average and low scores indicate the individual does not say the scale's content is descriptive of him- or herself. This may be an accurate characterization, or it may indicate an unwillingness to admit to the problems, or even an unawareness of the problems. In any event, item content has direct meaning for interpretation.

In addition to item content, Williams et al. (1992) presented empirically derived descriptors based on correlations between the Content Scales and external data (i.e., parent and treatment-staff ratings, record reviews) for the MMPI-A Content Scales. For each of the 15 MMPI-A Content Scales, we provide interpretations of elevated scores, first based on content and then on their associated descriptors. In most cases, the empirical descriptors provide validation for the content-based interpretations, as we will see in the following sections. The more general interpretive guidelines for the MMPI-A Content Scales are summarized in Table 11-1.

Table 11-1. General interpretive guidelines for the MMPI-A Content Scales

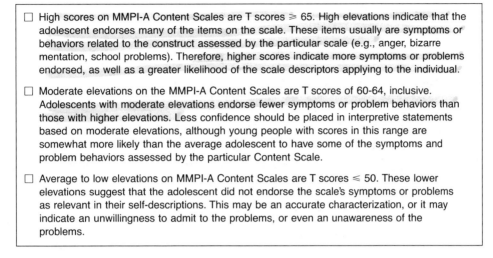

☐ High scores on MMPI-A Content Scales are T scores ≥ 65. High elevations indicate that the adolescent endorses many of the items on the scale. These items usually are symptoms or behaviors related to the construct assessed by the particular scale (e.g., anger, bizarre mentation, school problems). Therefore, higher scores indicate more symptoms or problems endorsed, as well as a greater likelihood of the scale descriptors applying to the individual.

☐ Moderate elevations on the MMPI-A Content Scales are T scores of 60-64, inclusive. Adolescents with moderate elevations endorse fewer symptoms or problem behaviors than those with higher elevations. Less confidence should be placed in interpretive statements based on moderate elevations, although young people with scores in this range are somewhat more likely than the average adolescent to have some of the symptoms and problem behaviors assessed by the particular Content Scale.

☐ Average to low elevations on MMPI-A Content Scales are T scores ≤ 50. These lower elevations suggest that the adolescent did not endorse the scale's symptoms or problems as relevant in their self-descriptions. This may be an accurate characterization, or it may indicate an unwillingness to admit to the problems, or even an unawareness of the problems.

Adolescent-Anxiety

Content-Based Interpretive Statements

Adolescents who score high on A-anx report many symptoms of anxiety, including tension, frequent worrying, nervousness, and difficulties sleeping (e.g., nightmares, disturbed sleep, difficulty falling asleep). They report problems with concentration, confusion, and inability to stay on task. Life is a strain for them, their difficulties are insurmountable, and they are under much stress. High scorers worry about losing their minds or going to pieces. They may feel that something dreadful is about to happen. They appear aware of their problems and how they differ from others.

Empirically Based Interpretive Statements

High-scoring adolescents are likely to be experiencing increasing family discord. Girls in clinical settings are likely to be depressed and have somatic complaints. Table 11-2 summarizes these descriptive statements.

Adolescent-Obsessiveness

Content-Based Interpretive Statements

Adolescent high scorers on A-obs report worrying excessively, often over trivial matters. They report great difficulty making decisions and frequently dread having to make changes in their lives. They have times when they are unable to sleep because of their worries. They are often regretful about things they may have said or done. They may ruminate about "bad words" or may count unimportant items. Others sometimes lose patience with them because of these behaviors.

Table 11-2. A-anx descriptors for the MMPI-A

☐ Adolescents with moderate to high elevations on A-anx report:
- Many symptoms of anxiety including nervousness, tension, and worrying
- Sleep difficulties (e.g., nightmares, disturbed sleep, problems falling asleep)
- Concentration problems, confusion, inability to stay on task
- Life is a strain, their problems are insurmountable
- Considerable stress
- Worries about losing their mind, going to pieces
- Fears about something dreadful happening
- Awareness of their problems and how they differ from others

☐ High scorers are likely to experience increasing family discord.

☐ High-scoring girls in clinical settings are likely to be depressed and have somatic complaints.

Table 11-3. A-obs descriptors for the MMPI-A

☐ Adolescents with moderate to high elevations on A-obs report:
- Worrying excessively, often over trivial matters
- Decision-making difficulties
- Dread of making changes in their lives
- Sleep difficulties because of worrying
- Regrets about things they may have said or done
- Ruminations about "bad words" or counting unimportant items
- Others sometimes losing patience with them because of these behaviors

☐ High-scoring girls are likely experiencing increasing family discord.

☐ High-scoring girls in clinical settings are likely to have suicidal thoughts among their obsessions and/or possible suicidal gestures.

☐ High-scoring boys in clinical settings are described by treatment staff as:
- Overly dependent and clinging to adults
- Anxious and overly concerned about the future
- Resentful, obsessed, worried, or preoccupied
- Having feelings of being bad or deserving punishment

Empirically Based Interpretive Statements

High-scoring girls are likely to have increasing disagreements with their parents. Girls in clinical settings may have suicidal thoughts among their obsessions or possible suicidal gestures. However, more serious suicide attempts were not associated with high A-obs scores. Clinical boys with elevated A-obs scores are seen by treatment staff as overly dependent and clinging to adults, anxious and overly concerned about the future, resentful, obsessed, worried, and preoccupied, often with feelings of being bad or deserving of punishment. Table 11-3 provides the A-obs interpretive guidelines.

Adolescent-Depression

Content-Based Interpretive Statements

Adolescents who score high on A-dep report many symptoms of depression.

Table 11-4. A-dep descriptors for the MMPI-A

☐ Adolescents with moderate to high elevations on A-dep report:
  • Many symptoms of depression
  • Frequent crying spells and fatigue
  • Several self-deprecative thoughts (e.g., beliefs that they have not lived the right kind of life, they are condemned, their sins are unpardonable)
  • Their future seems hopeless
  • Life is neither worthwhile nor interesting
  • Feeling blue
  • Sometimes thinking of killing themselves and/or wishing they were dead
  • Loneliness even when with other people
  • Feelings of uselessness or no one seems to care about them
  • Their future seems very uncertain
  • Periods when they are unable to "get going"
  • Other people are much happier than they
  • Hopelessness, not caring what happens, inclination to take things hard
  • Dissatisfaction with their lives

☐ High scorers in clinical settings are likely to have suicidal ideations and/or gestures.

☐ High-scoring girls in clinical settings have noticeable low self-esteem and depression.

☐ High-scoring boys in clinical settings could be evaluated for a history of sexual abuse.

☐ High-scoring girls in school settings are:
  • Less likely to have good grades
  • Less likely to be recognized for an outstanding personal achievement
  • More likely to be concerned with significant weight gain

Frequent crying spells and fatigue are problems. They have many self-deprecative thoughts, including believing that they have not lived the right kind of life, they are condemned, and their sins are unpardonable. Their future seems hopeless, life is neither worthwhile nor interesting. Most of the time they report feeling blue or wishing they were dead. Sometimes they may think of killing themselves. They report loneliness even when with other people and feeling useless or that no one seems to care about them. Their future seems too uncertain for them to make serious plans, and they have periods when they are unable to "get going." Others are seen as much happier. A sense of hopelessness, not caring what happens, as well as an inclination to take things hard, are other characteristics. They are dissatisfied with their lives.

Empirically Based Interpretive Statements

Suicidal ideations and/or gestures are associated with high-scoring boys and girls seen in clinical settings. Boys with high A-dep scores in clinical settings could be evaluated for a history of sexual abuse. Clinical girls are likely to have low self-esteem and depression noted as problems in their records. Girls in normative settings with elevated A-dep scores are less likely to have good grades or to be recognized for outstanding personal achievement. They are also more likely to be concerned with significant weight gain. The A-dep descriptors are included in Table 11-4.

Adolescent-Health Concerns

Content-Based Interpretive Statements

Adolescents with high scores on A-hea report numerous physical problems that interfere with their enjoyment of after-school activities and that contribute to significant school absence. They may report that their physical health is worse than their friends'. Their physical complaints cross several body systems. Included are gastro-intestinal problems (e.g., constipation, nausea and vomiting, stomach trouble), neurological problems (e.g., numbness, convulsions, paralysis, fainting and dizzy spells), sensory problems (e.g., hearing difficulty, poor eyesight), cardiovascular symptoms (e.g., heart or chest pain), skin problems, pain (e.g., headaches, neck pain), and respiratory problems. High scorers report worrying about their health and feeling that their problems would disappear if only their health would improve.

Empirically Based Interpretive Statements

Somatic complaints are verified as empirical descriptors of high-scoring adolescents. In addition, young people in normative settings are more likely to have both academic and behavioral problems in school, including poor grades, course failures, and suspensions. Parents of adolescents in clinical settings are likely to report numerous physical problems in their offspring including nausea and vomiting, pains, headaches, dizziness, rashes, and eye problems. Their parents may see them as fearful of school. Clinical girls are likely to report increasing disagreements with parents. Many other problems are associated with elevated A-hea scores in clinical boys. Their parents see them as very worried and anxious, accident and guilt-prone, clinging, fearful, and perfectionist. High-scoring boys may be less bright than others and are more likely to have lost weight. The A-hea descriptive statements are summarized in Table 11-5.

Adolescent-Alienation

Content-Based Interpretive Statements

High scorers on A-aln report considerable emotional distance from others. They believe that they are getting a raw deal from life and that no one cares about or understands them. They feel unliked by others and report an inability to get along with others. They report having no one, including parents or close friends, who understands them. They feel that others are out to get them and are unkind to them. They do not believe they have as much fun as other adolescents and would prefer living all alone in a cabin in the woods. They have difficulty self-disclosing and report feeling awkward when having to talk in a group. They may not appreciate hearing others give their opinions. Other people are seen as blocking their attempts at success.

Empirically Based Interpretive Statements

Adolescents with high scores on A-aln are less likely to report having good grades in school. Normative girls with high scores may have a problem with

Table 11-5. A-hea descriptors for the MMPI-A

☐ Adolescents with moderate to high elevations on A-hea report:
- Numerous physical problems that interfere with their enjoyment of after-school activities and contribute to significant school absence
- That their physical health is worse than their friends'
- Physical complaints across several body systems
- Gastro-intestinal problems (e.g., constipation, nausea and vomiting, stomach trouble)
- Neurological problems (e.g., numbness, convulsions, paralysis, fainting, and dizzy spells)
- Sensory problems (e.g., hearing difficulty, poor eyesight)
- Cardiovascular symptoms (e.g., heart or chest pain)
- Skin problems
- Pain (e.g., headaches, neck pain)
- Respiratory problems
- Worries about their health
- Feelings that their problems would be solved if only their health would improve

☐ High scorers in school settings are more likely to have both academic and behavioral problems in school, including poor grades, course failures, and suspensions.

☐ High-scoring boys may be less bright than others and are more likely to have lost weight.

☐ Parents of adolescents seen in clinical settings are likely to describe their offspring as:
- Having numerous physical problems (e.g., nausea and vomiting, pains, headaches, dizziness, rashes, and eye problems)
- Being fearful of school

☐ In addition, boys' parents also describe them as very worried and anxious, accident-prone, guilt-prone, clinging, fearful, and perfectionistic.

☐ Clinical girls are likely to report increasing disagreements with parents.

weight gain. Clinical girls have few or no friends and report increasing disagreements with parents. Clinical boys are noted to have social-skills deficit and low self-esteem. These interpretive statements are included in Table 11-6.

Adolescent-Bizarre Mentation

Content-Based Interpretive Statements

Adolescents scoring high on A-biz report very strange thoughts and experiences, including possible auditory, visual, or olfactory hallucinations. They characterize their experiences as strange and unusual, and believe there is something wrong with their minds. Paranoid ideations (i.e., beliefs that they are being plotted against or someone is trying to poison them) may also be reported. They may believe that others are trying to steal their thoughts and ideas, or control their minds. They may believe that evil spirits or ghosts possess or influence them.

Empirically Based Interpretive Statements

Boys and girls with elevated A-biz scores in normative settings experience numerous behavior and academic problems in school including poor grades, course failures, and suspensions. Adolescents in clinical settings are likely to

Table 11-6. A-aln descriptors for the MMPI-A

☐ Adolescents with moderate to high elevations on A-aln report:
- Considerable emotional distance from others
- Beliefs that they are getting a raw deal from life and that no one cares about or understands them
- Feeling unliked by others
- An inability to get along with others
- Having no one, including parents and close friends, who understands them
- Feelings that others are out to get them and are unkind to them
- That they do not have as much fun as other adolescents
- They would prefer living all alone in a cabin in the woods
- Having difficulty self-disclosing
- Feeling awkward when having to talk in a group
- Not appreciative when others give their opinions
- Seeing others as blocking their attempts at success

☐ High scorers are less likely to report having good grades in school.

☐ High-scoring girls in school settings are likely to report a weight gain.

☐ High-scoring clinical girls have few or no friends and report increasing disagreements with parents.

☐ High-scoring clinical boys have social-skill deficits and low self-esteem.

Table 11-7. A-biz descriptors for the MMPI-A

☐ Adolescents with moderate to high elevations on A-biz report:
- Very strange thoughts and experiences, including possible auditory, visual, and olfactory hallucinations
- Strange and unusual experiences
- Beliefs that there is something wrong with their minds
- Paranoid ideations (i.e., beliefs that they are being plotted against or someone is trying to poison them)
- Beliefs that others are trying to steal their thoughts, ideas, or control their minds
- Evil spirits or ghosts possess or influence them

☐ High scorers in school settings report many serious behavior and academic problems, including poor grades, course failures, and suspensions.

☐ Adolescents in clinical settings are likely to show bizarre or psychotic behaviors.

☐ Clinical girls are likely to come from disruptive families characterized by parents or siblings with arrest records.

☐ Clinical boys may have had a child-protection worker assigned to them in the past, and the treatment staff is likely to observe them exhibiting strange behaviors and mannerisms.

---

show bizarre or psychotic behaviors. Clinical girls are likely to come from disruptive families characterized by parents or siblings with arrest records. Clinical boys may have had a child protection worker assigned to them. Treatment staff are likely to observe strange behaviors and mannerisms in boys with elevated A-biz scores. The A-biz interpretive descriptors are available in Table 11-7.

Adolescent-Anger

Content-Based Interpretive Statements

Adolescents with high scores on A-ang report considerable anger-control problems. They often feel like swearing, smashing things, or starting a fist-fight. Not surprisingly, they frequently get into trouble for breaking or destroying things. They report having considerable problems with irritability and impatience with others. They have been told that they throw temper-tantrums to get their way. They especially do not like others to hurry them or to get ahead of them in a line. They indicate that they are hot-headed and often have to yell in order to make a point. Occasionally they report getting into fights, especially when drinking.

Empirically Based Interpretive Statements

Adolescents with elevated A-ang scores are very likely to act-out in school or at home. Not unexpectedly, the intensity of the acting-out behaviors increases in clinical settings. Both boys and girls in these settings are likely to have histories of assaultive behaviors. Both parents and treatment staff observe numerous instances of anger-control problems, resentfulness, impulsivity, impatience, variable moods, and other externalizing behaviors. These young people may be overly interested in violence and aggression.

Clinical boys with high A-ang scores may also be seen as overly clinging and dependent by treatment staff. Although resentful, they are also attention-seeking, self-condemning, and anxious about the future. They may feel deserving of punishment. Clinical boys could be evaluated for a possible history of sexual abuse. High-scoring clinical girls are likely to have had court appearances. Their parents describe them as aggressive and delinquent, which is also confirmed by treatment staff. They may act-out sexually with promiscuity and provocative clothing and behaviors. Treatment staff are likely to report a need to supervise these girls around boys. The A-ang descriptive statements are summarized in Table 11-8.

Adolescent-Cynicism

Misanthropic attitudes are held by adolescents scoring high on A-cyn. They believe that others are out to get them and will use unfair means to gain an advantage. They look for hidden motives whenever someone does something nice for them. They believe that it is safer to trust no one because people make friends in order to use them. Others are seen as inwardly disliking to help another person, and they are on guard when people seem more friendly than they expect. They feel misunderstood by others, and see others as very jealous of them. Empirically derived descriptors are yet to be determined for A-cyn. Content-based interpretive descriptors for A-cyn are summarized in Table 11-9.

Table 11-8. A-ang descriptors for the MMPI-A

☐ Adolescents with moderate to high elevations on A-ang report:
- Considerable anger-control problems
- Feeling like swearing, smashing things, or starting a fist-fight
- Getting into trouble for breaking or destroying things
- Considerable problems with irritability and impatience
- Throwing temper tantrums to get their way
- Not liking others to hurry them or get ahead of them in a line
- Being hot-headed and having to yell in order to make a point
- Getting into fights, especially when drinking

☐ Adolescents with elevated A-ang are very likely to act-out in school or at home and, not unexpectedly, the intensity of the acting-out behaviors increases in clinical settings.

☐ High-scoring adolescents in clinical settings:
- Have histories of assaultive behaviors
- Are likely to be described by both parents and treatment staff as having anger-control problems, resentfulness, impulsivity, impatience, variable moods, and other externalizing behaviors
- Overly interested in violence and aggression

☐ High-scoring clinical boys:
- May be seen as overly clinging and dependent by treatment staff
- Although resentful, they are also attention-seeking, self-condemning, and anxious about the future
- May feel deserving of punishment
- May have a history of sexual abuse

☐ High-scoring clinical girls:
- Have had court appearances
- Are likely to be described as aggressive and delinquent by parents and treatment staff
- Act-out sexually with promiscuity, wearing provocative clothing, and behaving flirtatiously
- Need supervision around boys

Table 11-9. A-cyn descriptors for the MMPI-A

☐ Adolescents with moderate to high elevations on A-cyn report:
- Beliefs that others are out to get them and will use unfair means to gain an advantage
- Looking for hidden motives whenever someone does something nice for them
- Beliefs that it is safer to trust nobody because people make friends in order to use them
- Seeing others as inwardly disliking helping another person
- Being on guard when people seem more friendly than they expect
- Feeling misunderstood by others
- Seeing others as being very jealous of them

Adolescent-Conduct Problems

Content-Based Interpretive Statements

Adolescents scoring high on A-con report many different behavioral problems, including stealing, shoplifting, lying, swearing, breaking or destroying property, and being disrespectful and oppositional. They may report having legal difficulties and see no problems in trying to get around the law. Their peer group is often in trouble and can talk them into doing things they know they should not do. At times they may try to make other people afraid of them, just for the fun of it. They are entertained by another's criminal behavior, and do not blame people for taking advantage of others. They may admit to doing bad things in the past that they cannot tell anybody about.

Empirically Based Interpretive Statements

Elevated scores on A-con are related to the many very serious acting-out behaviors described above in its item content. High-scoring boys and girls, even from general-population school settings, are likely to have many behavior problems in school and are less likely to be doing well academically. There is a tendency for these problems to be acknowledged more readily by high-scoring girls compared with boys. Descriptors found for the normative girls included self-reported disciplinary and probation problems, suspension, course failures, and cheating or lying in school. This does not mean that high-scoring girls have more of these problems than boys, because even though the boys admit to fewer problems, their parents indicate otherwise (see below).

Adolescent high scorers on A-con are likely to use alcohol and other drugs. More problematic alcohol and drug use is evident in high scorers seen in clinical settings. In fact, high-scoring girls in clinical settings are likely to have had records indicating previous treatment for substance-abuse problems.

Adolescents in clinical settings show more extreme behaviors than the normative sample when A-con is elevated. Parents of both genders report many delinquent behaviors in their offspring, including lying, cheating, stealing, running away, and truancy. In addition, they describe high scorers as disobedient, impulsive, and swearing. Girls are more likely to report increasing family discord. Parents of high-scoring boys report even more behavior problems and less social competence at school than do parents of girls.

There is empirical evidence that high-scoring adolescents have court involvement for problems like stealing (girls), status offenses (girls), being placed on probation (girls), and violent nonstatus offenses (boys). Boys have a greater likelihood of having a child-protection worker assigned to them.

Treatment staff of high-scoring girls report numerous behavior problems, including anger-control problems, lying, unpredictability, volatility, being moody, cheating, bossy, and easily upset. These girls are seen as sexually active, provocative, and requiring supervision when around the opposite sex. They are likely to be impatient, resentful, persistent, and impulsive. They are unlikely to be seen as depressed. The A-con interpretive statements are summarized in Table 11-10.

Adolescent-Low Self-Esteem

Content-Based Interpretive Statements

Adolescents with high A-lse scores have very negative opinions of themselves, including being unattractive, lacking self-confidence, feeling useless, having little ability and several faults, and not being able to do anything well. They are likely to yield to pressure from others, changing their minds or giving

Table 11-10. A-con descriptors for the MMPI-A

☐ Adolescents with moderate to high elevations on A-con report:
  ● Many different behavior problems, including stealing, shoplifting, lying, swearing, breaking or destroying property
  ● Being disrespectful and oppositional
  ● Legal difficulties
  ● Having a peer group that is often in trouble and who talk them into doing things they know they should not
  ● At times trying to make other people afraid of them, just for the fun of it
  ● Being entertained by another's criminal behavior
  ● Not blaming people for taking advantage of others
  ● Admitting to doing bad things in the past they can tell no one

☐ Adolescent high scorers are likely to use alcohol and other drugs, with even more problematic alcohol and drug use evident in the high scorers seen in clinical settings. In fact, girls in clinical settings are likely to have had previous treatment for alcohol and drug problems.

☐ High-scoring adolescents are likely to have court involvement for problems like stealing (girls), status offenses (girls), being placed on probation (girls), violent nonstatus offenses (boys), and having a child-protection worker assigned to them (boys).

☐ High scorers are likely to have:
  ● The many serious acting-out behaviors described in A-con item content
  ● Many behavior problems in school and less likely to be doing well academically
  ● A tendency to acknowledge these problems more readily if a girl
  ● Self-reported disciplinary and probation problems, suspension, course failures, and being caught cheating or lying in school (particularly if a girl)

☐ High scorers in clinical settings:
  ● Show more extreme behaviors than the normative sample
  ● Have parents who report many delinquent behaviors including lying, cheating, stealing, running away, and truancy. Their offspring are seen as disobedient, impulsive, and swearing.

☐ Parents of high-scoring boys report even more behavior problems and less social confidence at school than the parents of girls.

☐ Treatment staff of high-scoring girls report numerous behavior problems, including anger control, lying, unpredictable behavior, volatility, moodiness, cheating, being bossy, and easily upset. These girls are likely to be sexually active, provocative, and require supervision when around boys. They are likely to be impatient, resentful, persistent, and impulsive, but are unlikely to be seen as depressed.

up in arguments. They tend to let other people take charge when problems have to be solved, and do not feel that they are capable of planning for their own future. They have difficulty accepting or believing compliments from others. They may get confused and forgetful.

Empirically Based Interpretive Statements

Girls in normative settings who score high on A-lse are more likely to report having poor grades and significant weight gain. They are less likely to report

Table 11-11. A-lse descriptors for the MMPI-A

☐ Adolescents with moderate to high elevations on A-lse report:
  - Very negative attitudes of themselves, including being unattractive, lacking self-confidence, feeling useless, having little ability, having several faults, and not being able to do anything well
  - Being likely to yield to pressure from others
  - Frequently changing their minds or giving up in arguments
  - Tendencies to let other people take charge when problems have to be solved
  - Feeling that they are not capable of planning their own future
  - Difficulties accepting or believing compliments from others
  - Confusion and forgetfulness

☐ Girls in normative settings with elevated scores are likely to report having poor grades and having significant weight gain. They are less likely to have had an outstanding personal achievement.

☐ High scorers in clinical settings are likely to be seen as having low self-esteem among their problems.

☐ Clinical girls are likely to be seen as depressed, with the possibility of suicidal thoughts and/or gestures. They are likely to have a history of learning disabilities and report increasing disagreements with parents.

☐ Clinical boys are seen as having poor social skills.

☐ High-scoring boys could be evaluated further for the possibility of a history of sexual abuse.

---

having a recent outstanding personal achievement. No correlates were found for the normative boys, which may be more related to the relative infrequency of low scores in boys than to differential validity for the genders.

Clinical boys, as well as girls in these settings, were likely to have low self-esteem noted as a problem in their treatment records. Boys were also seen as having poor social skills. High-scoring boys could be evaluated further for the possibility of a history of sexual abuse. Clinical girls were likely to be seen as depressed, with the possibility of suicidal thoughts and/or gestures. They were likely to have a history of learning disabilities and to report increasing disagreements with parents. The A-lse descriptors are summarized in Table 11-11.

Adolescent-Low Aspirations

Content-Based Interpretive Statements

High scorers on A-las are disinterested in being successful, particularly academically. They do not like to study or read about things, and they dislike science and lectures on serious topics. They may prefer work that allows them to be careless. Their expectations of success are low. They avoid reading editorials, believing that the comic strips are the only interesting part of a newspaper. They report difficulty starting things and quickly give up when things go wrong. They let other people solve problems and they avoid facing difficulties. They believe that others block their success. Others also tell them that they are lazy. They probably do not want to go to college.

Table 11-12. A-las descriptors for the MMPI-A

☐ Adolescents with moderate to high elevations on A-las report:
- Disinterest in being successful, particularly in academics
- Dislike of studying or reading about things
- Dislike of science and lectures on serious topics
- Preference for work that allows them to be careless
- Low expectations of success
- Avoidance of reading editorials and preference for the comic strips
- Difficulty starting things
- Quickly giving up when things go wrong
- Letting other people solve problems
- Avoiding facing difficulties
- Beliefs that others block their attempts for success
- Others tell them that they are lazy
- A disinterest in going to college

☐ High scorers, as expected from the item content, are more likely to:
- Have poor grades in school
- Be less willing to participate in school activities
- Perhaps have more school-related problems, particularly if a boy

☐ Boys in clinical settings are more likely:
- To be truant or avoid school
- To run away from home

☐ Girls in clinical settings are:
- More likely to be seen as acting-out sexually
- Less likely to report winning an outstanding prize or award

---

Empirically Based Interpretive Statements

As would be expected, given the item content of A-las, high scorers, regardless of setting, were more likely to have poor grades in school and less likely to participate in school activities. There is some possibility that high-scoring boys may also have more school-related problems. Boys in clinical settings are more likely to be truant or avoid school. They are also more likely to run away from home. Girls in clinical settings are more likely to be seen as engaging in sexual acting-out and less likely to report winning an outstanding prize or award. Table 11-12 summarizes the A-las interpretive guidelines.

Adolescent-Social Discomfort

Content-Based Interpretive Statements

Adolescents with high scores on A-sod find it very difficult to be around others. They report being shy and much prefer to be alone. They dislike having people around them and actively avoid others. They do not like parties, crowds, dances, or other social gatherings. They avoid initiating conversations. They report embarrassment when having to give an opinion to a group. Others indicate that it is hard to get to know them. They report having difficulty making friends and do not like to meet strangers.

Table 11-13. A-sod descriptors for the MMPI-A

☐ Adolescents with moderate to high elevations on A-sod report:
  ● Difficulty being around others and making friends
  ● Shyness and preferring to be alone
  ● Disliking having others around them and actively avoiding others
  ● Disliking parties, crowds, dances, or other social gatherings
  ● Avoidance of initiating conversations
  ● Embarrassment in having to give an opinion in a group
  ● Others find it hard to get to know them
  ● Dislike of meeting others

☐ High-scoring adolescents in school settings are unlikely to report use of alcohol and other drugs, perhaps owing to the strong role peer groups have in influencing such use.

☐ High-scoring boys are:
  ● More likely to avoid participation in school activities
  ● Very unusual in treatment settings

☐ High-scoring clinical girls are:
  ● Very unlikely to be in treatment for acting-out behavior problems
  ● Likely to have parents and treatment staff indicating that they do not engage in behavior problems including alcohol and drug use, sexual acting-out, or irresponsibility
  ● Instead seen as withdrawn, timid, fearful, physically weak, and a fringe participant in peer activities
  ● Uninterested in the opposite sex
  ● Have few or no friends
  ● Likely to be depressed
  ● May have eating problems

Empirically Based Interpretive Statements

High A-sod normative boys are more likely to avoid participation in school activities. They are less likely to report using alcohol or other drugs, perhaps because of the strong role peer groups have in influencing such use. There are no descriptors for clinical boys, again possibly because of the low frequency of high A-sod scorers among boys in treatment centers.

High-scoring normative girls are also unlikely to report using alcohol or other drugs. In clinical settings high A-sod scores in girls have an inhibitory effect on acting-out behaviors. Both parents and treatment staff are unlikely to describe high-scoring girls as having behavior problems, including alcohol and drug use, sexual acting-out, or irresponsibility. They are likely to be seen as withdrawn, timid, fearful, physically weak, and a fringe participant in peer activities. They show little interest in the opposite sex. They have few or no friends, are likely to be depressed, and have eating problems. Table 11-13 provides interpretive statements for A-sod.

Adolescent-Family Problems

Content-Based Interpretive Statements

Adolescents with high A-fam scores report considerable problems with their parents and other family members. Family discord, jealousy, fault-finding, anger, serious disagreements, lack of love and understanding, and limited communication characterize these families. These adolescents do not believe they can count on their families in times of trouble. They may wish for the day when they are able to leave their homes. They feel their parents frequently punish them without cause, and treat them more like children. They report that their parents dislike their peer group. They do not accept responsibilities around the home and may have run away. They may report having many beatings.

Empirically Based Interpretive Statements

As expected, elevated A-fam scores are associated with many problems in the family and reported increases in family discord. Some of these adolescents' problems spill over into the school setting. However, high A-fam scorers do not show the same asocial behaviors as do high scorers on A-con. Elevations on A-fam are not associated with problems with the courts and police, as are A-con elevations.

Normative adolescents who score high on A-fam reveal that in addition to overall family discord, there may be increases in parental marital problems. These adolescents report poor grades and more school problems, including suspensions. Normative girls high on A-fam are more likely to report weight gain, job loss, and failure on a major exam.

Parents of adolescents in clinical settings report numerous behavior problems in their offspring. Their reports are not limited to externalizing behaviors, as was true with elevations on A-con and A-ang. In addition to lying, cheating, stealing, and other externalizing behaviors, parents of high A-fam youth report somatic complaints, guilt, fearfulness, worrying, crying, clinging, timidity, and withdrawal as characteristic. Boys are seen by their parents as uncommunicative, secretive, sad, self-conscious, unloved, disliked, and lonely. Girls, in addition to being seen by parents as cruel, destructive, prone to fight, immature, and hyperactive, are also reported to be sad, secretive, and self-conscious.

Treatment staff are also less likely to describe these adolescents' problems solely with acting-out descriptors. Rather, high-scoring boys are seen as overly dependent and clinging, resentful, attention-seeking, anxious about the future, preoccupied, and having feelings of self-condemnation and blame. Girls, on the other hand, were seen as likely to act-out sexually by being promiscuous, provocative, and preoccupied by sex.

Hospital records indicated significant family-related problems in high scorers, including running away (boys), physical abuse (boys), and sexual abuse (girls). Recommendations for further assessment of these very serious problem areas are indicated for high scorers. Interpretive guidelines for A-fam are provided in Table 11-14.

Adolescent-School Problems

Content-Based Interpretive Statements

Numerous difficulties in school characterize adolescents scoring high on A-sch. They often may be upset by things that happen at school. Poor grades, sus-

Table 11-14. A-fam descriptors for the MMPI-A

☐ Adolescents with moderate to high elevations on A-fam report:
- Considerable problems with their parents and other family members
- Family discord, jealousy, fault-finding, anger, serious disagreements, lack of love and understanding, and limited communication
- Beliefs that they cannot count on their family in times of trouble
- Wishes for the day when they are able to leave home for good
- Feeling that their parents punish them without cause
- Beliefs that their parents treat them more like children
- Reports that their parents dislike their peer group
- They do not accept responsibilities around the home
- Possible runaway
- Possible beatings

☐ High scores on A-fam are associated with many of the problems reflected in the item content. Some of these problems do spill over into the school setting. However, elevated scorers on A-fam do not show the same asocial behaviors as do elevated scorers on A-con. Elevations on A-fam are not associated with problems with the courts and police as are elevations on A-con.

☐ Adolescents in school settings with elevated A-fam scores:
- Reveal possible increases in parental marital problems, in addition to overall family discord
- Report poor grades and more school problems including suspensions

☐ Girls in school settings are more likely to report weight gain, job loss, and failure on a major exam.

☐ Parents of adolescents in clinical settings report numerous behavior problems:
- Not limited to the externalizing behaviors associated with elevations on A-con and A-ang. In addition to the lying, cheating, stealing, and other externalizing behaviors, parents also report somatic complaints, guilt, fearfulness, worrying, crying, clinging, timidity, and withdrawal
- Boys especially are seen as uncommunicative, secretive, sad, self-conscious, unloved, disliked, and lonely
- Girls are likely to be seen as cruel, destructive, prone to fight, immature, hyperactive, but also sad, secretive, and self-conscious

☐ Treatment staff are also less likely to describe these adolescents' problems solely with acting-out descriptors:
- High-scoring boys are seen as overly dependent and clinging, resentful, attention-seeking, anxious about the future, preoccupied, and feeling self-condemnation and blame
- Girls are seen to act-out sexually by being promiscuous, provocative, and preoccupied by sex

☐ Boys are likely to have a history of running away.

☐ Interpretive reports should include recommendations of further assessment of the possibility of physical abuse, particularly for boys, and sexual abuse, particularly for girls.

pension, truancy, learning problems, negative attitudes toward teachers, and dislike of school are characteristic of high scorers. The only pleasant aspect of school for youth high on A-sch is their friends. They avoid participation in school activities or sports. School is a waste of time in their opinion. Others may consider them lazy. They report frequent boredom and sleepiness at school. Some of these individuals may report being afraid to go to school or missing school because of illness.

Empirically Based Interpretive Statements

Like A-fam, described above, elevations on A-sch indicate problems in primarily one setting, in this case the school. High scorers are quite likely to have both academic and behavior problems. Interestingly, the A-sch correlates are pretty much limited to school and do not include the asocial activities covered by A-con, the anger-control problems associated with A-ang, or the family discord assessed by A-fam.

As its item content implies, A-sch elevations are associated with a wide range of school problems, including poor grades, course failures, repeating a grade, disciplinary actions and probation, and suspensions. Parents of high scorers are unlikely to report that their offspring are socially competent in school. They report several school problems that can include poor school work, truancy, lying and cheating, impulsivity, disobedience at school and home, and concentration difficulties. They may also report more general behavior problems, including associating with a bad peer group, running away, alcohol and other drug use, stealing, swearing, and secretiveness.

Their hospital records revealed many school-related problems as well. Truancy and school avoidance were characteristic responses of both boys and girls. Boys were more likely to run away, act irresponsibly, and have a history of drug use, particularly amphetamines. They could be further evaluated for a history of sexual abuse. Clinical girls were characterized by histories of academic underachievement and/or learning disabilities. The A-sch interpretive guidelines are provided in Table 11-15.

Adolescent-Negative Treatment Indicators

High scorers on A-trt describe several attitudes and behaviors that are unlikely to be conducive to psychotherapy. High scores indicate very negative attitudes toward physicians or mental-health professionals. They do not believe that others are capable of understanding them or care much about what happens to them. They also report great unwillingness to discuss their problems with others and indicate that there are some issues that they would never be able to share with anyone. They report being nervous when others ask them personal questions and have many secrets they feel are best kept to themselves. They are unwilling to take charge and face their problems or difficulties. They report several faults and bad habits that they feel are insurmountable. They do not feel they can plan their own future. They will not assume responsibility for the negative things in their lives.

Treatment outcome studies are needed to verify whether the negative attitudes toward mental-health professionals, ability to change, and desire to change affect the course of psychotherapy. Until these studies are completed, high scores can be interpreted as reflecting attitudes that may contribute to difficulties in psychotherapy outcome. Williams et al. (1992) note that this scale is not simply a measure of general maladjustment. Table 11-16 provides descriptors for A-trt.

Table 11-15. A-sch descriptors for the MMPI-A

☐ Adolescents with moderate to high elevations on A-sch report:
  • Numerous difficulties in school
  • Being easily upset by things that happen at school
  • Poor grades, suspension, truancy, learning problems, negative attitudes toward teachers, and dislike of school
  • Only pleasant aspect of school is their friends
  • Avoidance of participation in school activities or sports
  • School is a waste of time
  • Others may consider them lazy
  • Frequent boredom and sleepiness in school
  • Possible fears of going to school or missing school because of illness

☐ Elevations on A-sch indicate problems in primarily one setting, in this case the school. High scorers are quite likely to have both academic and behavior problems. As was the case with A-fam, the A-sch correlates are setting-specific and do not include the asocial activities covered by A-con, the anger-control problems associated with A-ang, or the family discord assessed by A-fam.

☐ Similar to the item content described above, A-sch elevations are also associated with:
  • A wide range of school problems
  • Poor grades, course failures, repeating a grade, disciplinary actions and probation, and suspensions

☐ Parents of high scorers seen in clinical settings:
  • Are unlikely to report that their offspring are socially competent in school
  • Describe many school behavior problems (e.g., poor school work, truancy, lying and cheating, impulsivity, disobedience at school and home, and concentration difficulties)
  • May also report more general behavior problems, including associating with a bad peer group, running away, alcohol and other drug use, stealing, swearing, and secretiveness

☐ School-related problems, including truancy and school avoidance, were confirmed in the treatment records of these young people.

☐ Clinical boys are more likely to run away, act irresponsibly, and may have a history of drug use, particularly amphetamines.

☐ Clinical boys could be further evaluated for a history of sexual abuse.

☐ Clinical girls are characterized by histories of academic underachievement and/or learning disabilities.

Integrating Information into Interpretive Reports

This chapter and the previous one describe the numerous scale descriptors associated with elevations on the MMPI-A validity, standard, and supplementary scales (see Chapter 10), and the new MMPI-A Content Scales. The task of integrating all these potential descriptors into an integrated report may at first seem daunting. However, much of the information presented in Chapter 8 about the integration of MMPI-2 inferences into interpretive reports applies equally well to the MMPI-A. The remainder of this chapter presents some modifications in the basic strategy for writing MMPI reports. The reader may wish to consult Chapter

Table 11-16. A-trt descriptors for the MMPI-A

☐ Adolescents with moderate to high elevations on A-trt describe several attitudes and behaviors that are unlikely to be conducive to psychotherapy:
- Very negative attitudes toward physicians or mental-health professionals
- Others are incapable of understanding them
- Others do not care what happens to them
- Great unwillingness to discuss problems with others
- Indications that they will not be able to share some issues with anyone
- Reports of nervousness when others ask them personal questions
- Reports of many secrets best kept to themselves
- Unwillingness to take charge and face their problems or difficulties
- Several faults and bad habits that are unsurmountable
- An inability to plan their own future
- An unwillingness to assume responsibility for the negative things in their lives

☐ Treatment outcome studies are needed to verify whether the negative attitudes toward mental-health professionals, ability to change, and desire to change affects the course of psychotherapy. Until these studies are completed, high scores can be interpreted as indicating attitudes that may be attributed to difficulties in psychotherapy outcome. Low scores on A-trt should not be interpreted as indicating a potential for psychotherapy, unless future studies indicate such an association.

8 for information about this basic interpretive strategy and its use with the MMPI-2.

As we do for the MMPI-2, we recommend approaching an MMPI-A interpretation with a series of questions, some identical to those suggested in Chapter 8 for MMPI-2 interpretations. However, the questions are modified for the MMPI-A for several reasons. Some of the questions for the MMPI-A interpretive strategy highlight unique developmental issues and characteristics (e.g., the importance of school adjustment, the prevalence of acting-out problems during adolescence, and negative peer-group influences). Because there is less research available on the use of the MMPI with adolescents, we are more limited in making some of the inferences that have been established for adults (e.g., the interpretive guidelines appearing in Chapter 8 about the likelihood of an acute mood state or those about dominance as a personality characteristic). These MMPI-2 inferences have not been validated for adolescents. Furthermore, adolescence is a time of tremendous growth and change, which makes us more cautious in making long-term predictions about adjustment, severity of the disorder, or trait-based personality characteristics. Perhaps longitudinal studies using the MMPI-A will allow us to make these long-term predictions at a future time.

Table 11-17 presents an outline of questions to address during an MMPI-A interpretation. Answers to these questions come primarily from the descriptors associated with the various MMPI-A indicators, scales, and subscales that are elevated in an individual's profile. These questions and their answers can be grouped into sections of an MMPI-A interpretive report, including validity considerations, symptoms and behaviors, alcohol and other drug problems, interpersonal relationships, strengths, diagnostic hypotheses, and treatment recommendations. Table 11-18 provides this suggested outline for an MMPI-A

Table 11-17. Questions for MMPI-A interpretations

1. Are there any extra-test factors that can explain the MMPI-A results?
2. What are the individual's response attitudes?
3. What are the individual's reported symptoms and behaviors? What is the likelihood of acting-out behaviors? If present, are the acting-out problems likely to be seen across settings or in specific settings? How severe is the acting-out likely to be?
4. Do problems in school play a significant role in the adolescent's clinical picture? What, if any, are they likely to be?
5. Does the adolescent admit to having a problem with alcohol or other drugs? Does she or he have the potential for developing such a problem?
6. What are the individual's interpersonal relationships like? Are there negative peer-group influences? Are family problems significant? How does he or she respond to authority? Are alienation, cynicism, or isolation a factor?
7. Does the MMPI-A suggest a need for evaluation of possible physical or sexual abuse?
8. What strengths or assets are apparent in the individual?
9. What are the diagnostic implications of the MMPI-A profile?
10. What treatment implications or recommendations are suggested from the MMPI-A including:
    - Is this individual in need of psychological treatment at this time?
    - How aware is the individual of his or her problems?
    - How credible is the individual's self-report?
    - Is the individual willing to disclose personal information to the therapist?
    - How motivated is the individual for treatment?
    - Is the individual capable of gaining insight into his or her problems?
    - Is he or she amenable to treatment? Is the individual willing to change his or her behavior?
    - Are there specific treatment needs suggested by the MMPI-A?
    - Are there negative personality features that could interfere with the treatment relationship?

interpretive report. In the following sections, we will describe further each of these questions and their place in the interpretive report.

Extra-Test Information

Consideration of demographic and setting characteristics is as important in interpreting the MMPI-A as it is for the MMPI-2. The accuracy of an MMPI-A interpretation is enhanced by knowledge of these important extra-test characteristics. For example, in presenting Tony's case in Chapter 10, we note that his Hispanic ethnicity suggests that English may not be his primary language. If this is true, his responses to an MMPI-A administered in English might not give as accurate a description of his problems as would the Spanish version of the instrument. Before we proceeded with our MMPI-A interpretation, we verified that Tony had the required sixth-grade reading level in English for the test.

Chapter 8 describes several demographic and setting characteristics for the MMPI-2 that also apply to the MMPI-A. The reader should consult that chapter since we do not repeat them here. The importance of gender and setting for MMPI-A interpretations is highlighted in many of the guidelines for the various MMPI-A scales presented in this chapter and the previous one. Slightly different descriptors apply depending upon the adolescent's gender or setting (i.e., a

Table 11-18. Form of an MMPI-A interpretive report

Name _____   Age and Grade _____

Setting _____   Gender _____

Validity Considerations
_____
_____

Symptoms and Behaviors
_____
_____

Alcohol and Other Drug Problems
_____
_____

Interpersonal Relationships
_____
_____

Strengths
_____
_____

Diagnostic Hypotheses
_____
_____

Treatment Recommendations
_____
_____

school population or treatment facility). The tables summarizing the interpretive guidelines for each scale indicate how the descriptors may differ depending upon gender and setting.

Any unusual extra-test characteristic or circumstance that might influence the individual's responses to the MMPI-A items should be noted at the beginning of the interpretive report, perhaps in the section on validity considerations. For example, if the interpreter is uncertain about the young person's ability to read or comprehend the items, this should be noted and followed up with an examination of the validity indicators, particularly the VRIN and TRIN scales.

There are several other important extra-test variables that we will illustrate with two examples. Extreme responding to the MMPI-A content may occur if the individual recently experienced a catastrophic life event (e.g., a sexual assault or witnessing the death of a parent). In this case, it would be important to discuss this extra-test information in the diagnostic considerations section of the report. An individual with a history of alcohol or drug problems may respond affirmatively to the items indicating hallucinations because of experiences while intoxicated. This may cause elevations on the scales associated with psychotic processes (e.g., Sc, A-biz) that should not be interpreted as indicating the presence of a psychotic disorder. Again, this and similar information should be noted in relevant sections of the interpretive report.

Response Attitudes

The first step in any MMPI interpretation is an examination of the validity of the individual's self-report. As we saw in Chapters 3 and 10, there are some response styles that are so problematic (e.g., inconsistent responding, an all-false pattern) that no MMPI-2 or MMPI-A scale should be interpreted. With other response attitudes (e.g., defensiveness) the profile can be interpreted by including cautionary statements about potentially compromising validity. In other cases the validity pattern reveals an honest and open response style. The first section of an MMPI-A interpretive report should begin with a description of the individual's response attitudes as revealed by his or her scores on the validity scales and indicators.

Assessing Symptoms and Behaviors

Answers to the third question in Table 11-17 about the individual's symptoms and behaviors form a major section in an MMPI-A interpretation. Descriptors associated with high and moderate scale elevations provide the sources for this section of the report. MMPI-A interpretations rely on these scale elevations and not on the code-type approach described in Chapter 8 for the MMPI-2. Test interpretation begins with a review of the descriptors associated with any MMPI-A scale that is elevated (generally defined as T scores greater than or equal to 65 for high elevations and T scores of 60-64, inclusive, for moderate elevations) in the individual's MMPI-A profiles. Confidence that a descriptor applies to the individual is greatest for those descriptors coming from highly elevated scales, scales with the strongest evidence for their validity, scales rather than subscales, and those descriptors that replicate across MMPI-A scales.

As is true with the MMPI-2, there may be times when an individual's scale elevations on the MMPI-A produce conflicting descriptors. For example, 15-year-old Mandy obtained elevations over 80 on Si and A-sod, along with a highly elevated A-fam score of 75 and a Pd score of 64. None of the other Content Scales associated with acting-out problems was elevated. Descriptors for Si and A-sod are similar, and in addition to withdrawal, shyness, and timidity, include less likelihood of engaging in acting-out behaviors and of having parents report delinquent behaviors. On the other hand, A-fam elevations are associated with numerous behavior problems, including parental reports of lying, cheating, stealing, and other acting-out behaviors. Her moderate elevation on Pd provides replication of these acting-out behaviors as well. It is noteworthy that A-fam elevations are also associated with withdrawal and timidity, which provides additional verification for the Si and A-sod descriptors.

The general guidelines described above for resolving discrepancies are not very helpful for interpreting Mandy's MMPI-A scores since Si, A-sod, and A-fam are all scales evidencing strong validity and Mandy's scores on all three scales are highly elevated. Si and A-sod descriptors suggesting less likelihood of acting-out provide replication across scales, although the item overlap between these two scales is high and likely contributes to this descriptor overlap. Should the acting-out descriptors from A-fam and Pd be discounted in her interpretation?

Although Mandy's significant problems in social relationships should be prominently highlighted in her MMPI-A interpretation, her potential for acting-out should not be dismissed because of her Si and A-sod elevations. Earlier data from Hathaway and Monachesi (1963) suggested that when both "excitatory" (i.e., scales positively associated with delinquency like Pd) and "inhibitory" (i.e., scales with a negative association with delinquency like Si) scales are elevated, the acting-out descriptors are more likely to apply than the inhibitory ones. However, Mandy's potential for acting-out is less than if she had elevations on the other scales associated with acting-out like A-con and may be limited to the family setting. She does not fit the personality profile of individuals belonging to a destructive peer group, and this should be noted in her MMPI-A interpretation. She would likely have difficulty relating to other adolescents in treatment for more typical delinquency problems.

As is true with the MMPI-2, interpretation of Mandy's scores on Si, A-sod, A-fam, and Pd demonstrates how seemingly conflicting MMPI-A correlates can result in useful personality descriptions. In cases where differing correlates cannot be resolved, they should be noted in the report. (See the section below on alcohol and other drug problems for another example.)

School Problems

The MMPI-A provides a more direct assessment of school-related problems than did the original instrument. Two new scales deal directly with school, A-sch and

A-las. Both academic and behavior problems are covered. Since these two scales are content-based, they will be elevated only if the young person describes problems in these areas. Some young people may not view school as problematic, even though they are quite troubling to teachers and school officials. Elevations on other scales (e.g., Pd, A-con) include school problems that should be interpreted even in the presence of low scores on A-sch or A-las.

School problems can be included in the symptoms and behaviors section of the interpretive report. However, if the psychologist is working in a school setting, he or she may wish to have a separate section in the report for school behavior and problems. A separate section on school may better meet the needs of the referral source in these circumstances.

Problems with Alcohol and Other Drugs

One of the advantages in using the MMPI-A to assess psychopathology during adolescence is its alcohol and other drug problem scales. There are three separate scales developed to discriminate adolescents with alcohol or other drug problems from those with different types of psychopathology. In addition, elevations on several clinical and Content Scales are associated with alcohol or other drug use. Scores on the MAC-R, ACK, and PRO scales should be examined to determine if they are elevated. The ACK scale indicates whether the young person openly acknowledges having problematic alcohol or other drug use, the other two scales indicate a personality style associated with a proneness for developing such problems.

There is a great likelihood of the individual having and acknowledging alcohol and drug problems if all three scales are elevated. If MAC-R and PRO are elevated, but ACK is not, the likelihood of a problem in this area is high, but the young person is unwilling to admit to it. If an ACK elevation is present in the absence of MAC-R or PRO elevations, as well as in the absence of exaggeration or malingering, then the adolescent is showing an atypical problem in this area.

A more equivocal pattern of scores occurs with elevations on only MAC-R or PRO. Until future research suggests otherwise, it may be best in this case to indicate in the interpretive report that the evidence is equivocal about the presence on an alcohol or other drug problem. Scores from 17-year-old Stan's MMPI-A will be used to illustrate this. Stan scored low on both ACK and PRO (50 and 43, respectively), but was very high on MAC-R at a T score of 70. There was no evidence of defensiveness in his profile, in fact to the contrary (e.g., he had high elevations on three of the standard scales and six Content Scales). Two of his highest elevations were on Si and A-sod, which suggest less likelihood of problem use. Given this, the alcohol and other drug problem section in his interpretive reads as follows:

Stan's scores on the alcohol and other drug problem scales suggested a mixed picture of his potential for developing serious problems in this area. He had some of the personality features associated with individuals who have problems in this area (e.g., risk-taking), yet he did not acknowledge having problematic alcohol and drug use, nor is it likely he belonged to a peer group who used drugs or alcohol. Given his willingness to admit to many other problem areas and his openness in his approach to the MMPI-A, problematic alcohol and other drug use may be less relevant in his current circumstances than the many other problem areas described in this report.

Interpersonal Relationships

Si, its subscales, and A-sod are the primary sources for information about the individual's interpersonal behavior. However, as we saw in Chapter 8 about the MMPI-2, other scales have descriptors related to interpersonal relationships that can be included in this section. In addition, several of the Content Scales describe characteristics that are relevant to an individual's relationships with others (e.g., A-aln, A-ang, A-cyn, and A-fam). The content of PRO suggests that an elevation on it raises the possibility of belonging to a negative peer group. These descriptors should be highlighted in a section of the interpretive report about interpersonal relationships (Table 11-18).

Sexual or Physical Abuse

Data collected during the MMPI Restandardization Project revealed that elevations on several MMPI-A scales were associated with sexual or physical abuse in clinical boys or girls. The base rate for physical abuse in the clinical sample was 34% (30% boys; 40% girls). Likewise, the base rate for sexual abuse was 29% (16% boys; 48% girls). These base rates were determined from the 696 adolescents (N = 412 boys; N = 284 girls) in the clinical sample whose hospital or school records were summarized by research assistants using a record review form. Rates of abuse were determined by this review of records, not from self-report.

The associations between abuse and the MMPI-A scales were included as descriptors in the interpretive guidelines of the relevant scales for adolescents in clinical settings. Like all other MMPI-A correlates, the abuse descriptors will apply to some, but certainly not all, individuals with elevated scores. In general, the higher the T score, the greater likelihood of any descriptor applying. However, the abuse correlates should never be interpreted as confirmation that a given individual has been abused. Rather, elevations on these scales suggest that a careful evaluation is needed in this area. Furthermore, these descriptors should be limited to adolescents in clinical settings with similar base rates of abuse. Recommendations for further evaluation of possible abuse could be included in the treatment recommendations section of the MMPI-A report.

Boys with histories of sexual abuse noted in their treatment records are more likely to have elevations on Pt, Sc, A-dep, A-ang, A-lse, A-fam, and A-sch. It is interesting that several of these scales measure internalizing symptoms (e.g., anxiety, depression, low self-esteem) which are relatively uncommon in boys in treatment settings. However, only between 21% to 28% of boys with elevations of 60 or above on these scales have histories of sexual abuse recorded in their charts. While this is above the base rate for boys for sexual abuse (16%), one cannot use this scale correlate to accurately predict sexual abuse. Similarly, sexual abuse in girls is related to three MMPI-A scales (Pd, Sc, and A-fam). The rate of sexual abuse in girls with elevations of 60 or higher on these scales varies between 56% to 59%. Again, although this is higher than the base rate of 48% for girls, it does not accurately predict sexual abuse for individual girls. Only one MMPI-A scale, Pd, was associated with a history of physical abuse and only in boys.

Perhaps the most appropriate use of the abuse descriptors is simply to facilitate a discussion with the young person about whether any abuse has occurred. An MMPI-A feedback session may be helpful to begin this discussion. In the feedback session the young person could be told that some adolescents with scale scores similar to his or hers have been abused and the clinician would like to help if he or she has a similar problem. Of course, in settings with high base rates of abuse, assessment of abuse should not be limited to the MMPI-A, but should include other techniques as well. The MMPI-A may prove to be a useful tool for research into the psychological aftermath of abuse.

Strengths

Although the MMPI and its successors are primarily measures of psychopathology and not indicators of personality strengths, there are some MMPI-A descriptors that can be categorized in this area. It is useful to have such a section in an MMPI-A report, particularly when giving feedback to the young person, his or her parents, or school staff. Some of the Harris-Lingoes subscales offer examples of possible strengths (e.g., Hy_1—Denial of Social Anxiety, comfortable around others, finds it easy to talk with others; Pd_3—Social Imperturbability, confident in social situations, willing to defend his or her strong opinions). In some cases, extreme emotional distress can be interpreted as an asset for treatment because the young person will be more motivated to make difficult changes in his or her life.

Diagnostic Considerations

The last two sets of questions in Table 11-17 and the corresponding last two sections of an interpretive report (Table 11-18) rely on information from the MMPI-A, as well as on other sources of information about the individual. In arriving at a possible diagnosis, the clinician integrates information from the MMPI-A to form an impression of the individual's overall symptoms, behaviors, likelihood of alcohol or other drug problems, interpersonal relationships, and strengths. From this, the clinician can consult the current diagnostic manual to see if the MMPI-A description of the adolescent coincides with any of the current diagnostic categories. Unfortunately, less research is available in relating the MMPI-A to diagnostic categories common during adolescence than was described in Chapter 8 for the MMPI-2.

Treatment Implications or Recommendations

Similar treatment-related questions presented in Chapter 8 for the MMPI-2 are relevant to the MMPI-A and are included in Table 11-17. Some of the answers to these questions can come from an elevation on the A-trt scale, which should be interpreted as an indication of the presence of negative attitudes toward mental-health treatment that may interfere with building a therapeutic relationship. However, treatment outcome studies are needed to determine whether these negative attitudes predict poor prognosis for psychotherapy. Low scores on A-trt should not be interpreted.

Other MMPI-A descriptors can provide answers to the treatment-relevant questions in Table 11-17. Noncompliance with the MMPI-A instructions indicated by the validity scales suggests an unwillingness to reveal problems or even an unawareness of problems that does not bode well for psychotherapy. The types of problems revealed by elevated scale scores suggest problem areas to concentrate on in treatment, as well as giving an indication of the need for treatment.

An MMPI-A Interpretive Worksheet

With all the different scales and potential descriptors available on the MMPI-A, it is helpful to begin writing an interpretive report by summarizing the information using worksheets such as the ones presented in Tables 11-19 and 11-20. Similar worksheets could also be used to facilitate MMPI-2 interpretation. The worksheet in Table 11-19 allows the interpreter to list the various descriptors and their sources, and to make an initial evaluation of the probability that the descriptors are associated with the individual (i.e., by using the certainty column on the worksheet). The interpreter can also indicate if the scale descriptor is verified by another MMPI-A scale (i.e., using the verification column on the worksheet). The worksheet in Table 11-19 is organized into the same sections described in Table 11-18 for an interpretive report (i.e., symptoms and behavior; alcohol and other drug problems; interpersonal relationships; and strengths). Because the diagnostic hypotheses and treatment recommendations sections of an MMPI-A interpretive report require information from sources in addition to the MMPI-A indicators, a separate worksheet is provided for them in Table 11-20.

Scale elevation is used to determine the certainty of whether the descriptor applies to the individual, with T scores ≥ 65 indicating high certainty. Moderate certainty is attributed to descriptors based on other scores. A "+ moderate" classification is used for descriptors from T scores of 60-64, inclusive, in the certainty column on the worksheet (Table 11-19). "Moderate−" certainty is used for subscale elevations ≥ 65, because the subscales are less psychometrically sound. "Moderate−" certainty is also used with any descriptors based on Content Scale elevations that are average or low (i.e., T scores ≤ 50). The verification column in Table 11-19 indicates whether the descriptor is associated with another elevated MMPI-A scale (i.e., whether it replicates within the MMPI-A profile).

Table 11-19. MMPI-A interpretive worksheet for descriptors

SYMPTOMS AND BEHAVIORS			
Source	Descriptor	Certainty	Verification
ALCOHOL AND OTHER DRUG PROBLEMS			
Source	Descriptor	Certainty	Verification
INTERPERSONAL RELATIONSHIPS			
Source	Descriptor	Certainty	Verification
STRENGTHS			
Source	Descriptor	Certainty	Verification

Note: Source indicates which MMPI-A scale or subscale accounts for the descriptor. Certainty refers to the scale's or subscale's elevation. Verification indicates whether the descriptor is associated with another MMPI-A scale elevation.

The information in Table 11-19 is listed by single scales and comes entirely from the individual's MMPI-A profile. On the other hand, information about diagnostic hypotheses and treatment recommendations combines information across MMPI-A scales and uses the clinician's knowledge about the adolescent's problems from other sources, resulting in hypotheses about diagnosis and treatment. The interpretive worksheet for these two sections of the report is presented in Table 11-20. For this process, information is integrated across the MMPI, combined with extra-test information about the individual and based on the clinician's experience in evaluating and treating similar adolescents.

In determining a diagnostic or treatment hypothesis, the clinician integrates the information presented in Table 11-19 to form an impression of the individual. Diagnostic hypotheses and treatment recommendations are based on the clinician's knowledge and experience in treating adolescents with similar problems. The Table 11-20 worksheet allows for an assessment of the likelihood, based on the MMPI-A, of whether these diagnostic or treatment hypotheses apply, using probable or possible as indicators. The last column in Table 11-20 provides space to note whether any other data (e.g., interviews; psychological tests; school, parent, or agency reports) confirm the MMPI-A hypotheses. In the next section of this chapter we will use these two worksheets to summarize Tony's MMPI-A findings.

Highlight Summary: Integrating Tony's MMPI-A

We ended Chapter 10 with 14-year-old Tony, a black Hispanic eighth grader being assessed with the MMPI-A to help the staff in his special school plan for his psychological and educational needs. Tony was placed in the special school because of numerous behavior problems including theft, for which he was on court-ordered probation, fighting, truancy, and oppositional behavior. Surprisingly, Tony's MMPI-A standard scale scores did not correspond with the severity of his already identified behavior problems. However, the MMPI-A alcohol and other drug use problem scales (MAC-R, ACK, and PRO) suggested a severe problem in this area.

Figure 11-1 presents his MMPI-A Content Scales profile, which can be used for further elaboration of his problems in the MMPI-A interpretive report. Tony's scores on the MMPI-A Content Scales provide several sources of inferences. Tony is well above the T-score cut-off of 65 on two Content Scales, A-con and A-ang. As Tables 11-8 and 11-10 reveal, these scales are associated with very serious behavior problems. Accordingly, Tony is much more likely to experience problems such as stealing, shoplifting, lying, destroying property, and being disrespectful and oppositional. He is quite likely to be part of a peer group that frequently talks him into doing things he knows he should not. Poor academic performance and school behavior problems are also quite likely. His A-con score also indicates alcohol and drug problems, providing additional support for the interpretation of his MAC-R, ACK, and PRO elevated scores.

Tony may also have a history of running away from home, and his parents would likely confirm many behavior problems, including lying, cheating, stealing, disobedience, impulsivity, and swearing. His parents likely are aware of his school behav-

Table 11-20. MMPI-A interpretive worksheet for diagnostic and treatment hypotheses

DIAGNOSTIC HYPOTHESES			
Diagnosis	Sources	Likelihood Based on MMPI-A	Extra-Test Confirmation
TREATMENT RECOMMENDATIONS			
Recommendation	Sources	Likelihood Based on MMPI-A	Extra-Test Confirmation

Note: Sources indicate which MMPI-A scales or subscales account for the diagnosis or recommendation. The likelihood column allows the interpreter to express the degree of confidence (i.e., "probable" or "possible") in the MMPI-A based hypotheses or recommendations applying to the adolescent. Extra-test confirmation can be obtained from interviews, parents, school teachers, social-service agencies, juvenile courts, or other psychological test data, as well as from any other sources used in psychological evaluations.

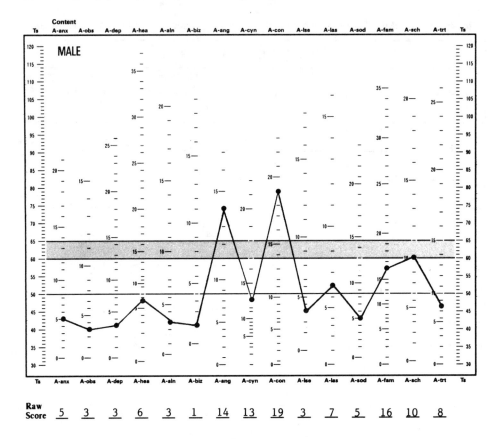

Raw
Score   5   3   3   6   3   1   14   13   19   3   7   5   16   10   8

Figure 11-1. Tony. MMPI-A Content Scales profile

ior problems and see him as less socially competent than other boys, given his elevation on A-con.

Anger control is a significant issue for Tony with his elevated A-ang score. He is likely to lose control, swear, smash things, or start a fight. He is prone to be impatient and irritable with others. Temper tantrums may be a frequent response to get his way. He may have a history of aggressive or assaultive acts and be overly interested in violence and aggression. On the other hand, he may also be dependent and clinging in relationships with adults. Although he can be resentful, he is also attention-seeking, self-condemning, and anxious about the future.

The possibility of abuse should be assessed, given the association of scores on A-ang and sexual abuse in boys. However, his profile should not be cited as providing evidence of sexual abuse. Rather, it would be much more consistent with available research to include a statement in his report calling for further assessment of the possibility of abuse. Given the description of Tony's concerns for his mother's and other family members' safety (including his own) during episodes of heavy drinking by his father, a call for an assessment of possible abuse (not just limited to sexual abuse) is warranted.

Tony's A-fam score did not reach an interpretable level (T score = 57). This means that he did not report having any more family problems than many other adolescents. However, his other elevations suggest that even though he did not use the MMPI-A item content to describe significant family discord, his home life is highly unlikely to be problem-free, given the family problems associated with elevations on A-con and A-ang.

Notably, given his current placement, the A-sch scale was only moderately elevated at a T score of 60. Certainly, school-related problems should be part of his MMPI-A interpretation, which would also be consistent with his scores on A-con and A-ang. His average A-las score is interesting with his history and the MMPI-A indications of a significant conduct disorder (i.e., his score on A-con). Tony's A-las score suggests that he has not given up on achievement in school and that he has some interest in academic topics. This is something his school environment may use as a resource. His average A-las score is consistent with his reported interest in school extracurricular activities like band and sports, and his teacher's reports that he does excel when he chooses to do so. His moderate elevation on A-sch and average A-las score, along with his above-average performance in some subjects and enjoyment of sports and band, suggest the possibility of structuring his school environment to increase his motivation and performance, particularly if his behavior and substance-abuse problems can be better controlled.

Comments

Tony's MMPI-A descriptors are listed on the interpretive worksheet presented in Table 11-21. Included in Table 11-21 are several descriptors with high certainty that have been verified by other MMPI-A scales. These should be emphasized in the interpretive report. Tony's descriptors present a fairly consistent pattern of behavior problems. Table 11-22 presents his interpretive worksheet for diagnostic and treatment hypotheses. Again, many of these hypotheses are listed as probable because they have been verified by other MMPI-A scales. Many of the diagnostic and treatment hypotheses are also confirmed by extra-test data from Tony's parents, school, or court records. Others are listed as to be confirmed by additional assessment.

Tony's MMPI-A Content Scales profile demonstrated how some of these new features of the instrument can be used to provide richer inferences about a troubled adolescent's symptoms and behavior. The original validity scales, combined with information from the new indicators (F_1, F_2, VRIN, TRIN), increases our confidence that he has an interpretable profile. His standard scale profile is less revealing than many. From it we infer that Tony has a greater activity level than many adolescents, is somewhat more likely to act-out, and is sociable with limited, if any, social anxiety (Chapter 10).

His MAC-R score, along with ACK and PRO, were much more revealing of problems, as was his MMPI-A Content Scales profile. A more descriptive picture of his behavior problems was revealed by these scales. From this, a psychologist can write a narrative report highlighting Tony's problems that would include conduct disorder and substance-abuse problems. Listing out all the descriptors on a worksheet highlighted the prominence of multiple drug-use problems (Table 11-22). The

Table 11-21. Tony's MMPI-A interpretive worksheet for descriptors

SYMPTOMS AND BEHAVIORS

Source	Descriptor	Certainty	Verification
Ma	Academic underachievement	+ Moderate	Yes
Ma$_1$	Perceives others as dishonest and selfish, justifying his similar behaviors	Moderate −	Yes
MAC-A	Exhibitionistic, risk-taker	High	Yes
A-con	Court involvement for serious behavior problem is possible	High	No
A-con	Numerous behavior problems including stealing, shoplifting, vandalism, lying, cheating, running away	High	Yes
A-con	School-related problems including truancy and academic difficulties	High	Yes
A-con	Parents well aware of these behavior problems in home and at school	High	Yes
A-con	Impulsive, disobedient, swearing	High	Yes
A-ang	Anger-control problems, irritability	High	Yes
A-ang	Impatience	High	Yes
A-ang	Fighting	High	Yes
A-ang	History of assaultive behavior	High	Yes
A-ang	Overly interested in violence	High	No
A-ang	Variable moods	High	No
A-ang	Anxious and self-condemning	High	No
A-sch	Wide range of school problems (poor grades, failure, repeating grade, disciplinary action, probation, suspensions)	+ Moderate	Yes
A-sch	Truancy	+ Moderate	Yes
A-sch	Runaway, irresponsibility	+ Moderate	Yes

ALCOHOL AND OTHER DRUG PROBLEMS

Source	Descriptor	Certainty	Verification
Ma	Experience with drugs, possibly amphetamines	+ Moderate	Yes
ACK	Readily acknowledges having problems with alcohol or other drugs	High	Yes
MAC-R	Personality style consistent with those having alcohol or other drug problems	High	Yes
PRO	Personality style consistent with those having alcohol or other drug problems	High	Yes
A-con	Likely to use alcohol or other drugs	High	Yes
A-sch	Drug use history, possibly amphetamines	+ Moderate	Yes

INTERPERSONAL RELATIONSHIPS

Source	Descriptor	Certainty	Verification
Si	Socially extraverted and outgoing	High	Yes
MAC-R	Socially extraverted	High	Yes
PRO	Likely to be involved with a peer group who uses alcohol or other drugs	+ Moderate	Yes
A-con	Belongs to a peer group who is frequently in trouble	High	Yes
A-con	Disrespectful and oppositional	High	Yes
A-con	May like to frighten others for fun, thinks it is OK to take advantage of others	High	Yes
A-ang	Resentful, impatient, impulsive	High	Yes
A-ang	Clinging, dependent, attention-seeking	High	Yes

Table 11-21. Tony's MMPI-A interpretive worksheet for descriptors, continued

STRENGTHS			
Source	Descriptor	Certainty	Verification
Ma	Enthusiasm, interests in many things, animated approach to problems	+ Moderate	No
A-las	Average score suggests has some interests in academic pursuits	Moderate −	No

Note: Source indicates which MMPI-A scale or subscale accounts for the descriptor. Certainty refers to the scale's elevation with "high" indicative of scales with T scores $\geqslant$ 65; "+ moderate" indicating scales with T scores of 60-64, inclusive; and "moderate − " indicating subscales with T scores $\geqslant$ 65 or interpretations based on Content Scales with average to low scores ($\leqslant$ 55). Verification indicates whether the descriptor is associated with another MMPI-A scale elevation.

psychologist can also draw upon his or her training and experience with adolescents with similar problems to make therapeutic suggestions to the school staff involved with Tony's education and rehabilitation.

A treatment plan for Tony's acting-out behaviors would emphasize externalizing problems perhaps best controlled with clear expectations and behavioral contracting (Table 11-22). Tony's abuse of drugs and alcohol must be addressed in any therapeutic approach. An evaluation of possible abuse and attention to family issues are suggested by his profile. Tony has some academic interests that can be used in his school planning. He may respond to a strong, nurturing adult role model who frequently verbalizes expectations and fairly applies the stated contingencies.

Table 11-22. Tony's MMPI-A interpretive worksheet
for diagnostic and treatment hypotheses

DIAGNOSTIC HYPOTHESES

Diagnosis	Sources	Likelihood Based on MMPI-A	Extra-Test Confirmation
Conduct disorder, undifferentiated type.	A-con, A-ang, PRO, MAC-R	Probable	Interview, school, parents, court records
Alcohol abuse	MAC-R, ACK, PRO, A-con	Probable	Interview, school, parents
Cannabis abuse	MAC-R, ACK, PRO, A-con	Probable	Interview, parents
Amphetamine abuse	Ma, A-sch, MAC-R, ACK, PRO, A-con	Possible	To be determined
Other drug use/abuse	MAC-R, ACK, PRO, A-con	Possible	To be determined

TREATMENT RECOMMENDATIONS

Recommendation	Sources	Likelihood Based on MMPI-A	Extra-Test Confirmation
Treatment of a significant alcohol or other drug-use problem	Ma, ACK, MAC-R, PRO, A-con, Asch	Probable	Interview, school, parents
Treatment focusing on control of externalizing behaviors with clear expectations and behavioral contracting	A-con, A-sch	Probable	Interview, school, parents
May respond to a nurturing adult role model who frequently verbalizes expectations and fairly applies the stated contingencies	A-ang	Probable	School
Evaluation of sexual abuse	A-ang, A-sch	Possible	To be determined
May feel he has done some things that are so bad he cannot reveal them	A-con	Possible	To be determined
Has some academic interests that may be built upon	A-las	Possible	School

Note: Sources indicate which MMPI-A scales or subscales account for the diagnosis or recommendation. The likelihood column allows the interpreter to express the degree of confidence (i.e., "probable" or "possible") in the MMPI-A-based hypotheses or recommendations applying to the adolescent. Extra-test confirmation can be obtained from interviews, parents, school teachers, social-service agencies, juvenile courts, or other psychological test data, as well as any other sources used in psychological evaluations.

Chapter 12

Computerized MMPI-2 and MMPI-A
Interpretive Reports

In years past, if often took several days to have an MMPI administered, scored, and interpreted, and a report of the test results generated that could be used to provide personality feedback to the individual. Today electronic computers play an important role in mental-health services and have all but eliminated the lag time between test administration and reporting. The following situation illustrates a relatively common type of clinical test application:

A woman enters a community mental health center for an initial appointment to see a psychologist about the problems she has been having. In an initial session with an intake professional, she is asked to discuss her reason for referral and is given a briefing on the clinical evaluation procedures used in the clinic. Then she is ushered into a private room and seated at a computer console.

In the testing room, she receives instructions on how to respond to the questions that are presented on the TV screen and begins to respond to them by pressing the proper key on the keyboard. After completing the computerized test she is given a few minutes' break while the computerized narrative report is generated by the computer and given to the psychologist.

Shortly thereafter, the client is introduced to the psychologist, who has now had an opportunity to review the computer-based MMPI-2 report and already has an understanding of the patient's symptoms, possible diagnostic issues to address, possible long-standing personality characteristics, the client's openness to sharing personal information with the clinician, the likely need for therapy, and probable prognosis for treatment if that is the recommendation.

Many practitioners in contemporary clinical settings find that electronic computers are indispensable tools for collecting, processing, and interpreting psychologist test data. Computer processing of test protocols provides clinicians with immediate results on the MMPI-2 or MMPI-A. Rapid access to MMPI-2/MMPI-A information facilitates assessment and enhances treatment planning early in the intervention, even in the initial session. Computer-based interpretation usually provides the clinician with more extensive personality information than is typically available to practitioners using traditional test-scoring and interpretation approaches. Because of the amount of time it takes to handscore MMPI-2 or MMPI-A scales, the tendency is to use as few measures as possible. If computer scoring is used, a larger number of test indexes can be more efficiently incorporated.

Most contemporary clients are accustomed to seeing computer-based information, such as bank statements, grade reports, and so forth, and usually accept or even prefer information processed through a computer. Computerized MMPI-2 and MMPI-A reports can be used to provide test feedback to clients, which enhances and facilitates the clinical interaction (Butcher, 1990a; Finn & Butcher, 1990).

In this chapter, we describe computer-based MMPI-2 and MMPI-A scoring and interpretation and explain how computerized (often referred to as automated) interpretation works. Examples of computer-generated MMPI-2 and MMPI-A reports illustrate the kind of information that is provided through this service. Later in the chapter we examine several important issues in computer-based interpretation.

Automated Interpretation of Personality Tests

Meehl (1954) reviewed the literature on clinical prediction and evaluated the relative effectiveness of clinical and actuarial (use of objectively derived rules and information) methods at predicting and describing behavior. He found that assessment approaches using objective classification rules consistently outperformed those based on intuitive or clinical strategies. One of Meehl's students (Halbower, 1955) demonstrated that objectively derived correlate information for particular test indexes (i.e., MMPI profiles) could be automatically applied to new cases with a high degree of accuracy. This objective assessment approach (see the discussion in Chapter 5) spawned the development of a number of MMPI "cookbooks" or codebooks that served as the interpretive base for computer assessment systems.

The use of electronic computers for the interpretation of MMPI profiles has a long history. Electronic computers became widely available in the 1960s, prompting several psychologists to develop automated test interpretation systems by simply programming a computer to apply predetermined test correlates for specific test scores or combinations of MMPI scores. The first computer-based interpretation system for the MMPI was developed by Pearson and Swenson in 1961 at the Mayo Clinic in Rochester, Minnesota (Rome et al., 1962). This program demonstrated that Meehl's actuarial approach to test interpretation could be implemented effectively with the electronic computer. A library of over 100 personality and symptomatic behaviors, which had been associated with certain test scores, was stored in the computer and programmed to print when the specified test scores were in the interpretable range. The computer output included an MMPI profile along with a listing of up to six of the relevant descriptors from the statement library. This computer interpretation system, though limited in scope, was readily accepted by the psychology and medical staffs at the Mayo Clinic (Pearson & Swenson, 1967; Pearson, Swenson, Rome, Mataya, & Brannick, 1965).

In subsequent years, several other more comprehensive and sophisticated MMPI interpretation programs were developed. The computer program developed by Fowler (1969) for Roche Laboratories was particularly impressive since it provided personality and symptomatic information about clients in a highly objective format. More recent computer-based MMPI programs have become even more elaborate in that they typically provide extensive information in a readable, narrative report format (Fowler 1987).

Three general types of computer-based MMPI or MMPI-2 interpretation programs have been developed, differing largely in terms of complexity. The first and simplest type of program was the "cookbook" or codebook approach, the second type is the automated clinician, and the third type is the complex decision model. These different approaches are described below in more detail.

The Automated Cookbook

In this approach, the psychologist simply programs the test correlates to be automatically listed when certain test scores are obtained. This approach was exemplified by the innovative Mayo Clinic study developed by Pearson et al. (1965).

The Automated Clinician

The second approach to computer-generated psychological reports has been referred to as the automated clinician (Fowler, 1969). Most of the commercially available computerized psychological test reporting programs are of this variety. They are computerized lists of statements or paragraphs that can be associated with particular test scores or profile types. The computer is programmed to look up the stored information for a particular set of test scores or indexes. It is important to realize that most such systems are not strictly actuarial because they incorporate clinical inferences and hypotheses that may or may not have been validated against external criteria.

The Complex Decision Model

The third approach to computer-based test interpretation involves a somewhat greater use of the rapid combinatory powers of the computer than simply a look-up or listing function. In this approach, the computer is programmed to combine data and make more complex decisions following more elaborate decision rules. This approach is somewhat more complicated than the other approaches because the procedures making specific higher level decisions more closely simulate a clinician's judgment processes in that numerous possible scale combinations are specified in order for relatively specific decisions to be made (Butcher, 1989b). The complex decision model is an "expert system" encapsulating specialist knowledge about a particular domain and making intelligent decisions within that area of expertise (Forsyth & Naylor, 1986.) For example, an individual's "Potential for Addiction" might be classified into several categories such as highly likely, likely, problems possible, or not likely. The following illustrate a set of MMPI-2 complex decision rules that could be used to define these categories:

If any of the following conditions are present classify the profile as "Addictive Problems are highly likely":

If the T score for MAC-R is greater than or equal to a T score of 70

If the T score for APS is greater than or equal to a T score of 70
If the T score for AAS is greater than or equal to a T score of 70
If the T scores for D, PD, and Pt are greater than or equal to a T score of 80
If the profile fails to meet any of the prior conditions then go to the next set

If any of the following conditions are present classify the profile as "Addictive Problems likely":

If the T score for MAC-R is greater than or equal to a T score of 65
If the T score for APS is greater than or equal to a T score of 65
If the T score for AAS is greater than or equal to a T score of 65
If the T scores for D, PD, and Pt are greater than or equal to a T score of 70
If the profile fails to meet any of the prior conditions then go to the next set

If any of the following conditions are present classify the profile as "Addictive Problems possible":

If the T score for MAC-R is greater than or equal to a T score of 60
If the T score for APS is greater than or equal to a T score of 60
If the T score for AAS is greater than or equal to a T score of 60
If the T scores for D, PD, and Pt are greater than or equal to a T score of 65
If the profile fails to meet any of the prior conditions then go to the next set

If all of the following conditions are present classify the profile as "Addictive Problems are not likely":

If the T score for MAC-R is less than a T score of 59
If the T score for APS is less than a T score of 59
If the T score for AAS is less than a T score of 59
If the T scores for D, PD, and Pt are less than a T score of 59

Options for Obtaining Computer-Based MMPI-2 and MMPI-A Reports

There are several options for administering and processing MMPI-2 protocols to obtain a computer-based MMPI-2/ MMPI-A report. Many of these options were briefly described in Chapter 2. The present chapter provides more detail about the MMPI-2 and MMPI-A scoring and interpretation services provided by National Computer Systems [NCS] (P.O. Box 1416, Minneapolis, MN 55440. Phone 1-800-627-7271).

Mail-In Service

Clinicians using the mail-in service administer the booklet versions of the MMPI-2 or MMPI-A to the client and mail or express mail the answer form to NCS for processing. The completed report is sent to the clinician by return mail within 24 hours of receipt. Practitioners with a low volume of patients and ample time to process the MMPI-2 (for example, if the therapist sees the patient on a weekly basis) can use this option. This is probably the most cost-effective test-processing option if time is not a factor and there is a low volume of clients assessed.

Fax Machine

With the advent of facsimile machines, data processing at a remote site becomes quite efficient. The completed MMPI-2 or MMPI-A answer sheet can be administered and faxed to National Computer Systems. The responses are recorded and processed at NCS and the report is faxed back to the practitioner. This allows prompt turnaround almost anywhere in the world. The fax submission option for test processing is also cost-efficient in that no computers or telecommunications equipment (other than a telephone and a fax machine) are needed for immediate access to computerized reports. The clinician needs to have a telephone line dedicated to the facsimile machine or have a multipurpose fax machine for maximum efficiency.

In-Office Processing by Microcomputer

Practitioners with access to a microcomputer can obtain immediate processing of the MMPI-2 or MMPI-A in their office with or without using a booklet and answer sheet. Clients can actually be given the MMPI on-line (see Chapter 2) and their responses immediately scored and used to generate a complete interpretive report. Another option, if the practitioner does not wish to dedicate a computer for test administration purposes, is to administer the MMPI-2 or MMPI-A by paper and pencil methods and then have a clerk key enter the item responses onto a computer file. The computer file can then be used to score and interpret the MMPI-2 profiles. This is a relatively cost-efficient approach since it only requires about eight minutes for an individual to key enter an entire answer sheet and even less with practice. There are problems with this procedure, the most evident being human error in entering the client's responses.

Optical Scanning of Answer Sheets

Practitioners or clinics with a high volume of tests to process, say five or six per day, may find that on-line administration or key entry of test responses by clerical staff can be cumbersome and inefficient. An attractive and relatively cost-effective option is to use an optical scanner to read and process the item responses. The optical scanner, which is directly wired to the computer, operates much like a copying machine to read the paper answer sheet. Instead of producing a paper copy, however, the scanner records the answers into a data file that can be processed by the computer. The MMPI scores can be computed and the protocol processed by the computer. The answer sheet is fed into the scanner, and within seconds the computer processes the scores and begins to print out the report.

Computer-Based MMPI-2/MMPI-A Narrative Reports

In this section, we will describe how an electronic computer can construct a narrative report from the information available on the MMPI-2 or MMPI-A scales. There are several misconceptions about computer-based interpretation that must first be clarified. First, let's begin by describing what a computerized report is *not*.

1. An MMPI-2/MMPI-A computerized report is not a purely scientific or actuarially based personality description. The necessary information for a complete actuary is not yet available, consequently most computer interpretation systems incorporate some clinically derived hypotheses, as well as actuarially combined data.

2. An MMPI-2/MMPI-A computerized personality report is not designed for use by individuals who are not trained in working with the MMPI-2 or MMPI-A. Computerized reports provide interpretive hypotheses to be used in conjunction with other clinical or test information by trained interpreters.

3. A computerized report is not an independent or "stand alone" psychological evaluation. It should be considered an aid to psychological interpretation and not an end in itself.

Computerized personality reports are summaries of hypothesized characteristics, symptomatic behavior, or other descriptions that are generated by a computer using specified test indexes that have been related empirically or theoretically to the behavior in question. Computerized reports are best considered as professional-to-professional consultations. Automated interpretation systems are analogous to reference books that serve as a convenient source of information for consultation as needed. These systems are ethical to use when following the Computerized Testing Guidelines of the American Psychological Association (American Psychological Association, 1986). They provide summaries of behavior-test relations and clinically derived or postulated relationships. The practitioner must decide how well the computerized prototype actually fits the patient in question.

The data base for MMPI-2/MMPI-A interpretations can come from several sources: the established empirical literature for MMPI-2/MMPI-A scales and indexes; correlates for special scales such as the Mf, MAC-R, APS, AAS, Si, Es, A-sch, ACK; predictive decisions or personality descriptions based on scale relationships or indexes (e.g., the Megargee Rules for adult correctional settings or the Goldberg Index for adult inpatients); problems or themes reflected through the MMPI-2/MMPI-A Content Scales, the Harris-Lingoes subscales, the MMPI-2 Critical Items; and, finally, the clinical experience of the system developer. These reports or automated clinicians vary in their comprehensiveness and accuracy in describing and predicting behavior depending, in part, on how closely they follow validated test correlates.

A number of computerized interpretive reports are available for the MMPI-2, including the Caldwell Report developed by Alex Caldwell, Roger Greene's MMPI Adult Interpretive System, and the Minnesota Report, described in the following section. A new version of the Minnesota Report is available for adolescents, as is an interpretive report by Robert Archer.

The Minnesota Report

The Minnesota Report, a series of computerized interpretation systems for the MMPI, was developed to aid clinicians in their clinical assessment (Butcher, 1987; 1989a; 1989b; 1991; Butcher & Williams, 1992). The Minnesota Report was developed with several goals in mind. The information included in the statement library of the various interpretive systems was based as closely as possible on established, replicable research data with the goal of providing highly generalizable and accurate descriptions. These systems take into account differences in MMPI-2/MMPI-A profiles across settings (i.e., the base rates of the population under consideration).

The MMPI-2/MMPI-A Minnesota Reports usually follow a plan that allows for the following operations:

1. The first step in computerized interpretation involves processing the raw answers by scoring relevant scales, compiling appropriate indexes, and storing the information in accessible disk reference files.

2. The next step involves determining profile validity, eliminating invalid records, drawing profiles, and printing out a summary of the client's validity scale pattern.

3. Next, the stored data files are searched for relevant scale scores and indexes to determine the appropriate prototypal information to apply to the case. The computer is programmed to search the stored data base (reference files or look-up tables) to locate the relevant personality and symptom information for particular scale scores in the protocol, that is, for the highest clinical scales or code type for the MMPI-2. The prototype information for the clinical scale or code type is supplemented with information from the content scales and the supplementary scales such as APS or AAS in the MMPI-2 or ACK and PRO in the MMPI-A.

4. Finally, the computer prints out a narrative report that addresses the validity of the self-report, summarizes the individual's symptomatic status, describes personality characteristics and significant problems. The interpretive programs also generate hypotheses about diagnostic possibilities and suggest treatment plans.

Several systems are available for the Minnesota Report:

1. The Minnesota Report: Adult Clinical System provides MMPI-2 reports developed for a number of specific clinical settings, including adult inpatient, adult outpatient, college counseling, correctional, medical settings, and chronic pain programs.

2. The Minnesota Report: Personnel Selection System was developed to provide reports for job applicants in occupations for which the MMPI-2 is used (i.e., those in which there is great public responsibility or high stress). The specific occupations include: nuclear power plant employees, police officers, airline pilots, fire department personnel, medical and psychological personnel, and ministerial candidates.

3. The Minnesota Report: Alcohol and Drug Treatment Program was developed specifically for use with clients who have or are thought to have substance-abuse problems. Information on profile type frequency, likelihood of substance abuse as measured by APS and MAC-R, and whether the individual has acknowledged problems with alcohol or drugs is included.

4. Minnesota Report for Adolescents (MMPI-A) was developed for the following settings: outpatient mental health, inpatient mental health, correctional, drug-alcohol treatment, medical, and school.

The interpretive reports were written in a format that would be clinically useful and would meet the clinician's needs for information on symptom description, diagnostic hypotheses, and treatment considerations. The interpretive system was designed to allow for easy modification as new research findings on the MMPI-2 and MMPI-A emerge.

Case Illustration for the Minnesota Report: Adult Clinical System

For our illustration of the Adult Clinical System of the Minnesota Report we will use the case with which you have already obtained a high degree of familiarity, the case of Alice. Alice's computer-generated MMPI-2 report, shown in Figure 12-1 (see the basic and Content Scale profiles reproduced in Chapter 8, p. 197) indicates that many of the elements from the basic profile, the content profile, and the supplementary profile that were explored in earlier chapters have been incorporated in the computer narrative report.

The computer report based on Alice's validity-scale pattern notes that her MMPI-2 profile is interpretable and is likely to be a good indication of her present personality functioning. The computer report also indicates that her cooperative approach toward the testing was likely to suggest a favorable treatment prognosis. Individuals with this pattern are likely to be willing to share personal information in therapy.

Alice's MMPI-2 standard scale profile pattern, with the high point scale 7 and prominent elevation on scale 8, was employed in the narrative report. Therefore,

Figure 12-1. Computer-Based Interpretation of the MMPI-2 for Alice (see Chapter 8 for discussion)

Profile Validity
This client's approach to the MMPI-2 was open and cooperative. The resulting MMPI-2 profile is valid and probably a good indication of her present level of personality functioning. This may be viewed as a positive indication of her involvement with the evaluation.

Symptomatic Pattern
The client appears to be anxious and tense, and is having difficulty concentrating or making routine decisions. She ruminates a great deal and feels worried, guilty, and depressed.

She seems insecure, and she is experiencing generalized fears that are difficult for her to control. She feels that her life is falling apart. She may be feeling panicky as well as worried about possible health problems. She reports no significant sex-role conflicts.

Interpersonal Relations
She is somewhat shy and insecure, nonassertive in social situations, and apparently ineffective and often covertly hostile in dealing with others. She also seems quite guilt-prone and ruminates excessively about personal and interpersonal failings. Furthermore, her perfectionistic standards and rather moralistic attitudes are likely to create relationship problems for her. Her feelings of inadequacy may impair close intimate relationships.

The content of this client's MMPI-2 responses suggests the following additional information concerning her interpersonal relations. She feels a moderate degree of family conflict at this time, and reported some troublesome family issues. She feels that her family life is not as pleasant as that of other people she knows.

Behavioral Stability
She is apparently highly distressed, and this might have a situational component. This appears to be an acute state which may subside as stress dissipates, or as treatment produces symptom relief. Her interpersonal style is not likely to change significantly if retested at a later date.

Diagnostic Considerations
Psychiatric patients with this profile are often diagnosed as having an anxiety disorder or a compulsive personality disorder. Phobic or obsessive-compulsive behavior is likely to be present.

Treatment Considerations
Since they desire symptom relief for anxiety and tension, individuals with this profile tend to be quite motivated for help and tend to remain in treatment for a long time. However, they are likely to rationalize, intellectualize, and ruminate at great length in psychotherapy, and may find it difficult to focus on specific topics. They may also be somewhat hostile or sarcastic toward the therapist.

Some individuals with this profile respond to relaxation or desensitization therapy for their fears. Since these clients are passive and nonassertive and have difficulty openly expressing their anger, they might benefit from assertiveness training or stress inoculation training.

If psychological treatment is being considered, it may be profitable for the therapist to explore the client's treatment motivation early in therapy. The item content she endorsed includes some feelings and attitudes that could be unproductive in psychological treatment and in implementing self-change.

Note: This MMPI-2 interpretation can serve as a useful source of hypotheses about clients. This report is based on objectively derived scale indexes and scale interpretations that have been developed in diverse groups of patients. The personality descriptions, inferences, and recommendations contained herein need to be verified by other sources of clinical information since individual clients may not fully match the prototype. The information in this report is most appropriately used by a trained, qualified test interpreter, and should be considered confidential.

her high anxiety, insecurity, concentration problems, and inability to function was highlighted in the symptomatic pattern. These are essentially the same personality features and problems that were addressed in the interpretive section in Chapter 8. The computer-based report incorporated high likelihood descriptors in the symptom section of the report. As the clinical interpretation of Alice's profile showed in Chapter 8, the computerized report considered the general problem area of anxiety disorder to be important in her clinical diagnosis.

The computer-based report concluded that psychological treatment was indicated in Alice's case and that she is likely to be motivated to become involved because of her feelings of discomfort. The report also noted a number of problems that would likely become central in her treatment, including her family conflicts and her nonassertiveness in interpersonal relationships.

Case Illustration of the Minnesota Report for Alcohol and Drug Treatment Settings

The Minnesota Report for Alcohol and Drug Treatment Settings is illustrated with the case of Mr. Jenkins. The patient, a 42-year-old salesman, (see the case description in Chapter 7) was being evaluated for admission to an inpatient alcohol treatment program at the insistence of his employer after a series of work problems related to alcohol use. His wife also refused to continue in their marriage unless he sought treatment for his alcoholism. She reported that he had been very irresponsible by drinking all night and frequently missing work the next day. He reportedly physically abused his wife on two occasions while drinking. He carelessly spends money by running up debts on his credit cards and by writing checks when he does not have money in the bank. His wife reported that she has had to borrow money several times to cover his bank overdrafts. His wife has attempted to get him to go into alcohol treatment on several occasions, but he has always refused, saying that he doesn't have a problem with alcohol. She recently left him after an incident in which he drank excessively, was arrested for drunken driving, and was very abusive toward the family. She took him back only after he agreed to go to the alcohol treatment program.

Mr. Jenkins's MMPI-2 basic profile is shown in Figure 12-2; the Content Scale profile in Figure 12-3; the supplementary scale profile is presented in Figure 12-4, and the narrative report summarizing the profile information in Figure 12-5.

The first step in using Mr. Jenkins's Minnesota Report is to determine whether the report is an appropriate match for his current behavior and personality. This can be done by evaluating his validity pattern and appraising whether the pattern of behavior he has been exhibiting is accurately portrayed by the report. The validity paragraph addresses the generally open and cooperative manner in which he was willing to disclose problems. Some symptom exaggeration might be present. The narrative report is considered to be a good indication of his present personality functioning. Second, the major pattern of symptoms he

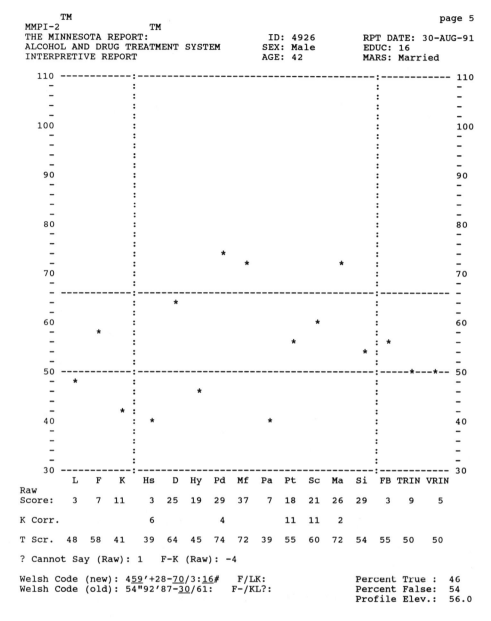

```
 110 ------------:-------------------------------------------:------------ 110
   -            :                                             :            -
   -            :                                             :            -
   -            :                                             :            -
 100            :                                             :          100
   -            :                                             :            -
   -            :                                             :            -
   -            :                                             :            -
  90            :                                             :           90
   -            :                                             :            -
   -            :                                             :            -
   -            :                                             :            -
  80            :                                             :           80
   -            :                                             :            -
   -            :                      *                      :            -
   -            :                    *                    *   :            -
  70            :                                             :           70
   -            :                                             :            -
   - -----------:------------------------------------------- :------------ -
   -            :    *                                        :            -
   -            :                                             :            -
  60            :                                  *          :           60
   -       *    :                                             :            -
   -            :                            *                :            -
   -            :                                     *  : *  :            -
  50 -----------:-------------------------------------------:-----*---*-- 50
   -    *       :                                             :            -
   -            :              *                              :            -
   -            :                                             :            -
   -          * :                                             :            -
  40          : *                     *                       :           40
   -            :                                             :            -
   -            :                                             :            -
   -            :                                             :            -
  30 -----------:-------------------------------------------:------------ 30
         L   F   K   Hs   D   Hy  Pd  Mf  Pa  Pt  Sc  Ma  Si  FB TRIN VRIN
Raw
Score:   3   7  11    3  25  19  29  37   7  18  21  26  29   3   9    5

K Corr.              6           4           11  11   2

T Scr.  48  58  41   39  64  45  74  72  39  55  60  72  54  55  50   50

? Cannot Say (Raw): 1    F-K (Raw): -4

Welsh Code (new): 459'+28-70/3:16#     F/LK:            Percent True :  46
Welsh Code (old): 54"92'87-30/61:      F-/KL?:          Percent False:  54
                                                        Profile Elev.: 56.0
```

Figure 12-2. Mr. Jenkins. The Minnesota Report:™ basic scales profile

has been experiencing as reported by his wife, his impulsive and irresponsible behavior, appears to be clearly addressed in the report. The two highest scores in the client's MMPI-2 profile, scales 4 and 9, are commonly found in individuals who are in alcohol treatment programs. Over 15% of inpatient treatment cases produce this two-point profile pattern.

```
        TM                                                        page 6
MMPI-2                      TM
THE MINNESOTA REPORT:                      ID: 4926        RPT DATE: 30-AUG-91
ALCOHOL AND DRUG TREATMENT SYSTEM          SEX: Male       EDUC: 16
INTERPRETIVE REPORT                        AGE: 42         MARS: Married
```

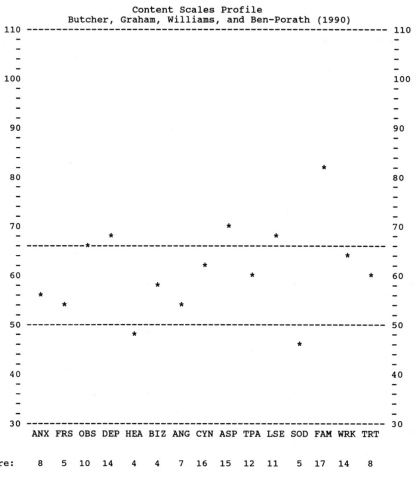

```
                        Content Scales Profile
               Butcher, Graham, Williams, and Ben-Porath (1990)
    110 --------------------------------------------------------------- 110
      -                                                                 -
      -                                                                 -
      -                                                                 -
      -                                                                 -
    100                                                                 100
      -                                                                 -
      -                                                                 -
      -                                                                 -
     90                                                                 90
      -                                                                 -
      -                                                                 -
      -                                                      *          -
     80                                                                 80
      -                                                                 -
      -                                                                 -
      -                                                                 -
     70                                       *                         70
      -                                                *                -
      - -----------*--------------------------------------------------- -
      -                               *                       *         -
     60                                       *                    *    60
      -    *                                                            -
      -       *                            *                            -
      -                           *                                     -
     50 --------------------------------------------------------------- 50
      -                   *                                             -
      -                                              *                  -
      -                                                                 -
     40                                                                 40
      -                                                                 -
      -                                                                 -
      -                                                                 -
     30 --------------------------------------------------------------- 30
        ANX FRS OBS DEP HEA BIZ ANG CYN ASP TPA LSE SOD FAM WRK TRT

Raw
Score:   8   5  10  14   4   4   7  16  15  12  11   5  17  14   8

T Score: 55  54  66  68  48  57  53  62  69  60  67  45  82  63  59
```

Figure 12-3. Mr. Jenkins. The Minnesota Report:™ Content Scales profile

The narrative report points to a number of factors that need to be considered in his treatment planning. Although he reports considerable problems with low morale, low self-esteem, and family conflicts, he may have difficulties dealing with these issues in therapy since he tends to have long-standing personality problems that may insulate him from external feedback. His typical behavior appears to involve externalizing blame rather than changing his behavior. His antisocial and acting-out tendencies might frustrate treatment efforts. The narra-

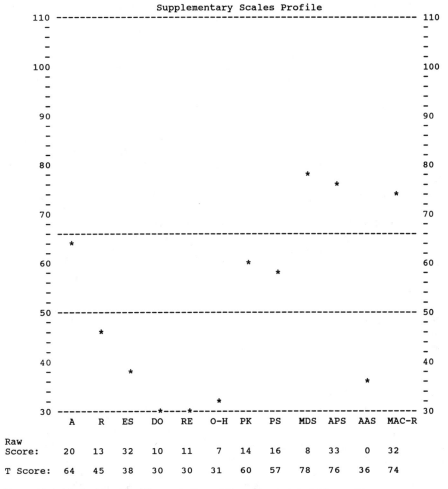

Figure 12-4. Mr. Jenkins. The Minnesota Report:™ supplementary scales profile

tive report provides a somewhat negative appraisal of his treatment potential, indicating that he might seek therapy, perhaps to appease his wife's demands, but may have difficulty implementing positive behavior change. His lack of acknowledgment of alcohol or drug problems, as noted by the report, will likely be a deterrent to treatment success since he apparently denies that problems exist. Any treatment program aimed at dealing with his alcohol or drug use would need to confront this problem denial in the early sessions if appropriate motivation for change is to be obtained.

Figure 12-5. Computer-Based Interpretation of the MMPI-2 for Mr. Jenkins

Profile Validity
This is a valid MMPI-2 profile. The client was quite cooperative with the evaluation and appears to be willing to disclose personal information. There may be some tendency on his part to be overly frank and to exaggerate his symptoms in an effort to obtain help. These hypotheses should be kept in mind when evaluating the clinical patterns reflected in the profile.

Symptomatic Pattern
The client appears to have long-standing impulse-control problems. Extraverted, uninhibited, and rather self-indulgent, he has a low frustration tolerance and a need for constant stimulation that cause him to behave recklessly or irresponsibly at times. Many individuals with this pattern use alcohol or drugs to excess. He apparently has an exaggerated sense of importance and may have grandiose plans. He has a gift for charming others and for appearing self-confident, but he may actually feel quite insecure and inadequate.

He becomes involved in numerous activities, does not follow through sufficiently on commitments, and tends to deny problems and to blame them on moods and overactivity, and he may explode angrily when he becomes frustrated. Many individuals with this profile develop problems of alcohol or drug abuse.

His MMPI-2 profile code, including Pd and Ma, is the most frequent two-point code among men in alcohol- or drug-abusing populations. Over 15.5% of men in substance-abuse treatment programs have this pattern. It should be noted that this high-point code occurs somewhat less frequently in the normative population (7.9%) and at a considerably lower level of elevation than in alcohol- and drug-abusing samples. This MMPI-2 profile configuration contains the most frequent high point, the Pd score, among alcohol-and drug-abusing populations. Over 24% of the men in substance-abuse treatment programs have this pattern, although it is not particularly frequent among men in the normative population (7.9%).

He experiences some conflicts concerning his sex-role identity, appearing somewhat passive and effeminate in his orientation toward life. He may appear somewhat insecure in a male-oriented role, and he may be uncomfortable in relationships with women. His interests, in general, are more characteristic of women than of men. He tends to be quite passive and submissive in interpersonal relationships, and he may make concessions in an effort to avoid confrontation. In addition, he may have a low heterosexual drive.

In addition, the following description is suggested by the content of this client's responses. He has endorsed a number of items suggesting that he is experiencing low morale and a depressed mood. The client's recent thinking is likely to be characterized by obsessiveness and indecision. Although he may be socially assertive and project a positive social image to others, his response content indicates a rather negative self-view that indicates he thinks little of himself. He reports holding some antisocial beliefs and attitudes, admits to rule violations, and acknowledges a history of antisocial behavior in the past. He seems to have an overinflated view of himself, and he seems to resent others making demands on him. He seems to have had much past conflict with authority and is quite resentful of societal standards of conduct.

Interpersonal Relations
A natural ability to charm, persuade, or even con others is usually found in individuals with this profile. They are very sociable and outgoing, but their relationships are usually quite superficial and manipulative. They tend not to be open and honest in relationships. His marriage does not seem to provide him with sufficient pleasure or happiness. He may be experiencing marital discord at this time.

Figure 12-5. Computer-Based Interpretation of the MMPI-2 for Mr. Jenkins, continued

In addition, the following description is suggested by the content of this client's responses. He tends to approach social relationships with some caution and skepticism. He views his home situation as unpleasant and lacking in love and understanding. He feels like leaving home to escape a quarrelsome, critical situation and to be free of family domination.

Behavioral Stability

The relative scale elevation of the highest scales in his clinical profile reflects high profile definition. If he is retested at a later date, the peak scores on this test are likely to retain their relative salience in his retest profile pattern.

This pattern of behavior shows a number of long-standing personality characteristics. Some individuals with this profile tend to "burn out" in later life and act out less, in which case a different pattern of symptoms might occur, including somatic distress, anxiety, and depression.

Diagnostic Considerations

Individuals with this profile are usually diagnosed as having a personality disorder. The possibility of a cyclothymic disorder should be evaluated, however. Excessive alcohol or drug use could be a central part of his clinical picture.

The content of his responses underscores the antisocial features in his history. These factors should be taken into consideration in arriving at a clinical diagnosis.

His extremely high score on addiction-proneness indicators suggests great proclivity to the development of an addictive disorder. Further evaluation of substance use or abuse problems is strongly recommended.

Treatment Considerations

Individuals with this profile tend not to seek psychological treatment on their own and are often seen in therapy only at the insistence of others. They may be seen in family therapy, for example. They may appear to be cooperative and to "enjoy" therapy for a time, but they usually resist any demands that they alter their behavior because they are not very introspective and see little reason to change.

Individuals with this profile assume little responsibility for their problems. Their acting-out behavior is likely to be destructive to treatment planning. The fact that he acknowledges having few or no problems with alcohol or drugs should be taken into consideration in treatment planning.

Examination of item content reveals a considerable number of problems with his home life. He feels extremely unhappy and alienated from his family. He related that he feels his home life is unpleasant and feels pessimistic that the situation will improve. Any psychological intervention will need to focus on his negative family feelings if treatment progress is to be made.

Note: This MMPI-2 interpretation can serve as a useful source of hypotheses about clients. This report is based on objectively derived scale indexes and scale interpretations that have been developed in diverse groups of patients with special emphasis on alcohol- and drug-abuse populations. The personality descriptions, inferences, and recommendations contained herein need to be verified by other sources of clinical information since individual clients may not fully match the prototype. The information in this report should most appropriately be used by a trained, qualified test interpreter. The information contained in this report should be considered confidential.

Case Illustration of The Minnesota Report
for Personnel Screening

The nuclear power company conducting the present evaluation, like most nuclear facilities, typically incorporates a personality screening instrument in its pre-employment program following recommendations of the Nuclear Regulatory Commission (Nuclear Regulatory Commission, 1984). The pre-employment screening program for the nuclear power company involves obtaining several types of information, including a background check, an interview to determine work experience conducted by the operations department, a clinical interview by the psychology staff, and the MMPI-2.

The applicant for one of the technical positions advertised was a 34-year-old woman, Eva B., who had previously been employed for 11 months as a technical assistant in a large chemical company. She was terminated from this employment before the end of her probationary period. No reasons were given for her termination. The Minnesota Report for Personnel Screening based on her MMPI-2 profile is illustrated in Figures 12-6, 12-7, and 12-8.

The applicant's relevant personal history, interview, and psychological test information were evaluated by the psychology staff in making their final employment determination. From the interview and history information, the staff was particularly concerned that the applicant lacked appropriate social skills and tended to interact negatively with others. This hypothesized lack of interpersonal skills might adversely influence her ability to work effectively on a team. In addition, the staff considered that her inability to perform to the satisfaction of her employer in her previous job might reflect both an inability to work in a cooperative team environment and possibly an inability to learn critical elements of the job.

The applicant's qualifications and psychological adjustment were discussed in the employment staffing conference after the evaluation was completed. Based upon her previous employment difficulties, her lack of experience in a nuclear facility, and the psychological adjustment difficulties she was likely experiencing (as assessed by the MMPI-2), it was decided not to offer her the position.

Case Illustration of the Minnesota Report for the MMPI-A

Computer-based interpretation of the MMPI-A will be illustrated by having the MMPI-A profiles of the case of Tony (see Chapters 10 and 11) analyzed by the Minnesota Report for the MMPI-A. Elements of Tony's MMPI-A performance that are picked up by the computer and incorporated in the narrative report will be noted. The MMPI-A basic and Content Scale profiles are presented in Figures 12-9 and 12-10 and the computer-generated narrative report is presented in Figure 12-11. The Minnesota Report is tailored to specific settings. Tony's MMPI-A could have been evaluated for a school setting but was processed to receive an outpatient mental-health report because of his referral problem.

The computer-based report addresses several aspects of the client's MMPI-A profile. First, Tony's validity scale performance is described in the Profile Validity

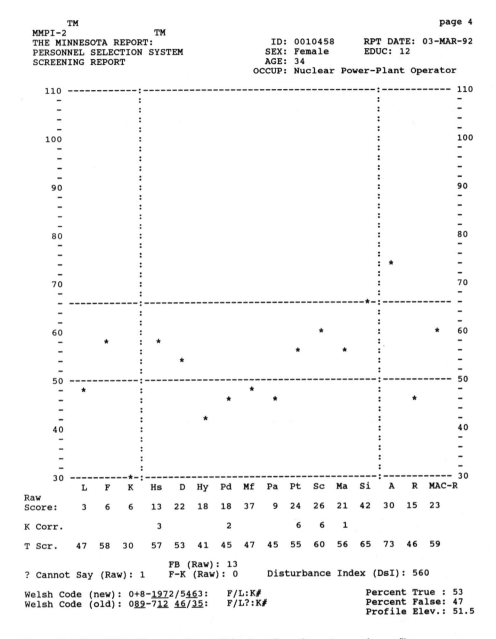

Figure 12-6. Eva B. The Minnesota Report:™ basic and supplementary scales profile

section of the report. Since all of his validity scales were clearly within the normal range, actually very near the mean score of 50, the computer-generated report accepts the profile as a valid and interpretable performance. No special limitations or interpretive caveats were noted in the validity section of the report.

Next, the computer narrative report addresses Tony's performance on the MMPI-A standard scales. In most cases, this section would incorporate an ex-

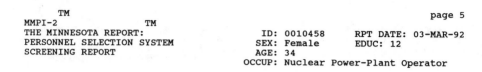

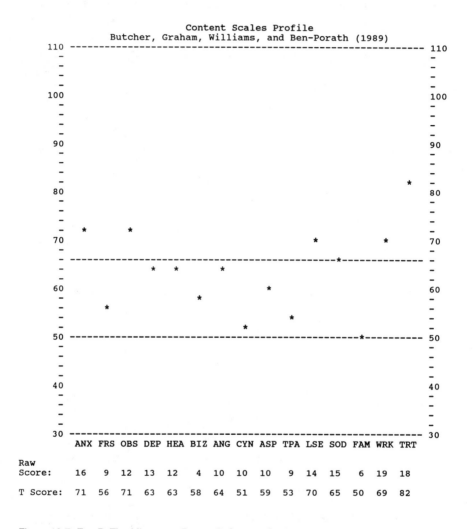

Figure 12-7. Eva B. The Minnesota Report:™ Content Scales profile

tended discussion of the empirical correlates of the most salient clinical scales. Since Tony's clinical scales were essentially in the normal range, with only one scale (scale 9) elevated above a T score of 60, the Symptomatic Pattern section is somewhat modest in its behavioral description. Only a few personality charac- teristics are inferred for individuals with moderate scores on scale 9; these center around overactivity and rebellious behavior. In this computer-based report, Tony's profile is placed in the perspective of other individuals with these peak

```
        TM                                                          page 1
MMPI-2                   TM
THE MINNESOTA REPORT:                        ID: 0010458      REPORT DATE: 03-MAR-92
PERSONNEL SELECTION SYSTEM
SCREENING REPORT
```

```
                         _____
                               OPENNESS TO EVALUATION
                         _____

    OVERLY       QUITE                    OVERLY
    FRANK        OPEN        ADEQUATE      CAUTIOUS     GUARDED      INDETERMINATE

    ------------X-----------------------------------------------------------------
```

```
                         _____
                              SOCIAL FACILITY
                         _____

    EXCELLENT     GOOD       ADEQUATE      PROBLEMS      POOR        INDETERMINATE
                                           POSSIBLE

    --------------------------------------------X----------------------------------
```

```
                         _____
                             ADDICTION POTENTIAL
                               (STANDARD LEVEL)
                         _____

               NO APPARENT   PROBLEMS
    LOW          PROBLEM      POSSIBLE     MODERATE      HIGH        INDETERMINATE

    --X---------------------------------------------------------------------------
```

```
                         _____
                              STRESS TOLERANCE
                         _____

    HIGH          GOOD       ADEQUATE      PROBLEMS      LOW         INDETERMINATE
                                           POSSIBLE

    ---------------------------------------------------X--------------------------
```

```
                         _____
                             OVERALL ADJUSTMENT
                         _____

                                           PROBLEMS
    EXCELLENT     GOOD       ADEQUATE       POSSIBLE     POOR        INDETERMINATE

    ------------------------------------X-----------------------------------------
```

Her responses to the MMPI-2 items suggests that she may have psychological problems at this time.

An individual with this level of social introversion is not likely to feel very comfortable in positions that have many interpersonal demands.

This applicant should be evaluated further to determine if she has adjustment problems.

NOTE: This MMPI-2 report can serve as a useful guide for employment decisions in which personality adjustment is considered important for success on the job. The decision rules on which these classifications are based were developed through a review of the empirical literature on the MMPI-2 with "normal-range" individuals (including job applicants) and the author's practical experience using the test in employment selection. The report can assist psychologists and physicians involved in personnel selection by providing an "outside opinion" about the applicant's adjustment. The MMPI-2 should NOT be used as the SOLE means of determining the applicant's suitability for employment. The information in this report should be used by qualified test interpretation specialists ONLY.

Figure 12-8. Eva B. The Minnesota Report:™ Personnel Selection System Screening Report

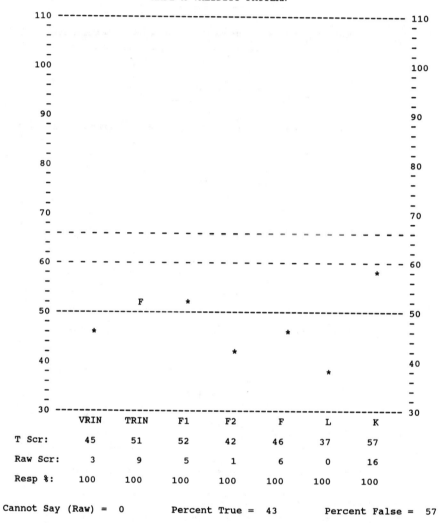

```
                TM                              ID: 18058                Page 1
                                                AGE: 14
MMPI-A                      TM                   GENDER: Male
THE MINNESOTA REPORT:                           SETTING: Outpatient Mental Health
ADOLESCENT INTERPRETIVE SYSTEM                  RPT DATE: 03-MAR-92


                        MMPI-A VALIDITY PATTERN

      110 ----------------------------------------------------------- 110
        -                                                              -
        -                                                              -
        -                                                              -
        -                                                              -
      100                                                              100
        -                                                              -
        -                                                              -
        -                                                              -
       90                                                              90
        -                                                              -
        -                                                              -
        -                                                              -
       80                                                              80
        -                                                              -
        -                                                              -
        -                                                              -
       70                                                              70
        -                                                              -
        - - - - - - - - - - - - - - - - - - - - - - - - - - - - - -    -
        -                                                              -
       60 - - - - - - - - - - - - - - - - - - - - - - - - - - - - - -  60
        -                                                    *         -
        -                                                              -
        -              F        *                                      -
       50 ----------------------------------------------------------- 50
        -                                                              -
        -        *                                  *                  -
        -                                                              -
        -                              *                               -
       40                                               *              40
        -                                                              -
        -                                                              -
        -                                                              -
       30 ----------------------------------------------------------- 30
              VRIN     TRIN     F1      F2      F       L       K

T Scr:         45       51      52      42      46      37      57

Raw Scr:        3        9       5       1       6       0      16

Resp %:       100      100     100     100     100     100     100
```

Cannot Say (Raw) = 0   Percent True = 43   Percent False = 57

Figure 12-9a. Tony. The Minnesota Report:™ basic scale profile

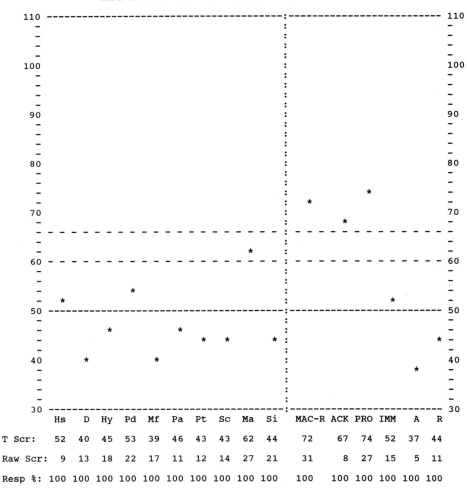

TM
MMPI-A   TM
THE MINNESOTA REPORT:
ADOLESCENT INTERPRETIVE SYSTEM

```
               MMPI-A BASIC AND SUPPLEMENTARY SCALES PROFILE

  110 -------------------------------------:------------------------- 110
    -                                      :                           -
    -                                      :                           -
    -                                      :                           -
    -                                      :                           -
  100                                      :                          100
    -                                      :                           -
    -                                      :                           -
    -                                      :                           -
   90                                      :                           90
    -                                      :                           -
    -                                      :                           -
    -                                      :                           -
   80                                      :                           80
    -                                      :                           -
    -                                      :            *              -
    -                                      :   *                       -
   70                                      :       *                   70
    -                                      :                           -
    - - - - - - - - - - - - - - - - - - - -:- - - - - - - - - - - - -  -
    -                                      :                           -
    -                                *     :                           -
   60 - - - - - - - - - - - - - - - - - - -:- - - - - - - - - - - -    60
    -                                      :                           :
    -                   *                  :                           -
    - *                                    :                  *        -
   50 -------------------------------------:------------------------- 50
    -           *             *            :                           -
    -                           *   *      *:                  *  -
   40      *          *                    :                 *        40
    -                                      :                           -
    -                                      :                           -
    -                                      :                           -
   30 -------------------------------------:------------------------- 30
       Hs   D   Hy  Pd  Mf  Pa  Pt  Sc  Ma  Si   MAC-R ACK PRO IMM   A   R

T Scr:  52  40  45  53  39  46  43  43  62  44    72    67  74  52  37  44

Raw Scr: 9  13  18  22  17  11  12  14  27  21    31     8  27  15   5  11

Resp %: 100 100 100 100 100 100 100 100 100 100   100   100 100 100 100 100
```

Welsh Code: 9-41/63078 2:5#   K/F:L#

Figure 12-9b. Tony. The Minnesota Report:™ supplementary scales profile

```
                                          ID: 18058              Page 5
              TM                          AGE: 14
MMPI-A                      TM            GENDER: Male
THE MINNESOTA REPORT:                    SETTING: Outpatient Mental Health
ADOLESCENT INTERPRETIVE SYSTEM           RPT DATE: 03-MAR-92
```

MMPI-A CONTENT SCALES PROFILE

```
 110 ------------------------------------------------------------ 110
  -                                                                -
  -                                                                -
  -                                                                -
  -                                                                -
 100                                                              100
  -                                                                -
  -                                                                -
  -                                                                -
  -                                                                -
  90                                                               90
  -                                                                -
  -                                                                -
  -                                                                -
  80                                        *                      80
  -                                                                -
  -                                  *                             -
  -                                                                -
  70                                                               70
  -                                                                -
  - - - - - - - - - - - - - - - - - - - - - - - - - - - - - - - -
  -                                                                -
  -                                                                -
  60 - - - - - - - - - - - - - - - - - - - - - - - - - * - - -     60
  -                                                *                -
  -                                                                -
  -                                            *                    -
  -                                                                -
  50 ------------------------------------------------------------ 50
  -                    *               *                            -
  -                                       *                    *    -
  -         *                                         *             -
  -              *         *     *                                  -
  40          *                                                     40
  -                                                                -
  -                                                                -
  -                                                                -
  30 ------------------------------------------------------------ 30
      A- anx obs dep hea aln biz ang cyn con lse las sod fam sch trt

 T Scr:     43  40  41  48  42  41  74  48  79  45  52  43  57  60  46

 Raw Scr:    5   3   3   6   3   1  14  13  19   3   7   5  16  10   8

 Resp %:   100 100 100 100 100 100 100 100 100 100 100 100 100 100 100
```

Figure 12-10. Tony. The Minnesota Report:™ Content Scales profile

scores by a description of the relative frequency of his profile type in both clinical and normative samples. The report also addresses the adolescent's self-perceptions by analyzing two MMPI-A Content Scales. His low scores on the A-las and A-lse scales were taken to indicate that he tends to view himself in generally positive ways.

Although, few symptoms were noted from the standard profile, the computer report does take note of several negative symptomatic behaviors through the

```
        TM                                ID: 18058                    Page 2
MMPI-A                                    AGE: 14
                    TM                    GENDER: Male
THE MINNESOTA REPORT:                     SETTING: Outpatient Mental Health
ADOLESCENT INTERPRETIVE SYSTEM            RPT DATE: 03-MAR-92
```

VALIDITY CONSIDERATIONS

This adolescent's approach to the MMPI-A was open and cooperative. The
resulting MMPI-A profile is valid and is probably a good indication of his
present level of personality functioning. This may be viewed as a positive
indication of his involvement with the evaluation.

SYMPTOMATIC BEHAVIOR

His MMPI-A clinical scales profile is only moderately elevated on Ma,
which is associated with enthusiasm, wide-ranging interests, and an
animated approach to problems. Very limited information is provided on his
clinical scales profile about any psychological problems. He may
overestimate his capabilities and overextend himself at times. His zeal and
intensity may lead to misunderstandings with teachers, parents, or other
authority figures.

Adolescent boys with this MMPI-A clinical profile configuration have one of
the most frequent high-point scales, the Ma score, found in adolescent
treatment units. Over 10% of boys in treatment programs have this
well-defined high point in their profile. It should be noted that this
high-point score is also the most frequent peak for well-defined profile
configurations in the normative sample (over 12%), although it usually has
a lower level of elevation than in treatment samples.

His MMPI-A Content Scales profile reveals important areas to consider in
his evaluation. He described significant behavioral problems including
stealing, lying, destroying property, and swearing. These problems are
likely to cut across settings, including school and home. He may be
assaultive or aggressive when he is angry, and he may be interested in
violence.

INTERPERSONAL RELATIONS

His social behavior might be punctuated with periods of moodiness and open
expression of negative feelings. Descriptions about his interpersonal
relationships are apparent from his MMPI-A Content Scales profile. He
reports being irritable and impatient with others, and he may throw temper
tantrums to get his way.

BEHAVIORAL STABILITY

The relative scale elevation of the highest scales in his clinical profile
reflects high profile definition. If he is retested at a later date, the
peak scores on this test are likely to retain their relative salience in
his profile pattern.

```
        TM                                ID: 18058                    Page 3
MMPI-A                                    AGE: 14
                    TM                    GENDER: Male
THE MINNESOTA REPORT:                     SETTING: Outpatient Mental Health
ADOLESCENT INTERPRETIVE SYSTEM            RPT DATE: 03-MAR-92
```

DIAGNOSTIC CONSIDERATIONS

The relatively low elevation of his MMPI-A clinical scales does not provide
sufficient information to formulate a clinical diagnosis. Additional
information from other sources is needed to arrive at a diagnosis.

Figure 12-11. Computer-Based Interpretation of Tony's MMPI-A Profile (see discussion in Chapter 11)

His elevated Conduct Problems Scale score suggests the possible presence of an oppositional-defiant disorder or a conduct disorder.

He obtained very high scores on all three of the alcohol and drug problem scales, which is indicative of serious problems in this area. He probably engages in risk-taking behaviors and tends toward exhibitionism. He likely belongs to a peer group who use alcohol or other drugs. His involvement in an alcohol- or drug-using lifestyle should be further evaluated.

He has endorsed items that confirm his increasing involvement with alcohol or other drugs. He acknowledges that his use is problematic and reports being criticized for it. He may feel that alcohol or other drugs facilitate social interactions, thus serving as a coping strategy.

TREATMENT CONSIDERATIONS

Adolescents with this clinical scales profile admit to few symptoms that require mental health intervention. Unless problems are revealed in the other MMPI-A profiles or through other sources of assessment, this individual may see no reason to enter therapy at this time. However, his Content Scales profile suggests conduct disturbances that might best respond to behavioral treatment methods.

His elevated scores on the alcohol and drug problem scales indicate an important treatment concern. He has acknowledged some problems in this area, a valuable first step for intervention.

Conditions in his environment that may be contributing to his aggressive and hostile behaviors could be explored. Adolescents with anger-control problems may benefit from modelling approaches and rewards for appropriate behaviors. Stress inoculation training or other cognitive behavioral interventions could be used to teach self-control. Angry outbursts during therapy sessions can provide opportunities for him to learn about his impulse-control problems and to practice new skills.

He did endorse content suggesting a desire to succeed in life. School may have some positive aspects for him. This could be an asset to build on during treatment.

```
        TM                              ID: 18058              Page 4
MMPI-A                                  AGE: 14
                 TM                     GENDER: Male
THE MINNESOTA REPORT:                   SETTING: Outpatient Mental Health
ADOLESCENT INTERPRETIVE SYSTEM          RPT DATE: 03-MAR-92
```

NOTE: This MMPI-A interpretation can serve as a useful source of hypotheses about adolescent clients. This report is based on objectively derived scale indexes and scale interpretations that have been developed with diverse groups of clients from adolescent treatment settings. The personality descriptions, inferences, and recommendations contained herein need to be verified by other sources of clinical information because individual clients may not fully match the prototype. The information in this report should most appropriately be used by a trained, qualified test interpreter. The information contained in this report should be considered confidential.

```
                                   ID: 18058              Page 6
        TM                         AGE: 14
MMPI-A              TM             GENDER: Male
THE MINNESOTA REPORT:             SETTING: Outpatient Mental Health
ADOLESCENT INTERPRETIVE SYSTEM    RPT DATE: 03-MAR-92
```

SUPPLEMENTARY SCORE REPORT

	Raw Score	T Score	Resp %
Depression Subscales (Harris-Lingoes):			
Subjective Depression (D1)	4	39	100
Psychomotor Retardation (D2)	4	46	100
Physical Malfunctioning (D3)	4	55	100
Mental Dullness (D4)	2	43	100
Brooding (D5)	1	41	100
Hysteria Subscales (Harris-Lingoes):			
Denial of Social Anxiety (Hy1)	1	38	100
Need for Affection (Hy2)	3	41	100
Lassitude-Malaise (Hy3)	4	50	100
Somatic Complaints (Hy4)	4	50	100
Inhibition of Aggression (Hy5)	4	59	100
Psychopathic Deviate Subscales (Harris-Lingoes):			
Familial Discord (Pd1)	4	53	100
Authority Problems (Pd2)	6	67	100
Social Imperturbability (Pd3)	3	48	100
Social Alienation (Pd4)	1	32	100
Self-Alienation (Pd5)	2	41	100
Paranoia Subscales (Harris-Lingoes):			
Persecutory Ideas (Pa1)	4	50	100
Poignancy (Pa2)	1	36	100
Naivete (Pa3)	4	50	100
Schizophrenia Subscales (Harris-Lingoes):			
Social Alienation (Sc1)	3	40	100
Emotional Alienation (Sc2)	0	37	100
Lack of Ego Mastery, Cognitive (Sc3)	1	41	100
Lack of Ego Mastery, Conative (Sc4)	2	42	100
Lack of Ego Mastery, Def. Inhib. (Sc5)	5	57	100
Bizarre Sensory Experiences (Sc6)	3	44	100

```
                                      ID: 18058              Page 7
            TM                        AGE: 14
MMPI-A                 TM             GENDER: Male
THE MINNESOTA REPORT:                 SETTING: Outpatient Mental Health
ADOLESCENT INTERPRETIVE SYSTEM        RPT DATE: 03-MAR-92
```

	Raw Score	T Score	Resp %
Hypomania Subscales (Harris-Lingoes):			
Amorality (Ma1)	5	66	100
Psychomotor Acceleration (Ma2)	8	57	100
Imperturbability (Ma3)	5	62	100
Ego Inflation (Ma4)	4	48	100

	Raw Score	T Score	Resp %
Social Introversion Subscales (Ben-Porath, Hostetler, Butcher, & Graham):			
Shyness / Self-Consciousness (Si1)	5	46	100
Social Avoidance (Si2)	1	43	100
Alienation--Self and Others (Si3)	4	40	100

Uniform T scores are used for Hs, D, Hy, Pd, Pa, Pt, Sc, Ma, and the Content
Scales; all other MMPI-A scales use linear T scores.

content of the individual's responses and through the MMPI-A supplementary scales. Specifically, the report addresses the adolescent's high scale elevations on the A-con and A-ang Content Scale scales, indicating that these are likely to indicate aggressive acting-out behavior. In addition, the narrative report incorporates a discussion of the adolescent's likelihood of developing drug- or alcohol-abuse problems and of his willingness to acknowledge that he has had problems with alcohol or drugs. These severe behavioral problems, highlighted by the computer report, are important features of Tony's present problem situation that need to be considered in treatment planning. Overall, the computer-based narrative report pointed to several major problem areas in Tony's test performance that could guide the clinician into fruitful areas of exploration.

Evaluation of Computer Interpretation Systems

Research studies comparing the relative accuracy of computer-generated reports with those written by a trained clinician are not available. Most of the computer-report evaluation research has employed a research strategy in which a clinician rates acceptability of or satisfaction with the report relative to how it describes the behavior of a client (Moreland, 1987).

Validity of Narrative Reports

Three recent empirical validation studies have been published. Moreland and Onstad (1985) found that computerized psychological reports produced for actual patients were judged by clinicians to be significantly more accurate than random reports. Muller and Bruno (1986) found the Minnesota Personnel Report to be effective in discriminating problem police applicants from non-problem applicants. The most comprehensive empirical validation study of computer-based MMPI reports was conducted by Eyde and her colleagues (Eyde, Kowal, & Fishburne, 1987; 1991). These investigators compared the relative accuracy of computerized MMPI reports published by seven commercial scoring and interpretation companies: Behaviordyne, Caldwell, Applied Innovations, Psych Systems, Minnesota Report (NCS), Western, and Tomlinson Report. The investigators submitted MMPI answer sheets for several patients to each computer assessment service. They separated the computer-generated statements, disguised their source, and gave the statements to raters familiar with the actual cases to evaluate for accuracy. Once the ratings were complete, the investigators reassembled the statements into their original context and computed accuracy ratings for each of the seven reports.

Eyde et al. (1991) concluded that "Despite the large amount of empirical evidence available for the MMPI and its potential for actuarial prediction, the outputs of CBTI systems for the MMPI for individuals were found to vary significantly in their rated relevance, accuracy, and in their usefulness in case dispositions" (p. 111). In comparison with other available systems, the Minnesota Report "received the highest number of accuracy ratings and the lowest number of inaccuracy ratings for the clinical cases" (p. 104).

Table 12-1. Comparability of overall adjustment ratings of airline pilots (N = 262) by clinicians and computer-based decision rules

MN Personnel Report			Clinician Rating		
Rating		Adequate	Problems Possible	Problems Likely	Raw Total
Excellent	1	2.4	—	—	1.9
Good	2	42.5	20.0	—	35.9
Adequate	3	53.6	43.3	3.0	48.5
Problems Possible	4	1.4	25.7	24.0	6.5
Poor	5	—	10.0	64.0	7.3
Total		79.0%	11.5%	9.5%	100.0%

Source: Butcher, 1988.

Classification Accuracy of the Computer-Based Decision Rules

To assess whether the Minnesota Report Personnel Decision Rules generate credible personality ratings, a study was conducted to compare computer-based ratings with those made by experienced clinicians. The MMPI profiles of 262 airline pilot applicants were rated as to their overall adjustment by three trained clinicians and also processed by the computer. The clinicians rated applicants, using their MMPI profiles, on a three-point scale of "Adequate," "Problems Possible," and "Problems Likely." The computer rated adjustment in terms of "Excellent," "Good," "Adequate," "Problems Possible," and "Poor." The results of the study are shown in Table 12-1

When the expert clinicians rated an applicant as "Adequate," 98.5% of the time the computer also rated the applicant as "Adequate" or better in terms of adjustment. When the clinicians rated the MMPI profile as "Problems likely," the computer agreed 88% of the time. For clear decisions (adequate or poor) agreement was obtained in 89.5% of the cases. A total of 11.5% of the cases were rated by the clinicians as "Problems possible." In these marginal adjustment cases, the computer rules classified 36.7% of them as "Problems possible" or "Poor" in adjustment and 63.3% of the cases as adequate or better.

This study showed that a computer program designed to rate an applicant's MMPI profiles for psychological adjustment accurately simulated the decisions of clinicians (Butcher, 1988). This generally high level of agreement between computer-rated and clinician-rated decisions shows that complex clinical judgments can be reliably made by computer. This study did not address external validity since information about the actual adjustment of the applicants was not available.

The personnel decision classification system involves the application of a very complex set of contingency rules to assign "ratings of adjustment." As shown in the study with airline pilot applicants, these ratings have a high degree of comparability with ratings made by expert clinicians evaluating the same MMPI profiles. It is likely that computer-based psychological assessment will be greatly expanded in the future. Future assessments will likely include greater utilization of more complex computerized assessment paradigms to exploit more fully the flexibility and power of the computer in combining assessment information into evaluations.

Issues Concerning Computer-Based MMPI-2 and MMPI-A Interpretation

Computer-based MMPI-2 and MMPI-A reports can be incorporated in a test battery and can provide the practitioner with very valuable information if appropriate cautions are taken and their limitations recognized. There are several caveats to keep in mind when considering the use of computer-generated test reports. First, the practitioner must ensure that the report is appropriate for the case in question and that the information provided in the report matches the test variables produced by the client. Second, care must be taken to employ the most pertinent information and, if necessary, ignore any information of limited relevance. This process, of course, requires that the user have a high degree of familiarity with the test itself. There are other issues with respect to "care and storage" of computerized outputs that require careful consideration. We will examine these issues pertinent to using computer-generated information in clinical assessment in more detail.

The Limited Range of Available Test Correlates for the MMPI-2/MMPI-A

Although many studies in the past 25 years have catalogued empirical correlates for the various MMPI scales and indexes, the data base for the MMPI, MMPI-2, and MMPI-A does not, at present, provide for interpretation of all possible profile configurations in a strictly actuarial manner. Given that the full range of MMPI code possibilities are not well delineated empirically, the clinical experience of the program developer will determine the make-up of the reports that are generated. Decisions about which components to employ in developing a computer interpretation program clearly influence the accuracy and generalizability of the report. As Fowler noted (1987), it is therefore important, in choosing a computer-based interpretation program, to evaluate carefully the expertise of the system developer. Most of the existing MMPI computer interpretation programs extrapolate from the available research information base to interpret all cases submitted to the service. For example, little actuarial data exist for some codes such as the 1-9-6 code. The interpretation will likely be based on some combination of the two-point codes or single-scale elevations of the three component scales, depending upon the experience of the computer program developer. The approach the program developer chooses will determine the nature of the resulting narrative report.

Determining the Prototypal Match: Does the Computerized Report Actually Fit the Client?

Computer-based test interpretations are best viewed as resource consultations. The computer reporting service provides scoring, indexing, profiling, and listing of relevant test variables along with the narrative statements considered to be most appropriate for the particular test scores. Some of the statements or predictions incorporated in the report may not apply to every patient with a given profile type. It is the responsibility of the test user to determine if the computer-generated statments are accurate for the particular client. Computer-based MMPI-2 and MMPI-A reports are based on modal or typical descriptions. It is very important for the practitioner to determine if the computer-based report is appropriate for the patient being assessed. That is, does the information being provided by the report actually apply to the client?

Several factors are important in determining if the profile and the prototypal descriptions match the individual in question. First, a proper match can be determined only if the clinician is both familiar with the MMPI-2 or MMPI-A measures and associated empirical descriptors and also sensitive to the client's actual behaviors and problems. Important to the determination of prototypal match is the clinician's judgment that the behaviors and symptoms obtained from external sources, such as interviews or other test data, are congruent with the hypotheses generated by the computer. The practitioner needs to have a knowledge of the special limiting factors that might influence a particular case, for example, whether the client was blind, had a limited educational background, or was from a different culture.

It is also important for the practitioner to evaluate test validity to ensure that the protocol is interpretable before the personality descriptions and symptoms are attributed to the client. Finally, the issue of profile definition needs to be addressed for the particular client's profile. If the profile is not well-defined, that is, if it has many scale scores falling at nearly the same level of elevation, the profile report is less likely to provide specific and reliable information about a client than are those profiles with very high profile definition.

The Role of the Computerized Output in the Assessment Report

How is the computerized narrative output used in developing a clinical report? Computer-based outputs are not "stand alone" clinical reports. Rather, they are best conceptualized as a documented resource or working hypotheses analogous to one's notes obtained from a textbook, actuarial tables, or an informed colleague.

High probability statements for a particular profile appear in the narrative output as hypotheses about the client. The practitioner determines the congruence and strength of this information in characterizing the client in question. Information that is confirmatory and fits into the clinical picture that is beginning to emerge from other data sources, such as interview, background information, or other test data, may be given a high degree of credence and be included as primary considerations in the evaluation. Many practitioners incorporate the actual wording from the narrative computer output if the information is considered highly relevant for the case.

Some aspects of a particular computerized narrative might appear to the practitioner as relatively unimportant to a case or as not adding particularly useful information to the assessment. For example, a computer-generated statement that "the client shows a lack of impulse control and might act-out in an impulsive manner" may not be particularly new or useful information if the client in question is being evaluated in a pre-sentencing investigation after having been convicted of a gruesome murder. The practitioner chooses the information that best fits the case and the purpose of the evaluation.

Where Are Computerized MMPI-2 and MMPI-A Outputs Filed?

As noted earlier, computer-based reports are usually viewed as professional-to-professional consultations analogous to information from a textbook or from a consultation with a specialist in a particular area. The computer scores and narrative reports generated on a particular case can be viewed as the practitioner's working notes from which he or she derives hypotheses or inferences about the client. As working documents in the early stages of a diagnostic evaluation, computerized reports and scores should be kept in the practitioner's working file along with other materials used and notes kept during the assessment process. Computerized narrative outputs are usually not stored in the patient's chart where they might, perhaps at a later date, be mistaken for the complete report on the case. States have different requirements about the storage of assessment information. Therefore the practitioner should be aware of the legal requirements.

In some settings, computer-based narrative reports are placed in patient's charts, along with other completed reports and pertinent documents, after the psychological evaluation is complete. Practitioners who find this to be the working practice at his or her particular facility should take care to add a summary statement to the output that clarifies the extent to which it entered into the final report on the client.

Limiting Patients' Access to Their Computerized MMPI-2 and MMPI-A Reports

The computer-based MMPI-2 or MMPI-A report should be viewed as resource material that can provide a number of useful hypotheses, personality descriptions, and test inferences about clients. Clinicians often find that a computerized report is a valuable aid in providing test feedback to clients (Butcher, 1990a; Finn & Butcher, 1990). However, care should be taken to limit patient access to reports. Reports should not be provided to clients to keep since there is great potential for misuse and misunderstanding. Computer-generated narrative reports are technical documents developed for professionals and not written for clients' self-use.

Computer-Based Psychological Test Interpretation: Consumer Qualifications

The American Psychological Association has established guidelines for determining user qualifications to purchase computer-based MMPI-2 reports (American Psychological Association, 1986). Most computer reporting services follow the user qualification guidelines and determine if potential subscribers are qualified to use the reports. For example, according to the National Computer Systems user qualification scheme, Minnesota Reports are made available to "fellows, members, and associate members of the American Psychological Association, as well as to psychologists, physicians, and marriage and family therapists licensed by the regulatory board of the state in which they practice."

The final chapter of the book has focused on the use of electronic computers to score and interpret the MMPI-2 and MMPI-A. Computer-based interpretive reports can provide the clinician with a convenient "outside opinion" concerning a client's symptoms and behavior based on MMPI-2 or MMPI-A scores. Information based upon the most likely empirical descriptors, prominent content themes, and supplementary scales are integrated into a narrative report.

Epilogue

You have, by reading to this point in the book, gained a great deal of background information and interpretive guidelines for using the MMPI-2 and MMPI-A in clinical assessment. For the beginner, who is learning about objective personality assessment for the first time, there has been a great deal to digest. For the previous MMPI user, who is making the transition to MMPI-2 and MMPI-A, some re-thinking of established measures and new dimensions has been required although many traditional aspects have been maintained. We anticipate that further readings that you may do on the MMPI and its variants will further confirm for you, as it has for us, that the MMPI has a very special place in applied psychology. It is an instrument that was initially developed out of a pragmatic orientation to understanding personality and has been reinforced by thousands of psychologists and psychiatrists who have conducted research on it over the past fifty years.

We hope that this introduction to the clinical interpretation of the MMPI-2 and MMPI-A will enable you, comfortably and effectively, to interpret profiles of your clients. We have tried to include only those measures that have stood the test of time or, in the case of the new measures, show substantial promise earned through empirical verification. Our goal throughout the book has been to illustrate the scales and interpretive process with abundant case material. It is through clinical application that the MMPI has earned the respect and allegiance of so many people across the world. We believe that the MMPI-2 and MMPI-A will follow in that tradition.

References

Altman, H., Gynther, M. D., Warbin, R. W., & Sletten, I. W. (1973). Replicated empirical correlates of the MMPI 8-9/9-8 code type. *Journal of Personality Assessment, 37,* 369-371.

American Psychiatric Association (1952). *Diagnostic and statistical manual of mental disorders.* Washington, DC: American Psychiatric Association.

American Psychiatric Association (1968). *Diagnostic and statistical manual of mental disorders (2nd ed.) (DSM-II).* Washington, DC: American Psychiatric Association.

American Psychiatric Association (1980). *Diagnostic and statistical manual of mental disorders (3rd ed.) (DSM-III).* Washington, DC: American Psychiatric Association.

American Psychiatric Association (1987). *Diagnostic and statistical manual of mental disorders (3rd ed.-revised) (DSM-III-R).* Washington, DC: American Psychiatric Association.

American Psychological Association (1986). *American Psychological Association guidelines for computer-based tests and interpretations.* Washington, DC: American Psychological Association.

Archer, R. P. (1984). Use of the MMPI with adolescents: A review of salient issues. *Clinical Psychology Review, 4,* 241-251.

Archer, R. P. (1987). *Using the MMPI with adolescents.* Hillsdale, NJ: Lawrence Erlbaum.

Archer, R. P., Gordon, R. A., Giannetti, R. A., & Singles, J. M. (1988). MMPI scale clinical correlates for adolescent inpatients. *Journal of Personality Assessment, 52,* 707-721.

Armentrout, D., Moore, J., Parker, J., Hewett, J., & Feltz, C. (1982). Pain patient subgroups: The psychological dimensions of pain. *Journal of Behavioral Medicine, 5,* 201-211.

Arnold, P. D. (1970). *Recurring MMPI two-point codes of marriage counselors and "normal" couples with implications for interpreting marital interaction behavior.* Unpublished doctoral dissertation, University of Minnesota.

Barrett, R. K. (1973). *Relationship of emotional disorder to marital maladjustment and disruption.* Unpublished doctoral dissertation, Kent State.

Barron, F. (1953). An ego strength scale which predicts response to psychotherapy. *Journal of Consulting Psychology, 17,* 327-333.

Beck, E. A., & McIntyre, S. C. (1977). MMPI patterns of shoplifters within a college population. *Psychological Reports, 41,* 1035-1040.

Ben-Porath, Y. S. (1989). Evaluating the validity of MMPI-2 profiles. In J. N. Butcher & J.R. Graham (Eds.), *Topics in MMPI-2 interpretation.* MMPI-2 Workshops, Department of Psychology, University of Minnesota.

Ben-Porath, Y. S., & Butcher, J. N. (1989a). Psychometric stability of rewritten MMPI items. *Journal of Personality Assessment, 53,* 645-653.

Ben-Porath, Y. S., & Butcher, J. N. (1989b). The comparability of MMPI and MMPI-2 scales and profiles. *Psychological Assessment: A Journal of Consulting and Clinical Psychology, 1,* 345-347.

Ben-Porath, Y. S., Butcher, J. N., & Graham, J. R. (1991). Contribution of the MMPI-2 scales to the differential diagnosis of schizophrenia and major depression. *Psychological Assessment: A Journal of Consulting and Clinical Psychology, 3,* 634-640.

Ben-Porath, Y. S., Hostetler, K., Butcher, J. N., & Graham, J. R. (1989). New subscales for the MMPI-2 Social Introversion (Si) Scale. *Psychological Assessment: A Journal of Consulting and Clinical Psychology, 1,* 169-174.

Bernstein, I., & Garbin, C. (1983). Hierarchical clustering of pain patients' MMPI profiles: A replication note. *Journal of Personality Assessment, 47,* 171-172.

Berry, D. T., Wetter, M. W., Baer, R. A., Widiger, T. A., Sumpter, J. C., Reynolds, S. K., & Hallam, R. A. (1991). Detection of random responding on the MMPI-2: Utility of F, Back F, and VRIN scales. *Psychological Assessment: A Journal of Consulting and Clinical Psychology, 3*, 418-423.

Boerger, A. R., Graham, J. R., & Lilly, R. S. (1974). Behavioral correlates of single scale MMPI code types. *Journal of Consulting and Clinical Psychology, 42*, 398-402.

Bogue, D. (1985). *The population of the United States: Historical trends and future projections*. New York: The Free Press.

Bohn, M. J. (1979). Management classification for young adult inmates. *Federal Probation, 43*, 53-59.

Booth, R. J., & Howell, R. J. (1980). Classification of prison inmates with the MMPI: An extension and validation of the Megargee typology. *Criminal Justice and Behavior, 7*, 407-422.

Bradley, L. A., Prokop, C. K., Margolis, R., & Gentry, W. D. (1978). Multivariate analysis of the MMPI profiles of low back pain patients. *Journal of Behavioral Medicine, 1*, 253-272.

Bradley, L. A., & Van der Heide, L. H. (1984). Pain-related correlates of MMPI profile subgroups among back pain patients. *Health Psychology, 3*, 157-174.

Brown, M. N. (1950). Evaluating and scoring the Minnesota Multiphasic "Cannot Say" items. *Journal of Clinical Psychology, 6*, 180-184.

Brown, P. L., & Berdie, R. F. (1960). Driver behavior and scores on the MMPI. *Journal of Applied Psychology, 44*, 18-21.

Burisch, M. (1984). Approaches to personality inventory construction. *American Psychologist, 39*, 214-227.

Butcher, J. N. (Ed.). (1972). *Objective personality assessment: Changing perspectives*. New York: Academic Press.

Butcher, J. N. (1979). Use of the MMPI in personnel selection. In James N. Butcher (Ed.), *New developments in the use of the MMPI*. Minneapolis: University of Minnesota Press.

Butcher, J. N. (1984). Current developments in MMPI use: An international perspective. In J. N. Butcher & C. D. Spielberger (Eds.), *Advances in personality assessment* (Vol. 4, pp. 83-92). Hillsdale, NJ: Lawrence Erlbaum.

Butcher, J. N. (1985). Current developments in MMPI use: An international perspective. In J. N. Butcher & C. D. Spielberger, (Eds.), *Advances in personality assessment* (Vol. 4). Hillsdale, NJ: Lawrence Erlbaum.

Butcher, J. N. (1987). Computerized clinical and personality assessment using the MMPI. In J. N. Butcher (Ed.), *Computerized psychological assessment*. New York: Basic Books.

Butcher, J. N. (1988). *Personality profile of airline pilot applicants*. Unpublished materials, MMPI-2 Workshops, Department of Psychology, University of Minnesota.

Butcher, J. N. (1989a, August). *MMPI-2: Issues of continuity and change*. Paper presented at the Ninety-Seventh Annual Convention of the American Psychological Association, New Orleans, LA.

Butcher, J. N. (1989b). *User's guide for the Minnesota Clinical Report*. Minneapolis: National Computer Systems.

Butcher, J. N. (1989c). *User's guide for the Minnesota Personnel Report*. Minneapolis: National Computer Systems.

Butcher, J. N. (1989d). *MMPI-2 profile of depressed inpatients*. Unpublished materials, MMPI-2 Workshops, Department of Psychology, University of Minnesota.

Butcher, J. N. (1990a). *Use of the MMPI-2 in treatment planning*. New York: Oxford University Press.

Butcher, J. N. (1990b). Education level and MMPI-2 measured psychopathology: A case of negligible influence. *MMPI-2 News and Profiles, 1* (2), 2.

Butcher, J. N. (1991). *User's guide to the Alcohol and Drug Treatment System*. Minneapolis: National Computer Systems.

Butcher, J. N., Aldwin, C., Levenson, M., Ben-Porath, Y. S., Spiro, A., & Bossé, R. (1991). Personality and aging: A study of the MMPI-2 among elderly men. *Psychology of Aging*.

Butcher, J. N., & Harlow, T. (1985). Psychological assessment in personal injury cases. In A. Hess & I. Wiener (Eds.), *Handbook of forensic psychology*. New York: John Wiley & Sons.

Butcher, J. N., Dahlstrom, W. G., Graham, J. R., Tellegen, A., & Kaemmer, B. (1989). *MMPI-2 (Minnesota Multiphasic Personality Inventory-2): Manual for administration and scoring*. Minneapolis: University of Minnesota Press.

Butcher, J. N., & Finn, S. (1983). Objective personality assessment in clinical settings. In M. Hersen, A. E. Kazdin, & A. S. Bellack (Eds.), *The clinical psychology handbook*. New York: Pergamon.

Butcher, J. N., Graham, J. R., Dahlstrom, W. G., & Bowman, E. (1990). The MMPI-2 with college students. *Journal of Personality Assessment, 54*, 1-15.

Butcher, J. N., Graham, J. R., Williams, C. L., & Ben-Porath, Y. S. (1990). *Development and use of the MMPI-2 Content Scales*. Minneapolis: University of Minnesota Press.

Butcher, J. N., & Hostetler, K. (1990). Abbreviating MMPI item administration: Past problems and prospects for MMPI-2. *Psychological Assessment: A Journal of Consulting and Clinical Psychology, 2*, 12-21.

Butcher, J. N., Jeffrey, T., Cayton, T. G., Colligan, S., DeVore, J., & Minnegawa, R. (1990). A study of active duty military personnel with the MMPI-2. *Military Psychology, 2*, 47-61.

Butcher, J. N., Keller, L. S., & Bacon, S. (1985). Current developments and future directions in computerized personality assessment. *Journal of Consulting and Clinical Psychology, 53*, 803-815.

Butcher, J. N., & Owen, P. (1978). Survey of personality inventories: Recent research developments and contemporary issues. In B. Wolman (Ed.), *Handbook of clinical diagnosis*. New York: Plenum.

Butcher, J. N., & Pancheri, P. (1976). *Handbook of cross-national MMPI research*. Minneapolis: University of Minnesota Press.

Butcher, J. N., & Pope, K. S. (1990). MMPI-2: A practical guide to clinical, psychometric, and ethical issues. *Independent Practitioner, 10*, 33-40.

Butcher, J. N., & Tellegen, A. (1966). Objections to MMPI items. *Journal of Consulting Psychology, 30*, 527-534.

Butcher, J. N., & Williams, C. L. (1992). *User's guide to the Adolescent Interpretive Report for the MMPI-A*. Minneapolis: National Computer Systems.

Butcher, J. N., Williams, C. L., Graham, J. R., Archer, R. P., Tellegen, A., Ben-Porath, Y. S., & Kaemmer, B. (1992). *MMPI-A (Minnesota Multiphasic Personality Inventory for Adolescents): Manual for administration, scoring, and interpretation*. Minneapolis: University of Minnesota Press.

Capwell, D. F. (1945a). Personality patterns of adolescent girls. I. Girls who show improvement in IQ. *Journal of Applied Psychology, 29*, 212-228.

Capwell, D. F. (1945b). Personality patterns of adolescent girls. II. Delinquents and nondelinquents. *Journal of Applied Psychology, 29*, 289-297.

Capwell, D. F. (1953). Personality patterns of adolescent girls: Delinquents and nondelinquents. In S. R. Hathaway & E. D. Monachesi (Eds.), *Analyzing and predicting juvenile delinquency with the MMPI* (pp. 29-37). Minneapolis: University of Minnesota Press.

Cheung, F. M. (1985). Cross-cultural considerations for the translation and adaptation of the Chinese MMPI in Hong Kong. In J. N. Butcher & C. D. Spielberger (Eds.), *Advances in personality assessment* (Vol. 4, pp. 131-158). Hillsdale, NJ: Lawrence Erlbaum.

Cheung, F. M., & Song, W. Z. (1989). A review on the clinical applications of the Chinese MMPI. *Psychological Assessment: A Journal of Consulting and Clinical Psychology, 1*, 230-237.

Cheung, F. M., Song, W. Z., & Butcher, J. N. (1991). An infrequency scale for the Chinese MMPI. *Psychological Assessment: A Journal of Consulting and Clinical Psychology, 3*, 648-653.

Clavelle, P., & Butcher, J. N. (1977). An adaptive typological approach to psychological screening. *Journal of Consulting and Clinical Psychology, 45*, 851-859.

Colby, F. (1989). Usefulness of the K correction in MMPI profiles of patients and nonpatients. *Psychological Assessment: A Journal of Consulting and Clinical Psychology, 1*, 142-145.

Colligan, R. C., Osborne, D., Swenson, W. M., & Offord, K. P. (1983). *The MMPI: A contemporary normative study*. New York: Praeger.

Colligan, R. C., & Offord, K. P. (1989). The aging MMPI: Contemporary norms for contemporary teenagers. *Mayo Clinic Proceedings, 64*, 3-27.

Constantinople, A. (1973). Masculinity-femininity: An exception to a famous dictum? *Psychological Bulletin, 80*, 389-407.

Costello, R. M., Hulsey, T. L., Schoenfeld, L. S., & Ramamurthy, S. (1987). P-A-I-N: A four-cluster MMPI typology for chronic pain. *Pain, 3*, 199-209.

Crewe, J. C., & Crewe, D. L. (1973). Sex! Who needs it? Not the MMPI! *Pupil Personnel Services, 2*, 13-14.

Cronbach, L. J. (1960). *Essentials of psychological testing*. (2nd ed.). New York: Harper.

Dahlstrom, W. G. (1980). Altered versions of the MMPI. In W. G. Dahlstrom & L. E. Dahlstrom (Eds.), *Basic readings on the MMPI* (pp. 386-393). Minneapolis: University of Minnesota Press.

Dahlstrom, W. G., & Butcher, J. N. (1964). *Comparability of the taped and booklet versions of the MMPI.* Unpublished manuscript.

Dahlstrom, W. G., Lachar, D., & Dahlstrom, L. E. (1986). *MMPI patterns of American minorities.* Minneapolis: University of Minnesota Press.

Dahlstrom, W. G., Panton, J. H., Bain, K. P., & Dahlstrom, L. E. (1986). Utility of the Megargee-Bohn MMPI typological assignments: Study with a sample of death row inmates. *Criminal Justice and Behavior, 13,* 5-17.

Dahlstrom, W. G., & Welsh, G. S. (1960). *An MMPI handbook: A guide to use in clinical practice and research.* Minneapolis: University of Minnesota Press.

Dahlstrom, W. G., Welsh, G. S., & Dahlstrom, L. E. (1972). *An MMPI handbook: Volume I, Clinical interpretation.* Minneapolis: University of Minnesota Press.

Dahlstrom, W. G., Welsh, G. S., & Dahlstrom, L. E. (1975). *An MMPI handbook: Volume II, Research applications.* Minneapolis: University of Minnesota Press.

Delk, J. (1973). Some personality characteristics of skydivers. *Life-Threatening Behavior, 3,* 51-57.

Drake, L. E. (1946). A social I-E scale for the MMPI. *Journal of Applied Psychology, 30,* 51-54.

Drake, L. E., & Oetting, E. R. (1959). *An MMPI codebook for counselors.* Minneapolis, Minnesota: University of Minnesota Press.

Edinger, J. D. (1979). Cross-validation of the Megargee MMPI typology for prisoners. *Journal of Consulting and Clinical Psychology, 47,* 234-242.

Edinger, J. D., Reuterfors, D., & Logue, P. E. (1982). Cross-validation of the Megargee MMPI typology: A study of specialized inmate populations. *Criminal Justice and Behavior, 9,* 184-203.

Egeland, B., Erickson, M., Butcher, J. N., & Ben-Porath, Y. S. (1991). MMPI-2 profiles of women at risk for child abuse. *Journal of Personality Assessment, 57,* 254-263.

Ehrenworth, N. V., & Archer, R. P. (1985). A comparison of clinical accuracy ratings of interpretive approaches for adolescent MMPI responses. *Journal of Personality Assessment, 49,* 413-421.

Endicott, N. A., & Jortner, S. (1966). Objective measures of depression. *Archives of General Psychiatry, 15,* 249-255.

Eyde, L., Kowal, D., & Fishburne, F. (1987, August). *Clinical implications of validity research on computer based test interpretations of the MMPI.* Paper presented at the Ninety-Fifth Annual Meeting of the American Psychological Association, New York, NY.

Eyde, L., Kowal, D., & Fishburne, F. (1991). In T. B. Gutkin & S. L. Wise (Eds.), *The computer and the decision making process* (pp. 75-123). Hillsdale, NJ: Lawrence Erlbaum.

Fink, A., & Butcher, J. N. (1972). Reducing objections to personality inventories with special instructions. *Educational and Psychological Measurement, 32,* 631-639.

Finn, S. (1990). *Providing client feedback with the MMPI-2.* Paper presented at the 25th Annual Symposium on Recent Developments in the Use of the MMPI, Minneapolis, Minnesota.

Finn, S., & Butcher, J. N. (1990). Clinical objective personality assessment. In Hersen, M., Kazdin, A. E., & Bellack, A. S. (Eds.), *The clinical psychology handbook* (2nd ed.). New York: Pergamon.

Fishburne, F., Eyde, L., & Kowal, D. (1988, August). *Computer-based test interpretations of the MMPI with neurologically impaired patients.* Paper presented at the Ninety-Sixth Annual Convention of the American Psychological Association, Atlanta, GA.

Fordyce, W. (1987). *Use of the MMPI with chronic pain patients.* Paper presented at the Ninth International Conference on Personality Assessment, Brussels, Belgium.

Forsyth, R., & Naylor, C. (1986). *The hitch-hikers guide to artificial intelligence: IBM PC version.* London: Chapman & Hall.

Fowler, R. D. (1969) Automated interpretation of personality test data. In J. N. Butcher (Ed.), *MMPI research developments and clinical applications.* New York: McGraw-Hill.

Fowler, R. D. (1985). Landmarks in computer-assisted psychological test interpretation. *Journal of Consulting and Clinical Psychology, 53,* 748-759.

Fowler, R. D. (1987). Developing a computer based test interpretation system. In J. N. Butcher (Ed.), *Computerized psychological assessment.* New York: Basic Books.

Fowler, R. D., Jr., & Athey, E. B. (1971). A cross-validation of Gilberstadt and Duker's 1-2-3-4 profile type. *Journal of Clinical Psychology, 27,* 238-240.

Gallucci, N. T. (1987). The influence of elevated F-scales on the validity of adolescent MMPI profiles. *Journal of Personality Assessment, 51,* 133-139.

Gilberstadt, H., & Duker, J. (1965). *A handbook for clinical and actuarial MMPI interpretation.* Philadelphia: Saunders.

Goldberg, L. R. (1965). Diagnosticians vs. diagnostic signs: The diagnosis of psychosis vs. neurosis from the MMPI. *Psychological Monographs, 79* (Whole No. 602).

Goodstein, L. D. (1954). Regional differences in MMPI responses among male college students. *Journal of Consulting Psychology, 18,* 437-441.

Gottesman, I. I., Hanson, D. R., Kroeker, T. A., & Briggs, P. (1987). Appendix C: New MMPI normative data and power-transformed T-score tables for the Hathaway-Monachesi Minnesota cohort of 14,019 15-year-olds and 3,674 18-year-olds. In R. P. Archer, *Using the MMPI with adolescents* (pp. 241-297). Hillsdale, NJ: Lawrence Erlbaum.

Gottesman, I. I., & Prescott, C. A. (1989). Abuses of the MacAndrew MMPI Alcoholism Scale: A critical review. *Clinical Psychology Review, 9,* 223-258.

Gough, H. G. (1947). Simulated patterns on the MMPI. *Journal of Abnormal and Social Psychology, 42,* 215-225.

Gough, H. G. (1950). The F minus K dissimulation index for the MMPI. *Journal of Consulting Psychology, 14,* 408-413.

Gough, H. G., McClosky, H., & Meehl, P. E. (1951). A personality scale for dominance. *Journal of Abnormal and Social Psychology, 46,* 360-366.

Gough, H. G., McClosky, H., & Meehl, P. E. (1952). A personality scale for social responsibility. *Journal of Abnormal and Social Psychology, 47,* 73-80.

Gough, H. G., McKee, M. G., & Yandell, R. J. (1955). *Adjective Check List analyses of a number of selected psychometric and assessment variables.* Officer Education Research Laboratory. Technical Memorandum, OERL-TM-55-10.

Graham, J. R. (1973). *Behavioral correlates of simple MMPI code types.* Paper presented at the 8th Annual Symposium on Recent Developments in the Use of the MMPI, New Orleans, LA.

Graham, J. R. (1977). *The MMPI: A practical guide.* New York: Oxford University Press.

Graham, J. R. (1987). *The MMPI: A practical guide* (2nd ed.). New York: Oxford University Press.

Graham, J. R. (1988, August). *Establishing validity of the revised form of the MMPI.* Paper presented at the Ninety-Sixth Annual Convention of the American Psychological Association, Atlanta, GA.

Graham, J. R. (1989, August). The meaning of elevated MacAndrew Alcoholism scale scores for nonclinical subjects. Paper presented at the Ninety-Seventh Annual Convention of the American Psychological Association, New Orleans, LA.

Graham, J. R. (1990). *MMPI-2: Assessing personality and psychopathology.* New York: Oxford University Press.

Graham, J. R., & Butcher, J. N. (1988, March). *Differentiating schizophrenic and major affective disorders with the revised form of the MMPI.* Paper presented at the 23rd Annual Symposium on Recent Developments in the Use of the MMPI, St. Petersburg, FL.

Graham, J. R., & Lilly, R. (1986). *Linear T-scores versus normalized T-scores: An empirical study.* Paper given at the 21st Annual Symposium on Recent Developments in the Use of the MMPI, Clearwater Beach, FL.

Graham, J. R., & McCord, G. (1985). Interpretation of moderately elevated MMPI scores for normal subjects. *Journal of Personality Assessment, 49* (5), 477-484.

Graham, J. R., Schroeder, H. E., & Lilly, R. S. (1971). Factor analysis of items on the social introversion and masculinity-femininity scales of the MMPI. *Journal of Clinical Psychology, 27,* 367-370.

Graham, J. R., Smith, R., & Schwartz, G. (1986). Stability of MMPI configurations for psychiatric inpatients. *Journal of Consulting and Clinical Psychology, 54,* 375-380.

Graham, J. R., & Strenger, V. E. (1988). MMPI characteristics of alcoholics: A review. *Journal of Consulting and Clinical Psychology,* 197-205.

Graham, J. R., Timbrook, R., Ben-Porath, Y. S., & Butcher, J. N. (in press). Code-type congruence between MMPI and MMPI-2: Separating fact from artifact. *Journal of Personality Assessment.*

Graham, J. R., Watts, D., & Timbrook, R. (1991). Detecting fake-good and fake-bad MMPI-2 profiles. *Journal of Personality Assessment, 57,* 264-277.

Grayson, H. M. (1951). *Psychological admission testing program and manual.* Los Angeles: Veterans Administration Center, Neuropsychiatric Hospital.

Greene, E. B. (1954). Medical reports and selected MMPI items among employed adults. *American Psychologist, 9,* 384.

Greene, R. L. (1980). *The MMPI: An interpretive manual*. New York: Grune & Stratton.

Greene, R. L. (1982). Some reflections on "MMPI short forms: A literature review." *Journal of Personality Assessment, 46*, 486-487.

Greene, R. L. (1991). *The MMPI-2/MMPI: An interpretive manual*. Boston: Allyn and Bacon.

Greene, R. L., Weed, N. C., Butcher, J. N., Arredondo, R., & Davis, H. G. (1992). A cross-validation of MMPI-2 substance abuse scales. *Journal of Personality Assessment, 58*, 405-410.

Grossman, L. S., Haywood, T. W., Ostrov, E., Wasyliw, O., & Cavanaugh, J. L. (1990). Sensitivity of MMPI validity indicators to motivational factors in psychological evaluation of police officers. *Journal of Personality Assessment, 55*, 549-561.

Guthrie, G. M. (1952). Common characteristics associated with frequent MMPI profile types. *Journal of Clinical Psychology, 8*, 141-145.

Gynther, M. D. (1961). The clinical utility of "invalid" MMPI F scores. *Journal of Consulting Psychology, 25*, 540-542.

Gynther, M. D. (1972a). *A new replicated actuarial program for interpreting MMPIs of state hospital inpatients*. Paper presented at the 7th Annual Symposium on Recent Developments in the Use of the MMPI, Mexico.

Gynther, M. D. (1972b). White norms and Black MMPIs: A prescription for discrimination? *Psychological Bulletin, 78*, 386-402.

Gynther, M. D., Altman, H., & Sletten, I. W. (1973). Development of an empirical interpretive system for the MMPI: Some after-the-fact observations. *Journal of Clinical Psychology, 29*, 232-234.

Gynther, M. D., Altman, H., & Warbin, R. W. (1972). A new empirical automated MMPI interpretive program: The 2-4/4-2 code type. *Journal of Clinical Psychology, 28*, 498-501.

Gynther, M. D., Altman, H., & Warbin, R. W. (1973a). A new actuarial-empirical automated MMPI interpretive program: The 4-3/3-4 code type. *Journal of Clinical Psychology, 29*, 229-231.

Gynther, M. D., Altman, H., & Warbin, R. W. (1973b). A new empirical automated MMPI interpretive program: The 2-7/7-2 code type. *Journal of Clinical Psychology, 29*, 58-59.

Gynther, M. D., Altman, H., & Warbin, R. W. (1973c). A new empirical automated MMPI interpretive program: The 6-9/9-6 code type. *Journal of Clinical Psychology, 29*, 60-61.

Gynther, M. D., Altman, H., & Warbin, R. W. (1973d). Interpretation of uninterpretable MMPI profiles. *Journal of Consulting and Clinical Psychology, 40*, 78-83.

Gynther, M. D., Altman, H., Warbin, R. W., & Sletten, I. W. (1972). A new actuarial system for MMPI interpretation: Rationale and methodology. *Journal of Clinical Psychology, 28*, 173-179.

Gynther, M. D., & Petzel, T. P. (1967). Differential endorsement of MMPI F scale items by psychotics and behavior disorders. *Journal of Clinical Psychology, 23*, 185-188.

Gynther, M. D., & Shimunkas, A. M. (1965). More data on MMPI F > 16 scores. *Journal of Clinical Psychology, 21*, 275-277.

Halbower, C. C. (1955). *A comparison of actuarial versus clinical prediction to classes discriminated by MMPI*. Unpublished doctoral dissertation, University of Minnesota.

Hall, G. S. (1904). *Adolescence: Its psychology and its relations to physiology, anthropology, sociology, sex, crime, religion, and education* (Vols. 1 & 2). New York: D. Appleton and Company.

Hanson, R. W., Moss, C. S., Hosford, R. E., & Johnson, M. E. (1983). Predicting inmate penitentiary adjustment: An assessment of four classificatory methods. *Criminal Justice and Behavior, 10*, 293-309.

Harris, R. E., & Lingoes, J. C. (1955, 1968). *Subscales for the MMPI: An aid to profile interpretation*. Mimeographed materials. Department of Psychiatry, University of California.

Hart, R. (1984). Chronic pain: Replicated multivariate clustering of personality profiles. *Journal of Clinical Psychology, 40*, 129-133.

Hart, T. R., McNeill, J. W., Lutz, D. J., & Adkins, T. G. (1986). Clinical comparability of the standard MMPI and the MMPI-168. *Professional Psychology: Research and Practice, 17*, 269-272.

Hathaway, S. R. (1947). A coding system for MMPI profiles. *Journal of Consulting Psychology, 11*, 334-337.

Hathaway, S. R. (1956). Scales 5 (Masculinity-Femininity), 6 (Paranoia), and 8 (Schizophrenia). In W. G. Dahlstrom & L. E. Dahlstrom (Eds.), *Basic readings on the MMPI*. Minneapolis: University of Minnesota Press.

Hathaway, S. R. (1965). Personality inventories. In B. Wolman (Ed.) *Handbook of clinical psychology*. New York: McGraw-Hill.

Hathaway, S. R., Hastings, D. W., Capwell, D. F., & Bell, D. M. (1953). The relationship between MMPI profiles and later careers of juvenile delinquent girls. In S. R. Hathaway & E.D. Monachesi (Eds.), *Analyzing and predicting juvenile delinquency with the MMPI* (pp. 70-80). Minneapolis: University of Minnesota Press.

Hathaway, S. R., & McKinley, J. C. (1940). A multiphasic personality schedule (Minnesota): I. Construction of the schedule. *Journal of Psychology, 10,* 249-254.

Hathaway, S. R., & McKinley, J. C. (1942). A multiphasic personality schedule (Minnesota): III. The measurement of symptomatic depression. *Journal of Psychology, 14,* 73-84.

Hathaway, S. R., & McKinley, J. C. (1942). *The Minnesota Multiphasic Personality Schedule.* Minneapolis, Minnesota: University of Minnesota Press.

Hathaway, S. R., & Meehl, P. E. (1952). *Adjective check list correlates of MMPI scores.* Unpublished materials.

Hathaway, S. R., & Monachesi, E. D. (Eds.). (1953a). *Analyzing and predicting juvenile delinquency with the MMPI.* Minneapolis: University of Minnesota Press.

Hathaway, S. R., & Monachesi, E. D. (1953b). Personality characteristics of adolescents as related to their later careers . . . Part I. Introduction and general findings. In S. R. Hathaway & E. D. Monachesi. (Eds.), *Analyzing and predicting juvenile delinquency with the MMPI* (pp. 87-108). Minneapolis: University of Minnesota Press.

Hathaway, S. R., & Monachesi, E. D. (1957). The personalities of pre-delinquent boys. *Journal of Criminal Law, Criminology, and Political Science, 48,* 149-153.

Hathaway, S. R., & Monachesi, E. D. (1961). *An atlas of juvenile MMPI profiles.* Minneapolis: University of Minnesota Press.

Hathaway, S. R., & Monachesi, E. D. (1963). *Adolescent personality and behavior: MMPI patterns of normal, delinquent, drop-out, and other outcomes.* Minneapolis: University of Minnesota Press.

Hathaway, S. R., Reynolds, P., & Monachesi, E. D. (1969). Follow-up of the later careers and lives of 1000 boys who dropped out of high school. *Journal of Consulting and Clinical Psychology, 33,* 370-380.

Hedlund, J. L. (1977). MMPI clinical scale correlates. *Journal of Consulting and Clinical Psychology, 43,* 739-750.

Helmes, E., & McLaughlin, J. D. (1983). A comparison of three MMPI short forms: Limited clinical utility in classification. *Journal of Consulting and Clinical Psychology 51,* 786-787.

Herjanic, B., & Campbell, W. (1977). Differentiating psychiatrically disturbed children on the basis of a structured interview. *Journal of Abnormal Child Psychology, 5,* 127-134.

Herkov, M. J., Archer, R., & Gordon, R. A. (1991). MMPI response sets among adolescents: An evaluation of the limitations of the subtle-obvious subscales. *Psychological Assessment: A Journal of Consulting and Clinical Psychology, 3,* 424-426.

Hill, H. E., Haertzen, C. A., & Glaser, R. (1960). Personality characteristics of narcotic addicts as indicated by the MMPI. *Journal of General Psychology, 62,* 127-129.

Hjemboe, S., Almagor, M., & Butcher, J. N. (in press). Empirical assessment of marital distress: The Marital Distress Scale (MDS) for the MMPI-2. In C. D. Spielberger & J. N. Butcher (Eds.), *Advances in personality assessment* (Vol. 9). Hillsdale, NJ: Lawrence Erlbaum.

Hjemboe, S., & Butcher, J. N. (1991). Couples in marital distress: A study of demographic and personality factors as measured by the MMPI-2. *Journal of Personality Assessment, 57,* 216-237.

Hoffmann, N. G., & Butcher, J. N. (1975). Clinical limitation of three Minnesota Multiphasic Personality Inventory short forms. *Journal of Consulting and Clinical Psychology, 43,* 32-39.

Johnson, D. L., Simmons, J. G., & Gordon, B. C. (1983). Temporal consistency of the Meyer-Megargee inmate typology. *Criminal Justice and Behavior, 10,* 263-268.

Johnson, J. H., Butcher, J. N., Null, C., & Johnson, K. N. (1984). Replicated item level factor analysis of the full MMPI. *Journal of Personality and Social Psychology, 47* (1), 105-114.

Katz, M. M. (1968). A phenomenological typology of schizophrenia. In M. M. Katz, J. O. Cole, & W. E. Barton (Eds.), *The role and methodology of classification in psychiatry and psychopathology.* Public Health Printing Office.

Keane, T. M., Malloy, P. F., & Fairbank, J. A. (1984). Empirical development of an MMPI subscale for the assessment of combat-related posttraumatic stress disorder. *Journal of Consulting and Clinical Psychology, 52,* 888-891.

Keller, L. S., & Butcher, J. N. (1991). *Use of the MMPI-2 with chronic pain patients*. Minneapolis: University of Minnesota Press.

Kelly, C. K., & King, G. D. (1978). Behavioral correlates for within-normal limit MMPI profiles with and without elevated K in students at a university mental health center. *Journal of Clinical Psychology, 34*, 695-699.

Kennedy, T. D. (1986). Trends in inmate classification: A status report of two computerized psychometric approaches. *Criminal Justice and Behavior, 13*, 165-184.

Klinefelter, D., Pancoast, D. L., Archer, R. P., & Pruitt, D. L. (1990). Recent adolescent MMPI norms: T-score elevation comparisons to Marks and Briggs. *Journal of Personality Assessment, 54*, 379-389.

Klinge, V., Culbert, J., & Piggott, L. R. (1982). Efficacy of psychiatric inpatient hospitalization for adolescents as measured by pre- and post-MMPI profiles. *Journal of Youth and Adolescence, 11*, 493-502.

Klinge, V., Lachar, D., Grisell, J., & Berman, W. (1978). The effects of scoring norms on adolescent psychiatric drug users' and non-users' MMPI profiles. *Adolescence, 13*, 1-11.

Koss, M. P. (1979). MMPI item content: Recurring issues. In J. N. Butcher (Ed.), *New developments in the use of the MMPI* (pp. 3-38). Minneapolis: University of Minnesota Press.

Koss, M. P., & Butcher, J. N. (1973). A comparison of psychiatric patients' self-report with other sources of clinical information. *Journal of Research in Personality, 7*, 225-236.

Koss, M. P., Butcher, J. N., & Hoffmann, N. G. (1976). The MMPI critical items: How well do they work? *Journal of Consulting and Clinical Psychology, 44*, 921-928.

Lachar, D. (1974). *The MMPI: Clinical assessment and automated interpretation*. Los Angeles: Western Psychological Services.

Lachar, D. (1979). How much of a good thing is enough?: A review of T. A. Fashingbauer & C. A. Newmark. *Short forms of the MMPI. Contemporary Psychology, 24*, 116-117.

Lachar, D., Klinge, V., & Grisell, J. L. (1976). Relative accuracy of automated MMPI narratives generated from adult norm and adolescent norm profiles. *Journal of Consulting and Clinical Psychology, 44*, 20-24.

Lachar, D., & Wrobel, T. A. (1979). Validating clinicians' hunches: Construction of a new MMPI critical item set. *Journal of Consulting and Clinical Psychology, 47*, 277-284.

LaPlace, J. P. (1952). *An exploratory study of personality and its relationship to success in professional baseball*. Doctoral dissertation. Columbia University (DA, 1952, 12, 592).

Leon, G., Gillum, B., Gillum, R., & Gouze, M. (1979). Personality stability and change over a thirty-year-period—middle age to old age. *Journal of Consulting and Clinical Psychology, 47*, 517-524.

Levenson, M. R., Aldwin, C. M., Butcher, J. N., de Labry, L., Workman-Daniels, K., & Bossé, R. (1990). The MAC scale in a normal population: The meaning of "false positives." *Journal of Studies on Alcohol, 51*, 457-462.

Lewandowski, D., & Graham, J. R. (1972). Empirical correlates of frequently occurring two-point MMPI code types: A replicated study. *Journal of Consulting and Clinical Psychology, 39*, 467-472.

Lewinson, P. M. (1968). Characteristics of patients with hallucinations. *Journal of Clinical Psychology, 24*, 423.

Lichtenberg, P. A., Skehan, M. W., & Swensen, C. O. (1984). The role of personality, recent life stress and arthritic severity in predicting pain. *Journal of Psychosomatic Research, 28*, 231-236.

Lilienfeld, S. (March, 1991). *Assessment of psychopathy with MMPI and MMPI-2*. Paper presented at the 26th Annual Symposium on Recent Developments in the Use of the MMPI (MMPI-2), St. Petersburg, FL.

Litz, B. T., Penk, W., Walsh, S., Hyer, L., Blake, D. D., Marx, B., Keane, T. M., & Bitman, D. (1991). Similarities and differences between Minnesota Multiphasic Personality Inventory (MMPI) and MMPI-2 applications to the assessment of post-traumatic stress disorder. *Journal of Personality Assessment, 57*, 238-254.

Long, K. A., & Graham, J. R. (1991). The Masculinity-Femininity Scale of the MMPI-2: Is it useful with normal men? *Journal of Personality Assessment, 57*, 46-51.

Louscher, P. K., Hosford, R. E., & Moss, C. S. (1983). Predicting dangerous behavior in a penitentiary using the Megargee typology. *Criminal Justice and Behavior, 10*, 269-284.

Lubin, B., Larsen, R. M., & Matarazzo, J. (1984). Patterns of psychological test usage in the United States 1935-1982. *American Psychologist, 39*, 451-454.

Lubin, B., Larsen, R. M., Matarazzo, J., & Seever, M. (1985). Psychological assessment services and psychological test usage in private practice and military settings. *Psychotherapy in Private Practice, 4,* 19-29.

MacAndrew, C. (1965). The differentiation of male alcoholic outpatients from nonalcoholic psychiatric outpatients by means of the MMPI. *Quarterly Journal of Studies on Alcohol, 26,* 238-246.

MacAndrew, C. (1986). Toward the psychometric detection of substance misuse in young men: The SAP scale. *Jounral of Studies on Alcohol, 47,* 161-166.

Marks, P. A., & Seeman, W. (1963). *The actuarial description of abnormal personality.* Baltimore: Williams & Wilkins.

Marks, P. A., Seeman, W., & Haller, D. L. (1974). *The actuarial use of the MMPI with adolescents and adults.* Baltimore: Williams and Wilkins.

McCreary, C. (1985). Empirically derived MMPI profile clusters and characteristics of low back pain patients. *Journal of Consulting and Clinical Psychology, 53,* 558-560.

McGill, J., Lawlis, G. F., Selby, D., Mooney, V., & McCoy, C. E. (1983). Relationship of MMPI profile clusters to pain behaviors. *Journal of Behavioral Medicine, 6,* 77-92.

McKenna, T., & Butcher, J. N. (1987). *Continuity of the MMPI with alcoholics.* Paper given at the 23rd Annual Symposium on Recent Developments in the Use of the MMPI, Seattle, WA.

McKinley, J. C., & Hathaway, S. R. (1940). A multiphasic personality schedule (Minnesota): II. A differential study of hypochondriasis. *Journal of Psychology, 10,* 255-268.

McKinley, J. C., & Hathaway, S. R. (1944). The MMPI: V. Hysteria, hypomania, and psychopathic deviate. *Journal of Applied Psychology, 28,* 153-174.

McKinley, J. C., Hathaway, S. R., & Meehl, P. E. (1948). The MMPI: VI. The K scale. *Journal of Consulting Psychology, 12,* 20-31.

Meehl, P. E. (1954). *Clinical versus statistical prediction: A theoretical analysis and a review of the evidence.* Minneapolis: University of Minnesota Press.

Meehl, P. E., & Hathaway, S. R. (1946). The K factor as a suppressor variable in the MMPI. *Journal of Applied Psychology, 30,* 525-564.

Megargee, E. I. (1984). A new classification system for criminal offenders: VI. Differences among the types on the Adjective Checklist. *Criminal Justice and Behavior, 11,* 349-376.

Megargee, E. I. (1991, March). *Assessing felons with the Megargee Classification System for the MMPI and MMPI-2.* Paper presented at the 26th Annual Symposium on Recent Developments in the Use of the MMPI (MMPI-2), St. Petersburg, FL.

Megargee, E. I., & Bohn, M. J. (1977). A new classification system for criminal offenders: IV. Empirically determined characteristics of the ten types. *Criminal Justice and Behavior, 4,* 149-210.

Megargee, E. I., Cook, P. E., & Mendelsohn, G. A. (1967). Development and validation of an MMPI scale of assaultiveness in overcontrolled individuals. *Journal of Abnormal Psychology, 72,* 519-528.

Megargee, E. I., Rivera, P., & Fly, J. T. (March, 1991). *MMPI-2 and the Megargee Offender Classification system.* Paper presented at the 26th Annual Symposium on Recent Developments in the Use of the MMPI (MMPI-2), St Petersburg, FL.

Meikle, S., & Gerritse, R. (1970). MMPI "cookbook" pattern frequencies in a psychiatric unit. *Journal of Clinical Psychology, 26,* 82-84.

Meresman, J. F. (May, 1992). *The ability of the MMPI-2 to discriminate between responders and nonresponders in the treatment of depression.* Paper presented at the 27th Annual Symposium on Recent Developments in the Use of the MMPI (MMPI-2), Minneapolis, MN.

Moldin, S. O., Gottesman, I. I., Rice, J. P., & Erlenmeyer-Kimling, L. (1991). Replicated psychometric correlates of schizophrenia. *American Journal of Psychiatry, 148,* 762-767.

Monachesi, E. D. (1948). Some personality characteristics of delinquents and nondelinquents. *Journal of Criminal Law and Criminology, 38,* 487-500.

Monachesi, E. D. (1950a). Personality characteristics and socioeconomic status of delinquents and nondelinquents. *Journal of Criminal Law and Criminology, 40,* 570-583.

Monachesi, E. D. (1950b). Personality characteristics of institutionalized and noninstitutionalized male delinquents. *Journal of Criminal Law and Criminology, 41,* 167-179.

Monachesi, E. D. (1953). The personality patterns of juvenile delinquents as indicated by the MMPI. In S. R. Hathaway & E. D. Monachesi (Eds.), *Analyzing and predicting juvenile delinquency with the MMPI* (pp. 38-53). Minneapolis: University of Minnesota Press.

Moreland, K. L. (1987). Computerized psychological assessment: What's available. In J. N. Butcher (Ed.), *Computerized psychological assessment*. New York: Basic Books.

Moreland, K. L., & Onstad, J. (1985, March). *Validity of the Minnesota Clinical Report I: Mental health outpatients*. Paper presented at the 20th Annual Symposium on Recent Developments in the Use of the MMPI, Honolulu, HI.

Moss, C. S., Johnson, M. E., & Hosford, R. E. (1984). An assessment of the Megargee typology in lifelong criminal violence. *Criminal Justice and Behavior, 11*, 225-234.

Motiuk, L. L., Bonta, J., & Andrews, D. A. (1986). Classification in correctional halfway houses: The relative and incremental predictive criterion validities of the Megargee-MMPI and LSI systems. *Criminal Justice and Behavior, 13*, 33-46.

Mrad, D. F., Kabacoff, R. I., & Duckro, P. (1983). Validation of the Megargee typology in a halfway house setting. *Criminal Justice and Behavior, 10*, 252-262.

Muller, B., & Bruno, L. (1986). *The MMPI and Inwald Personality Inventory for psychological screening of police candidates*. Paper presented at the 21st Annual Symposium on Recent Developments in the Use of the MMPI, Clearwater Beach, FL.

Murray, J. B. (1963). The Mf scale of the MMPI for college students. *Journal of Clinical Psychology, 19*, 113-115.

Nelson, L. (1987). Measuring depression in a clinical population using the MMPI. *Journal of Consulting and Clinical Psychology, 55*, 788-790.

Nelson, L., & Cicchetti, D. (1991). Validity of the MMPI depression scale for outpatients. *Psychological Assessment: A Journal of Consulting and Clinical Psychology, 3*, 55-59.

Nichols, D. (1987). Interpreting Wiggins MMPI content scales. *Clinical Notes on the MMPI*, No 10. Minneapolis: National Computer Systems.

Nuclear Regulatory Commission (1984). *Guidelines for nuclear power plant access*. NRC 10 CFR Parts 50 & 73. Washington, DC: Nuclear Regulatory Commission.

Pancoast, D. L., & Archer, R. P. (1988). MMPI adolescent norms: Patterns and trends across four decades. *Journal of Personality Assessment, 52*, 691-706.

Panton, J. H. (1959). MMPI profile configurations among crime classification groups. *Journal of Clinical Psychology, 15*, 305-308.

Parkison, S., & Fishburne, F. (1984). MMPI normative data for a male active duty Army population. In *Proceedings of the Psychology in the Department of Defense, Ninth Symposium* (USAFA-TR-84-2, pp. 570-574). Colorado Springs, CO: USAF Academy Department of Behavioral Sciences.

Pearson, J. S., & Swenson, W. M. (1967). *A users guide to the Mayo Clinic automated MMPI program*. New York: The Psychological Corporation.

Pearson, J. S., Swenson, W. M., Rome, H. P., Mataya, P., & Brannick, T. L. (1965). Development of a computer system for scoring and interpretation of the Minnesota Multiphasic Personality Inventory in a medical setting. *Annals of the New York Academy of Sciences, 126*, 682-692.

Persons, R. W., & Marks, P. A. (1971). The violent 4-3 MMPI personality type. *Journal of Consulting and Clinical Psychology, 36*, 189-196.

Peterson, C. D. (1989). *Masculinity and femininity as independent dimensions on the MMPI*. Unpublished doctoral dissertation, University of North Carolina, Chapel Hill.

Piotrowski, C., & Lubin, B. (1990). Assessment practices of health psychologists: Survey of APA Division 38 clinicians. *Professional Psychology Research and Practice, 21*, 99-106.

Pope, K. S. (1990). Seven clinical, ethical, and legal pitfalls in using psychological tests. *MMPI-2 News and Profiles, 1*, 2-3.

Prokop, C. K., Bradley, L. A., Margolis, R., & Gentry, W. D. (1980). Multivariate analyses of the MMPI profiles of low back pain patients. *Journal of Personality Assessment, 44*, 246-252.

Reese, P. M., Webb, J. T., & Foulks, J. D. (1968). A comparison of oral and booklet forms of the MMPI for psychiatric inpatients. *Journal of Clinical Psychology, 24*, 436-437.

Rempel, P. P. (1958). The use of multivariate statistical analysis of the Minnesota Multiphasic Personality Inventory in the classification of delinquent and nondelinquent high school boys. *Journal of Consulting Psychology, 22*, 17-23.

Rome, H. P., Swenson, W. M., Mataya, P., McCarthy, C. E., Pearson, J. S., Keating, F. R., & Hathaway, S. R. (1962). Symposium on automation technics in personality assessment. *Proceedings of the Staff Meetings of the Mayo Clinic, 37*, 61-82.

Roper, B., Ben-Porath, Y. S., & Butcher, J. N. (1991). Comparability of computerized adaptive and conventional testing with the MMPI-2. *Journal of Personality Assessment, 57,* 278-290.

Rosen, A. (1958). Differentiation of diagnostic groups by individual MMPI scales. *Journal of Consulting Psychology, 17,* 217-221.

Saccuzzo, D. P., Higgins, G., & Lewandowski, D. (1974). Program for psychological assessment of law enforcement officers: Initial evaluation. *Psychological Reports, 35,* 651-654.

Savacir, I., & Erol, N. (1990). The Turkish MMPI. In J. N. Butcher & C. D. Spielberger (Eds.), *Advances in personality assessment* (Vol. 8). Hillsdale, NJ: Lawrence Erlbaum.

Schill, T., & Wang, T. (1990). Correlates of the MMPI-2 Anger Content Scale. *Psychological Reports, 67,* 800-802.

Schlenger, W. E., & Kulka, R. A. (1987). *Performance of the Keane-Fairbank MMPI scale and other self-report measures in identifying post-traumatic stress disorder.* Paper presented at the American Psychological Association meetings, New York, NY.

Schlenger, W. E., Kulka, R. A., Fairbank, J. A., Hough, R. L., Jordan, B. K., Marmar, C. R., & Weiss, D. S. (1989). The prevalence of post-traumatic stress disorder in the Vietnam generation: Findings from the National Vietnam Veterans Readjustment Study: Report from Research Triangle Institute, Research Triangle Park, NC.

Schofield, W. (1956). Changes following certain therapies as reflected in the MMPI. In G. S. Welsh and W. G. Dahlstrom (Eds.), *Basic readings on the MMPI in Psychology and Medicine.* Minneapolis: University of Minnesota Press.

Schretlen, D. (1988). The use of psychological tests to identify malingered symptoms of mental disorder. *Clinical Psychology Review, 8,* 451-476.

Schwartz, M. F., & Graham, J. R. (1979). Construct validity of the MacAndrew Alcoholism Scale. *Journal of Consulting and Clinical Psychology, 47,* 1090-1095.

Serkownek, K. (1975). *Subscales for Scales 5 and 0 of the Minnesota Multiphasic Personality Inventory.* Unpublished materials.

Shaffer, J. W., Ota, K. Y., & Hanlon, T. E. (1964). The comparative validity of several MMPI indices of severity of psychopathology. *Journal of Clinical Psychology, 20,* 467-473.

Sieber, K. O., & Meyers, L. S. (1992). Validation of the MMPI-2 Social Introversion Subscales. *Psychological Assessment: A Journal of Consulting and Clinical Psychology, 4,* 185-189.

Silver, R., & Sines, L. K. (1962). Diagnostic efficiency of the MMPI with and without K correction. *Journal of Clinical Psychology, 18,* 312-314.

Simmons, J. G., Johnson, D. L., Gouvier, W. D., & Muzyczka, M. J. (1981). The Myer-Megargee inmate typology: Dynamic or unstable? *Criminal Justice and Behavior, 8,* 49-54.

Sines, J. O. (1966). Actuarial methods in personality assessment. In B. A. Maher (Ed.), *Progress in experimental personality research.* New York: Academic Press.

Snyder, D. K., & Regts, J. M. (1990). Personality correlates of marital satisfaction: A comparison of psychiatric, maritally distressed, and nonclinic samples. *Journal of Sex and Marital Therapy, 16,* 34-43.

Spanier, G. B., & Filsinger, E. E. (1983). The dyadic adjustment scale. In E. E. Filsinger (Ed.), *Marriage and family assessment* (pp. 155-168). Beverly Hills: Sage.

Stein, K. B. (1968). The TSC Scales: The outcome of a cluster analysis of the 550 MMPI items. In P. McReynolds (Ed.), *Advances in psychological assessment* (Vol. 1, pp. 80-149). Palo Alto, CA: Science & Behavior Books.

Streiner, D. L., & Miller, H. R. (1986). Can a good short form of the MMPI ever be developed? *Journal of Clinical Psychology, 42,* 109-113.

Taft, R. (1961). A psychological assessment of professional actors and related professions. *Genetic Psychology Monographs, 64,* 309-383.

Tellegen, A. (1988). The analysis of consistency in personality assessment. *Journal of Personality, 56,* 621-663.

Tellegen, A. (1991). *Development of consistency measures for the MMPI-A.* Paper presented at the Ninety-ninth Annual Convention of the American Psychological Association.

Tellegen, A., & Ben-Porath, Y. S. (1992). The new Uniform T-scores for the MMPI-2: Rationale, derivation, and appraisal. *Psychological Assessment: A Journal of Consulting and Clinical Psychology, 4,* 145-155.

Terman, L. M., & Miles, C. (1936). *Sex and personality: Studies in masculinity and femininity*. New York: McGraw-Hill.

Thatte, S., Manos, N., & Butcher, J. N. (1987, July). *Cross-cultural study of abnormal personality in three countries: United States, India, and Greece*. Paper presented at the 10th Annual Conference on Personality Assessment, Brussels, Belgium.

Timbrook, R., Graham, J. R., Keiller, S., & Watts, D. (1991, March). *Failure of the Wiener-Harmon Subscales to discriminate between valid and invalid profiles*. Paper presented at the 26th Annual Symposium on Recent Developments in the Use of the MMPI (MMPI-2), St. Petersburg, FL.

Urmer, A. H., Black, H. O., & Wendland, L. V. (1960). A comparison of taped and booklet forms of the MMPI. *Journal of Clinical Psychology, 16*, 33-34.

Vincent, K. R. (1990). The fragile nature of MMPI codetypes. *Journal of Clinical Psychology, 46*, 800-802.

Walsh, S., Penk, W., Brett, T., Litz, T., Keane, T. M., Bitman, D., & Marx, B. (August, 1991). *Discriminant validity of the new MMPI-2 Content Scales*. Paper given at the Ninety-ninth Convention of the American Psychological Association, San Francisco.

Walters, G. (1986). Correlates of the Megargee Criminal Classification System: A military correctional system. *Criminal Justice and Behavior, 13*, 19-32.

Warbin, R. W., Altman, H., Gynther, M. D., & Sletten, I. W. (1972). A new empirical automated MMPI interpretive program: 2-8 and 8-2 code types. *Journal of Personality Assessment, 36*, 581-584.

Wauck, L. A. (1950). Schizophrenia and the MMPI. *Journal of Clinical Psychology, 6*, 279-282.

Weed, N., Ben-Porath, Y. S., & Butcher, J. N. (1990). Failure of the Wiener-Harmon MMPI subtle scales as predictors of psychopathology and as validity indicators. *Psychological Assessment: A Journal of Consulting and Clinical Psychology, 2*, 281-283.

Weed, N. C., Butcher, J. N., Ben-Porath, Y. S., & McKenna, T. (1992). New measures for assessing alcohol and drug abuse with the MMPI-2: The APS and AAS. *Journal of Personality Assessment, 58*, 389-404.

Weed, N. C., Butcher, J. N. & Williams, C. W. (in preparation). Development of the Alcohol and Drug Problem Scale (PRO) and the Alcohol and Drug Problem Acknowledgment Scale (ACK).

Welsh, G. S. (1948). An extension of Hathaway's MMPI profile coding. *Journal of Consulting Psychology, 12*, 343-344.

Welsh, G. S. (1951). Some practical uses of MMPI profile coding. *Journal of Consulting Psychology, 15*, 82-84.

Welsh, G. S. (1956). Factor dimensions A and R. In G. S. Welsh & W. G. Dahlstrom (Eds.), *Basic readings on the MMPI in psychology and medicine*. Minneapolis: University of Minnesota Press.

Wiener, D. N. (1948). Subtle and obvious keys for the MMPI. *Journal of Consulting Psychology, 12*, 164-170.

Wiggins, J. S. (1966). Substantive dimensions of self-report in the MMPI item pool. *Psychological Monographs, 80* (22, Whole No. 630).

Wiggins, J. S. (1969). Content dimensions in the MMPI. In J. N. Butcher (Ed.), *MMPI: Research developments and clinical applications* (pp. 127-180). New York: McGraw-Hill.

Wilcockson, J. C., Bolton, B., & Dana, R. H. (1983). A comparison of six MMPI short forms: Code type correspondence and indices of psychopathology. *Journal of Clinical Psychology, 39*, 968-969.

Williams, C. L. (1981). Assessment of social behavior: Behavior role play compared with *Si* scale of the MMPI. *Behavior Therapy, 12*, 578-584.

Williams, C. L. (1982). Can the MMPI be useful to behavior therapists? *The Behavior Therapist, 3*, 83-84.

Williams, C. L. (1986). MMPI profiles from adolescents: Interpretative strategies and treatment considerations. *Journal of Child and Adolescent Psychotherapy, 3*, 179- 193.

Williams, C. L., Ben-Porath, Y. S., & Hevern, V. W. (1991, March). *Item level improvements for the MMPI-A*. Paper presented at the 26th Annual Symposium on Recent Developments in the Use of the MMPI (MMPI-2 and MMPI-A), St. Petersburg, FL.

Williams, C. L., & Butcher, J. N. (1989a). An MMPI study of adolescents: I. Empirical validity of the standard scales. *Psychological Assessment: A Journal of Consulting and Clinical Psychology, 1*, 251-259.

Williams, C. L., & Butcher, J. N. (1989b). An MMPI study of adolescents: II. Verification and limitations of code type classifications. *Psychological Assessment: A Journal of Consulting and Clinical Psychology, 1*, 260-265.

Williams, C. L., Butcher, J. N., Ben-Porath, Y. S., & Graham, J. R. (1992). *MMPI-A Content Scales: Assessing psychopathology in adolescents*. Minneapolis: University of Minnesota Press.

Williams, C. L., Butcher, J. N., & Graham, J. R. (1986, March). *Appropriate MMPI norms for adolescents: An old problem revisited*. Paper presented at the 21st Annual Symposium on Recent Developments in the Use of the MMPI, Clearwater, FL.

Williams, H. L. (1952). *Differential effects of focal brain damage on the MMPI*. Doctoral dissertation, University of Minnesota, Minneapolis.

Wolf, S. W., Freinek, W. R., & Shaffer, J. W. (1964). Comparability of complete oral and booklet forms of the MMPI. *Journal of Clinical Psychology, 20,* 375-378.

Wolfson, K. T., & Erbaugh, S. E. (1984). Adolescent responses to MacAndrew Alcoholism scale. *Journal of Consulting and Clinical Psychology, 52,* 625-630.

Woodworth, R. S. (1920). *The Personal Data Sheet*. Chicago: Stoelting.

Wrobel, N. H., & Lachar, D. (in press). *Refining adolescent MMPI interpretations: Moderating effects of gender in prediction of descriptions from parents*. Manuscript submitted for publication.

Zager, L. D. (1983). Response to Simmons and associates: Conclusions about the MMPI-Based Classification System's stability are premature. *Criminal Justice and Behavior, 10,* 310-315.

Index

James N. Butcher is professor of psychology at the University of Minnesota. He is author of numerous articles and books on the MMPI, including *A Handbook of Cross-National MMPI Research*, with Paulo Pancheri (Minnesota, 1976), *New Developments in the Use of the MMPI* (Minnesota, 1979), *MMPI-2 in Psychological Treatment* (1990), and coauthor, with Carolyn L. Williams, John R. Graham, and Yossef S. Ben-Porath, of *Development and Use of the MMPI-2 Content Scales* (Minnesota, 1990). Butcher is editor of the American Psychological Association's journal *Psychological Assessment*. He was a member of the MMPI Restandardization and Adolescent Project Committees.

Carolyn L. Williams is associate professor of epidemiology in the School of Public Health, University of Minnesota. She is coauthor of the *MMPI-A Manual* and coauthor, with James N. Butcher, Yossef S. Ben-Porath, and John R. Graham, of *MMPI-A Content Scales: Assessing Psychopathology in Adolescents* (Minnesota, 1992). In addition, she has published extensively on refugee mental health. Her most recent book is *Mental Health Services for Refugees* (1991), coedited with Joseph Westermeyer and Ahn Nga Nguyen.